Iain,

With many thanks for
your many contributions to the
development of IALS

Clive Cupin

27.9.85

INTERLANGUAGE

PAPERS IN HONOUR OF
S. PIT CORDER

INTERLANGUAGE

ALAN DAVIES

C. CRIPER

A. P. R. HOWATT

editors

EDINBURGH UNIVERSITY PRESS

© Edinburgh University Press 1984
22 George Square, Edinburgh

British Library
Cataloguing in Publication Data

Interlanguage.
1. Languages, Artificial
I. Davies, A.   II. Criper, C.
III. Howatt, A. P. R.
401'.3   PN8008
ISBN 0 85224 499 1

Set in Linoterm Times by
Speedspools, Edinburgh
and printed in Great Britain by
Redwood Burn Limited,
Trowbridge

Contents

v

Contents

Participants at the Interlanguage Seminar

Richard Allwright — Department of Linguistics,
University of Lancaster

Roger Andersen — University of California at Los Angeles

Ellen Bialystok — Department of Psychology,
York University, Canada

Gillian Brown — Department of Language and Linguistics,
University of Essex

Christopher Brumfit — University of London Institute of Education

S. Pit Corder — Burnside Cottage, Braithwaite,
Keswick, Cumbria

Clive Criper — Institute for Applied Language Studies,
University of Edinburgh

Alan Davies — Institute for Applied Language Studies,
University of Edinburgh

Dan Douglas — English Language Institute,
Wayne State University, Detroit

Rod Ellis — St Mary's College, Strawberry Hill,
Twickenham, Middx.

Claus Faerch — Department of English,
University of Copenhagen

Sacha W. Felix — Department of Linguistics,
University of Passau, Germany

Susan Gass — Department of Linguistics,
University of Michigan

Birgit Harley — The Ontario Institute for Studies in Education

Evelyn Hatch — University of California at Los Angeles

Ben Heasley — Department of Linguistics,
University of Edinburgh

A. P. R. Howatt — Department of Linguistics,
University of Edinburgh

Gabriele Kasper — University of Aarhus,
Denmark

Eric Kellerman — University of Nijmegen
Patsy M. Lightbown — Concordia University,
Montreal

Participants

Paul Meara — Department of Applied Linguistics,
Birkbeck College, London University

Keith Mitchell — Department of English Studies (foreign students),
University of Edinburgh

Clive Perdue — Gral, Paris-VIII and Max-Planck-Institut für
Psycholinguistik, Nijmegen

Jacquelyn Schachter — University of Southern California

John H. Schumann — University of California at Los Angeles

Larry Selinker — University of Michigan

Michael Sharwood Smith — University of Utrecht

Merrill Swain — The Ontario Institute for Studies in Education

Ray E. Underwood — British Council,
London

H. G. Widdowson — University of London,
Intitute of Education

Henning Wode — Englisches Seminar der Universität Kiel,
Germany

Helmut Zobl — Universite de Moncton

Introduction

Pit Corder retired from the Chair of Applied Linguistics at the University of Edinburgh in September 1983. His professional career took him, after fifteen years with the British Council, first to the University of Leeds and then to Edinburgh where he led the development of applied linguistics over the next twenty years.

Pit Corder's publications reflect the range of his interests and their development over time. His early interests in the pedagogic application of descriptions of English grammar and in the teaching of language by television led to his books *An Intermediate English Practice Book* (1960), *English Language Teaching and Television* (1960) and *The Visual Element in Language Teaching* (1966). His lead in the design of courses in applied linguistics and in the establishing of a coherent discipline of applied linguistics in relation to language teaching produced *Introducing Applied Linguistics* (1973) and the first three volumes of the *Edinburgh Course in Applied Linguistics* (1973–5), edited with Patrick Allen. Corder had always been interested in error analysis and written about it but it was not until the early 1970s that he combined this with a growing interest in second-language acquisition, thereby establishing 'interlanguage' as a theoretical study, further defining the core of applied linguistics. His book *Error Analysis and Interlanguage* (1981) brought his papers in this field together.

It is too soon to form a rounded assessment of Corder's contribution to applied linguistics, but two judgements can be made now and it is unlikely that we will wish to go back on them. The first is that, with the team he assembled in Edinburgh between 1965 and 1975, he made applied linguistics a coherent discipline which was neither 'linguistics for language teachers' nor English language teaching. The view he always presented of applied linguistics was eclectic; his encouragement to his colleagues was generous; the inspiration he provided was that of intellectual curiosity. Pit Corder's direction made Edinburgh the leading department of applied linguistics, certainly in Britain and probably internationally. His colleagues and students went on to establish their own university departments both at home and overseas.

The second judgement is that in this later work on interlanguage he has been largely responsible for the creation of a model of second-language acquisition which has a claim to be called a theory. He always regretted the lack of interest in interlanguage in Britain and had to look to colleagues elsewhere for collaboration, particularly in North America and in Europe where he is held in very high regard. No doubt he has had occasion to think ruefully that 'a prophet is not without honour save in his own country and among his own people'. It is never easy to distinguish between 'mere speculation' and theory-building. If his work had been more empirical there might have been greater awareness in Britain of his contribution to theory. His North American and European colleagues were entirely clear about this. For them Pit Corder was *the* theory maker and if there does now exist a theory of interlanguage and of second-language acquisition then it is because of Pit Corder's thinking and writing about the issues. He himself has never disdained the label 'speculation' not only because it can be another name for theory but also because speculation necessarily precedes the empirical work that leads to the development of theory.

To mark Pit Corder's retirement his colleagues arranged an international Seminar on Interlanguage Studies in his honour.

The papers collected in this volume form the proceedings of the Seminar held in Edinburgh in April 1984. Its purpose was to arrive at a considered view of the present state of the art in interlanguage; and it is partly with that purpose in mind that we arranged for the early publication of the Proceedings. Four areas of investigation were considered important, those of universals, the role of strategies including those appropriate for the mother tongue (L1), the analysis of interlanguage (IL) data, and the implications for language teaching. Papers were invited in these four areas, the intention being to cover both theoretical and empirical studies. Discussants were also commissioned. The contents page lists the areas as arranged for the Seminar. This division of the field of IL provided a satisfactory map for participants and it was afterwards agreed that all the major areas had been covered with the exception of a review of empirical work in the phonology of IL. This had been included in the original design but the late illness of one of the invited participants forced us to leave a gap here. (Elaine Tarone was sorely missed at the Seminar.)

This volume of the Proceedings contains all the position papers which were prepared for the Seminar and circulated in advance. It also contains the discussants' papers for each session. Each session began with the discussant's formal statement, after which the writers of the position papers were invited to reply and then a general discussion ensued. Discussion summaries are also included in the present volume, but it should be noted that they are intended only as a precis of the main contributor's responses to the discussants (where appropriate) and the arguments that followed thereafter. Normally no attempt is made to attribute comments to individual speakers. The purpose of the volume is therefore to capture the views of the participants at the time of the Seminar and does not in any sense seek to provide reworked and edited revisions. It is a first attempt at a state of the art in 1984, and our hope is that it may help re-create some of the excitement of the meeting and at the same time represent, with some reliability, what measure of agreement there is as to what IL studies have established so far and what uncertainty and real disagreement remain. Selinker provides a Summing Up in which he evaluates the degree of consensus that exists in the main IL areas. Finally, Corder's Epilogue reminds us that in IL studies as in all academic activity there is a human element.

Applied linguistics has gradually shifted the focus of its concern since it emerged as an independent academic discipline in the mid-1950s. It came into being with the intention of making available to language teachers and others the insights, techniques and methods of description derived from the linguistic sciences. Its purpose was to help language teachers understand more about language, first as an education they may have missed in their own studies and second as a training which might benefit them professionally and thereby improve language teaching. Two major developments have taken place since. The first, during the 1960s, brought a fusion between the practice of language teaching and the theoretical and descriptive concerns of the linguistic sciences. The outcome was a re-definition of applied linguistics which no longer recognized the direct unilateral application of linguistics to language teaching, but which aimed to relate the content areas of linguistics more closely to the special requirements and contexts of language teaching. Increasingly, the area of linguistics that seemed most relevant was socio-linguistics, which encouraged the application of studies of language varia-tion to the teaching of language for specific purposes and communicative language teaching in general. Throughout this development the focus was always on language and on the outcome of learning. The assumption was that language learners were reaching towards some final product: acquiring English for Medicine, developing their reading knowledge, improving their listening comprehension, performing 'communicatively', etc., but it was always a product and the direction of training and research in applied linguistics was towards planning for and describing that product.

The second development, beginning in the early 1970s, came about, it now appears, partly by accident, partly through the influence of work in psycholinguistics, and partly because of the inadequacy of the product model. The 'accident' was the availability of the techniques of error analysis which had been much exercised as a tool of contrastive analysis but which was left without an apparent purpose when contrastive analysis lost its theoretical rationale. Error analysis continued in use but as a means of plotting the learner's development and not of mapping the relations between the target language and the mother tongue. The influence of psycholinguistics was an inevitable overflow from work on child language acquisition which presented an obvious model for second-language acquisition since, it was argued, there are necessarily parallels between learning a second and a first language. Or, if the parallels are not exact, then employing the same research procedures will point to the differences. Both these reasons were still concerned with language even though they seemed to focus more on learning. The third reason was necessary in order to move the central interest from language as an 'object' of learning on to language learning itself. This had to do with the growing feeling that SLA was not necessarily like child language acquisition, that learners of second languages were not concerned with final outcomes (i.e. with becoming native speakers), but rather with partial outcomes, and that in SLA the major focus must be on process. Of course all processes are in one sense minor outcomes, but what gave SLA its excitement was the concept of interlanguage, which united the theoretical interest in SLA as distinct from child language acquisition and the practical interest in the systematicity of the learner's language at all stages. We have yet to realize the potential of such a construct, namely, that there are acceptable and usable levels of achievement in language learning which do not approximate native speaker outcomes. What interlanguage may yet do is to provide a satisfactory explanation of this 'partialness', i.e. it may be that second-language learning is actually promoted by the recognition and rewarding by teachers not only of correct part-knowledge but also of incorrect part-knowledge. This second development may, if it is carried through, dramatically change the concerns and the perception of applied linguistics.

If learners are regarded seriously and not as denizens of some language limbo then what they can do and what they know *while learning* is an important question. Like children, their state is not merely that of travellers (though, of course, it is that as well). Several names were suggested for the learner's system: transitional competence (Corder 1967), approximative system (Nemser 1971) and interlanguage (Selinker 1972). Selinker's term caught on and is now used in two distinct ways. The first is the general use: i.e. any synchronic state of SLA may be regarded as an IL, thus all learners exhibit interlanguage. It is an interesting question, of course, whether native speakers also exhibit IL, but this is perhaps a question that should not be asked – *not* because it opens the Pandora's Box of the definition of the native speaker but because it trivializes and renders vacuous the whole concept. IL needs to be restricted to second- and foreign-language learners and has value as a categorization of learning states in a second or foreign language. The second use of IL is much more rigorous and concerns a particular hypothesis of SLA. The IL hypothesis states that learning a second language is systematic. What kind of system is so far unresolved. What share of the system belongs to universal language-learning constraints, what effect cognitive learning demands have, what role the L1 plays, what place learning and performance strategies have and to what extent external factors (i.e. the situation) make a difference, these are all open questions. In the same way without prejudice to the answers that might be given to any of these questions, we are also faced with claims about the unchangeable sequence of learning, and the so-called 'natural order of morpheme acquisition' (Krashen 1981) has been suggested as a touchstone for all such studies. SLA is pre-theoretical, it delineates an area of professional interest. IL, on the other hand, is highly theoretical and presents a view of SLA which is systematic and system-friendly.

Many of these open questions were discussed at the Edinburgh Seminar. They reflected two quite distinct approaches to the field. Two voices emerged during the seminar, by no means always from the same people; but sufficiently distinct and coherent for some attempt at description to be made. The two voices spoke for different views or attitudes *towards the same data*: this is unsurprising since many academic disciplines represent differing starting-points, e.g. some parts of sociology and psychology, or biology and physiology.

One view was largely linguistic, the other largely psychological. Furthermore, a third view, the educational, shifted backwards and forwards between the linguistic and the psychological, sometimes aligning itself with one, sometimes with the other. Some such division, however, kept surfacing, if only in the mind of the present writer.

The *linguistic* view stresses product, i.e. the acquisition of whatever it is that native speakers of the target language have acquired. It therefore views IL from a normative position (i.e. that of the target language system). For instance, it has stressed the importance of the morpheme studies – both on the grounds of their value as linguistic indicators and also because they represent a usable methodology. This represents a challenge to the alternative view which dismisses the morpheme studies as trivial in the sense that it requires a demonstration of some equivalent methodology which would show that context is indeed salient. The linguistic view is basically universal, assuming that context is not in itself critical and that the evidence of IL like all 'exceptional languages' is finally unitary, i.e. that it adds to our knowledge of language structure. Indeed, this is a very attractive view: we do not need to accept this incorporation of 'exceptional languages' (i.e. creoles, pidgins, aphasic language, sign language, interlanguage, etc.) within language itself, but rather we can consider them as test beds for a general theory of language. If such a theory applies to exceptional languages, its own claim to explanatory adequacy becomes compelling.

The status of contrastive analysis among linguists has never been very high mainly because they are not primarily concerned with learning or with pedagogy. Contrastive analysis to them represents, therefore, familial language relationships which are not subject to argument or interpretation except in marginal cases of language contact or of language borrowing. But linguistics has traditionally interested itself in the evolution of languages and in that context has taken a severely Darwinian line, i.e. a rejection of the inheritance of acquired characteristics. What has surfaced, therefore, in the discussion on transfer has been general agreement: an agreement inevitable from the linguistic point of view, that *of course* L1 transfer takes place; and a shift of opinion on the psychological side, which had itself abandoned contrastive analysis after the discrediting of behaviourism, has fostered the view that after all there must be interference from the L1 and that the aim must be to incorporate within one area of study L1, plus target language, plus the IL itself.

The *psychological* view, stressing the importance of process as against product, partly no doubt because 'product' in cognitive learning is never finally reached, took the view that IL was a necessary autonomous system which required to be studied and described in its own terms. To try to extend IL to cover both exceptional languages and L1 was regarded as unhelpful and, potentially, a trivialization of the useful concept of IL by being made too powerful. It is not surprising within this view therefore that the same IL data can be analysed both as an autonomous system and as a normative one. For the same reason, this second view is less interested in exceptional languages as evidence about language than in IL as evidence about learning. Equally, this second view prefers to combine all strategies under the *learning* umbrella, regarding so-called communication strategies as either ad hoc adjustments or as subsets of learning strategies. This second view emphasizes the value of discourse in IL as further evidence for learning and disassociates 'true' discourse studies from those which use discourse material to collect examples of morpheme performance.

There was a third view which switched its allegiance and which can appropriately be labelled educational. A distinction was made between communication and learning strategies, the implication being that education is interested in both. Again, the educational view as against the psychological one was that speculation is as valuable (some thought more valuable) than empirical research. Quite what claim was being made here was hard to see. What was clear was that Pit Corder's own tradition as a master speculator (see above) was being tacitly invoked. It was equally clear that *both* speculation (i.e. theory-creating) and empirical investigation were essential.

The educational view, whch had aligned itself alternatively with the linguistic and the psychological views, itself came under attack from both the other groups towards the end of the Seminar because of its interest in *action* and *action research*. The educational view seems to be that IL is a learning state which is amenable to teaching even though it is so little described. Making teachers 'aware' of the phenomenon 'sensitizes' them to learners' problems. This view was directly challenged by non-educationists who argued that it was premature and that, as Bloomfield advised, we should 'wait upon science'. Paradoxically then, we can view the educational position as being concerned with the implications of research rather than with its applications; or, as Corder remarked, implied and not applied linguistics is what the discipline perhaps should be called.

But in the event we were agreed on perhaps four things: first, that L1 has an influence on SLA, second, that IL is still in such a state of flux that application requires caution, third that there is some value in restricting the term IL to SLA, and fourth, that it is important that languages other than English are investigated both for the sake of IL theory and to prevent IL becoming excessively narrow and abstract.

Acknowledgements

The twin enterprise of a large international Seminar and the publication of its proceedings can succeed only through the help and encouragement of a number of people. We are grateful to Dr Burnett, Principal, Edinburgh University, and Professor Asher, Head of the Linguistics Department for inaugurating the Seminar, to the British Council and the Institute for Applied Language Studies for financial help, to the Institute staff for back-up over a long period, and to the University Staff Club for opening its facilities to the Seminar. The Seminar discussions were carefully reported and appear now as Discussion Summaries: for the clarity of these valuable reports we must thank Tony Howatt and his team of post-graduate students, Ian McGrath, Bisimwa Nhakta Kuderwa, Bidemi Okanlawon, Maria Pavesi and Regina Weinert. Ian McGrath must be thanked for help with the assembling of the list of references. I would also like to thank the staff of Edinburgh University Press for their confidence in the book and the professional and speedy support they have provided.

Particular thanks are due to Myint Su for organising the much enjoyed social programme of the Seminar, to Lynda Lawson for all the administrative and secretarial work associated with the Seminar and the book, and to my fellow editors for professional care and skill.

Abbreviations

ESL   English as a Second Language

IL   Interlanguage

L1   First Language or Mother-tongue

L2   Second Language

NP   Noun Phrase

SLA   Second Language Acquisition

PART ONE

A UNIVERSAL HYPOTHESIS

1. The Empirical Basis for the
Universal Hypothesis in Interlanguage Studies

1. Introduction

In this paper I will present empirical evidence for the universal hypothesis in IL studies. First, I will review the literature on the role of universal implicational hierarchies in second-language acquisition and second, I will present specific results from research I have recently conducted investigating the role of universal implicational hierarchies in second-language acquisition.

Before beginning the review of relevant studies, I would like to make clear the approach I am taking and in particular delimit the areas that I am and am not dealing with. The word 'universal' in the second-language acquisition literature has appeared in a variety of contexts. For example, many researchers have discussed 'universals of acquisition'. The discussion in this area has been most evident in the literature on morpheme acquisition. Within this body of research, researchers have attempted to determine the universal acquisition order, or accuracy order, of morphemes. That is, the attempt is to determine a universal order of acquisition independent of native-language background (Bailey, Madden and Krashen 1974; Dulay and Burt 1974).

Still another approach dealing with universals relates to the discussion of universals of language use (production, perception, metalinguistic judgements, etc.) as opposed to those of language form. The particular processes that have received the greatest emphasis in L2 acquisition research are: transfer, generalization, fossilization, processes which are common to all learners in acquiring a second language. An example in this area is that of Taylor (1975) who suggests processes such as generalization of target-language material and transfer of native-language information are subsets of the same cognitive process: use of prior linguistic knowledge, in the first case based on the L2 and in the second based on the L1.

The two approaches discussed thus far can be classified as dynamic approaches in that they are concerned with developmental universals (cf. Baudouin de Courtenay (1972) for a distinction between dynamic/static aspects of language). A crucial aspect of this area of research is the starting point of L2 acquisition. Is something like the native language the starting point with restructuring taking place until the final product is reached, the final product being a linguistic system which is more or less target-like? Or is there a continuum of increasing complexity as suggested by Corder (1977b, 1983a)? He suggests that the starting point for learners is 'an earlier stage of their [learners] own linguistic development' (Corder 1983a, 91). He further asserts that the starting point is a 'more basic, possibly *universal*, grammar. This could be expressed as the mother tongue stripped of all its specific features' (emphasis mine; 1983a, 91).

There is another major area of consideration – what we might call a more static area. The issue within this paradigm is: what constraints are there on the formation of ILs? One approach is to consider what is universal to all ILs. If this approach is to contribute to an understanding of the nature of language, one must then extend these results beyond the class of inter-languages to a consideration of how these universals relate to properties of natural languages. A second approach, and the one taken in this paper is to begin with the range and limits of variation of natural languages and deter-mine how interlanguages do and do not follow the same constraints. The first approach begins with the IL and the second with language universals. While I have adopted the second in this paper due primarily to my own research in this area, I firmly believe that it is only through a multiplicity of approaches to IL studies that we will begin to fit the pieces of the IL puzzle together.

Considering universals from a static framework, there are two diverg-ent approaches that have been taken – one a Chomskyan approach and the other a Greenbergian approach.

Within the Chomskyan paradigm a universal grammar is comprised of universals of language (both formal and substantive) derived from an in-depth investigation of a language. The evidence for universals within this paradigm comes from a *detailed* analysis of a language. Furthermore, the detail necessary precludes the possibility of examining a large number of languages. Universal grammar in fact defines the class of possible human languages. Additionally, it is claimed that universal properties are innate and it is *because* of their innateness that children are able to construct abstract grammars in a relatively short amount of time. (See Cook (in press) for an excellent description of the Chomskyan paradigm as it relates to second language acquisition.)

The second paradigm that is generally considered within the context of language universals is that of Greenberg (1966), elaborated upon by such scholars as Hawkins (1983), Comrie (1981), Keenan (1978b), Thompson (1978) and others. The focus within this approach is on the 'search for regularities in the ways that languages vary, and on the constraints and principles that underlie this variation' (Hawkins 1983, 6). The type of language data used in this tradition is based more on surface features than are the data within a Chomskyan tradition. Hence, it is possible (and necessary) to consider a wide range of languages in the determination of universals. For example, consider the typological universal that subject-object-verb languages generally have preposed rather than postposed adjectives. A general cross-linguistic statement of this sort is not discoverable on the basis of a single language. Within this framework, two types of universals have been noted: (1) absolute and (2) statistical or universal tendencies (Comrie 1984). The former are properties which are shared by all languages and the latter, determined by considering all languages or those of a particular typology, are properties which are common to many languages. Absolute universals are directly witnessed in every (investigated) language. Statistical universals are not present as surface-true generalizations for at least one language. For a fuller discussion of these issues and a critical review see Hawkins (1983) and Comrie (1981).

The above brief discussion has not been intended as an exhaustive list of the different ways in which the term universal has been used within a linguistic and SLA framework. Rather, it was intended to show that there are many ways in which universals have been discussed. This clarification is necessary in order to put my remarks on universals within a proper perspective. What I will focus on in this paper is the literature which deals with universal constraints on interlanguages from a Greenbergian perspective. Secondly, I will deal with both static and dynamic aspects of this perspective, considering not only constraints or influencing factors on grammars, but also the ways in which grammars change and universals affect grammars as a function of increased proficiency in a target language.

2. Universal Constraints on Interlanguages – a Literature Review

Within linguistic theory universal generalizations are believed to hold true for natural languages. However, the concept of 'natural language' is ill-defined. Little attention has been paid to defining a natural language because there has been little need for such a consideration. Precisely what falls under the rubric of natural language is not clear. It is generally accepted that the languages people learn as children, such as English, Spanish, French, etc., are natural languages. It is also clear that systems such as Fortran and Pascal are not. In fact Adjémian's (1976) definition of natural language 'any human language shared by a community of speakers and developed over time by a general process of evolution' would categorize the above-mentioned language systems in the same way. However, this definition does not deal with the crucial question: what is a language? Is Pascal a human language? Is it shared by a community? Does it develop by a general process of evolution? There are ways in which we could conceive of Pascal (or music for that matter) which would result in an affirmative answer to all of the above questions. Yet, it seems that we would want to rule Pascal, or music, out in a discussion of language universals. Thus, ILs present the kind of challenge that forces a precision in definition. One way to begin to come to grips with the notion of 'natural language' is to consider ways in which ILs do and do not share well-defined characteristics of languages, such as English, Italian, etc. Selinker (1972) claimed that ILs are systematic in the sense of natural languages and are thus subject to analysis. Adjémian further claimed that ILs are subject to the same kind of linguistic constraints as natural languages. In other words ILs will not violate language universals. Thus, since sentences such as

He said that John is happy

(where *he* and *John* are coreferential) are impossible in natural languages because *he* both precedes and commands *John,* we would not expect a similar IL sentence to occur. Much headway has been made in the description of ILs, that is, in determining the systematicity of ILs. On the other hand, relatively little concern has been given to the interaction of language universals and a learner's developing grammar. Thus, the claim regarding universals has in large part been made without being tested against IL data and without a careful definition of 'language'. An important point, and one which potentially discriminates between 'natural languages' and ILs is that ILs are much more of an individual phenomenon than are 'natural languages'. While there might be something like a Spanish-English IL and there might be 'things' which all Spanish speakers learning English 'do', it is probably also the case that the grammars for any two individuals of the same native language and the same target language differ in some significant way.

Before discussing the work in this area and thus evaluating the claim that ILs *are* subject to universal constraints, it is necessary to examine different types of universals. Previous arguments have assumed that all types of universals will have the same effect. It is this assumption that I would like to challenge. In so doing, I will argue that if some universals do not appear to have an effect on learner-grammars, it does not necessarily invalidate the claim itself since there may be a priori predictions we can make about which universals will and will not constrain ILs. Furthermore, it may be necessary to distinguish between absolute constraints and an overall shaping factor. Because ILs involve more than a single linguistic system, interactions arise which may be unlike what occurs within a single linguistic system. Furthermore, because the ways in which two linguistic systems interact for any given individual may in some respects be unique to that individual, it may be more appropriate to talk about shaping influences rather than absolute constraints.

To begin to investigate systematically the question of universals, one must consider the source of a universal. Why is a universal a universal? Gass and Ard (1984) identified five major sources for language universals: (1) physical basis (e.g. the shape of the vocal tract), (2) human perceptual and cognitive apparatus and processing capabilities, (3) language acquisition device (and/or a neurological device for language use), (4) historical change and (5) interaction (see also Hawkins 1983; Dryer 1980; Grosu and Thompson 1977). These categories are not intended as the only sources, but only as representative of the most common explanations generally given to the 'rationale' behind a universal. They serve as a useful framework within which one can begin to examine the influence of universals on second-language grammars. In Gass and Ard (1984) we presented evidence which suggests that those universals which arise from language change are least likely to be an influencing or shaping factor on ILs. Those that stem from either a physical basis or processing and cognitive constraints are predicted to have the greatest effect. As an example consider the universal accessibility hierarchy proposed by Keenan and Comrie (1977). On the basis of cross-linguistic data they claimed that there is a hierarchy of relative clause types which a language can relativise. Keenan and Bimson (1975) and Givón (1975), while suggesting different explanations for the universal, both provide explanations which fall within the perceptual/cognitive domain. Hence, we would predict that there would be an effect on developing learner-grammars. To support this, in Gass (1979 and 1980) I presented data from second-language learners relating to this particular universal. Those data can be summarized as follows: (1) learners generally follow the pattern of the hierarchy in terms of accuracy of RC production, avoidance of structure, frequency of production, and judgements of grammaticality, (2) native language and target language factors play a counterbalancing role, resulting in non-hierarchical orderings in some instances. On the other hand there are examples of universals which do not seem to have an effect on L2 acquisition. Ard (1975), Givon (1971), Jeffers and Lehiste (1979) suggest that the mechanism through which many word order universals arise is the creation of new items and structures. That is, word-order relationships are motivated by diachronic factors. Given that in many cases the factors which motivated the universal are distanced from the synchronic grammar, there is no direct connection between the two and there is little reason to expect that those particular universals will affect L2 grammars. For example, in a given language A B may be the only possible order of elements simply because there is no series of historical changes through which B A could have arisen. If so, it does not follow that B A would be any harder to process or harder to learn than A B. In Gass and Ard (1984), we presented data from English learners of German, Spanish learners of English and English learners of Spanish to show that at least in the domain of word order the predictions are borne out. While a more detailed discussion is beyond the scope of this paper, it is important to realize the possible differential effects of universals since an argument which relies on universals as a monolithic phenomenon in dealing with their effect on L2 developing grammars will exclude potentially explanatory information.

In addition to my own theoretical work on relative clauses, I have also presented evidence from a pedagogical perspective (Gass 1982) in which I showed that within an instructional framework, generalizability occurred in accordance with the principles of the accessibility hierarchy discussed above. Students who were given instruction on a universally more difficult position were able to generalize their knowledge to an easier position, whereas the same generalizability did not occur from the easy positions to the more difficult ones.

Another prediction of the accessibility hierarchy is that pronominal reflexes are more likely in some relative-clause positions than in others. Hyltenstam (in press) found that the deletion/retention of pronominal copies in relative clauses by L2 learners could be accounted for in terms of the tenets of the accessibility hierarchy. Tarallo and Myhill (1983) in their investigation of the acquisition of relative clauses by English L1 learners of German and Portuguese (right-branching languages) and Chinese and Japanese (left-branching languages) found similar results. Higher hierarchical positions were easier to relativize than lower ones. As with my study not all of their results could be explained on the basis of language universals. L1- and L2-specific facts were necessary to adequately account for the data.

Evidence from a different syntactic domain comes from Dryer (1980) who presented a universal hierarchy of sentential complements suggesting as its basis cognitive principles. According to Dryer's hierarchy, given below, complements are most likely to occur in clause-final position and least likely in clause-internal position:

clause final > clause initial > clause internal

Given the basis of the universal it is expected that L2 learners will behave in accordance with its principles. Frawley (1981) found that the hierarchical orderings suggested by Dryer were also followed by L2 learners. They used more clause-final sentential complements than clause-initial complements than clause-internal ones.

Schmidt (1980) in her investigation of coordinate structures found that the types of coordination used by L2 learners followed universal constraints. In her study she examined such coordination phenomena as represented in the following sentences:

John plays the violin and Mary the piano

and

John typed and Mary mailed the letter

but

*John the violin and Mary plays the piano.

Her data came from German, Finnish, Mandarin, Japanese and Arabic L1 speakers learning English. She found that while some of the coordinated structures that these learners produced were not L2-like nor L1-like, they did *not* violate universal constraints.

Gundel and Tarone (1983) examined instances of pronominal anaphora by L2 learners. Based on prior work by Gundel (1978a, 1978b and 1980), they considered universal syntactic and pragmatic conditions on anaphora, finding that these conditions are not violated in IL grammars.

Wode (this volume) reports on negation in L1 German, L1 English, L2 German (L1 English) and L2 English (L1 German) claiming that all examples of negation which occur in these data are also typologically possible in the world's languages. That is, none of the negative forms which appear in the learner data (in this case either L1 or L2) violate constraints of negation in natural languages.

Similarly Selinker and Douglas (forthcoming) present data first presented in Selinker (1969) from Hebrew learners of English regarding postverbal adjuncts to the verb. They present both the attested forms and logically possible but unattested forms in their data set. What is interesting is the fact that the unattested forms can be accounted for on the basis of constraints on human languages in that the unattested structures do not, to the best of my knowledge, appear in natural languages (I thank Helmut Zobl, personal communication, for pointing this out).

In the area of semantics Kumpf (1982) presented evidence from untutored learners to suggest that the tense/aspect system of those learners did not correspond to the system of either the native language or the target language. She speculated that in such cases the IL 'system reflects the capacity of humans to create . . . unique form to meaning to function relationships' and importantly, these newly created systems will correspond to universal principles of natural languages. For example, one of her subjects had created an aspectual system, basically a morphological means of marking completed versus non-completed action, unlike that of either the target language or the native language system. To explain this learner's 'novel' system, she points to evidence from the world's languages as well as from child language that aspect is primary to tense. Further evidence comes from Guiora (personal communication) who claimed that most children cannot deal with time abstractly until they are about nine year's old. Thus, Kumpf's subject's system corresponds to what would be predicted on the basis of universal principles.

In a different type of study, also dealing with tense/aspect systems, Gass and Ard (1984) investigated grammaticality judgements of tense/aspect systems by L2 learners. We found that those parts of the tense/aspect system which were closer to a universal core were accepted as grammatical in the L2 with significantly greater frequency than those items which were more distant. The more distant items were not accepted even in instances where the native language used the translation equivalent with roughly the same function. We presented independent linguistic evidence that the progressive in a sentence such as

I am driving a car now

has more of the 'coreness' of the progressive than a sentence like

I am flying to New York tomorrow.

Learners in fact accepted the former as grammatical more often than the

9

latter. This was the case even for subjects whose native language has both possibilities. Similarly, Kellerman (1978b) in examining acceptability of polysemous lexical items found that those meanings which were closer to the 'core', that is were more 'basic' in meaning, were more likely to be accepted in the L2 than those which were furthest from the core. For example, Dutch learners of English were more likely to select

He broke his leg

as acceptable in English than

He broke his word

despite the fact that both are acceptable in Dutch and in English.

In the area of phonology there are even less data available. Tarone (1980a and in press) has investigated syllable-structure preference in IL phonology. In her work, based primarily on Korean, Cantonese and Portuguese learners of English, she found evidence of a preference for open (consonant-vowel) syllables independent of native-language background. Crucial to the interpretation of this preference, is the fact that the only syllable type shared by *all* languages is the consonant-vowel syllable (Clements and Keyser 1983). They propose that 'the syllable type consonant-vowel belongs to the grammar of all languages' (Clements and Keyser 1983, 28). The learners in Tarone's study 'simplified' the syllable structure by means of either deletion or epenthesis so that the resulting structure is a universally preferred one. As with the data reported on for other areas of the grammar, universal tendencies were not the sole determining factors in shaping IL phonology. Clear evidence of native-language influence could also be found.

A study also based on syllable structure is that of Sato (1983a). She presented data from two Vietnamese children learning English. However, her results were not compatible with Tarone's. The two Vietnamese children did not show a tendency to use open syllables. While Sato does not offer an explanation as to why this discrepancy occurs, it should be noted that at times native- or target-language influences are strong enough to counter the influence of universals (cf. Gass and Ard 1984). Just why this might have been the case in these data (if that is the appropriate explanation) is in need for further exploration.

Eckman (1984) investigated the question of violations of language universals in non-native languages. In considering data from phonology and syntax, he found that when violations of universal constraints do occur, they can be accounted for on the basis of the contact situation. In other words, there are explanations based on either the native or the target language to justify the violation. He claims that there is a constraint on ILs such that when violations of language universals occur, they can be accounted for by native- or target-language facts. As an example, consider the data he presents in Eckman (1981). His data come from the acquisition of final voice contrasts by Spanish and Mandarin learners of English. English has a voice contrast in word final position. Neither Spanish nor Mandarin has a contrast. With regard to universals, it is to be noted that no language has a rule of schwa paragoge (Sanders 1979 cited in Eckman 1981), a rule which inserts a schwa following a word-final voiced abstruent. Thus, if universal constraints are followed, speakers of these languages are predicted to resolve the final voiced contrast 'problem' in some way other than by adding a schwa word-finally. In the L2 speech of the Spanish speakers in Eckman's sample, the subjects 'resolved' the problem by devoicing in word-final position. On the other hand, Mandarin learners of English do use a rule of schwa paragoge even though it violates a universal prohibition against such a rule. What is crucial is that even though the rule per se does not exist, there are NL *motivating* factors for such a rule in Mandarin; there are not for Spanish. It is only in the former case where the universal restriction is violated.

Another example concerning universal constraints and ILs comes from Eckman, Moravcsik and Wirth (forthcoming), although here the evidence is conflicting. They investigated two universals set forth by Greenberg et al. (1978) concerning possible consonant sequences. They found that for the most part the universals were supported in the ILs of their subjects. That is, the implicational relationships of consonant clusters in 'natural languages' is also found in ILs. However, they did find some counterexamples. Unfortunately, the explanation which they gave has to do with the lack of instrumental measurements. While the results are generally supportive of the influence of universals, we do not know (1) the etiology of the universal or (2) the strength of the counterexamples. Instrumental analyses of their data may, as they say, eliminate the counterexamples or, on the other hand, they may create new ones. There is not enough information to determine whether this is an actual counterexample to universal influences or whether the apparent counterexamples are explainable in terms of the native language, target language or universal source.

A final example from phonology comes from Broselow (1983). In her work she discusses epenthesis in the IL of Cairene and Iraqi Arabic learners of English. Her specific focus of attention is on language transfer; however, she argues that transfer cannot be understood without reference to language universals since transfer does not occur in just those instances in which the target language, in this case English, violates universal principles.

I now turn to work I have recently completed investigating the acquisition of complex sentences by L2 learners. Specifically, I investigate the interaction of a universal implicational hierarchy and language-specific facts.

3. Complex Sentences

3.1. Background

Languages of the world differ in the domain of word order both in terms of (1) the order of canonical elements in a sentence (subject-verb-object versus subject-object-verb versus verb-subject-object, etc.) and (2) the rigidity of those elements. In English, for example, word order is necessary for determining relationships between elements in a sentence. In a sentence with a noun$_1$-verb-noun$_2$ sequence, the first noun is taken as the subject of the sentence and the second as the object. If the order of elements differs (noun$_2$-verb-noun$_1$), there is a concomitant change in meaning. (I am excluding the possibility of intonational contours affecting meaning changes.) Hence, given typical intonation, the two sentences differ significantly in meaning:

> The boy loves the doll.
> The doll loves the boy.

The scope of investigation of this study is sentence interpretation of complex sentences. I deal specifically with differences in interpretation among sentences in which the main verb is or behaves like *promise, tell* or *ask.* The interpretation of complex sentences with *promise, tell* or *ask* as the main verb is dependent on the verb in the main clause. Specifically, sentence pairs such as the following have the same surface syntactic pattern: NP-verb NP-infinitive-prepositional phrase. However, the interpretation of these sentences is quite different:

> The boy told the girl to go to school
> The boy promised the girl to go to school.

In the first sentence the subject of *go* is *girl,* the object of the main verb *tell.* In fact, this pattern is the predominant one in English. On the other hand, in the second sentence, the subject of *go* is *boy,* that is, the subject of the main verb. Chomsky (1969, 1972) in investigating the acquisition of English complex structures by children found that appropriate sentence interpretation was influenced by the frequency of the syntactic pattern in English. In her work, she found that children interpreted the *promise* sentences as if they followed the syntactic patterns of the *tell* sentences. Hence, in sentences such as the second one, children interpreted the sentence as if the *girl* were to go to school, not the boy. Correct sentence interpretation was therefore more accurate on the *tell* sentences than on the *promise* sentences.[1]

In the SLA literature, a number of studies relating to Chomsky's study have appeared. d'Anglejan and Tucker (1975) investigated the promise/ tell/ask distinction among adult French native speakers learning English at two levels of proficiency. Their results suggest little difference in the acquisition of sentence types like the *tell/promise* pair above. Incorrect interpretation of these sentences was approximately the same with 25 per cent errors on the *promise* sentences and 19 per cent errors on the *tell* sentences for the lower-level students and 4 per cent and 5 per cent respectively for the more advanced group. An interesting finding occurred on sentences such as:

> The child asked the teacher to leave the room

and

> The teacher asked the child to leave the room

which are ambiguous for many speakers of English, although there is a preferred interpretation. In the second sentence both groups overwhelmingly selected the *child* as the subject of the second verb. On the other hand, in the first sentence where syntactic and semantic information are in conflict there is a progression from using primarily semantic information by beginning students to a primary use of syntactic information by native speakers with the advanced ESL learners being in between.

In a replication of d'Anglejan and Tucker's work, Cooper, Olshtain, Tucker and Waterbury (1979) and Bongaerts (1983) investigated the acquisition of complex structures by Hebrew and Cairene Arabic native speakers (Cooper et al.) and Dutch (Bongaerts). A direct comparison with the d'Anglejan and Tucker results is difficult since one cannot easily compare proficiency levels. Nonetheless, their results suggest similar although not identical results. The Cooper et al. subjects showed slightly more divergence between the *promise, tell* sentence types, however, in all cases there were fewer errors on the *tell* type sentences than on the *promise* sentences.

Berent (1983) in a study involving L2 learners and prelingually deaf adults found that the error rate of *promise* sentences was higher than that of *tell* sentences, but less than that of the ambiguous *ask* sentences.

The study I report on here investigates the acquisition of *promise/tell/ask* sentences by adult L2 learners as a function of syntactic/semantic and pragmatic factors. This study departs from earlier treatments of complex sentences in that it deals with this set of sentences not as a unitary syntactic phenomenon, but rather as a function of the role relationships between the two NPs in the sentence. The relationship is largely determined by universal factors.[2]

3.2. Universal Topicality Hierarchy

This study deals with universal hierarchies and their interaction with language-specific facts.[3] It has been established cross-linguistically (Givón 1976; Duranti 1979; Hawkinson and Hyman 1974; Morolong and Hyman 1977) that not all elements are equally likely to be selected as topics. The universal ordering of elements is given below:

human > animate > inanimate.

The implicational hierarchy is to be interpreted in such a way that there is a greater likelihood for a human noun to be selected as a topic than for an animate noun to be selected as a topic than for an inanimate noun to be selected as a topic. This ordering is independent of syntax.

How semantic information such as that implicit in the topicality hierarchy interacts in actual language use with language-specific syntactic facts is a question of theoretical import. For example, generative and interpretive semantics assume a *single* direction of interpretation between syntax and semantics. Dressler (1977) on the other hand proposes a bidirectional influence. The way syntax and semantics are found to interact as evidenced by L2 data may shed light on this issue. Further, knowledge of what kinds of syntactic and semantic information may be more or less susceptible to interaction can result from a study of interaction in language use. With regard to theories of L2 acquisition, these results shed light on not only the kind of linguistic information which is used but also on the ways in which it is used in the acquisition of an L2. A language like English in which there is general dominance of syntax is a fertile ground to investigate syntactic/ semantic interactions. Importantly, L2 learners provide us with a way to investigate the resolution of semantic/syntactic conflicts in a way which is not possible with monolingual speakers at a single point in time since

TABLE 1. Subjects

Native Language	2	3	4	5	Total
Chinese	1	1	1		3
Arabic	6	6	10	12	34
Spanish	6	10	16	16	48
Korean	1		1	1	3
Greek	1				1
Portuguese		1	1		2
Finnish		1	1		2
Japanese		2	5	6	13
Serbocroatian			1		1
Thai				1	1
Italian				1	1
Turkish				2	2
Total	15	21	36	39	111

conflicts per se are not readily observable in a static situation. Distance is necessary in order to 'see' the resolution. Diachronic change (time) is one sort of distance, acquisition is another.

3.3 Procedure

3.3.1. Subjects. The subjects for this study were 111 learners of English, ranging in proficiency from level two to level five of a five-level intensive course program at the English Language Institute of the University of Michigan. The distribution of levels and native languages can be seen in Table 1.

3.3.2. Methodology. Each subject was presented with either fourteen or twenty-one sentences,[4] each followed by a question designed to elicit the subject's interpretation of the sentence. (See Appendix A for a listing of the sentences used.) The sentences varied not only in terms of verb type (*ask/ promise/tell*), but also in terms of the two NPs and their place on the topicality hierarchy. Hence, the design of the experiment was such that

syntactic and semantic information at times converged and at others con-
flicted. Information, then, was either complementary or competitive (cf.
also Bates and MacWhinney 1979, 1981; Bates, McNew, MacWhinney,
Devescovi and Smith 1982).

TABLE 2. Results of *tell* sentences where both NPs are of equal
status on the topicality hierarchy

NPs	Level			
	2	3	4	5
human/human	2-3	1-9	0-10	1-14
Ex. The boy told				
the girl to go.				
animate/animate	1-4	1-8	1-11	1-13
Ex. The dog told				
the cat to go.				
inanimate/inanimate	2-3	0-9	6-8	1-15
Ex. The chair told				
the table to go.				

3.4. Results and Discussion

This section is divided into five parts. First, I deal with the topicality
hierarchy in relation to the *tell* sentences, second with the *promise* verbs.
This is followed in 3.4.3 by a discussion of these results. In section 3.4.4 the
results of the *ask* sentences are given and finally in section 3.4.5 the *ask*
sentences are discussed.

TABLE 3. Results of *tell* sentences where syntactic and
semantic information converge

NPs	Level			
	2	3	4	5
inanimate/animate	1-5	0-10	2-12	1-15
Ex. The chair told				
the dog to go.				
inanimate/human	1-8	3-8	1-7	0-8
Ex. The chair told				
the man to go.				
animate/human	1-4	2-7	1-13	1-15
Ex. The dog told				
the man to go.				

3.4.1. Tell sentences. In Tables 2–5 I present the results for the *tell* verbs as a
function of both proficiency levels and the relationship of the NPs vis-à-vis
the topicality hierarchy. In Table 2 are the results of those sentences in which

15

both NPs have the same status on the topicality hierarchy. Recall that the native English interpretation is such that the second NP is the subject of the lower verb. Results are listed in terms of the number of responses to the first

TABLE 4. Results of *tell* sentences where syntactic and semantic information conflict

NPs	Level			
	2	3	4	5
animate/inanimate	5-4	8-3	4-5	4-4
Ex. The dog told the chair to go.				
human/inanimate	3-2	5-4	6-8	1-15
Ex. The woman told the table to go.				
human/animate	1-5	0-10	2-12	1-15
Ex. The man told the dog to go.				

versus the second NP. Thus, a response such as 2–3 is to be interpreted in such a way that, given the sentence

The woman told the man to go home,

two subjects responded that it is the *woman* who should go home and three responded that the *man* should go home.

In Table 3 are the results of those sentences in which the second NP is higher on the topicality hierarchy than the first NP. Thus, from the perspective of *both* syntax *and* semantics, we predict that learners would choose this

TABLE 5. Results of *promise* sentences where both NPs are of equal status on the topicality hierarchy

NPs	Level			
	2	3	4	5
human/human	8-1	7-4	8-1	8-0
animate/animate	6-3	8-3	6-3	8-0
inanimate/inanimate	7-2	8-1	9-3	13-0

NP as the subject of the verb, that is, as the doer of the action. As can be seen, there is a very strong tendency for the correct syntactic and semantic choice to be made at all levels. In fact, the strength of the choice of the second NP in this group is slightly stronger than the strength of the second NP in the equal-status in Table 2.

In Table 4 we present the results of those sentences in which semantic and syntactic information are in conflict. These are the sentences in which the first NP is higher on the hierarchy. The conflict arises in that syntactically it is the second NP which is the subject. Here the choice of the second NP is less clear than in the results presented in Tables 1 and 2.

3.4.2. Promise *sentences*. In Tables 5–7 are the results of the *promise* sentences. In Table 5 are the results of those sentences which have NPs of equal status vis-à-vis the topicality hierarchy. Again, as with the *tell* sentences, the results are in the direction of target-language interpretation.

TABLE 6. Results of *promise* sentences where syntactic and semantic information converge

NPs	Level			
	2	3	4	5
animate / inanimate	3-2	5-4	9-3	12-1
human / inanimate	7-2	9-2	8-1	8-0
human / animate	5-4	6-5	9-3	13-0

In Table 6 are the results of those sentences in which syntactic and semantic information are in conformity.

In Table 7 I present the results for those sentences in which there is a conflict in syntactic and semantic information.

TABLE 7. Results of *promise* sentences where syntactic and semantic information conflict

NPs	Level			
	2	3	4	5
inanimate / animate	3-3	4-5	11-3	15-1
inanimate / human	2-4	5-5	9-5	14-2
animate / human	6-3	8-3	9-0	7-1

3.4.3. *Discussion of* tell *and* promise *sentences*. The results that I have presented show an interesting developmental progression in terms of the effects of universal hierarchies on the acquisition of syntax. With specific reference to the *tell* sentences, we see that in those sentences in which there is no conflict of information, the general tendency is for the correct English interpretation to occur.

TABLE 8. Results of *ask* sentences with NPs of unequal status

NPs	Level			
	2	3	4	5
animate / inanimate	100-0	100-0	100-0	88-12
inanimate / animate	0-100	20-80	17-83	8-92

On the other hand, where there is conflict, semantics (the hierarchical relationships of the NPs) has a stronger effect at earlier stages of proficiency with syntax 'winning' only at the later stages. The line representing conflicting information has only 50 per cent correct responses initially. (These

17

findings are consistent with the earlier studies reported on in L2 acquisition.) This becomes particularly clear if we compare the results of Tables 3 and 4 for the same role relationships, but with reversed orders. These tables are combined in Table 8.

If we look for example at the inanimate/human as opposed to the human/inanimate relationship, we see very different results. In the first case, where the topicality hierarchy predicts that it will be the human noun that will be selected as the subject and syntactic constraints of English also predict that the human noun will be selected, there is an overwhelming preference at all proficiency levels to select the human nouns. However, in the second case, the topicality hierarchy (a semantically based hierarchy) predicts that the human noun will be selected and syntax predicts that the inanimate noun will be selected. Initially, that is, at the earlier proficiency levels, there is a preference for the human noun to be chosen whereas by the fourth level the preference begins to favour the inanimate noun and finally by level 5, the inanimate noun is overwhelmingly preferred. In levels 2, 3 and 4 the conflict is apparent. No one noun is the obvious choice. However, we do see a direction in the choice (in levels 2 and 3 in favour of semantics and in level 4 in favour of syntax). It is only at the most proficient level that these students have learned to separate out the dominant role of syntax in English. Thus, it seems that part of learning the syntax of a language involves learning the relative importance and strength of syntactic constraints. Of additional interest here is the way pragmatics affects both syntax and semantics. Consider the third row in Table 2 where both NPs are inanimate. Given real-world knowledge the sentences given represent a situation which of all the situations is the most unlikely to occur. This is reflected in the results in that neither syntax nor semantics is the dominant choice. In other words, the pragmatics of the situation dominates, not permitting a clear dominance of either syntax or semantics. A similar pattern is seen in Table 4, also in the bottom row. The results for these sentences differ from the other sentences within this group. While they represent conflicting information, they are also sentences which are very likely to occur. In this case the pragmatics of the situation promotes results which are more typical of converging rather than conflicting information.

The situation is even more complex if we consider the strength of the 'pull' for only those sentences in which there is conflicting information. We can see that there is differential strength depending not only on the order of NPs, but also on the place of the NP on the hierarchy. When the relationship is either human or animate as the first NP and inanimate as the second, the higher one on the hierarchy 'wins' out (at least at a time when, in general, semantics has the overall dominant role), but when the relationship is human to animate, the effect of the hierarchy is felt to a lesser degree and syntactic constraints dominate (even before learners have 'realized' the overall importance of syntax in English). It is interesting to note again that the 'real-world knowledge' affects the semantic/syntactic interaction in that in a situation which is unlikely to occur (animates telling inanimates) (Table 4) syntax never dominates, with both syntax and semantics taking a secondary role to pragmatics. On the other hand, as mentioned, with the two highest elements on the hierarchy (humans and animates) (Table 4), syntax dominates at all levels of proficiency. The role of pragmatics in the acquisition of syntax has, to my knowledge not received attention in the L2 literature. The only example I have been able to find comes from Zobl (in press). He presents evidence from the L2 acquisition of children, suggesting that successive 'chunks' such as

Man go. He go in there

in which the noun subject and the prepositional phrase are separated into two chunks are necessary to reduce the amount of new information in each of the information chunks. He suggests that this illustrates the way in which pragmatics influences syntactic structure. His suggestion shows the importance of considering interacting parts of the grammar to account for L2 production data. This is clearly similar to the findings of this paper. While we are not dealing with production here, it is clearly the case that syntactic interpretation is dependent on factors other than just syntax.

TABLE 9. Results of *ask* sentences with NPs of equal status

NPs	Level			
	2	3	4	5
human*/human	100-0	100-0	100-0	94-6
human/human*	33-66	36-64	30-70	63-37

* The asterisked NP is that NP which is most likely to be the subject of the second verb, given knowledge of real-world relationships.

The results of the *promise* sentences are even more complex than the *tell* sentences. The trend in these sentences is similar to that of the *tell* sentences. For example, consider the animate/human relationship. In both the *tell* and the *promise* sentences, syntax appears to have a greater impact on the animate/human sentences (for *promise*) and human/animate (for *tell*) than on the other sentences. From level 2 through level 5, the correct syntactic choice is made even though the 'strength' with which it is selected differs.

Looking at Table 9 we see that reversed relationships for animate/inanimate and human/inanimate nouns initially show reverse tendencies. By level 4, syntax has had a clear impact, a greater one than in the *tell* sentences. Thus, it does not appear that learners, in dealing with *promise* sentences follow the syntactic constraints of the larger class of *tell* sentences. To the contrary, we have seen that syntax dominates 'earlier' in the *promise*

19

than in the *tell* sentences. The fact that *promise* is unlike the majority of verbs may serve to make it more salient, allowing the learners to access and sort out the relevant syntactic and semantic information. It is again interesting to note the difference in responses on those sentences in which there is conflicting syntactic/semantic information. As with the *tell* sentences the greatest change comes in those sentences where there is maximum divergence in the hierarchical positions – that is, the inanimate/human sentences.

Again, however, there is more than meets the eye. As with the *tell* sentences, where there is equal status of NPs, syntax dominates. Where there is unequal status, but where there is convergence (Table 6), syntax also dominates but to a lesser degree than with the *tell* sentences (Table 3). This may be due to the fact that even though there is convergence, there is also conflict with other syntactic patterns in the language. The situation is perhaps best understood by considering Table 10 which presents the areas in which non-syntactic information dominates.

TABLE 10. Tables 3 and 4 combined

NPs	Level			
	2	3	4	5
inanimate/animate	1-5	0-10	2-12	1-15
animate/inanimate	5-4	8-3	4-5	4-4
inanimate/human	1-8	3-8	1-7	0-8
human/inanimate	3-2	5-4	6-8	1-15
animate/human	1-4	2-7	1-13	1-15
human/animate	1-5	0-10	2-12	1-15

On the *tell* sentences the error rate was 32 per cent where there was a conflict of information, but only 9 per cent where information converged. On the other hand, the error rate was approximately the same for the *promise* sentences, 27 per cent versus 22 per cent. Thus, in general, the conflicting information stemming from language universals has a greater effect on the *tell* sentences than on the *promise* sentences. This, we surmise has to do with the already present syntactic conflict of the *promise* sentences vis-à-vis other complex sentences.

3.4.4. Ask sentences. The sentences tested in this category are:

> The child asked her mother to have a cookie

and

> The woman asked her child to have a cookie

where the syntax leads to an ambiguous interpretation, although for most speakers there is a preferred interpretation. In cases of potential ambiguity, pragmatic factors, such as role relationships, are likely to play a major role in sentence interpretation. In addition two sentences were tested in which the two lowest elements on the topicality hierarchy are manipulated.

>The chair asked the dog to have a cookie

and

>The dog asked the chair to have a cookie.

In Table 11 are the results for those sentences in which there is a differential role relationship based on the topicality hierarchy (the above pair of sentences). Results are presented in terms of percentages of answers to a given NP.

TABLE 11. Tables 6 and 7 combined

NPs	Level			
	2	3	4	5
animate/inanimate	3-2	5-4	9-3	12-1
inanimate/animate	3-3	4-5	11-3	15-1
human/inanimate	7-2	9-2	8-1	8-0
inanimate/human	2-4	5-5	9-5	14-2
human/animate	5-4	6-5	9-3	13-0
animate/human	6-3	8-3	9-0	7-1

TABLE 12. Percentage of errors

	Conflict of information	Convergence of information
tell	32	9
promise	27	22

In Table 12 are the results based on those sentences in which there is equal status in terms of the topicality hierarchy, but in which there are differences in terms of the pragmatics of the sentences.

3.4.5. Discussion of ask *sentences.* On the *ask* sentences, where the syntax allows for more than one interpretation, semantics dominates throughout. (It is important to note that ambiguity is not seen by all native speakers of English.) Perhaps the most interesting result of these sentences is the level 5 responses to one of the previous sentences repeated here.

>The woman asked her child to have a cookie.

The preferred syntactic interpretation is for the second noun to be the subject of the second verb. In addition, the preferred interpretation based on pragmatic factors is for the child to have the cookie. Yet, the predominant choice for level 5 subjects was 'woman'. As stated earlier, part of what is involved in learning the syntax of an L2 is learning the relative strength of syntax in relation to other aspects of language. However, there is no reason to assume that when the relative importance of syntax is straightened out, that learners will have learned to consider the *appropriate* aspects of syntax. In fact, this seems to be what has happened here. There is a switch away from pragmatic/semantic factors. The learners are keying in on a particular aspect of the syntactic structure. They are focusing on 'who controls the asking' and infer that that is the person who will have the cookie. (I thank Josh Ard for pointing out this interpretation of the *ask* sentences to me.) Thus, they are looking at the specific facts about the syntax surrounding *ask*, although in this case the information leads to the incorrect syntactic choice. A similar result is found in a study of Italian speakers learning English by Gass (forthcoming) where the learners figured out the importance of syntactic factors, although they zeroed in on incorrect aspects of syntax. Note that this does not occur with the results presented in Table 11, where the lack of strength (inanimate noun) of the semantic factors is not enough to override syntactic dominance. Inanimates are unlikely to control the asking. These results clearly point to the importance of not attributing single strategies to L2 learners even in dealing with the same syntactic structure.

3.5. Implications

Pulling together the findings of this study I have attempted to show that language universals, in this case based on a semantic-based hierarchy, affect the acquisition of syntax. The acquisition of the syntax of complex sentences cannot be understood in isolation. Universals (seen in the role of the topicality hierarchy) interacted with the language-specific facts of English.

There are also implications for the nature of hierarchical relationships, as frequently put forth in linguistic theory. Mathematical orderings such as $a > b > c$ do not imply equal distancing between a and b and b and c. Within theoretical linguistics and SLA research, to my knowledge, there has been little concern with the strength of relationships or with the distancing between elements. It was seen here that syntax was differentially affected by different hierarchical role relationships suggesting that non-specified distances in linear hierarchical relationships may capture linguistically real relationships, but do not capture psycholinguistically real ones. The results are only the beginning in our quest to understand the resolutions of competing aspects of language and thus to understand the nature of influencing factors in second-language acquisition. Clearly, syntax, semantics and pragmatic acquisition cannot be understood as isolated grammatical components with a unidirectional information flow.

4. Conclusion

In conclusion, in this paper I have shown ways in which universals affect developing grammars. I have shown in particular that the acquisition of syntax cannot be adequately described without recourse to language universals. I have further suggested in this paper and elsewhere (Gass and Ard

1980; Gass and Ard 1984) that L2 data may indeed provide us with a window on language universals in the sense of testing and verifying their universality and the strength with which they operate. This notion has been reiterated by others, for example, Comrie (1984), Kumpf (1982) and Sharwood Smith (1980). If it is the case that linguistic theory and L2 acquisition theory can make important contributions to each other, then, as Ard (1983) points out, we do not have an example of an 'applied' field, as the word is commonly used. Rather we do have an example of an 'applied' field in the original sense of the word – a folding together of information.

Notes

1) Chomsky's study deals with other sentences as well. However, given the limitations of the design of the present study, I was only able to limit the domain of inquiry to the particular sentence types illustrated in 11 and 12 in Appendix A.

2) Sentences with *promise* are generally considered to be in a unique class. However, this may not be accurate depending on one's definition of that class. Sentences like 'I agreed with him to go' are similar to the *promise* sentences, the difference being in the form of the object (with or without a preposition). I thank Josh Ard for pointing this out to me.

3) The study was actually concerned with two hierarchies (topicality and person), but for the sake of brevity I will limit my discussion only to the topicality hierarchy. A fuller description appears in Gass (forthcoming).

4) The actual number given was dependent on the number of subjects available at a given proficiency level.

Appendix A: Sentences used in the present study:

1. The women advised the men to go home.
2. The chair told the dog to leave.
3. The chair promised the dog to leave.
4. The chair told the table to leave.
5. The boy told the dog to leave.
6. The table promised the boy to leave.
7. The child asked her mother to have a cookie.
8. The girl told the chair to leave.
9. The dog told the boy to leave.
10. The woman allowed her husband to go.
11. The dog asked the chair to have a cookie.
12. The dog told the chair to leave.
13. The dog promised the cat to leave.
14. The table told the boy to leave.
15. The girl promised the chair to leave.
16. The dog promised the boy to leave.
17. The man warned the woman to leave immediately.
18. The boy promised the girl to leave.
19. The woman asked her child to have a cookie.
20. The woman advised her husband to drive carefully.
21. The boy promised the dog to leave.
22. The chair promised the table to leave.
23. The girl persuaded the boy to study hard.
24. The chair asked the dog to have a cookie.

25. The dog told the cat to leave.
26. The boy told the girl to leave.
27. The man ordered his boss to walk slowly.
28. The dog promised the chair to leave.

2. *Discussant*

Introduction

S. Gass raises many interesting questions in her paper – too many for me to discuss fully. I will therefore merely take up two of the issues she discusses, try to take them a little further, and include some of the other aspects of the 'universal hypothesis' she mentioned in her introduction as phenomena she does not deal with. Her main question seems to me to be: What is the nature of the universal hypothesis in IL studies?

From this question there follow two sub-questions: Are ILs natural languages? Do linguistic universals constrain the second language acquisition process, and if so, in what way? The first sub-question is mentioned by Gass in her discussion of previous work in determining the systematicity of interlanguages. The second sub-question is investigated in more detail in her experiment on complex sentences. There is a second issue I see arising from Gass' paper which I think is worth keeping distinct from the above set of questions, namely: What is the role of linguists' descriptions in studies in SLA?

1. Why Study Adult Language Acquisition?

Before turning to these questions, I want to ask a preliminary question: Why is it interesting to study the acquisition of a *second* language by adults, rather than linguistics or child language acquisition or aphasia? In other words, what is it that study of SLA can contribute to our knowledge which study of these related disciplines cannot?[1]

Consider first of all the type of subject studied. We are dealing with a cognitively developed, very sophisticated communicator, who has full command of one linguistic system (his L1), and knows how to use it appropriately. This is, for different reasons, in contradistinction both to aphasia and child language studies.

The subject is communicating during the time he is acquiring the second language with target-language-linguistic means which are by definition limited in comparison with those of the native speaker of that language. He has therefore to resort to other communicative means beyond what he has of the target-language in order to try to get his message across. The non-target-language-means he has at his disposal are – for different reasons – again

25

different from those of the child or the aphasic. In other words, SLA studies contribute specifically to our understanding of how languages operate and are acquired because the cognitive and linguistic development of the subject are disentangled, and furthermore because the major disturbing factor we have to deal with – the subject's L1 – can in principle, be fully controlled for.

What he successively acquires of the target language will presumably depend on the input he receives, and the success he feels he is having with the use of his IL at any given time. He will stop making the effort to acquire, presumably, when he achieves the communicative success he wants with the means he has (the 'given motivation' caveat of Corder 1967). As adult learners can fossilize (Selinker 1972), but do not necessarily fossilize (Neufeld 1979), (i.e. the 'critical period' hypothesis on its own is insufficient explanation), a satisfactory account of the acquisition process will have to examine all of the following:

1) the type and quantity of the target-language input, and the subject's perception of it (what elements are salient, easy, etc. for him) through the filter of the linguistic knowledge he already has; perceived relative ease of acquisition, if you will;

2) the internal systematicity of the IL at any given time, and the (degree of success of) the uses to which it is put;

3) more global socio-psychological phenomena of the type Schumann's (1978a) pidginization hypothesis examines.

Again (Corder 1967) the question of explaining the process looks different for child language acquisition and aphasic reacquisition. Linguistics is different again. Theoretical linguists, on their different paths towards a definition of the notion 'possible human language', take as their primary object of study the systems of languages – thus the subject becomes implicitly or explicitly 'ideal'. It may be felt by them to be methodologically important to look at the use of complete and incomplete systems in seeking independent explanations for their discoveries (see section 2), but in the first instance it is their problem, not ours.

The development linguists have traditionally been most interested in, takes the form of explaining the historical evolution of already fully-fledged systems: the role of extra-linguistic phenomena in this evolution has been a subject of debate since before Saussure.

These broad considerations can, indeed must, be broken down into finer detail. But I hope that as such they suffice to suggest that, taken together, they are specific to the study of adult SLA and can provide insights into the acquisition of a new linguistic system from a cognitively developed starting-point, the role that knowledge of one fully-fledged linguistic system may have in the acquisition of another, sophisticated communication with 'simple codes' (Corder), insights which may prove interesting to compare with insights from sister disciplines concerned with the processing of natural languages by humans. I suggest too that these questions can be asked of 'social' and 'educational' acquisition (Klein 1981b).

2. The Nature of the Universal Hypothesis in IL Studies

But I have presupposed a fundamental question in Gass' paper; is IL a natural language? Gass distinguishes 'static' and 'dynamic' approaches to IL studies although I am not clear just how watertight she herself wants this distinction to be. The former suggests to me a less data-oriented tradition in the field which is perhaps best summed in the title of Adjémian's important paper 'On the *nature* of interlanguage *systems*'. This tradition has addressed questions of the type Gass mentions: what constraints are there on the formation of ILs? What linguistic constraints must all ILs follow? The latter suggests to me a more data-oriented tradition concerned with tracing developmental sequences and with problems of language use, best represented by the empirical studies undertaken in West Germany during the past ten years. There is definitely no watertight distinction between these two traditions.[2]

An important idea in Adjémian's (1976) article is the following:

Given modern beliefs in linguistics and psychology that human languages form a definable set, it would be curious if learner languages turned out not to fit into the set of possible human languages.

It follows, then, that: 'ILs are subject to the same kind of linguistic constraints as (other) natural languages'.

One ensuing debate (Arditty and Perdue 1979; Frauenfelder et al. 1980; Tarone 1982) revolved around:

1) the specific status of ILs within this set, and turned on whether a *system,* called IL, 'had' distinctive features such as fossilization, backsliding, permeability, etc. In other words, it was trying to determine what is peculiar to the L2 learner's internalized grammar by appealing to what L2 learners do, and thereby to what other subjects do not do;

2) the idea that universal constraints of the type Gass mentions should also apply to ILs. Moreover, it was suggested (Frauenfelder et al. 1980) that IL data could provide relevant evidence and counterevidence concerning those constraints.

Gass seems in her paper to follow this tradition when she suggests that the field should help in providing a more precise definition of natural language: 'One way to begin to come to grips with the notion of "natural language" is to consider ways in which ILs do and do not share well-defined characteristics of languages such as English, Italian, etc.', and in her examination of the shaping influences of universals on IL development.

I mention this debate on Adjemian's article simply because I took part in it, and because I now feel there are more productive ways to approach IL studies, for the following reasons:

1) On the level of knowledge, if we agree that learner languages are systematic (Corder, Selinker) and have been learned, then they do fit into

the set of possible human languages, as Adjémian surmised, because they were learned. From this perspective, the differences between ILs and languages such as English, Italian, etc. will be merely quantitative (Arditty and Perdue 1979);

2) SLA is not the only testing ground, perhaps not even the best testing ground, for linguists' analyses of what they themselves would term – with terminological variations – the knowledge of the competent adult native speaker;

3) The road between what fully-fledged languages have and what learners/ speakers do is long (passing, for the bilingual, by constructs such as 'psycho-typology', see Kellerman). Specifically, it is not clear (to me at least) at what level of abstraction a generalization over the surface structure of sentences of languages has explanatory relevance for the processing of linguistic elements, or vice versa. Certainly, establishing a correlation will not do. Suppose adult native speakers of a language produced relative clauses with a frequency corresponding to Keenan and Comries' accessibility hierarchy, and that furthermore, experimental investigation found reaction times corresponding to the same hierarchy for the same subjects: this explains nothing in itself. The explanation would come, I assume, from system-independent phenomena such as real-time processing constraints, memory limitations, etc. The experimental work would be testing Keenan's or Givón's explanation of the universal, not seeing if the universal were replicated;

4) I assume that normal adult speakers are normal adult speakers, in other words they have (Gass, p.4) the physical, perceptual and cognitive attributes of adult human beings (precisely those that Gass claims to have the greatest shaping effect on second language grammars). Much of the research described by Gass in her paper gives empirical evidence suggesting that this is indeed the case: thus the studies she cites which show that adult learners have the same behavioural tendencies as adult natives are particularly unrevealing.

3. Studies in SLA and the Role of Linguistic Descriptions

For Gass then, the question of interest is tracing the 'shaping influences' of universals on SLA, or more strongly, is that SLA provides 'a window on language universals in the sense of testing and verifying their universality and the strength with which they operate'. Comrie (1984) comments on the use made of his own work – the Keenan/Comrie accessibility hierarchy – in SLA in much the same way: given two possible formulations of the accessibility hierarchy as a tendency or as an absolute, and given the results of research in SLA, we have 'a clear instance where data from SLA give at least some indication as to which of two competing approaches one should take in the statement of a language universal, in this case that the conceptually simpler tendency has greater validity than the conceptually more complex exceptionless absolute universal'. SLA is here, then, indirect evidence for the greater validity of one formulation of a universal over another.

Here, applied linguistics has not really changed. The linguist finds the interesting hypotheses, the IL researcher tests them, though the interest is now acquisition rather than teaching. Worse, the linguists have done the leg-work and provide facts generalizable over many linguistic systems (the universals). The IL-researcher can then safely assume that they are indeed attested cross-linguistically and apply them to students of English as a foreign language. I will try to show in section 4 that things are not so straightforward, and that we need our own cross-linguistic studies.

Regarding linguists' descriptions of languages, that is, of French, Spanish, etc., three possibilities are of interest:

1) the linguist's description is right;

2) the linguist's description is relevant;

3) the linguist's description is lacking (because wrong, or irrelevant, or whatever).

The conclusions Gass draws from her experiment seem to presuppose (2) and probably – give or take some refinements – (1), although this latter is not so important. (2) is the important case, because at best (2) must come as a pleasant surprise; we haven't the right to expect linguistic descriptions of the adult native norm to correspond systematically to our preoccupations. Many researchers have pointed out that if ILs are analysed exclusively in terms of the SL and target language categories, their own internal systematicity is in danger of going unnoticed. For example, frequently used terms in the universal approach Gass refers to are 'subject, verb, object': I would hesitate in assigning 'verb' – the category or the function – correctly and unambiguously in many early utterances of immigrant workers.

For the SL and target language systems, (3) is relatively easy to deal with. Kellerman and his collaborators are trying to work out for themselves the syntax and semantics of conditional clauses in SL Dutch in order to be able to account for an interesting bit of U-shaped behaviour in relatively advanced Dutch learners of English, but the acquisitional phenomenon motivated the description, not vice versa.

Perhaps it is illegitimate to level this type of criticism at the questions Gass addresses with the subjects she has: educated students of English learning it to be able to study a course at university, i.e. advanced learners. However, if one wants to make generalizable (more universal) characterizations of adult SLA, working exclusively from pre-existing descriptions of (complex sentences of) the adult norm will preclude in too many cases the possibility of generalization (3).

4. Some Generalizable Phenomena

In suggesting that SLA researchers cannot always find available relevant descriptions (of the SL, or of the target-language input), I of course do not want to suggest that there cannot be fruitful insights bearing directly on the questions I outlined at the beginning of this discussion to be obtained from linguists' descriptions of languages (as there can from the other sister disciplines mentioned). The examples below have to do with well-established linguistic categories – aspect, tense, (in)definitely referring NPs – and involve an examination of the communicative functions the adult acquires target-language means for expressing, the choice he makes amongst the linguistic devices the target language offers for expressing these functions, and the (often idiosyncrasic) use he makes of these devices.

To illustrate this, I will briefly discuss two studies with target-language English, and two studies with target-language German that I am acquainted with. The reasons for choosing these studies is that they deal with data that is communicatively oriented – both use narratives, the German studies also using film or picture re-telling tasks – and above all, that the subjects in question tell good stories. I read them with pleasure, and understand them without having to analyse them: with the usual caveats about the distance between the event and the transcription, the speakers achieve communicative success.

Temporal Reference

The English studies are Kumpf's work (1982), together with related work by Flashner (1982). Kumpf found that one of her subjects created an idiosyncrasic aspectual opposition – marked by $V + \phi$ versus $V + ing$ – and meaning 'completed versus incompleted'. Flashner found the same opposition marked respectively by $V + ed$ versus $V + \phi$, and argued, plausibly, that the opposition is the important thing. Morphological markings on the verb conveyed, then, aspectual rather than temporal oppositions.

Now, it may be that these subjects' systems correspond to the predictions of universal principles because (Gass, p.6):
1) aspect is primary to tense in the world's languages;
2) aspect is primary to tense in child language acquisition.[4]
But given the evidence so far, I could equally argue that English, the target language of the subjects in question, also has the means to make reference to time by adverbs ('then', 'after'), by prepositional phrases, and some more complex expressions; and the speaker of English can also use discourse organizing principles such as implicit reference, sequencing, framing, etc., and that the subjects handled temporal reference by use of simple adverbs and these latter means, successfully (after all I enjoyed the narratives), leaving the aspectual opposition to morphological markings; i.e. studying the grammaticization of one semantic opposition is insufficient because the interplay of this with other parts of the system is ignored.

Kumpf's own conclusion – 'aspect is somehow primary to tense in terms of grammaticizing temporal systems' – will not do as such. It suffices to look at one other target language. Research into learner varieties of German

(Stutterheim 1982, HPD 1978) also show that an aspectual category, which Stutterheim characterizes as 'a state of affairs over a given time' is indeed used systematically early on. It is, however expressed by a simple adverb – immer – the same grammatical category that is used by these learners to express concepts such as 'now', 'then', at the same stage. We need our own cross-linguistic studies.[5] There are, however, phenomena which are potentially generalizable here, which have to do with how languages function: it is possible to isolate recurring semantic categories, used by real subjects to achieve definable functions in discourse, and expressed idiosyncratically by real subjects with different syntactic-lexical means. The following example attempts to take this idea a little further.

Word Order and Reference

The example of German concerns the acquisition of structures of the noun phrase involving a lexical head. HPD (1978) inferred a developmental order from their cross-sectional study as follows: first of all, the bare noun was used; secondly, there followed a two-item stage where numerals, quantifiers and articles accompanied the noun in the order given; thirdly, adjectives accompanied nouns; then came three-item combinations, then more complex constructions.

As I said earlier, the acquisition of linguistic means to express communicative functions can be determined by:

1) the input, and the way the input is perceived by the subject in terms of relative linguistic ease of acquisition, for example;

2) the importance of the communicative function itself.

The progression described by HPD goes from the syntactically simple to the syntactically more complex. But this does not explain the relative internal ordering of quantifiers, determiners or adjectives. One could imagine (Klein) that quantification is communicatively more 'important' than determination which itself is more important than attribution, and so on. This speculation could be based on the linguistic observation that there are languages without determiners but (I think) none without numerals, or it could be based on observation of the functions the informants are observed (or assumed) to have to fulfill in interactions, etc. However, syntactic complexity as such will not do.

Carrol and Dietrich have written on the relationship between reference and word order in early varieties of German. Dietrich's (1982) Turkish subject and the two subjects (one Italian, one Turk) whom Carrol and Dietrich (1983) study in greatest detail show a marked tendency to reserve utterance-initial position (or pre-verbal position in those utterances where there are recognizable verbs), for definitely referring noun (phrases), and second (or post-verbal) position for indefinitely referring noun (phrases), and in these positions there is a virtual absence of articles. One informant did use articles, or some other linguistic means to mark the definite/

indefinite status of noun (phrases) which did not obey the above distribution.

I further examined the (approximately 150) lexical noun phrases of Carrol's and Dietrich's two subjects and noticed that over 90 per cent of these constructions were one- or two-place in terms of HPD's developmental order (most of the others being, arguably, set phrases). For the 'bare' nouns, the referential status could be determined, as stated, by their distribution. There is unsurprisingly, avoidance of redundant marking. But this can be taken further: if you can only 'manage' NPs with two places, using one place for an article and the other for a noun fills the structure. Whereas if you accompany your noun with, say, an adjective and keep the general distributional rule for indicating the referential status of NPs, you are achieving two functions with the syntactic means you have: unsurprisingly, the adjective + noun combinations there were (about 20 out of the 150) did follow the distributional rule for bare nouns.

These are small case studies. They tentatively support the existence of a two-place stage in the acquisition of the structure of the NP by spontaneous acquirers of German, tentatively suggest that the acquisition order within the two-word stage may be subject to individual variation, and suggest that the relatively late emergence of articles is not to be explained by determination being an unimportant function, but rather that the use of word order, allowing as it does the listener to infer the referential status of an NP, makes its explicit marking redundant. Obviously, the observed distribution of definitely and indefinitely referring noun phrases was linked by Dietrich and Carrol to the discourse phenomena of theme/rheme.

These studies illustrate (albeit succinctly) some points I have tried to make in the discussion in section 1 above:

1) the language production analysed had an internal systematicity which is not that of the target norm, and is only partially describable in terms of the target norm;

2) clever (pragmatically sophisticated) use of limited means can achieve communicative success (or be felt by the learner to achieve communicative success, the distinction is not important here);

3) the interplay of various linguistic/pragmatic means, and the balance that the subject achieves between them in a systematic learner variety can be compared (and, one hopes, generalized) across other cases of SLA;

4) discourse principles such as sequencing, theme/rheme organisation, etc. are of interest to disciplines related to SLA, and emerge particularly clearly in the data of adult acquirers, as these latter typically rely more heavily on them;

5) (1) and (2) combined go some way to explaining a phenomenon peculiar to SLA, namely Selinker's 'fossilization'.

5. Conclusion

Gass' paper is entitled 'The empirical basis for the universal hypothesis in interlanguage studies'. I see an ambiguity in the title:

1) there are SLA-independent universal hypotheses for which the SLA testing ground provides empirical evidence;

2) there are phenomena of SLA which can be generalized across different cases of SLA (and afterwards, compared with phenomena emerging from sister disciplines).

I take (1) to be Gass' preferred reading; (2) is mine.

Acknowledgements. Thanks to Eric Kellerman, Colette Noyau and – especially – Wolfgang Klein for comments on this version of this paper.

Notes

1) The following three paragraphs owe much to Corder (especially 1967 and 1971). I hope I have not misinterpreted him.

2) Similarly in first language acquisition studies, one assumes that the 'data-driven' versus 'theory-driven' studies distinction does not imply an ignoring of theoretical preoccupations on the part of the former, or of relevant data on the part of the latter.

3) There are also methodological considerations here to do with the generalizability of intuitional data, but this is not the place to discuss them.

4) I am not sure whether (1) and (2) deal with the marking of semantic categories or with the semantic categories themselves. Guiora's personal communication to Gras would seem to indicate that for (2), what is intended is that children acquire aspectual categories before temporal ones. If this is what is implied then reason (2) is irrelevant. The subjects in Kumpf's study were adults who can, one assumes, refer to time perfectly well in their first language. Reason (1) is interesting if what is meant is that more languages have (more) aspectual than tense markings, but still won't do entirely as the following discussion indicates.

5) Distinct from cross-linguistic studies of fully-fledged systems. Merely to draw a relationship between what fully-fledged systems have and what shows up in case-studies of the acquisition of one target language is insufficient because one finds *similar* semantic distinctions expressed by *different* formal means as one goes across different source-language / target-language pairs.

3. Summary of Discussion

Replying to the discussant, Gass expressed broad agreement with most of his comments, given certain reservations on points of detail, and accepted that the contrast between two different interpretations of the role of universals in interlanguage mentioned at the end of his paper represented alternative perspectives on important theoretical and methodological issues.

During the ensuing general discussion, a number of themes emerged which were reiterated in later sessions of the seminar. One concern the status of IL studies in both applied and general linguistics, and, in the view of at least one speaker, the specialist focus of IL research into learner languages and other cross-linguistic phenomena (piginization, creolization, etc.) helped to identify a specialist field of enquiry within applied linguistics. However, there was still a long way to go before it would be possible to elaborate a fully coherent theoretical framework for IL studies, and some anxiety was expressed that IL might become too data-oriented, if indeed it had not already become so. The mere observation of recurring phenomena was inadequate; what was required was a principled basis for explanation. One topic of relevance to this issue which was explored briefly was the problem of demarcation: there was, for instance, no adequate definition of the distinction between the acquisition of second languages by children and by older learners.

A second theme (which appeared repeatedly during the symposium) was the relationship between language and cognition. The discussion was not developed very far at this stage but the issue was noted as an immediate and unavoidable consequence of the commitment of IL studies to the investigation of interlingual communication.

PART TWO

EXPLAINING AND DESCRIBING LEARNING AND PERFORMANCE STRATEGIES

4. Strategies in Interlanguage Learning
and Performance

Models of L2 learning and communication have assigned a central role to the concept of strategies (Bialystok 1978; Krashen 1978b; Selinker 1972). Available accounts currently describe in considerable detail the occasions on which L2 learners use strategies as well as the specific strategies that are likely to occur. Less documented, however, is the theoretical basis of these strategies which might account for their relationship to learning and performance both in L2 accquisition and in other domains. The present paper is an attempt to develop a definition of strategies common to a number of domains, examine the cognitive basis of such a definition, and explore the implications of this definition for L2 learning and performance.

The search for a set of strategies that underlie the learning and use of a second language has been motivated by a number of concerns. Psychologically, the assumption is that the delineation of such strategies will provide access to the mental processes responsible for acquisition. Linguistically, strategies used by learners inform us of the learner's hypotheses about language – what is taken to be universal, what is subject to awareness, and so forth. Pedagogically, the intention is to instruct language learners in the strategies that have been shown to be effective for others in simplifying the imposing task of language learning. This disparity in goals, however, has led to a concomitant disparity in definition. Strategies, that is, are not always considered in the same terms where each of these alternate goals is concerned. The first problem, then, is to examine the definitions that have been proposed for this construct in second language acquisition. The second step is to explore the uses of the construct in other domains, in particular, first language acquisition, and distill from this variety of work a set of common assumptions and definitional constraints that apply as well to its use in applied linguistics. Finally, to be explanatory, the commonality found among the definitions of strategies must be based on some construct that is cognitive, or mental, or at least process-oriented in that it deals with mental functioning. In the final step, then, a cognitive framework is proposed in which a small number of mental processes can be shown to generate both the strategies used by children in L1 acquisition and by adults in L2 acquisition which nonetheless maintains the important distinction between these two activities.

Definitions of L2 Strategies

Two approaches to the problem of definition have been used. The first is to ostensively define the concept by generating structured lists of the exemplars of the concept. To this end, a variety of taxonomies and classifications of strategies for learning and communication have been proposed. The second is to attempt to delineate the concept theoretically, usually by comparing and contrasting it to other similar concepts. These attempts have produced a variety of definitions of strategies and procedures for distinguishing strategies from processes, techniques, tactics, and other efforts of language learning.

Following the first method of taxonomy, the classifications of strategies that have been proposed operate at two different levels. The first distinguishes broad classes by identifying strategies according to function. The classification is usually binary, distinguishing between pairs of learning, communication, production, perception, comprehension, social, and cognitive strategies. The second level documents the range of strategies that can occur to serve any of these functions. Thus, we have taxonomies of communication strategies (Tarone 1977), taxonomies of learning strategies (Rubin 1975; Stern 1975), taxonomies of social strategies (Wong-Fillmore 1979). Although the various strategies in the set may differ in their conditions of application, they share a common goal which is specified by the functional type.

These levels of classification correspond to levels of goal setting. If the goal is language learning, for example, then a strategy of 'communication' may be relevant since practising the language in real communicative exchanges promotes learning. But if the goal is communication, in that a learner is involved in a conversation but unequipped to continue, then lower level strategies to deal with specific problems in communication where words are unknown, for example, 'circumlocution', may be relevant. In these terms, the difference between strategies of learning and strategies of communication may be hierarchically related. In other contexts, the order may be reversed. The primary goal may be communication and a variety of communication strategies may be invoked, but at some point a specific problem arises in which a word is not available but is recognized as potentially relevant, and so a strategy for learning may be initiated. In this case, a set of learning strategies, such as 'appeal for assistance' followed by rehearsal may be deployed to deal with that communicative need. In both cases, though, goals are set and language learners draw from some set of strategies to meet those goals.

In these classification systems, it is undoubtedly the case that the strategies cited are effective means to achieve the ends stated. The problem is that the lists are not as delineated as would be required of a list that also serves a definitional function. There are numerous overlaps in which strategies of communication also serve as strategies of learning (e.g. appeal for assistance when one needs to remember the elicited item) and vice versa (e.g. memorization when only a short term need is recognized and the item immediately forgotten after that use). Moreover, the approach carries some inherent circularity. The type of strategy (learning, etc.) and its exemplars (memorization, etc.) continually assign definitional responsibility to the other.

The second approach to definition is to define the term itself. While the taxonomic approach takes differences between types of strategies as the problem, the definition approach takes differences between strategies and other similar events as the problem for definition. Faerch and Kasper (1983d) provide an informative review of a variety of such definitions that have been proposed for 'strategy' with an emphasis on distinguishing 'strategies' from other events such as 'plans' and 'processes'. As they rightly conclude from this review, the reader is left with little sense of an important theme to extract, and not much clarification on the issues. Some features which have been cited in these accounts are temporal constraints (Blum and Levenston 1978b), hierarchically related processes (Selinker 1972), and obligation or optionality (Bialystok 1978; Frauenfelder and Porquier 1979).

The theoretical definitions vary in content but point consistently to a few defining features. Corder (1977a), for example, proposes that 'communicative strategies . . . are a systematic technique employed by a speaker to express his meaning when faced with some difficulty'. Faerch and Kasper (1983d) define them as 'potentially conscious plans for solving what to an individual presents itself as a problem in reaching a particular communicative goal'. Tarone (1980b) offers a 'mutual attempt of two interlocutors to agree on a meaning in situations where requisite meaning structures are not shared'. Rubin (1975) referring to learning strategies, calls them 'the techniques or devices which a learner may use to acquire knowledge'.

Throughout these definitions, both theoretical and taxonomic, there are three consistent features that are either explicitly or implicitly incorporated. Two of these are identified by Faerch and Kasper (1983d) to be criterial to the notion of strategy; the third is implied by their description and by the descriptions of others. The three features are problematicity, consciousness, and intentionality.

Problematicity refers to the notion that strategies are adopted when problems in either learning or production are perceived. Strategies that is, are not part of the routine operations of language use. The criterion for *consciousness* can refer either to the learner's awareness that the strategy is being employed for a particular purpose, or the awareness of how that strategy might achieve its intended effect. Faerch and Kasper are careful to note, however, that consciousness is likely a matter of relative degree and that individual and situational constraints may determine the extent to which consciousness may be achieved. *Intentionality* refers to the learner's control over those strategies so that particular ones may be selected from the range of options and deliberately applied to achieve certain effects.

The concept of strategy in L2 learning and communication, then, seems consistently to refer to the use of devices to solve problems by learners who are in control of the selection of these devices and at least somewhat conscious of their application and effect. To what extent is this conception consistent with that used in other domains for describing similar concepts? The present claim is that the reliance of applied linguistic strategies on these three criteria obscures their similarity with the conception and functioning of strategies in other domains and therefore impedes attempts to develop process-related descriptions of their use. Two fields which should be consulted for their use of this construct are psychology and pedagogy, each of which assigns to strategies a somewhat different role. The objective is to identify some similarity for these various interpretations in order to achieve consistency of usage across fields and to have a means of relating this interpretation to some hypotheses about the process of language learning.

The use of the term 'strategies' in psychology and pedagogy points to two meanings. First is its use as a cognitive strategy in first language acquisition. For this purpose, the construct refers to the set of mental events that accompany language acquisition. Taken from the more general psycholinguistic literature (e.g. Clark and Clark 1977), these mental events are construed as sequences of operations that seem necessary to produce the specific observed outcomes. Second is its use as an educational strategy. The construct in these terms involves training novices to achieve more skilled levels of mastery in a particular area (see for review Pressley and Levin 1983). The difference between these uses is the extent to which the three criteria of consciousness, problematicity, and intentionality are imposed. Both refer to goal-related activities that have a developmental component, yet the educational use additionally assumes the three criteria to set the conditions of application. Hence the pedagogical interpretation of strategies is similar to that in applied linguistics for second language learning. Is there any similarity, then, between the interpretation of strategies as it is used in the psychological sense for L1 acquisition, and the sense used in applied linguistics and education? This comparison will be conducted by examining commonality between the possible strategies used in L1 and L2 acquisition.

Strategies in L1 Acquisition

Macnamara (1972) argued that children could not possibly learn the complex rules of the system, including all the exceptions to those rules in the short time it takes to master a first language if they treated the problem as one of learning a linguistic system. Rather, children must have some other 'strategy' for approaching language learning. That strategy is to figure out what meanings make sense in context, and then to map linguistic structures onto those meanings. Children, that is, learn meanings which are later related to structures. What are some of the strategies that comprise this hypothesis-testing approach to language learning by children? And to what extent are they appropriate procedures for adults learning a language later in life?

One important strategy is the use of context. Children, that is, assume that language has certain meanings because of their past experiences with that situation. Clark (1973a) found compelling evidence of that in an early study of semantic development. Her intention was to examine the order in which children learned the meanings for the spatial locatives 'in', 'on', and 'under'. Children were given some common objects and instructed to place them in certain relations to each other according to verbal commands using 'in', 'on', or 'under'. Her results showed that the interpretations of these terms depended entirely on children's experiences with the objects rather than with the verbal instructions. If an object had a supporting surface, for example, then things go 'on' it regardless of the particular word used. In a non-verbal replication of the study in which children were simply told to copy the experimenter's movements with respect to some objects, children created their arrangements in terms of the properties of the object, such as supporting surface, container, and not at all in terms of the instructions.

The use of context as a strategy in language learning has, it seems, clear application to second language learning. Adult second language learners make use of contextual information to predict possible meanings. One rather serious limitation of this strategy when used by adults, however, is that the adult uses of language are less determined by contextual constraints than are those of children (Snow and Ferguson 1977).

Another strategy fundamental to child L1 acquisition is the over-generalization of word meanings to new, usually inappropriate, situations. In the original descriptions of this characteristic of child speech, Clark (1973b) claimed that the overgeneralization was caused by the child's in-complete semantic entry for a word. A child, that is, may have only the feature (+4 legs) listed as the definition for 'dog'. Any event which satisfied that description, then, for example a horse, would be called a 'dog'. The question is whether the child actually believed that the labelled object, a horse, was equivalent to a dog, or whether that child was simply using some 'strategy' for labelling where the appropriate name was not available. In further tests of this hypothesis, others (Huttenlocher 1974; Anglin 1977) have found the latter explanation to be a better description. Children, that is, use the strategy of extending a limited vocabulary to describe a broader range of events. Overgeneralization in these terms is not a deviant process of language learning, but a productive strategic effort to use language.

Stated in these terms, overgeneralization can be related to events that occur in adult L2 learning. Frequently, words are selected for their 'high coverage', even though the speaker is well aware of their inaccuracy in that context. The strategy, that is, is equivalent for both children and adults. A limited vocabulary is used creatively to increase expressive power. Again, the difference is largely in the extent to which consciousness, problematicity, and intentionality are implicated when the strategy is used by different kinds of learners.

There are two examples in L2 learning research that illustrate how a strategy similar to overgeneralization is used. The first describes adult performance where adults are attempting to communicate with a limited vocabulary. The outcome of this situation is invariably to select words which are not quite accurate but convey certain features of the meaning. Blum and Levenston (1978b) have documented this use of language, which they call 'simplification' to show the systematicity in these extensions of word meanings for other purposes. Adults in these situations are not much different from the children referred to by Clark who erroneously overextend certain concrete nouns in the attempt to communicate. The difference is that we would be unlikely to cite cognitive deviancy as an explanation for the linguistic liberties taken by these struggling adult speakers.

The second example is children's use of certain aspects of a second language when they are in the process of learning two languages. Lightbown (1978) describes the use of the French question system by young English-speaking children learning French as a second language. They select certain terms and regularly overapply them on the basis of a few appropriate features. The term 'où', for example, would serve the functions for both where (où) and when (quand). In a counterpart study, Felix (1976) has shown that children learning English as a second language allow 'where' to also indicate both 'when' and 'why'. Again, the claim is that the basis of these uses of language is the same overgeneralization strategy used by children learning their first language. The difference in the L2 context is the extent to which we expect the learner to be aware of a problem, to be conscious of a solution, and to deliberately select a strategy.

A third strategy of considerable importance in children's language learning is the use of formulaic expressions that represent unanalysed 'chunks' of meaning. Bowerman (1982) argues that the child accumulates linguistic knowledge by adopting pieces of language and inserting them as wholes into contexts. The child is unaware of the relationship between such chunks as well as the internal structure of the chunks themselves. These chunks are progressively analysed to produce linguistic representations at a higher level of abstraction. The process of first language acquisition, on this view, rests heavily on the incorporation of large linguistic schemata into conversations.

SLA, too, proceeds to a great extent by the learner's use of large units of language which are only vaguely understood in their analysed forms. Again, the adult users of such a strategy may be more aware of this as an effective approach than are children, nonetheless, the behaviour is evident for both adult and child learners. Dechert (1982) refers to 'islands of reliability' for L1 and L2 speakers. These 'islands' are similar to the pre-fabricated chunks described by Hakuta (1974b). Raupach (1983) argues that one kind of strategy is to repeat whole phrases without adjustment, to avoid possible problems in variations. This produces a style of speech which both creates and exploits chunks of language. The patterns do not (necessarily) reflect error; they do reflect strategies in the sense of planned operations.

Other problems in learning encountered by children, cognitive rather linguistic, also involve the use of strategies but are different from those used for language learning in that there is less range in the possible variation. The strategies, that is, are determined primarily by the task, leaving less option-ality to the user. Conservation of fluids, for example, involves learning a set of appropriate strategies (Brainerd 1983), but the solution to the problem depends on selecting the correct ones. While the strategies themselves may be similar in many ways to those used in language learning, choosing the incorrect strategy, such as paying too much attention to the context or to perceptual 'chunks' of information, in this case the height of the beaker, will lead to failure in the problem. For language, any strategy will help a little and improve communication and learning.

Criteria for Interlanguage Strategies

The examples of children's learning strategies seem to characterize impor-tant aspects of adult L2 learning. Yet, clearly there are important differences between children and adults in their use of strategies. The three definitional differences that have been cited in reference to child and adult use of strategies are (i) consciousness, (ii) problem-related, and (iii) intentional selection. The argument here is that it is in the application of these criteria that children's strategic operations differ from those of adults. The implication is that if these three factors were controlled, then the role of strategies by children in first language acquisition would provide a model for the role of strategies by adults in L2 learning. Once the appropriate adjust-ments have been made with respect to differences between children and adults in terms of these three criteria, the emerging definition of strategies would satisfy the two constraints of being applied to domains other than L2 learning and resting in some cognitive mechanism.

The current literature on children's development of metacognition and the control of cognitive processes argues strongly for a view of development in which children's major learning problem during the early school years is not to fundamentally change the way in which they operate on information but rather to gain control of those operations (Brown 1975; Flavell 1977). This control of memory, study procedures, comprehension of text, etc. is necessary for the more complex symbolic acts of learning usually associated with schooling. These processes, too, seem to be largely responsible for the application of learning strategies as traditionally defined in the applied linguistics and educational literature. The criteria concerning consciousness, problematicity, and intentionality are essentially metacognitive skills. In these terms, pre-metacognitive children could not use strategies. Yet most views of early language acquisition carry a large component for the strategic effort of young children. Either the use of the term 'strategy' in these cases is unrelated to the interpretation in applied linguistics and young children are not strategic in their L1 acquisition, or the imposition of the three criteria which prevents access to strategies by pre-metacognitive children is unduly restrictive. Is it reasonable, then, to impose these criteria on adults when using the *same* strategies?

The need for consciousness as a criterion excludes children's use of the strategies, and so the assessment of the role of consciousness as a criterion for strategy use involves comparing the use of strategies by children and adults. If they are similar except for this feature, then it may be that consciousness is not a useful definitional property. The review of L1 acquisition strategies outlined above appears to indicate sufficient overlap in the approaches to language mastery taken by children and adults to warrant the conclusion that the same strategies, but without the necessity for consciousness of those strategies, are applied in both learning situations.

The criterial contribution of problematicity is assessed by comparing adult L2 learners not with children but with native speakers. Since ordinary communication is not usually considered to be 'problematic', could it be argued that native speakers use strategies for language learning and production? If native speakers rely on the same devices as do learners, then problematicity could not be the most decisive feature motivating strategy use. In NS speech, the relevant description seems to be that it is goal-oriented. The issue for a native speaker is not how to overcome a problematic impasse, but how to select appropriately from a range of options to achieve a communicative goal. Such goals may be considered to be problems, but at a different level. Strategies may apply to either level. Faerch and Kasper (1983) make a similar distinction by differentiating 'global goals' (e.g. writing a letter) from 'local goals' (e.g. how to execute that goal). It is in this sense of goal-orientedness that NS speech relies on strategies. Accordingly, the precise requirement for the recognition of a problem excludes an important aspect of strategic behaviour.

Finally, the criterion of intentionality needs to be examined in terms of the deliberate selective control adult L2 learners display when using these strategies. A variety of studies have examined the influence of proficiency, instructional differences, personality differences, type of word differences, and strategy effectiveness differences (Beebe in press; Bialystok 1983c; Corder 1977a; Haastrup and Phillipson 1983; Paribakht 1982). In all of these studies, very little difference in the selection of specific strategies could be attributed to any of these factors. Some differences in effectiveness were observed in which more proficient speakers could use these strategies more successfully. But the general issue of differences in intentionality regarding selection shows that whatever is responsible for the adoption of specific strategies seems to operate at a more abstract or more universal level than specific aspects of linguistic competence.

What is needed, then, is a definition of strategies for learning and communication that is sufficiently general that it can include both child and adult uses, overcoming the problem of the three restrictive criteria, yet sufficiently specific that it adds importantly to our understanding and clarification of the process of L2 learning and use. If the real difference observed in strategy use between adults and children, or between language learners and native speakers, is tied in with the factors of consciousness, problematicity, and intentionality, rather than with completely different constructs for the notion strategy, then those differences should be explained in terms of the three criteria. Rather than propose different definitions for strategy use in different language learning tasks, that is, it would be better to identify instead the factors that distinguish adults from children and language learners from native speakers in their application of some more universal, cognitively based set of strategies.

One possibility is to adopt a definition from Simon (1979) in which he claims that procedures (strategies) are means for 'performing a task as being composed of a fixed set of elementary information processes that are evoked by both aspects of the external environment and the internal representation of the problem' (p.85). This definition contains none of the three criterial features cited in the standard definitions, yet requires elaboration of another kind. Specifically, it requires that the external constraints and the internal mental mechanisms be identified and shown to be developmental, and second that the development of the elementary processes be explained. To what extent can this definition apply to problems in language learning and contribute to a conception of the role of strategies in interlanguage? What is necessary is a framework for understanding the cognitive system underlying SLA.

Cognitive Framework for Language Acquisition and Use

One means of conceptualizing language acquisition is in terms of a cognitive framework proposed elsewhere (Bialystok 1981; Bialystok and Ryan in press). This framework is based on two cognitive skills that are presumed to underlie the acquisition and use of language in either first or second language contexts. The first of these is called *analysis of knowledge* and refers to the extent to which the learner is able to represent the structure of knowledge along with its content. In unanalysed representations of language, only the meanings are coded; in analysed representations, both the meanings and the relationship between forms and those meanings are coded. Such analysed representations permit the learner to manipulate those form-meaning relationships to create particular structured uses of language. The ability to represent language in this way depends on the learner's ability to analyse a body of knowledge into structured categories and to operate on those structures. The second dimension, called *cognitive control* refers to the learner's ability to deliberately focus on relevant aspects of a problem and not be misled by distracting alternatives. Donaldson (1978) has argued that this is an essential ability for success in school and Piaget (1971) cites a similar ability as responsible for the onset of operational thought. In his terms, the child must learn to 'decenter' in order to give controlled attention to multiple aspects of a problem overcoming perceptual distractions, such as in conservation problems.

The way in which these cognitive dimensions operate in the acquisition and use of an interlanguage has been described elsewhere (Bialystok and Sharwood Smith 1984). Learners must gain mastery of the structure of knowledge so that the formal relationships are understood, and also control their attentional processes so that appropriate balances of forms and meanings are included. Strategies are involved in both these processes, not only as a facilitator when problems are perceived, but also in the more routine execution of these functions in language learning and production.

In communication, strategies which involve selecting other words to fill an IL lexical gap, such as paraphrase, synonymy, circumlocution, are classed as knowledged-based in that they depend on the relationships that exist in the code. Native speakers, too, use knowledge-based strategies in their attempts to select precise words to convey desired effects. Strategies which involve the focus of mental attention in the production of language are classed as control-based in that they relate to the use of the system rather than to the knowledge of the system. Some examples of control-based strategies would be to solve an IL lexical gap by incorporating context, gesture, L1, and the like, rather than by manipulating the L2 code itself.

In this dichotomy the strategies themselves do not irrevocably belong to a particular category. They fit with categories for theoretical reasons based on their source and function in language production. The category is not *defined* by the strategy, it is only illustrated by it. One needs a richer analysis of how the strategy was functioning in order to decide to which system it belongs. The approach, that is, is process-oriented rather than product-oriented. Rather than choosing (even unconsciously) a particular strategy, the learner/user relies on one of two processing resources relating either to the structure of the relevant knowledge base or the control procedures for executing the skill.

An example of how a single strategy may appear to belong to both categories but still function differently can be taken from Faerch and Kasper (1983d). They distinguish two forms of transfer of L1 into L2 speech. They claim the first is the result of interference of L1 habits which they interpret in a behaviourist model of performance. The second they claim is the result of active (conscious) use of L1 knowledge for problem-solving and they interpret this in a cognitive model of performance. A more parsimonious explanation, it seems, is to consider the first transfer to be a control-based strategy involved with execution and the second to be a knowledge-based strategy involved with the structure of lexicon. This removes the cumbersome need for both behaviourist and cognitive explanations within the same model as well as the difficulty of positing consciousness as a criterial distinction between them. Relative levels of consciousness may be attributed to either of these strategies.

This underlying basis in the analysed knowledge and cognitive control dimensions accounts for the 'elementary information processes' referred to in the definition adopted from Simon. The ability to execute any of these strategies depends not so much on contextually or individually determined factors, such as personality, task instructions, etc., but on the learner's developmental level with respect to analysed knowledge and cognitive control. Strategies requiring particularly high levels of these skills will not be executed by young children. It is likely that these skills must be developed, or re-developed, for each new content area, but that once established, the application of the skills to new content areas is relatively effortless. Thus, a child must first learn basic abilities with respect to analysed knowledge and cognitive control, apply them to L1 acquisition (probably as they are being developed), and possibly apply them later to L2 acquisition. This last step is presumably the easiest.

Flavell (1977) identifies three stages in the development of strategic ability. In Stage 1, the child is unable to perform the component skills that comprise the strategy. In Stage 2, the child is capable of executing the strategy but never uses it spontaneously. If instructed to do so, the child can use the strategy and benefit from its operation, but on a subsequent problem, will again avoid its use. Finally, in Stage 3, the child is able to recognize situations in which the strategy may be useful and spontaneously employs it.

This developmental model applies to the use of strategies in adult L2 acquisition as well. Adults are presumably capable of executing all the strategies (Stage 1) but may not use the appropriate strategy spontaneously (Stage 2). It seems, then, that movement from the first to the second stage is a matter of maturity in which the required levels of analysed knowledge and cognitive control are present. Movement from the second to the third stage, however, is a matter of experience with problem types in which possible strategies are consolidated and understood to be effective in these situations. Children begin in Stage 1; adult L2 learners begin in Stage 2.

Summary and Conclusions

The argument has been that the basis of strategies for L2 learning and production are rooted in the same cognitive mechanisms as are strategies in other domains, in particular, L1 acquisition. The developmental component of strategy use involves both the acquisition of cognitive skills to use these strategies where consciousness, problematicity, and intentionality are required and to learn the elementary operations that comprise the strategies. Both aspects of development were traced to the knowledge and control

47

systems that govern cognition.

The difference between the strategies of applied linguistics and education and those of L1 acquisition and cognitive development, then, is the presence of the three requirements of consciousness, problematicity, and intentionality. Adults, that is, are able to bring these features to problem solving because they are metacognitively mature. The roots of these strategies, though, can be observed in children solving similar problems. Children, that is, do the same things to learn language, to communicate, and to solve other cognitive tasks as do adults, but without the advantages of metacognition. So, the theoretical basis of the strategies used by adults in language learning and production is the cognitive operations evident from the earliest time in children attempting to learn their language and their problem solving skills. They are the same in that the mental mechanisms that propel them are the same; they are different in that the possibility for their intentional manipulation makes them capable of affecting performance in ways not possible for their automatic deployment by children.

In this analysis, the sophisticated strategies used by adults (and children) to solve complex problems was traced to a more primitive precursor of the same behaviour by children. These same strategies, that is, are elaborated in ways specified by cognitive development and then applied to new problems. The analysis is similar to one proposed by Corder (1978) to solve a rather different problem. His question was to determine a reasonable starting point for L2 acquisition by adult learners if a model of either a restructuring or a recreation continuum is not accepted. The starting point, he reasoned, could be neither a fully elaborated code from the learner's first language (restructuring) nor a null set (recreation). His solution was to posit a simple code based on the first language and consistent with the features of simplification noted in child language acquisition. Elaboration and restructuring of this code would eventually lead the learner towards the model of the target language. The argument presented here for strategy use is similar. Children always had and used essentially the same strategic devices that are evident in adult L2 learning and performance. The strategies used by children differ from those used by adults in elaboration and specificity.

The theoretical basis of strategies in interlanguage is the unconscious processes observed in children. They develop by elaborating the pool of available strategies through mastery of the component skills and by gaining conscious and intentional control over those strategies so that they may be used more effectively and more purposefully. Interlanguage has many of the properties of a natural language because it is generated by the same cognitive processes as those responsible for generating the child's first language. But it takes on the special features that are tailored to individuals and to situations because, in the hands (or minds) of metacognitively aware speakers, it can be redirected through the intentional introduction of particular strategies of learning and production.

5. Strategies in Production and Reception –
Some Empirical Evidence

Although the notions of learning and communication strategies are as old as interlanguage research itself, the last few years have witnessed an intensification of research into this area.[1] Communication strategies in the production of IL have received particular attention, and there is now a fair amount of empirical study of strategies used by L2 learners in communication with native speakers. Receptive strategies have so far been less explored, but this situation is changing. As regards learning strategies, it is equally possible to state that our knowledge of these is extensive as to state the opposite. This reflects the rather unclear notion of 'strategy', which has been developed differently in L1 acquisition research (with a very general meaning) and in research into IL communication (with a much more restricted meaning). Researchers probably agree that it is necessary to define strategies not only precisely but also in such a way that the notion does not encompass *all* process phenomena – otherwise there would be no difference in principle between strategic and non-strategic aspects of production, reception and learning. *How* this could be achieved, however, remains a moot question. In this paper I adopt a fairly restricted definition of strategy, which reflects the way most IL researchers have carried out empirical investigations into strategic aspects of IL communication.

My focus will be on IL strategies in the production and reception of speech, whereas learning strategies will not be dealt with.[2] The reason is that the few empirically based studies of L2 learning that investigate the contribution of strategies to learning are based on rather unclear, and very general, notions of 'learning strategies'.

1. Investigating Strategies – some Methodological Problems
Heffalumps and Strategies

As an illustration of some of the problems we are confronted by in the study of strategies, consider the following quotation from *Winnie-the-Pooh*.

> One day, when Christopher Robin and Winnie-the-Pooh and Piglet were all talking together, Christopher Robin finished the mouthful he was eating and said carelessly: 'I saw a Heffalump to-day, Piglet.'
> 'What was it doing?' asked Piglet.
> 'Just lumping along,' said Christopher Robin. 'I don't think it saw *me.*'
> 'I saw one once,' said Piglet. 'At least, I think I did,' he said. 'Only perhaps it wasn't.'
> 'So did I,' said Pooh, wondering what a Heffalump was like. (Milne 1926, 51)

Pooh and Piglet decide to trap a Heffalump, and Piglet's problems about the nature of Heffalumps are solved in the way that whatever he finds in the trap he will identify as a Heffalump. So when he finds Pooh with a honey-jar sticking onto his head, he does not doubt in the slightest that he has now seen a Heffalump!

How could Pooh and Piglet have improved on their method of catching a Heffalump? One possibility would have been to design the trap in such a way that only Heffalumps could be trapped – which would have demanded very careful consideration of both the formal and functional characteristics of the animal.[3] Such 'empirical traps' constitute one type of empirical procedure, widely used in IL research. But as we have just noted, the trap only works in a satisfactory way if designed so that we can be confident that whatever we trap is a strategy – and not a process with a honey-jar sticking onto its head!

A different possibility for Pooh and Piglet would have been to wander around in the forest looking for a Heffalump – which again would demand a previous clarification of the formal/functional characteristics of the animal. On their way they might get a good impression of the whereabouts of the Heffalump, of its behavioural characteristics, of the way it interacts with other animals. This represents the widely-used alternative to the empirical trap, by some considered a necessary stage *before* designing the controlled empirical investigation, by others the only valid way of obtaining information on phenomena which are basically socio-psychological, and which can only be appropriately described if they are not isolated from their proper social context.

Strategies in Learning and Communication – the Definitional Issue

IL researchers have occasionally expressed themselves in a way which seems to put strategies on the same ontological level as Heffalumps. Thus Selinker (1972) wrote: 'Concerning the notion "strategy" little is known in psychology about what constitutes a strategy . . .', implying that the problem was one of description rather than definition (however, the clause immediately following this says: 'a viable definition of it does not seem possible at present'). Furthermore, a number of studies which have had a significant impact on the development of research into IL strategies (e.g. Tarone, Cohen and Dumas 1976; Tarone 1977) have quoted examples of strategies rather than discussed the definitional basis of the concept (cf. Bialystok's discussion in this volume of ostensively defined strategies). Such studies have largely been based on a pre-theoretical, intuitive notion of strategies, and their major contribution to IL studies has been to help clarify the notion. In view of the socio-psychological nature of strategies, such clarification is a necessary prerequisite for systematic empirical investigations, as these can only be conducted if based on a model-related definition of the term.

There is considerable disagreement as to whether strategies should be considered a particular type of psycholinguistic process (see for example Selinker 1972), a particular type of psycholinguistic plan (see for example Sharwood Smith 1979 or Faerch and Kasper 1983d), or a particular type of interactional process (Tarone 1981). This disagreement tends to lead to confusion as it is not always clear what the larger learning or communication framework is within which strategies are assumed to function. Thus there exists the possibility that related notions are discussed under different headings in different models, just as the mere fact that the term strategy crops up in different types of research is no guarantee that the term carries identical denotations (cf. the discussion of this problem in Tarone 1980b). A systematic attempt at locating strategies within a larger context of IL production was made in Váradi (1980), completed 1973, and later attempts owe much to this pioneering study (e.g. Corder 1983; Faerch and Kasper 1983c). The situation is even less clear in the case of strategies in reception and learning, where few attempts have been made to relate strategies systematically to comprehensive models of reception and foreign language learning (but see Candlin 1981a; Faerch, Haastrup and Phillipson 1984; Faerch forthcoming; Kasper forthcoming for reception; Faerch and Kasper 1980a; Knapp-Potthoff and Knapp 1982 for learning).

Another major question concerns the criteria which mental and/or interactional phenomena have to satisfy to qualify as strategies. As discussed in Bialystok (this volume), three criteria are particularly widespread in IL studies: problematicity, consciousness and goal-relatedness/intentionality. One may postulate a hierarchical, hyponymic relationship between these in the following way;

Goal-relatedness

⇑

Consciousness

⇑

Problematicity

The relation is one of one way implication: problematicity implies consciousness and goal-relatedness, whereas the opposite is not necessarily the case. Without going into details, the figure tries to convey that goal-relatedness is a highly general aspect of human behaviour (one of the most fundamental, according to some ideologies); that consciousness (or more precisely, degrees of consciousness, cf. the discussion of this in Tarone, Frauenfelder and Selinker 1976; Sharwood Smith 1979; Faerch and Kasper 1983d) holds true of some goal-related communication; and finally that individuals may be conscious about behaviour without experiencing problems – whereas it can be argued that the existence of problems implies consciousness, at least if 'problem' is defined in subjective terms, as seen from the point of view of the interactors, and not from the point of view of the observer.

An important implication of the hierarchical relationship between the three sets of criteria is that if strategies are defined in terms of problematicity (a widely used criterion, cf. Jordens 1977; Kellerman 1977; Tarone 1977; Corder 1983c; Faerch and Kasper 1983b) the result is a highly specific concept which can be investigated fairly precisely. If, on the other hand, the criterion of goal-relatedness is selected, the result is a very broad concept of strategy, and it becomes difficult to differentiate between strategic and non-strategic learning and communication. It might therefore seem an easy choice to decide on the criterion. Experience is that this works all right for strategies in IL speech production, but that there are considerable problems in connection with reception and learning – areas within which it is much more difficult to draw categorical lines between 'problematic' and 'non-problematic' behaviour. In the following I first discuss strategies in IL production (section 2) before dealing with the more tricky area of strategies in the reception of speech (section 3).

2. Strategies in Production
Establishing a Taxonomy of Strategies

In his study of reduction strategies, Váradi (1980) analysed the written performance in L1 and IL (English) of nineteen Hungarian learners (intermediate level[4]). The learners produced four versions of a picture story:
1) original Hungarian version
2) original English version
3) translation of (1) into English
4) translation of (2) into Hungarian.

By comparing the L1 with the IL versions, and assuming that the L1 versions represented the learners' 'optimal message', Váradi was able to identify and categorize numerous instances of 'message adjustment', both at the semantic and at the formal level. The following types of reduction were particularly frequent:

generalization (e.g. using *ball* for 'balloon')
approximation (e.g. using *air ball* for 'balloon')
circumlocution[5] (e.g. using *line for drying wet clothes* for 'clothes-line')
paraphrase (e.g. using *quickly* for 'at a quick pace').

By and large, original IL texts and translations from Hungarian into IL exhibited the same features. Occasionally, however, translated versions were more elaborate and grammatical than original IL texts, which Váradi explains as partly due to learners varying their communicative intention when asked to repeat the same task, partly to 'the difference in language skills required in making a translation and in writing a composition'.

Tarone (1977) adopted a technique similar to that of Váradi: picture description in both L1 (Spanish, Turkish, Mandarin) and IL (English). Nine adult intermediate learners produced oral descriptions in both languages, after which the investigator went over the task again with the learner, probing for particular forms in English and clarifying learners' preferences. The analysis was based on transcriptions of the original record-ings, as well as on the subjects' retrospective statements. Tarone found that the following types of communication strategies provided a satisfactory tool for describing her data:

avoidance	(topic avoidance; message abandonment)
paraphrase	(approximation; word coinage; circumlocution)
conscious transfer	(literal translation; language switch)
appeal for assistance	
mime.	

Although later studies have added to these categories, the basic prin-ciples used for classifying communication strategies still follow those estab-lished by Tarone. As an exemplification:

Tarone (1977)	*Faerch and Kasper (in press)*	
avoidance	reduction	
paraphrase	FL based	⎫
conscious transfer	L1/L3 based	⎬ achievement
appeal for assistance	interactional	⎪
mime	non-linguistic	⎭

Tarone concludes that the learners investigated 'seem to exhibit decided preferences for certain types of strategies and not for others' (1977, 202). The following hypotheses are formulated:

1) that personality factors, rather than the learner's L1 background, will determine strategy preferences

2) that strategy preferences and L2 proficiency may be related, proficient learners preferring paraphrase (FL based) strategies.

The first-mentioned hypothesis is still largely unexplored, though sup-ported by Haastrup and Phillipson (1983, 154) for example. The relation-ship between strategy preferences and L2 proficiency has been investigated in a number of studies, some of which are discussed below (section 2).

An innovative aspect of Tarone's 1977 study is the use of introspective data as a supplement to performance data. Unfortunately, it is not clear from her description to what extent Tarone made use of the learners' meta-statements in analysing the data. The situation is different in Glahn's study of retrieval strategies (1980), which relied heavily on the use of introspective techniques. Twenty-six informants of differing language back-grounds (Danish, English, Spanish) performed a communication game (in pairs) in which one person had to describe eight pictures in French to his or her interlocutor. Immediately following the interaction, the investigator replayed the tape, and the informants were asked to stop it whenever they had a comment.[6] Various retrieval strategies were identified:

1) *waiting for the term to appear*

2) *appealing to formal similarity*

3) *retrieval via semantic fields* (informants said aloud words from the same semantic field in order to retrieve a word)

4) *searching via other languages* (e.g. retrieving French 'sol' from English 'soil')

5) *retrieval from learning situation* (e.g. retrieving 'mouton' by mentally looking up the chapter on 'les viandes' in the index to a French cookery book)

6) *sensory procedures* (e.g. staring hard at the floor to find a word for 'ground').

An interesting finding was that learners, especially the eighteen adults, had very clear ideas about their knowing a word or not: 'When looking at the pictures they immediately realized whether they did or did not possess a term in French' (1980, 122). Furthermore, the adult learners were often able to predict lexical gaps early enough to plan accordingly. The psychological presence of lexical gaps and lexical retrieval problems implied by Glahn's results support the feasibility of a definition of strategies in terms of problematicity.[7]

The three studies summarized so far have contributed both to the description of IL strategies in production and to the development of a research methodology. Let me briefly enumerate the most important features of the studies collectively:

1) Both L1 and IL data are obtained (Váradi, Tarone; cf. Selinker's (1972) proposal for relevant types of data in IL research).

2) Performance data are supplemented by introspective data (Tarone, Glahn).

3) Learner – native speaker as well as learner – learner communication is studied.

4) By choosing a specific research design, the experimenter controls the learner's 'intended messages'.

5) Experiments are set up in such a way that learners are bound to run into problems and consequently use communication strategies.

Investigating Variables in Strategy Use

That the proficiency level of the learner may influence strategy use was hypothesized by Tarone (1977), and has been investigated in a number of studies. Bialystok (1983b)[8] analysed strategies used by two groups of informants: sixteen grade-twelve students learning French in high school (ten from a 'regular' programme and six from an advanced class) and fourteen adults learning French in a Civil Service Foreign Language Training Programme. Informants were asked to instruct a native speaker of French to reconstruct a picture on a flannelboard. The informant was provided with the complete picture, the native speaker had at her disposal both correct and incorrect items. The reconstructor was required to speak as little as possible and to provide feedback primarily by putting items on the flannelboard.

The analysis was based on a transcribed sound-recording of the sessions. Strategies were identified and a figure calculated representing the average number of distinct strategies used for each unknown item. The following results were obtained (1983b, 108ff.):

1) All groups used the same number of strategies on average per item.

2) The grade-twelve advanced students used significantly fewer L1-based strategies than did the other two groups, but used L2-based strategies instead.

3) When correlated with scores for a proficiency test (cloze test), strategy results revealed no relation to proficiency with respect to the average number of strategies used, whereas a significant negative correlation was obtained between proficiency scores and use of L1-based strategies for the adult group (for the student group, no significant correlation was obtained). A further difference between the groups was that the adults varied their strategy use more than the students depending on the item to be communicated (1983b, 110).

A panel of seventeen native speakers of French assessed the effectiveness of the strategies used by the subjects. Bialystok summarizes the results as follows:

> The best strategies, it seems, are those which are based on the target language and take account of the specific features of the intended concept. The best strategy users, on the other hand, are those who have adequate formal proficiency in the target language and are able to modify their strategy selection to account for the nature of the specific concept to be conveyed. (1983, 116)

An important implication of Bialystok's findings is that linguistic competence ('formal mastery') strongly interacts with 'strategic competence" (Canale and Swain 1980), and that appropriate strategy use requires a minimal level of proficiency in the L2 (1983b, 115).

Paribakht (1982) further investigated the relationship between the use of strategies and learners' proficiency level in the L2. Two groups of Persian ESL students, representing different proficiency levels according to two proficiency tests,[9] were asked to explain pictures (concrete concepts) and abstract concepts (presented to the learners in their L1) to a native speaker of English. A similar task was conducted by 20 native speakers of English. Strategies were identified in the performance of the three groups and classified according to a taxonomy which contained four major categories:

1) *linguistic approach,* comprising 'semantic contiguity', 'circumlocution' and 'metalinguistic clues'

2) *contextual approach,* comprising 'linguistic context', 'use of TL idioms and proverbs', 'transliteration of L1 idioms and proverbs' and 'idiomatic transfer'

3) *conceptual approach,* comprising 'demonstration', 'exemplification' and 'metonymy'

4) *mime,* either replacing or accompanying 'verbal output'.

The low-proficiency groups (IL1) differed significantly from the high-proficiency group (IL2) and the native speaker group with respect to the following strategy types:

semantic contiguity, especially synonymy (IL1<IL2, native speaker)
transliteration of L1 idioms and proverbs (IL1>IL2, native speaker)
idiomatic transfer (abstract nouns only) (IL1>IL2, native speaker)
demonstration (IL1>IL2, native speaker).

Paribakht points out that 'idiomatic transfer' and 'transliteration of L1 idioms and proverbs' were the only L1-based strategies used by the learners (1982, 142). As an explanation of this she suggests, following Kellerman 1977, 1978a, that the learners' perception of the distance between Farsi (L1) and English (L2) may have reduced their willingness to use other types of L1-based strategies like 'foreignizing' and 'creating L2 cognates'. She concludes that:

> ... the presence of Idiomatic Transfer and the absence of TL [target language] idioms and Proverbs in the strategy list of [IL1] seem to suggest that for communicating in the TL, idiomatic and cultural aspects of L1 are among the last to be abandoned, while similar aspects of the TL are among the last to be acquired. (1982, 141–2)

This, in fact, is in contrast to Kellerman's findings, according to which perceived idiomaticity in L1 reduces subjects' willingness to transfer (Kellerman 1978a).

As regards the difference between concrete and abstract nouns, Paribakht found that 'circumlocution' was preferred by all groups for concrete concepts, whereas the conceptual approach was preferred for abstract nouns. However, the preferences were more outspoken for the high-proficiency than for the low-proficiency groups, which Paribakht interprets as indicative of greater differentiation in strategy use according to content.

It is perhaps not surprising that both Bialystok and Paribakht found that low-proficiency learners tended to use more L1-based strategies than high-proficiency learners: after all, it takes a certain amount of proficiency in the L2 to use L2-based strategies. What is more surprising is that the differences found by Bialystok and Paribakht were not even larger: Bialystok only found a statistically significant difference in her adult group, and Paribakht only found two types of L1-based strategies in her low-proficiency group, both of which to a large extent combine L1 and L2 features. Haastrup and Phillipson (1983), however, in a study of eight Danish learners of English in conversation with a native speaker, found that their learners made extensive use of a variety of L1-based strategies, including 'borrowing' and 'foreignizing' (1983, 154), even though the learners were in their sixth year of learning English at school. It therefore seems that variables other than proficiency level are relevant in determining how much learners make use of L1-based strategies. In addition to the already mentioned perceived distance between L1 and L2, both in linguistic and cultural terms, the following may be relevant (see also Palmberg 1982):

experience with previous non-school communication in the L2
learners' age
learners' knowledge of languages other than L1 and relevant L2
personality characteristics
type of content for which strategies are used (concrete/abstract)
type of situation in which communication takes place (real-life – test
situation).

Communication Strategies in Production – Methodological Problems

Three problems of a methodological kind are now discussed which in my
view need careful consideration before further progress can be made in the
study of IL strategies in production.
Taxonomy. Even given a consensus on the definition of communication
strategies (which may be difficult enough to achieve), there are serious
problems connected with the comparison of results from different studies
because taxonomies of strategies vary:

> The taxonomy of strategies developed for the present study was based on
> existing typologies, most notably that of Tarone (1977), but was conceptually
> reorganized. (Bialystok 1983b, 101)

> On the basis of the data collected in this study, certain major modifications were
> made in the existing taxonomies. (Paribakht 1982, 43)

It is probably unrealistic to expect IL researchers to agree on one
taxonomy of communication strategies as being ideal – which would facilitate the comparison of results. In view of this situation, it is mandatory that
studies contain precise information on the taxonomy used, illustrated by
examples, and the procedure followed in assigning strategies to individual
classes (e.g. how the problem of multiple classification is tackled; cf. the
discussion of this in Trosborg 1982). Also, it would be beneficial if more
studies were undertaken which accepted an already existing taxonomy
without changes and used this in an attempt to describe the relationship
between strategy use and background variables.
Experimental design. The nature of the tasks which subjects perform, the
instructions given and the interlocutors with whom subjects communicate all
exert a decisive influence on which strategies are used. The situation is
particularly clear within the area of interactional strategies ('appeals', etc.).
Tarone (1981b, note 1) explains how she experienced the situation, being
the native speaker eliciting data from her NNS subjects for her 1977 study:

> ... when a speaker used a communication strategy, I tried not to provide help
> because I didn't want to contaminate the results, and also I wanted as many
> examples of communication strategies as possible.

In Tarone and Yule (1983), it is reported that appeal to authority did
not occur in the data. Tarone and Yule explain this as due to the fact that in
NNS–NNS interaction, 'the listener cannot be assumed to have either the

information or the language to respond to such an appeal'. This is a very reasonable hypothesis, only it is clear from Tarone and Yule's description of their research procedure that listeners were *instructed* not to provide verbal feedback ('the other was asked to be the listener who would simply pay attention, without interrupting, to what the speaker said [. . .] The only feedback which the listener could provide the speaker was nonverbal [. . .]'). A similar instruction was used in Bialystok's study (1983b): '. . . the reconstructor refrained from speaking as much as possible. Feedback was provided by the items put on the flannelboard' (1983b, 105). In view of the fact that one of the objectives of Bialystok's study was 'to simulate real communicative exchange in which one of the interlocutors was a mono-lingual speaker of the target language' (1983b, 103), it is difficult to see how this is compatible with the restriction on providing feedback.

The procedure adopted by Bialystok would have been ideal, had the objective of her investigation been to describe the use of non-interactional strategies, rather than 'simulate real communicative exchange'. The question at stake is whether the analysis is specifically oriented towards clearly defined topics – which may allow for controlled experiments in situations that differ from real-life interaction, or whether the purpose is to describe the individual's 'strategic competence' in general. In the latter case, it may be advisable not to let interlocutors know the purpose of the interaction and to ask them to behave as normally as possible. This, however, has the important consequence that the interlocutor becomes an active party to the experiment, a party who may exert a decisive influence on the results obtained. Thus Paribakht notices that 'interlocutors had a contributing effect in the success or failure of communication [. . .] A speaker [. . .] was more likely to fail if the interlocutor wouldn't take an active role in the communication process' (1982, 158). Similarly, Haastrup and Phillipson (1983, 152) state that:

> In virtually all conversations the native speakers provoke communication dis-
> ruptions by occasionally asking an incoherent question. Furthermore, they vary
> in the degree to which they follow up learner contributions, particularly when
> these are opaque.

Therefore, if strategies are analysed in fairly uncontrolled types of communication, it is important *not* to consider learners' turns as the 'real' data, to be lifted out of the context in which they occur, while interlocutors' turns are reduced to being part of the elicitation measure (see also Faerch 1979). Rather, both the learner's and his or her interlocutor's performance constitute the relevant data. This means that analyses of learners' use of communication strategies in such situations should *ideally* be related to the interlocutors' use of strategies and to metalingual activities such as repair work and discourse regulation, all located within a wider context of dis-course analysis (cf. Tarone 1981b, Trosborg 1982). Taking this step does *not* mean that the criterion of problematicity has to be abandoned – although there seems to be a tendency for it to be generally ignored by researchers who describe communication strategies within a larger context of communicative interaction (see e.g. Tarone 1981b; Wagner 1983).

Identifying communication strategies. The following description is characteristic of early studies of communication strategies:

> For the sake of simplicity in analysis, [. . .] it is assumed that all correct target expressions [. . .] result from knowledge only. An L2 expression which differed from the L1 version is presumed to arise from the employment of a communication strategy. (Palmberg 1979, 55)

Strategies are here used as a means of accounting for errors in IL, an approach which is understandable considering the historical origin of strategies in IL research. However, if a distinction is made between strategic and non-strategic performance, the approach exemplified by Palmberg is problematic, as errors may be the result of rules and strategies need not result in errors (cf. Faerch and Kasper 1980b; Stedje 1982, 159). We therefore need other means of ensuring that what we analyse in performance can be considered the result of a strategy, rather than the application of an IL rule or the uncontrolled transfer of L1 knowledge (cf. Faerch and Kasper forthcoming a). Returning to the discussion of Piglet's and Pooh's attempt at catching a Heffalump, we may distinguish between the following two approaches to identifying communication strategies.

The empirical trap. An elicitation situation is constructed in such a way that the subject is forced to make use of communication strategies. Many of the investigations described above adopt this principle in that they have the subject communicate concepts for which s/he does not know the appropriate word. The result is a highly controlled type of elicitation with a focus on individual words rather than on subjects' more general communicative behaviour. Provided that subjects are pre-tested (to ensure that they don't know the words in question),[10] the procedure may be satisfactory for restricted purposes, e.g. in order to compare learners' use of L1- or L2-based strategies. There are, however, difficulties: the fact that problems can be identified and strategic solutions seen in the performance does not imply that a direct link can be established between the problem and the overt behavioural solution. This is attested in Faerch and Kasper (forthcoming b), from which the following description is taken.

Danish learners of German were asked to communicate to a native speaker of German five items which had been encircled in the learner's copy of a picture. The native speaker's task was to put circles around the items described by the learner. The interaction was tape-recorded and played back to the subject when she had completed the task (cf. Tarone 1977). In several places, learners identified intervening problems between the original problem (as expected by the experimentators) and the final – strategic – solution, as in the following example where a circle around a bow on a woman's dress is involved:

```
L    und die Frau auf das selbe Bild hat ja ein Kleid – –
NS
L    und – – 5 – (a) ah – auf ihre – äh rechte Arm – äh – –
NS
L    gibt es ja – äh – 3 – wie heisst es (b) äh – 3 – sie
NS
L    sie sie verliert ja nicht – äh – ihre Kleid wenn sie
NS              auf dem rechten Arm
L    ja diese haha zwei – –
NS                         ach du meinst wo sie also es
L         ja            ja . . .
NS   festgebunden hat
```

The learner here uses a functional description ('her dress does not come down') as a strategy, after having given the location ('on her right arm') of the item. Without any further information, we would have to interpret the hesitations and pauses in the second and third lines as indicative of her trying to find a strategy for communicating the word 'bow'. The introspective data, however, tell a different story:

Interviewer: (having stopped the tape at (a) – see transcript): what is your problem here?

Learner: I'm thinking about how to say that – er – it's like a string – you see I don't know – I'm thinking about a string I believe – I don't know – – what keeps the dress up – – I don't think so much about bow . . .

Interviewer: (having stopped the tape at (b) – see transcript): you said 'wie heisst es' – er – what did you want to achieve?

Learner: yes – – – erm – I believe I keep thinking about – – what – no no now I know I was thinking about er – I was trying to find the word for 'shoulder' what that's called – because er – then I could explain that the string was on her shoulder . . .

(Translated from Danish)

That example illustrates that even in a highly controlled experiment in which the problems to be communicated are clear-cut, subjects may handle the situation in such a way that new problems crop up. Occasionally, these surface in performance, but often they remain within the subject's head. Only introspective techniques can help us identify such problems, without a knowledge of which our description remains fragmentary.

Straying around in the forest. According to the alternative methodology, no attempt is made at eliciting strategic solutions to previously identified problems. Rather, learners are asked to communicate in as natural a situation as possible and the performance data are then screened for what may be considered the product of communication strategies. The difficulty with this approach is that the investigator first has to identify 'problems' before s/he can proceed to a description of strategic solutions.

Temporal variables (rate of articulation, pauses, drawls, repetitions, self-repairs and slips) may be interpreted as implicit strategy markers, whereas 'handicap signals' (like 'I don't know' as an aside) may function as explicit strategy markers (cf. Faerch and Kasper 1980b, 1983b; also Seliger 1980; Stedje 1982, 1983 for a related suggestion). However, this identification procedure can only provide a tentative analysis of the data, and recent analyses of temporal variables in IL speech (German learners of French and French learners of German) indicate that the interpretation may be rather uncertain:

> ... die Planungsindikatoren sind nicht 'eindimensional' zu interpretieren [...]: weder beziehen sie sich notwendigerweise auf das, was ihnen unmittelbar in der Äusserung folgt, noch reflektieren sie jeweils nur Schwierigkeiten, die dem Sprecher auf einer einzelnen, deutlich zu lokalisierenden Planungsebene erwachsen sind. (Möhle and Raupach 1983, 91)

A further difficulty is that proficient strategy users may become expert at concealing their use of strategies ('covert strategies'), e.g. by predicting a communicative problem and planning a strategic solution well in advance of the problem spot itself (Faerch and Kasper 1983b, 235). Such strategies can only be identified by means of introspective techniques.

3. Strategies in the Reception of Speech

Types of Procedures

When we move from communication strategies in the production of IL to strategies in speech reception, one thing becomes clear immediately: that the various criteria proposed by different IL researchers for defining strategies (cf. section 1) are largely based on considerations of speech production, and that it is difficult to transfer at least some of the criteria to speech reception. The problematicity of 'problematicity' as a defining criterion for receptive strategies is expressed in a number of studies, of which I shall only quote two:

> ... it seems to be the case in comprehension that problem-solving is rather the rule than the exception, which makes the notion of strategy rather vacuous ... (Kasper forthcoming)

> ... at least in speech perception, strategic competence may be of central importance, and operate not just in cases of communication breakdown, but constantly. (Tarone 1981b)

The quotations represent different approaches to handling the notion of strategy in speech reception:

1) applies the definitional criteria established for strategies in speech production directly and without modification;

2) operates with different concepts of strategies in different areas.

It may be possible to strike a compromise between these two positions by at the same time acknowledging the need for a common definitional basis of strategies in speech production, reception and foreign-language learning and acknowledging the fact that definitional criteria may function differently in different situations. Hence we may preserve 'problematicity' as a criterion if we accept that 'problematicity' needs to be given a specific characterization, which when applied to speech reception means locating the criterion within a wider model of speech reception. Without going into details, such a model may comprise:

1) procedures (mental) that utilize knowledge, linguistic or other, at various levels of delicacy for the interpretation of incoming speech (knowledge-driven or top-down processing)

2) procedures (mental) that utilize incoming data by decoding gradually larger segments, moving from phonological and morphological to syntactic and semantic decoding (data-driven or bottom-up processing)

3) procedures (behavioural) that utilize interpretive possibilities in the context, e.g. by means of repair work.

In the following, I shall discuss (1) and (2) together, before going into (3).

Procedures of Types (1) and (2)

Contemporary models of speech reception are generally 'interactive' in the sense that they see top-down and bottom-up processing as interrelated in complex ways (cf. Lesgold and Perfetti 1981). Hence it is difficult to maintain the position, adopted by Tarone (1981b), that the stage at which mental interpretive strategies operate, such as Bever's perceptual strategies (Bever 1970) (cf. procedures of type (1) above) precedes the stage at which grammatical rules are applied (cf. procedures of type (2) above). Indeed, the strategies proposed by Bever, which to a large degree rely on grammatical decoding, are generally considered examples of bottom-up processing (cf. Clark and Clark 1977, 58ff.). It therefore seems reasonable to abandon the sequential ordering of procedures of types (1) and (2) which, however, does not entail abandoning the difference in principle between the two types of procedures.

Procedures of types (1) and (2) are undoubtedly used by all listeners, whether they are exposed to their native language or to a foreign language, although the amount of top-down processing relative to bottom-up processing may vary with different situations. It is probably the case that the two types of procedure are generally activated unconsciously, without the individual experiencing a problem – which would exclude them from being 'strategic' in the narrow sense of the term. But as there is some evidence that procedures of types (1) and (2) may also be used in problem-solving situations (see below), they may be characterized as potentially strategic. In the following, I shall briefly report on a number of empirical studies aimed at clarifying learners' utilization of top-down and bottom-up processing in decoding foreign-language input.

In a study of reading comprehension, Carrell (1983) investigated the extent to which two groups of learners at different proficiency levels utilized top-down and bottom-up processing. Three variables were investigated:

1) *context* (presence or absence of title and picture, preceding text),

2) *transparency* (presence or absence of specific lexical items within text, e.g. *clothes* and *washing machine* versus *things* and *facilities*),

3) *familiarity* (presence or absence within reader of previous knowledge of the content of the text).

Two texts (from Bransford and Johnson 1973) were used, one dealing with a familiar, the other with an unknown topic. Each text was presented with and without context and in either of two versions: with and without transparent words. After having read the texts, the subjects (66 advanced and 42 high-intermediate learners) were asked to assess the difficulty they had had in reading the text on a 7-point scale, following which they were asked to note down as many ideas from the text as they could recall. Results from the two groups of learners were compared to results obtained from a group of native speakers of English. Carrell concludes that the native speakers utilized all three components of background knowledge: *context* used in top-down processing; *textual transparency clues* used in bottom-up processing; and *familiarity* with the topic, which had the effect that novel information was more memorable than familiar information. Neither group of learners utilized context or textual clues. Only the advanced group of learners were affected by the familiarity of the text, in the way native speakers were affected. Carrell (1983, 200) suggests that:

> . . . high-intermediate and even advanced ESL readers tend to be linguistically bound to a text. They may be processing the literal language of the text, but they are not making the necessary connections between the text and the appropriate background information. [. . .] They appear not to be efficient text processors. They are not utilizing context as a top-down cognitive processing mode to make appropriate predictions about the meaning of a text, nor are they utilizing textual transparency of lexical cues, as a bottom-up processing mode to build up a mental representation of the meaning of a text.

Carrell here distinguishes between 'literal processing' and top-down/bottom-up processing in a way which, unfortunately, is not very transparent. A different interpretation of her results, based on the distinction between top-down and bottom-up processing exclusively, would be that learners do not utilize information obtained via bottom-up processing for the purpose of top-down processing. Just to illustrate with one example, learners correctly interpret the meaning of *washing machine* (bottom-up processing) but fail to utilize this meaning for establishing a higher-level frame ('laundry instructions') which, again, might be used in processing the rest of the text in a top-down manner. According to this interpretation, Carrell's learners rely too much on bottom-up processing and miss out on the possibilities for top-down processing.

This re-interpretation of Carrell's results is in line with Kasper's analysis (Kasper forthcoming) of pragmatic comprehension in role-play situations between German learners of English and native speakers. Kasper found two areas in which learners misunderstood the native speaker's communicative intention: (1) phatic talk being interpreted as referential talk, and (2) misinterpreting the intended illocution of action-oriented speech acts. The two areas can be illustrated by the following examples:

1) (Learner (L) has taken on a holiday job as a strawberry picker on the native speaker's (E) farm.)
L: hello Mr Knox here I am again with my basket
E: oh hello Peter how are you
L: oh well I think I'm very fine now well it's a hard work but it's nice to have such good contact with people you see I like it

2) (L taking leave from her landlady with whom she stayed for two years. Emotional involvement in both parties.)
E: I've got some sandwiches ready for you here I hope it'll be enough
L: yes of course it will be enough

Kasper offers as an explanation of (1) that the advanced learner analysed the native speaker's utterance by means of bottom-up processing and 'failed to connect the reading "inquiry about L's well-being" to the frame "opening-sequence specific phatic talk"'', whereas top-down processing might have led to the correct interpretation of the native speaker utterance as a 'routine inquiry'. A similar explanation is provided for (2): the learner ignores a cue ('I hope') which, together with her knowledge of the pragmatics of leave-taking, would have enabled her to interpret the native speaker turn as a wish. Instead, she decodes the native speaker utterance 'literally', from the bottom, and misinterprets the native speaker wish as a request for information.

Both Carrell's and Kasper's study offer mutually supportive evidence from quite different quarters that at least in certain situations, learners over-rely on bottom-up processing, a finding which is the opposite of what Tarone hypothesized:

Because learners of nonprimary languages do not yet have a complete mastery of the linguistic rules of the target language, it must be the case that they rely quite heavily on the perceptual strategies [. . .] to decode meaningful elements and arrive at a hypothesis as to meaning. (Tarone 1981b)

Carrell emphasizes the need for contrastive studies, comparing learners' reading procedures in their native language and in a foreign language, in order to decide on the amount of transfer of top-down procedures. If more evidence can be accumulated that learners do not automatically transfer top-down procedures from their native-language reading habits to foreign-language reading (cf. the evidence reported in Clarke 1979), this leads on to a discussion of why this should be the case. Two possibilities seem particularly pertinent.

First, it might be hypothesized that specific activity types in the foreign-language classroom further bottom-up, rather than top-down, processing. This is suggested by Kasper in the discussion of her results. She points out that traditional activities in the German foreign-language classroom either encourage bottom-up processing (pattern-practice and sentence-to-sentence translation) or, at the advanced stages, top-down procedures which never reach the bottom level (literary analysis focusing on ideas, attitudes or problems contained in texts).

Second, it might be hypothesized that a prerequisite for using top-down processing successfully is that low-level cognitive operations are automatized. According to an interactive model of comprehension, top-down processing does not precede low-level decoding. High-level frames are matched against low-level cues (e.g. lexical items or parts of these), and one might speculate that learners have to devote too much energy to decoding low-level cues for high-level operations to take place efficiently.

In the two studies just reported on, no special attention was paid to the question of whether learners experience problems in comprehension. There are, however, a few studies which focus on top-down processing used 'strategically', for problem-solving. One of these is Cavalcanti (1983), who trained her informants (Brazilian learners of English) to think aloud when they paused in the process of reading an English text. The rationale for this is expressed by Cavalcanti (1983, 287–8) in the following way:

> The use of this procedure [. . .] assumes that the identification of pauses, i.e. potential problem situations caused by either the reader's inadequacy or by the reader's hyperinterest in parts of the text (or in the topic as a whole), results from a natural slowing down of the processing of information. It represents a shift from 'automatic' to 'controlled' processing in the reading (see Shiffrin and Schneider 1977).

Cavalcanti's study is of considerable methodological interest: it focuses on problems in the comprehension process, the informants are trained to introspect in a way which minimally interferes with the reading process itself, introspection is controlled by the reader herself and not by an observer, and last, but not least, informants read the way they normally read and not aloud, as in a number of other reading studies (see e.g. the overview in Cohen and Hosenfeld 1981).

Also of great methodological interest is a study conducted by Haastrup. The aim of this is to investigate how Danish learners of English at two proficiency levels solve lexical problems in reading by means of inferencing procedures (as discussed in Carton 1973; Faerch forthcoming). Learners, working in small groups (two or three together), discuss the meaning of a number of unknown words in a text and try to reach an agreement. The following extract, based on Faerch, Haastrup and Phillipson 1984, 97ff., illustrates the procedure, as well as the different types of cues that the participants bring into the discussion.

The group of three are discussing words in a text about the dangers of smoking. They come across the following sentence:

> You can regard it [the withdrawal symptom] as a mild syndrome, but it is a withdrawal syndrome and nicotine is an addictive drug.

Here follows an extract (translated into English) of the learners' discussion of 'addictive'.

> B: it is probably something like
> A: 'dependent on' or 'habit-forming' or something like that
> C: 'addictive' – 'addictive' what the hell do you think it means in this context [. . .] it may be a dangerous drug as well as
> A: 'habit-forming'
> C: can't we find something which sounds like 'addictive' – isn't there something in Latin
> B: oh no
> C: 'addere' – what does 'addere' mean in Danish [. . .]
> B: I've heard it in a song or something like that this expression 'I'm an addict'
> C: can you recall a few phrases before or after it
> B: something like 'you're an addict' [. . .]
> C: 'drug' [. . .] isn't there something called a 'drugstore' or the like
> A: a 'drugstore' – that's just a pub or something like that [. . .]'

The three learners utilize interlingual cues (Latin 'addere'), contextual cues (addictive drug), intralingual cues (drug – drugstore) and combinations of these. Final results from Haastrup's investigation are not yet available, but a preliminary analysis of the data obtained from 30 low-proficiency and 30 high-proficiency groups of learners seems to confirm one of the hypotheses being investigated, viz. that learners at the low-proficiency level are too dependent on bottom-up processing and don't utilize the potential of inferencing procedures for interpreting the meaning of unknown words.

Procedures of Type (3)

When learners apply procedures types (1) and (2) to incoming speech (written or spoken), the result is often partial comprehension (this is not unique for learner-native speaker communication, cf. Goffman's 'God save us from total comprehension'). It is feasible to distinguish between:

1) Partial comprehension in the sense of a mismatch between the speaker's communicative intention and the hearer's interpretation of this, unnoticed by the hearer and – possibly – by the speaker as well (cf. Brown: 'It would be interesting to know how many times a day we all arrive at a hypothesis about something which has been said to us which is, strictly, an incorrect hypothesis, but which is never revealed to us as incorrect because the opportunity for correction does not arise', 1977, 163).

2) Partial comprehension in the sense that the hearer experiences a mismatch between what s/he has been able to interpret (by means of procedures of types (1) and (2)) and something more which she believes the speaker to have intended.

Strategies aimed at clarifying receptive problems implied by the last-mentioned type of situation are referred to as *behavioural* by Faerch and Kasper (1980a). These strategies utilize communicative resources outside the hearer, typically located in the speaker. They therefore overlap with what in ethnomethodological terms is described as other-initiated repair work (cf. Schegloff, Jefferson and Sacks 1977). Two major types can be distinguished (cf. Brown 1977; Faerch forthcoming):

1) *General repair requests,* in which the hearer only requests a repair, without identifying the repairable:

    3) NS: y' you don't want to visit England particularly
        L: what
        NS: you don't *want* to visit England particularly
        L: no
    4) NS: how long how much time do you spend at the stables
        L: what
        NS: how how much time do you spend with the horses
        L: I don't know erm

A variant of general repair request is lack of uptaking (Faerch and Kasper 1982), where the hearer does not provide the speaker with positive feedback at a point where this is desired. This is a well-known situation in teacher-student communication in the classroom, where student uptaking is largely expressed non-verbally (gaze, head-nods, bidding). In conversation between native speakers, there is empirical evidence for back-channel information to occur at fairly regular intervals (cf. Oreström 1983, 128–30), which provides the interactional basis for speakers to interpret lack of uptaking as an (indirect) repair request.

2) *Specific repair requests,* in which the hearer identifies the repairable:

    5) NS: what time does your father have to go to work
        L: er *where* he's going to work
        NS: what time yeah what time
        L: oh – what time
        NS: I mean . . .
    6) NS: is it an exchange
        L: I don't know what that is
        NS: it means
    7) NS: d'you like going to the cinema
        L: to the what
        NS: the cinema
        L: yeah

It may be the case that learners tend to use fewer specific repair requests than native speakers. Thus Kasper (1981, 252) reports that whereas her native speakers, engaged in dyadic interaction with learners, used many specific repair requests, there was only one learner who used a specific repair request (and only once).

The learner's repair request forces the speaker to acknowledge the presence of a problem. Hence repair requests may elicit productive communication strategies (cf. Tarone forthcoming). In some cases, these strategies amount to nothing more than the speaker repeating what s/he has just said, possibly with more force (as in examples (3) and (5); cf. the discussion in Hatch 1983). Sometimes, the result is a repair which looks much more like the types of productive strategies discussed above, e.g. paraphrase or generalization (cf. example (4)).

There are few empirical studies of the way learners use behavioural strategies for solving receptive problems. Schwartz (1980) analysed repairs in video-recordings of pairs of learners of English. She found the same preference for self-repair as has been documented for communication between native speakers (by Schegloff, Jefferson and Sacks 1977). Other-repair was restricted to situations in which a learner made a lexical, syntactic or phonological error. Gaskill (1980) found a similar distribution of repair-types in his analysis of learner-native speaker interaction, with a clear preference for other-repair in situations where the native speaker was an experienced ESL instructor. In an analysis of six conversations between Danish learners and native speakers of English, Faerch and Kasper (1982) found a marked difference in repair types according to the proficiency level and personality of the learner. It is suggested that these differences reflect learners' differing needs for protective face work (see also Lauerbach 1982). Thus learners at high proficiency levels or ambitious learners may withhold explicit repair requests and fake comprehension, hoping that they will be able to understand when more input has been processed.

As was the case with strategies in IL production, this brings up the essential questions how individual learner characteristics influence strategy use, and whether or to what extent individual differences can be traced back to communicative patterns in the learners' L1 or to communication in the foreign language classroom. It is perhaps not a wild guess that some learners develop an ability to fake comprehension, rather than admit ignorance, when confronted by problems in classroom input. To the extent they rely on mental interpretive procedures (types 1 and 2), this is fine. Unfortunately, the (admittedly very few) results summarized above do not imply that this is done very effectively.

4. Conclusion

In section 1, three defining criteria for strategies were enumerated: goal-relatedness, consciousness and problematicity. In sections 2 and 3 I described the state of the art of research into strategies, adopting problema-ticity as the defining criterion. I hope to have shown that problematicity helps delimit, in a non-arbitrary way, a relevant field of study within the much wider field of (IL) speech production. As regards strategies in speech reception, the situation is equally clear-cut in the case of behavioural strate-gies, but much less so with respect to mental procedures: top-down as well as bottom-up processing is undoubtedly utilized both in (automatized) uncon-trolled processing and in situations in which the individual is conscious about the existence of a receptive problem. We may therefore be describing the same area of 'procedural knowledge' (Faerch and Kasper forthcoming c) irrespective of whether we focus on automatized or problematic reception. There may, however, be certain methodological gains if we focus on the way learners try to cope with receptive problems: rather than depend exclusively on methods of recall and rection time – methods that rely heavily on a *productive* reaction from the subject – we may try to develop introspective methods which much more directly inform us about receptive procedures. Needless to say, there are still many unresolved questions with respect to this, and whereas it is easy to state that introspection should be supplemented by performance description in speech production research, it is much more difficult to decide what introspective methods have to be 'triangulated' with, to increase validity, in research into speech reception.

The approach to the description of strategies in IL communication advocated above is based on the assumption that a definition of strategies, and the empirical investigations in accordance with this, will have to be established for each mode of communication separately, reflecting the general socio-psychological situation within which strategies are located. The implication is that we may have to juggle with different notions of strategy in IL production and in the reception of FL input, just as the notion may look different for native and for IL communication.

There are obvious problems associated with this approach, the most serious one being that in establishing different notions of strategies for different types or different modes of communication, we prevent ourselves from directly comparing, for example, strategies in L1 acquisition and in L2 learning. I'm not sure how important this objection is, as there exists a danger that we create an artificial psycholinguistic tertium comparationis simply by labelling different phenomena similarly. Furthermore, there is the important question to what extent it is reasonable for IL research to adopt concepts, models and methods directly and without modification from psycholinguistic research into L1 acquisition. I here agree entirely with Meara (1983, 131–2) who states that

> the way we have subordinated ourselves to the theoretical concerns of others is something that has done us lasting harm. The only way in which we are going to alter this state of affairs is for us to work out what our own priorities are, and then to become more self-confident and assertive about pursuing them.

My own priorities would be to investigate individual variation in strategy use, to relate this to learners' strategic competence and communicative behaviour in their L1 and to communicative patterns of interaction in the foreign-language classroom, and to bridge the gap between communication strategies and learning. Whether we need a notion of 'learning strategy' as something separate from learning processes or procedures in general I do not know, but it is important that IL research addresses the question of how communication strategies interrelate with, and possibly further, learning.

Notes

1) Cf. the historical overview in Faerch and Kasper (1983a).

2) 'Speech' is used throughout this paper as a convenient cover-term for spoken and written language.

3) Cf. Piglet's speculations: 'What was a Heffalump like? Was it Fierce? *Did* it come when you whistled? And *how* did it come? Was it Fond of Pigs at all? If it was Fond of Pigs, did it make any difference *what sort of Pig?*' (Milne 1926, 60-1)

4) The learners had been enrolled in an English course 16 hours a week for a period of either six or nine months, already having some knowledge of the language at the time when they entered the course.

5) 'Circumlocution' and 'paraphrase' are instances of 'formal replacement' in Váradi's typology. In the categorization of Faerch and Kasper (1983c), these would be characterized as formal reduction accompanied by achievement (assuming that the learners were in fact avoiding *clothes-line* and *at a quick glance,* which is perhaps dubious, cf. Váradi's own reservations (1983, 89).

6) Unfortunately, Glahn only describes the introspective procedure in connection with her first experiment, which was aimed at a grammatical area. It is unclear whether the procedure used in the experiment described above was the same, as I have interpreted the description.

7) Cf. also Möhle and Raupach: 'Wenn Pausen oder andere Verzögerungs-phänomene, die durch Wortsuche bedingt sind, den Sprechern in stärkerem Masse bewusst werden als alle anderen Verzögerungsphänomene, so hängt das vermutlich damit zusammen, dass die Behinderung des inhaltlichen Ausdrucksbedürfnisses hier am stärksten und am offensichtlichsten ist' (1983,79).

8) Bialystok's study has been included in spite of the fact that she defines communication strategies as 'all attempts to manipulate a limited linguistic system in order to promote communication' (1983b, 102), i.e. in a way which is considerably broader than a definition based on problematicity. The reason is that what Bialystok actually investigates is 'the use of communication strategies when appropriate target language vocabulary is lacking' (1983b, 103).

9) No details are given of the subjects' proficiency in English.

10) None of the studies reported on which utilized this approach (Tarone 1977; Glahn 1980; Paribakht 1982; Bialystok 1983a) report that pre-tests were admini-stered.

11) See also the discussion in Raupach (1983).

6. Discussant:

The approaches to learners' strategies adopted by Bialystok and Faerch are fundamentally different, as is brought out by the following:

> What is needed, then, is a definition of strategies for learning and communication that is sufficiently general that it can include both child and adult uses, overcoming the problem of the three restrictive criteria [problematicity, consciousness, and intentionality], yet sufficiently specific that it adds importantly to our understanding and clarification of the process of second language learning and use. (. . .) The theoretical basis of strategies in interlanguage is the unconcious processes observed in children (Bialystok, pp.45 and 48).

> A definition of strategies, and the empirical investigation in accordance with this, will have to be established for each mode of communication separately, reflecting the socio–pyschological situation within which strategies are located (Faerch, p.69)

Categorizations of reality, not least of L2 learners communicative and learning behaviour, inevitably reflect the analyst's epistemological interest, the difference between the two authors in theoretical stand being an excellent case in point: Bialystok's perspective is that of a cognitive psychologist wishing to reconstruct the principles involved in language acquisition and use, and the model she adopts is therefore highly general – in fact, it can be argued that it is not even specific to *language* processing but applies to cognitive information processing as such. Faerch's focus, on the other hand, is specifically on IL use and development, and within this field he addresses the specific differences between strategic and non-strategic L2 processing, and between strategies in production and reception. His ultimate interest in learners' strategies derives from educational concerns, which necessitates that learners' strategy use is related as precisely as possible to both situational and learner factors.

However, even among those who, like Faerch, take a more restricted IL perspective, approaches to learners' strategies are far from homogeneous, the theoretical positions adopted deriving from researchers' interests in different aspects of IL development and use. Let me illustrate this by three examples from studies of communication strategies in IL production. Dechert (1983) and Möhle and Raupach (1983) examine IL users' process of speech planning. Using temporal variables as planning indicators, they attempt to reconstruct the procedural knowledge that learners activate in speech production. As the planning process as such is seen as one of decision-making and problem-solving, no attempt is made to isolate a particular type of planning procedure as 'strategic'.

Wagner (1983) investigates the communicative acts which interlocuters perform in a specific type of discourse, an instruction task. The solution to this task is analysed within the framework of Rehbein's model of discourse, the 'Mustertheorie' (e.g. Rehbein 1977). In the instruction, the instructor solves his task by breaking down the overall goal into sub-goals which are reached by establishing and executing verbal plans. These goal-related activities are referred to by Wagner as strategies. Again, no attempt is made to single out a specific type of plan from the rest of the goal-directed plans of action as being 'strategic'.

Faerch and Kasper (1980a, 1983e) specify their ultimate concern with communication strategies as educationally motivated. Given that learners often get into situations where they experience their IL resources as insufficient or difficult to access, the authors assume that the operations employed to overcome such problems are particularly relevant for learners. Furthermore, in order to make learners aware of how to solve these problems as efficiently as possible, the problems must be accessible to learners' consciousness. Hence the authors' adoption of problem-orientedness and potential consciousness as defining criteria for communication strategies. The usefulness of communication strategies thus defined to foreign language teaching methodology and testing has been demonstrated in various ways (cf. the overview in Faerch and Kasper, in press).

The purpose of these examples is to illustrate how different research interests result in different notions of strategy, not to suggest any inherent superiority of any of these proposals. As long as scientific concepts and terms are explicitly defined and related to specific theories, their diversity is not only harmless but even mutually beneficial, as advocators of one approach can profit from the insights achieved on the basis of a different model. For instance, Dechert's discovery of 'islands of reliability' in IL performance and of their function in the planning process is perfectly compatible with Faerch and Kasper's notion of strategy – yet it took Dechert's model for the reconstruction of the planning processes in IL speech production to discover it. Likewise, Wagner identifies the discourse strategy 'handing over the verbalization to the more competent interlocuter', a strategy perfectly in line with Faerch and Kasper's definitional requirements, but which first became apparent in Wagner's discourse analytical framework. Thus, these approaches to strategies in IL production are complementary rather than mutually exclusive.

In a similar manner, Bialystok's 'search for the general' and Faerch's 'search for the specific' in strategy studies can be related to each other, not just in the trivial sense of the general including the specific but rather in that both authors adopt identical criteria for defining IL strategies. According to

Bialystok, the presence of problematicity, consciousness and intentionality (Faerch: goal-relatedness) differentiates the notion of strategy in IL and educational research from L1 acquisition research and developmental psychology. The same set of criteria singles out strategic from non-strategic IL use in Faerch's proposal, which may therefore be seen as comprised by Bialystok's model.

However, Faerch acknowledges that even within IL use, his main criterion, problematicity, does not equally apply across modalities. Whereas it efficiently delimits an interesting class of cognitive and behavioural operations in IL production, it does not function as well with respect to reception and learning. This becomes clear if one transfers 'problematicity' directly, the way it is characterized in production, to reception. One would then have to define as problematic situations in which IL knowledge which could directly match incoming L2 data is not available or accessible. This would partly restrict problematicity in reception to problems in bottom-up processing, partly ignore the important fact that even fully competent hearers regularly face deficient incoming data which cannot be decoded by immediately matching frames, but which require the activation of further knowledge sources to bridge the information gaps in the data (cf. Clark 1975). As for learning, the application of problematicity seems even more difficult to sustain, as the existence of a gap between available and desired knowledge, and thus of problematicity, is constitutive for any learning situation. One would therefore have to conclude that all activities geared at L2 learning are strategic, which leaves us with a rather unspecific notion of a learning strategy (as suggested, e.g., by Rubin 1975 and 1981).

Neither of the two papers under discussion take up all three strategy types. They both discuss productive communication strategies at length, which reflects the state of the art in IL strategy research with its emphasis on this particular stategy type. Bialystok also discusses learning strategies in L1 and L2 acquisition or learning, and Faerch goes into IL users' receptive strategies. In the remainder of these comments, I shall try to relate the three strategy types to each other by examining the contribution of receptive and productive communication strategies to L2 learning. The general relationship between learning and communication strategies, and the problem of disentangling them, has been pointed out by, for instance, Tarone (1981b), Bialystok (1983b), Corder (1983b) and Faerch and Kasper (1980a, 1983e), and I need not repeat their arguments here.

An account of learning strategies and the learning effect of communication strategies presupposes a model of L2 learning. In accordance with a cognitive view of language processing, it has been customary to conceive of language learning as a process of hypothesis formation and testing, as proposed by Chomsky and Miller (1963) for L1 acquisition and extended by Corder (1967) to L2 learning. The outcome of the L2 learning process is the learner's IL knowledge, whose components differ, among other things, in terms of their implicit or explicit mental representation or, in terms of Bialystok's recent suggestion, in the extent to which the knowledge is analysed. Moreover, IL knowledge has to be made accessible for productive and receptive purposes. This is achieved by the process of automatization, as a result of which IL knowledge can be activated with different degrees of cognitive control – compare Bialystok's control dimension. The following remarks will address the knowledge dimension only. As for terminology, I label strategies operating in the learner's mind exclusively as 'cognitive', and strategies which involve the interlocutor or other resources in the problem–solving task as 'interactive'.

When establishing hypotheses about L2 rules by means of cognitive communication strategies, learners can rely on two sources: the input they receive and their existing knowledge. Receptive cognitive strategies combine the two sources, whereas productive cognitive strategies operate on the learners's prior knowledge only.

In the case of the receptive strategy of inferencing, as discussed in Faerch's paper (see also Carton 1972; Bialystok 1978, 1983a; Rubin 1981), linguistic and other knowledge is used to interpret L2 input. In order for learning to take place, the input must have certain characteristics: it must not be immediately matchable by the learner's existing knowledge, yet it must be decodable by means of other knowledge sources and contextual cues. These conditions, however, are insufficient to determine which parts of the 'comprehensible input' (Krashen, e.g. 1982), or 'intake' (Corder 1967), are retained as part of the IL system, and which are just used for immediate comprehension and then forgotten. Little is known today about input requirements for learning, and it will therefore be an urgent task for future IL research to specifiy these factors.

By using productive cognitive communication strategies, learners activate their linguistic knowledge in order to solve production problems, for instance by transferring rules from L1/L3 or by generalizing within IL. The problem solutions can function as new hypotheses about L2 under two conditions: (1) The learner must believe that the solution is compatible with the L2 system. This excludes, for example, language switch from the L1-based strategies that can have a learning effect. (2) The learner must produce a problem-solution which extends her available resources. Among the IL-based strategies, this excludes paraphrase from being relevant for hypothesis formation, as this strategy involves the application, rather than the extension, of already available IL knowledge.

The cognitive strategies mentioned so far have in common that they can be employed either as communication strategies which have an impact on hypothesis formation as a side-effect, or specifically as learning strategies in situations where L2 learning rather than communication is in focus. This applies particularly to formal classroom learning situations. Apart from strategies which have this double function as learning and communication strategies, there are strategies which are exclusively relevant for learning – just as there are communication strategies which do not have a direct learning effect, such as language switch, paraphrase, non-linguistic strategies, and all avoidance or reduction strategies. Such cognitive learning strategies, which are not directly tied to communicative purposes, are mentioned, for instance, by Rubin (1981) under the category of 'deductive reasoning'. Some of these strategies can lead directly to hypothesis formation, such as 'comparing native/other language to target language to help identify regular similarities and differences' and 'inferring of grammatical rules and vocabulary by analogy'.

In addition to the cognitive strategies, IL rules may be established by means of interactive strategies. These are receptive or productive appeals for assistance addressed to the interlocutor or other resources; compare the receptive appeals, or other-initiated self-repairs, discussed in Faerch's paper. Appeals can elicit word explanations from an interlocutor in non-educational communication, or metalinguistic rule formation in a teaching context, to mention just two examples. The information thus gained may be directly integrated into the learner's IL system without first having had hypothetical status. However, it is doubtful whether this seeming shortcut is also an efficient way of learning. It may be the case that for IL rules to be retained in long-term memory and to stabilize, they have to pass through different developmental stages in which the learner's cognition is actively involved (cf. McDonough 1981, 31).

If we now turn to hypothesis testing, it is noticeable that cognitive communication strategies have no function here as hypothetical rules have already been established – hence there is no communication problem to be overcome with the help of these strategies. Cognitive communication strategies, we may therefore conclude, contribute to hypothesis formation only. However, testing out hypotheses, either as an end in itself or as a by-product of communication, can be viewed as a problem-solving activity, the problem being that the learner wants to find out whether a hypothetical rule is correct or not. By this I don't wish to imply that any application of a hypothetical rule qualifies as problem-solving. Rather, in order to test their hypothesis, learners must *attend* to both the hypothetical rule and the feedback they receive, and *draw conclusions* from matching the hypothesis against the feedback. If these conditions are satisfied, hypothesis-testing, and the activities used to this end, can comfortably be seen as a learning strategy.

There are various ways in which hypotheses can be tested out: by employing them receptively or productively, in communicative language use or metalinguistically (cf. Figure 1).

In *receptive* hypothesis testing, the learner activates the hypothetical rule and matches it against either of two forms of input: communicatively used input, which requires analysing the input in terms of the rule, or metalinguistically stated input, which allows for direct comparison between the hypothetical rule and the rule formulated by the sender of the input. However, even in the latter case, direct rule matching is only possible if the metalinguistic terms employed in the input are compatible with the learner's metalinguistic knowledge. *Productive* hypothesis testing can be achieved by the learner using the hypothesis for communicative purposes or by formulating it in metalinguistic terms. The latter strategy has been examined by Raabe (1982, in press), who refers to this type of hypothesis testing as 'pre-output data', i.e. utterances preceding the actual use of the (hypothetical) rule (e.g.'Isn't *ne* . . . *pas* a double negation?'). The interlocutor's

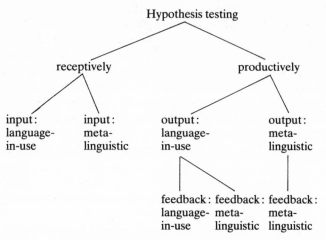

FIGURE 1. Ways of hypothesis testing.

feedback to learners' language-in-use output can again be formulated in either of two ways: (1) as a communicative act at the same functional level, from which the learner then has to induce the underlying rule and compare it to her or his rule (e.g. learner: 'Peter er were mad at James' – interlocutor: 'He was mad at him yes'); (2) as a metalinguistic statement, formulated either implicity ('He *was* mad at James') or explicitly ('You say "was" in the first and third person singular'). The learner's initiating language-in-use act thus allows for either an equivalent response or a 'world-shift' to metalinguistic discourse. A metalinguistically formulated hypothesis such as 'Is *money* a plural noun as in Danish?', however, conditions only metalinguistic statements as response (and again, the degree of explicitness is at the interlocutor's discretion).

It is true that the occurrence of these hypothesis testing strategies is probably strongly linked to specific learning or communication environments, the metalinguistic strategies being particularly likely to occur in educational contexts, as in Raabe's investigations, the language-in-use formulations seeming most usual in non-educational situations. However, it would be premature to discard any of them as irrelevant for one or the other context at the present stage of research. As classroom data show, teachers frequently use implicit language-in-use feedback moves, in particular when L2 functions as a means of communication rather than as the object of formal practice (cf. Kasper in press b). And learners, as well as their native or non-native interlocuters, use metalinguistic hypothesis testing and feedback moves in non-educational discourse (cf. Faerch 1979). Determining which of these hypothesis testing activities is the most efficient learning strategy for whom and under what conditions remains a task for future research.

7. Summary of Discussion

In responding to the discussant's comments, Bialystok summarised her position on the three major criteria for strategy-use. Problematicity, she said, should not be pressed too far since its over-emphasis on the notion of 'communicative impasse' (which was irrelevant to much IL speech) tended to interfere with further study. She placed greater stress on intentionality (whether consciousness was involved or not) as a more generally applicable criterion. The best way forward in the study of strategies, in her view, was to aim for generality in broad cognitive framework rather than search for language-specific strategies. Faerch in his comments repeated his concern that the study of IL comprehension strategies had been neglected and that this lack of interest was particularly unfortunate in a pedagogical context.

A number of contrasts were explored in the course of the general discussion. The first concerned the distinction, if there was one, between strategies of communication and strategies of learning. It was noted that among some SL learners (e.g. migrant workers) communication strategies could develop a high level of sophistication without apparently influencing the development of language, which seemed to fossilize at an early stage. Conversely, there was also evidence to show that not all L2 development need be communication-led and much seemed to depend almost exclusively on linguistic factors.

Secondly, there was the contrast between L1 and L2 strategies, and the general consensus was that, although there may well be differences in the ways that L1 and L2 learners apply their strategic competence to specific problems, it would be a serious mistake to look for separate L1 and L2 strategy-systems.

Among other topics considered by the group was the need for a more vigorous investigation of strategies of comprehension, but, in spite of general sympathy for the aims of such a project, it was pointed out by a number of speakers that there were formidable methodological problems in the way of pursuing it. The point was also made that there could usefully be closer links between research into communication strategies and input studies.

The session closed with broad agreement that the object of study was not a 'set' of more or less isolated strategies of various kinds, but a generalised strategic competence that was brought to bear on the learning task by different learners in different ways under varying conditions.

8. Cross-language Generalizations and the
Contrastive Dimension of the Interlanguage Hypothesis

Introduction

Of the numerous criticisms levelled against the classic formulation of the contrastive analysis hypothesis during the late sixties and early seventies, three are pertinent to the scope and objectives of this paper.

1). In spite of the claims made regarding learning difficulty and learning ease, the contrastive analysis hypothesis was not an acquisition theory; or, alternatively, it lacked one. There are two issues that need to be teased apart in this criticism. The first has to do with the dynamic aspect of language acquisition, which the contrastive analysis hypothesis did not take into consideration (cf. Zobl 1982). The second issue – the one that will concern us more – bears on the nature of the putative properties we ascribe to the language-learning device in order to explain the ultimate accomplishment within the empirical conditions under which it is achieved. The learning theory underpinning the contrastive analysis hypothesis was transfer, a general-purpose learning mechanism. I take it to be sufficiently well established that a general-purpose learning mechanism cannot account for the nature of language acquisition.

2) The contrastive analysis hypothesis did not take into account the inherent ease or difficulty of the various rule system of the L2. This criticism overlaps with the preceding one and the next.

3) The contrastive analysis hypothesis was unable to relate types of contrast and similarity to learning difficulty in any principled way. Thus, while interference was assumed to covary positively with language distance, the associated learning theory did not allow of such a straightforward interpretation. The less similarity there is between two tasks, the less likelihood there should be of proactive interference.

Despite these and other shortcomings, the contrastive analysis hypothesis has continued to attract the attention of applied linguists. In fact, it would not be an exaggeration to claim that research over the past decade has led to a sharpening of the contrastive analysis hypothesis. This enhanced precision is due largely to the incorporation of markedness measures into contrastive statements of learning difficulty (e.g., Eckman 1977; Gass 1979; Hyltenstam 1982). In the light of the advances brought about by this research we might therefore replace inadequacies (2) and (3) above with the more general formulation in (4):

4) The classic formulation of the contrastive analysis hypothesis lacked a sufficiently rich theory of language structure which would have permitted an evaluation of bilingual contrasts in terms of their crosslanguage status.

To our present list of shortcomings we might add yet a third. Even with the advent of generative transformational grammar, and its adoption by contrastive analysis, a distinction fundamental to that theory was disregarded, namely, that of abstract knowledge and the performance of that knowledge. Admittedly, contrastive grammars were generally not claimed to be anything more than 'competence' grammars, serving to pinpoint potential areas of conflict; yet in the analysis of learner data this distinction became lost. Learner performance in areas of contrastive difficulty was not examined with the aim of determining whether this difficulty resided in gaps in competence or gaps in processing routines. A rigorous application of this distinction would appear to be of benefit to the contrastive analysis hypothesis as well as the field of second-language learning, as Sharwood-Smith (1981) and Kellerman and Sharwood-Smith (to appear) have argued persuasively.

This paper will seek to address the topic 'the theoretical basis of the role of the L1 in interlanguage' from the vantage point afforded by the three inadequacies we have identified. The next section deals with inadequacies (1) and (2). Having remedied these somewhat, we will have the outline of a deductive structure from which to approach the topic.

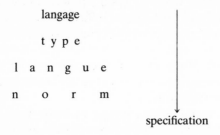

FIGURE 1. Scale of language differentiation
(adapted from Lehmann 1982).

Outlines of a Deductive Structure

A Scale of Language Specification

The view of language structure that will serve as a reference model for the presentation is diplayed in Figure 1. It is by no means novel. It views natural languages as instantiations of a set of universal principles and a series of structural options which, in their turn, more or less stringently define subsequent options until the level of langue is attained. As an example of the former we may take the biuniqueness of function-argument assignments (Bresnan 1982), which rules out the assignment of the same grammatical function to different arguments of a predicate and the assignment of different grammatical functions to the same argument. As an example of the latter we may take the implicational chain obtaining between inversion in yes/no questions and word order. If a language has inversion in yes/no questions, then it will have inversion in information questions. If it possesses the latter attribute, it will have wh-movement and clause-initial complementizers (Bresnan 1970). If it possesses this attribute as well, it will not be a rigid subject-object-verb language. We can conceive of this multi-layered structure as a scale of linguistic specification or differentiation. At the level of norm we reach the most conventionalized aspect of language. At this level system-internal constraints do not suffice to explain why certain available options have or have not been taken up.

The scale of specification can also be viewed as a centre/core-periphery model of language structure.[1] I propose that certain facts of word order typology belong to the centre; the minimum distance principle (Rosenbaum 1967), which represents the unmarked case for control; the lower portion of Dik's (1978) functional hierarchy for mapping thematic roles onto subject and object; the boundedness of phrases (Koster 1978a), and the principal of semantic dissonance (Keenan 1978b), to name just a few. The list has an illustrative function and is not meant to be exhaustive.

Ideally, we would wish to be able to account for the nature and distribution of centre/core properties in terms of an explicit theory of the acquisition faculty. Failing this, we are forced into a circular argumentation; that is, that core properties fall out the way they do because of the structure of the acquisition faculty. We will use this inferred structure to formulate claims about interlanguage patterning in the following sections. The chain of argumentation is anything but neat; yet for the moment it would appear to be unavoidable.

Before turning to this inferred structure, let us briefly examine the notion 'periphery'. I shall be using it in three distinct senses:

1) typological specialization, e.g., a grammaticized word-order language in the sense discussed by Thompson (1978), Berman (1980), Hawkins (1981) and Hammarberg and Viberg (1977). Typological specialization will also be used to refer to departures from core properties such as the boundedness of phrases (Koster1978a).

2) typological inconsistency, e.g., of the better known languages, German appears to be a typologically inconsistent language. The unmarked order in main clauses is subject-verb-object, it has prepositions, clause-initial complementizers and a possessed-possessor order with nominals. An array of arguments can also be adduced for the claim that German is subject-object-verb.

3) typological indeterminacy, e.g., distributions which appear to be neutral within and across language types. Dahl (1979), for example, points out that for languages with an uninflected negative particle there is no clear

correlation between language type and the pre-versus post-verbal position of the negator. Hence, two typologically close (subject-verb-object and postnominal modification) and genetically related languages like Spanish and French can differ exactly on that dimension. An even fuzzier distribution – one which will concern us later – is the order of time and place adverbials relative to the verb. Although theoretical considerations suggest that place adverbs should be positioned closer to the verb (cf. Smith 1978), languages seem to have considerable leeway. Selinker (1969) points to two dialects of Hebrew which differ on this very dimension.

Not all senses of the notion 'periphery' are to be identified with 'more marked'. While this is true of certain kinds of typological specialization such as grammaticized word order and typologically inconsistent properties, typologically indeterminate features do not necessarily translate straightforwardly into a marked value. Later on I will suggest that typological fuzziness may well be a reflection of the fact that two crucial components of the acquisition faculty – the projection procedure and the evaluation metric – are not, or are only minimally, involved in fixing properties displaying this peripheral characteristic.

In general, the core/centre-periphery distinction rests (1) on the degree of stringency with which a property is related to other attributes of a language type (e.g. backward gapping is stringently tied to subject-object-verb, but not the order of place and time adverbials) and (2) on the position of an attribute on the relevant typological hierarchy (e.g. Keenan and Comrie 1977; Dik 1978). The higher end of a typological hierarchy identifies those properties that show the least amount of variation cross-linguistically and whose implementation in languages is not subject to constraints or exceptions.

The Acquisition Device

The scope of the paper permits only a sketch of those components of the acquisition faculty that can be inferred from our scale of language differentiation. Essentially, I follow current assumptions within the extended standard theory, in particular Roeper (1981) and Williams (1981). The device consists of biologically specified constraints on the form of a human language. In addition, the device is equipped with a projection procedure (Zobl 1983a). It is activated upon exposure to data which uniquely define a correlated attribute of the language. In Williams' terminology (1981, 26), these represent 'free rides' for the language acquirer, i.e. knowledge he has in advance of encountering the correlated attribute. The postulation of uniquely defined projections follows from, among other things, a number of inviolable typological implications, e.g., if a language is verb-initial, then it will be prepositional. In addition, it is assumed that, upon exposure to a typologically central datum, the projection procedure generates a narrow range of options regarding what attributes will co-occur with it. Put differently, on the basis of the datum, or possibly a conjunction of crucial data, a mental pre-disposition is created as to the patterning of the type in other areas. These options are then checked against incoming data. We can tentatively assume that, as the periphery is approached, projections become indeterminate and the device ceases to operate. As has been suggested by Chomsky (1981c) and Cook (1983) it may well be that other learning strategies take over at this point.

The options generated by the projection procedure are not checked in random order. I assume an evaluation procedure which dictates the order in which the assumptions are tested. I adopt Williams' (1981) proposal that ease of disconfirmability dictates this order.

The preceding remarks apply to the acquisition faculty as it pertains to native language acquisition. While I believe that the device remains available for non-native acquisition, the acceptance of the L1 as a factor influencing interlanguage development would indicate the need for some modification. In Zobl (1980a, 1983b) and in Andersen (1983b) it is argued that, in many cases, structural areas of the L2 susceptible to influence from the L1 exhibit ambiguity, instability, or irregularity. In Zobl (1980b) it is suggested that transfer structures very often conform more closely to favoured processing heuristics (cf. Slobin 1973). These considerations have led me to propose that the L1 furnishes a very abstract auxiliary evaluation measure which, under certain well-defined conditions, is activated and supplants that of the acquisition device. (George (1972), I believe, was the first to view the L1 as a kind of evaluation measure.)

It is not too difficult to establish a connection between Williams' proposed ease of disconfirmability principle and the motivators of transfer that Andersen and I have identified. Opaque structures, for example, should be more inaccessible to disconfirmation of spurious derivations. In such a case, the evaluation metric furnished by the L1 is activated and transfer is promoted. Our sketch of the periphery in the preceding section suggests that typological inconsistency and typological indeterminacy may well represent two linguistic phenomena which invite a takeover by the auxiliary evaluation measure.

Before concluding this section, a remark is in order on the relationship of the L1 to the input filter and the parser. There now exist a number of L2 studies which demonstrate a difference in the pace with which learners of different L1s achieve productive control of an L2 structure (e.g., Schumann 1979; Keller-Cohen 1979; Jansen, Lallemann and Muysken 1981; Zobl 1982, in press b). What Corder (1978) has elsewhere termed 'rediscovery' in explanation of the more rapid development we can witness under conditions of broad L1–L2 structural congruence will be explored in relationship to the input filter and the parser.

The core/centre-periphery distinction in conjunction with the components of the acquisition faculty furnish a deductive structure from which we can approach our topic. It will permit us to arrive at a number of principled claims concerning the scope of L1 influence on interlanguage. Furthermore, it should allow us to assess the implications of various types of interlingual errors for a theory of adult L2 acquisition and to pinpoint structural domains where (outstanding) interlanguage data should bear crucially on such a theory. Finally, our deductive structure will provide additional theoretical support for the application of the competence-performance distinction to contrastive learning difficulty as well as a basis for deciding whether a particular instance of contrastive difficulty is due to the one or the other.

The Simple Codes Hypothesis
Preliminary Considerations

The study of interlanguage can be approached in a number of ways. One way is to think of it as dividing into two questions – the starting point for adult acquisition and the sequence of interim grammars between that starting point and the final state. With respect to the first issue, one advantage of the scale of linguistic specification would seem to be that it accommodates a broad spectrum of L2 learning phenomena.

At the [+ specification] end of the scale we can situate cases of minimal learning made possible by close genetic affinity. Cocoliche, the variety of Spanish spoken by Italian immigrants in Argentina, would appear to belong at this end (cf. Whinnom 1971). At the [− specification] end of the scale we approach views of adult L2 learning as espoused by Closs-Traugott (1977), who sees a return to a natural semantax in the creation of pidgins. The scale also accommodates Kellerman's (1978) notion of the learner's 'psycho-typology' of the L2, i.e., the perceived language distance. Finally, the scale takes into account the commonsense view that the L2 learner doesn't have to begin from scratch. In advance of any encounter with L2 data (s)he 'knows' that the L2 will contain means of forming questions, means of quantification, conjunction, deictic reference, etc. Not surprisingly, some of these show up very early. *One* functions as an indefinite article (Frith 1977) and NP conjunction emerges right from the beginning (Hakuta 1976).

Where on the scale of specification does the learner begin? It now seems to be beyond doubt (Hyltenstam 1978a; Corder 1977a; Bickerton 1975) that the L2 learning process does not commence with a fully specified L1 as its starting point. The empirical evidence for this is strong. It is supported by Kellerman's (1978, 1983b) and Jorden's (1977) studies on perceived transferability, by Silverstein's (1972) analysis of Chinook Jargon, and by a host of L2 studies in which learners avoid reproducing – or judging grammatical – marked forms or marked options of the L1 even though the L2 may have an equivalent (e.g., past tense for irrealis, Kellerman 1981; particle shift, Drubig 1972; preposition stranding, Adjemian and Liceras 1982).

In addition to the empirical evidence, there are compelling theoretical reasons why despecification must occur. Corder (1977b) analyses interlanguage in relation to two types of language continua – a restructuring continuum (e.g., historical change and decreolization) and an elaborative continuum (e.g., L1 acquisition and creolization). Corder points out that both the contrastive analysis hypothesis and early conceptions of interlanguage imply a restructuring continuum whereas interlanguage properly belongs to the complexificational continuum type. Using data from Bickerton (1975) on the Guyanese decreolization continuum and from a cross-sectional L2 study I have proposed elsewhere (Zobl, to appear) that restructuring presupposes prior despecification or unmarking. In restructuring, distinctions are lost and subsequently elaborated along different lines. (For an incisive demonstration of this, see Huebner, to appear). Thus, even under the older conception that interlanguage represents a successive restructuring of the L1 (a view I do not share), unmarking or despecification of the L1 grammar would have to take place for any movement to occur in the direction of the target.

There is another compelling reason which supports the simple-codes hypothesis: the learnability argument (Baker 1979). If a learner formulates an overly inclusive grammar, then on the assumption that (s)he does not receive negative evidence for the erroneous rule, a class of errors remains which is inaccessible to disconfirmation. Baker terms this class 'embarrassing' in contradistinction to the 'benign' class, which can be disconfirmed on the basis of positive evidence alone. L1 acquisition theory has come up with a number of proposals to meet this problem. Among these are two principles: the uniqueness principle (Wexler and Culicover 1980) and the disjunctive ordering principle (Roeper 1982). The first principle assumes that a learner proceeds on the assumption of a one-to-one relationship between base and surface strings and that where a one-to-two relationship is encountered, the alternate string is registered as a lexically governed construction. Thus, assuming infinitival complements to be unmarked, upon encountering 'I started playing', 'start' will be marked in the lexicon as permitting a second subcategorization frame. In this way, no general rule is formulated which would lead to 'embarrassing' errors such as "*I hope playing'. The second principle is designed to deal with the problem posed by various combinations of auxiliary and modal verbs in the English child's input. Nothing in the input will tell a child that the string 'he should must do it' is wrong. Roeper (1982) proposes to remedy this situation by invoking a principle which dictates that rules are ordered disjunctively until evidence to the contrary is encountered.

1. can
    must come
    have

This grammar is easily refuted on the basis of positive evidence. On the other hand, this is not the case with a conjunctively ordered grammar:

2. (can) (must) (have) come

The situation sketched for L1 acquisition is no different for the naturalistic L2 acquirer and probably only little different for the tutored L2 learner in light of several studies demonstrating random correction procedures which more often than not contain ambiguous or insufficient feedback on grammatical errors. If French-speaking learners let themselves be guided by their L1, utterances like 'she must can do it' would result. We must similarly assume the adoption of grammar (1) in order to prevent the generation of such strings as 'I have could do it', in analogy to the French 'j'ai pu le faire'. Impressionistically, I would say that such strings – particularly the latter – are rare in French-English interlanguage, suggesting that some version of Roeper's principle is indeed being followed.

TABLE 1. Distribution of quantifier phrase extraction from NP versus NP-movement in 'how many'-questions

Extraction from NP, e.g., How many you want __ N?	NP integrity, e.g., How many N you want __ ?
Oral production (N = 32)*	
2	16
Grammaticality judgement (N = 54)	
low-level	
1	13
low intermediate	
0	40

* Fourteen ineligible responses, e.g., *How many you want?*, *How many oranges?*, no question produced.

We can illustrate the theoretical necessity of adopting the uniqueness principle for L2 learning with reference to a French-English contrast discussed by White (1983). French permits extraction and wh-fronting of the NP quantifier 'combien' from an NP, e.g., 'Combien voulez-vous d'oranges?' as well as of the entire NP, e.g., 'Combien d'oranges voulez-vous?' Unless the learner drops the optional rule of French, which represents an exception to the boundedness of phrases, positive evidence alone would not rule out 'How many do you want oranges?' As far as this construction is concerned, let us consider some oral production data and some data from a grammaticality judgement task, both from low-level, adult French-speaking ESL learners (see Table 1).

On the grammaticality judgement task, only one out of 54 informants did not preserve the integrity of the NP. In the oral production task, a picture description, only two out of 16 informants produced an utterance in which 'combien' was extracted. The findings from this probe, then, indicate quite clearly that the overwhelming majority of responses respects the boundedness of the NP. To sum up, considerations of learnability would require that the L2 learner despecify his L1. The data we have presented above on a French-English contrast in quantifier information questions do not go counter to learnability requirements.

There is yet a third reason which lends theoretical support to the simple codes hypothesis. If acquisition proceeds on the basis of projections – as I think the evidence warrants – then the projection procedure can only function on those levels of our scale of language differentiation where options correlated with a certain attribute are narrowly or uniquely defined. For example, if a learner despecifies the lexical head phrasal categories of his L1, then (s)he is in a position to generalize phrasal expansions of one lexical head to others. No such procedure is possible if the L1 is not despecified.

The assumption that the projection procedure ceases to operate once we reach the [+ specified] end of our scale of linguistic differentiation has a further, interesting consequence. It is a commonplace that learners overgeneralize. For a theory of adult L2 acquisition, though, not all over-generalizations have equal import. I would like to argue that overgeneralizations which originate below the level of langue bear more directly on the nature of the adult acquisition faculty than those which originate at the level of langue. To illustrate this distinction, let us consider two examples of overgeneralization – 'I bringed' versus 'I am enough big to . . .'. The former is an overgeneralization at the level of langue. To properly appreciate the latter, we have to consider phrasal expansions in the typology represented by English, French, Spanish and related languages. Both adjectives and nouns share the feature [+N] in X-bar framework. For the category [+N] degree quantifiers occur in prehead position, e.g., 'enough money', 'too poor', etc. 'Enough', marks an exception, obligatorily requiring a shift to posthead position with adjectives. Thus, in the latter case the overgeneral-ization amounts to a projection which happens not to bear out due to an idiosyncracy of English. The former type of overgeneralization takes place at a superficial level and has probably been overvalued in its relevance for the nature of language acquisition in the past.

In concluding this section, I would like to indicate how the third theoretical argument fares against the empirical evidence. I have argued that in order for the projection procedure to operate, the L1 must be despecified. Consider, now, word order, a major dimension of language variation. Hawkins (1980) has noted that one of the strongest controllers of word order properties in languages is the order of adpositions, i.e., adposition + head versus head + adposition. The former correlates signifi-cantly with verb-object while the latter correlates significantly with object-verb. While the word order contrast verb-object versus object-verb does not appear to control other attributes quite as tightly, a uniform expansion of $\bar{V}$ and $\bar{P}$ (both $[-N]$ in an X-bar framework) is a significant generalization. We would therefore predict that where the L2 is unambiguous, the projection procedure excludes transfer of object-verb to verb-object. The evidence I am familiar with (Jackson 1981; Bell 1973) bears out this prediction. Furthermore, given verb-object and evidence for auxiliaries in the input, the projection device will project the order vVO and exclude the transfer of Vv, which would result in utterances of the type 'I run can'. (See Bell, where with one or two exceptions all auxiliary-infinitive combinations conform to the prediction.) While there is some evidence that word order in the NP is less tightly controlled than in the VP (Vincent 1976), on the assumption that expansions from V^2 and P^2 are projected to N, then NPs in the prehead, specifier position represent a loss in generalizability. This would explain why the transfer of English structures of the type NP's N (e.g., my father's brother) in English-French interlanguage is non-existent and is a late acquisition in French-English interlanguage. Facts such as these constitute positive evidence that the projection device is operative in expanding, P,V,N to the exclusion of typologically contrasting L1 word order.

Let us consider one more case. Disregarding for the moment the verb-object versus object-verb controversy, German like Swedish belongs to a typology that is known as verb-second, i.e., the finite verb appears in the second position of declarative main clauses. When adverbs, objects and prepositional phrases are topicalized, the verb remains in second position and the subject is shifted behind the verb. Although it is a defining feature of German, this rule rarely surfaces in German L1 interlanguage (Drubig 1972). There are three other properties which are also dropped in German L1 interlanguage. These are:

1) non-finite verb last with auxiliaries present, e.g.,

   Ich kann den Mann sehen
   I can the man see

2) particle shift to final position with main verbs, e.g.,

   Ich nehme den Hut ab
   I take the hat off

3) absence of verb raising in clause union, e.g.,

   Ich liess den Mann laufen
   I let/made the man run

A number of authors (e.g., Kielhöfer 1975; Drubig 1971) have presented data showing that, as a rule, errors based on construction (1) are sufficiently rare in the French or English speech of German learners. German learners apparently have to re-acquire particle shift in English L2 (Drubig 1971). Third, German learners produce errors of the type 'the farmers would not let drive the cars over their land' (Zydatiss 1973), a clear case of verb raising.[2] Now, according to Aissen (1974) and Harbert (1977), word order in clause union tends to parallel word order in simple sentences (Harbert 1977, 142) and that where the auxiliary and the main verb are adjacent, the embedded verb will wind up adjacent to the matrix verb. Thus, there exists a very good possibility that German speakers project 'let drive' on the basis of auxiliary-verb order in simple clauses. If we grant that example (2) above is produced by the same rule that shifts the non-finite verb, then German L1 interlanguage furnishes some weighty evidence in favour of typological despecification and L2 data-driven projections.

The Periphery

In the preceding section we presented three theoretical arguments in favour of the simple-codes hypothesis. While the first argument relies on insights into language change mechanisms, the second and third arguments make more precise claims about what needs to be despecified in order for acquisition to be accomplished. In this section we turn to what has been termed the periphery of language structure, and it is in this area that the deductive model leads us to expect 1L influence. There are at least three reasons for this. First, typological inconsistency in the L2 can prompt a takeover by the auxiliary evaluation device furnished by the L1. Second, typological indeterminacy is a reflection of the fact that the projection device and the primary evaluation measure are neutral, so to speak, vis-à-vis typological indeterminacy. This represents an opening for the L1. Third, I shall argue that certain kinds of typological specialization also lie outside the domain of the acquisition device, notably pragmatic word-order prominence.[3]

Typological Specialization

Typological research has identified a number of typological specializations such as subject prominence (Thompson 1978) or grammatical word-order prominence (Hammarberg and Viberg 1977), 'habere' languages (Issatschenko 1974), accusative versus ergative languages (Moravcsik 1978), to name just a few. Within the extended standard theory, language variation with regard to which nodes are bounding for subjacency has come under a good deal of scrutiny (Rizzi 1978; Sportiche 1982). Given limitations of space we can only consider a few briefly. Within our scale of differentiation, these specializations fall in the [+ specified] range and are therefore prime candidates for despecification in interlanguage.

Subject prominence. It now seems to be generally recognized that obligatory subject pronouns represent a typological specialization of SVO languages (cf. Berman 1980; Hammarberg and Viberg 1977). Berman claims that 'subject-weak' SVO languages like Hebrew typically lack non-referential subject pronouns (e.g., dummy 'it', 'there', indefinite 'they') and that they permit coreferent deletion in embedded clauses, in apparent violation of the tensed-S condition (Berman, p.760 fn.2):

dan$_i$ amar $_S$[COMP sĕ $_S$[PRO$_i$ yavo maxar]]
Dan   said   that ϕ will-come tomorrow

In Zobl (in press) it was found that French L1-English L2 interlanguage has subject pronoun omission in these contexts even though French has obligatory subjects. This finding led me to propose that subject prominence represents a typological specialization which is re-elaborated in L2 acquisition by all learners, irrespective of whether the L1 possesses this attribute.

'Habere' languages. Since all languages have a verb corresponding to 'esse' but not all languages have a verb corresponding to 'habere' (e.g., Russian, Classical Latin), 'Habere' represents a typological specialization (Issatschenko 1974). Issatschenko identifies a number of other properties associated with 'habere' languages, notably modal verbs expressing necessity, obligation, etc. Non-'habere' languages employ an 'esse'-adjective construction. I know of no systematic data on whether possessive 'have' poses a problem for learners whose L1 is a 'habere' language, although copula substitution for 'have' is fairly frequent. French L1-English L2 interlanguage abounds with 'esse' + adjective constructions for the expression of modality, e.g.,

Is possible to help you? (Can I help you?/Puis-je vous aider?)
Is necessary I go (I must/have to go/Je dois partir)

Since French and English have cognates, 'necessary'/'nécessaire', 'possible'/ 'possible' it may well be that these cognates promote an 'esse' construction. The question of whether such 'esse' constructions are a reflection of despecifying a 'habere' language might profitably be examined in French L1-German L2 interlanguage, for example, where adjectives like 'possible' and 'nécessaire' have no cognates in the L2.[4]

Case marking versus grammaticized word order. Hawkins (1981) proposes a typological classification of languages according to the degree to which surface-structure grammatical relations preserve the underlying predicate-argument structure. Building on a contrastive description of English and German he hypothesizes that case-marking languages will show more restrictions on changes in grammatical relations (e.g., raising to object, tough-movement) and that they will exhibit more restrictions on what thematic roles can be mapped onto the nominative subject and the accusative object. At this point let us refer to Dik's (1978, 70) semantic function hierarchy, which expresses the possibility of subject and object assignment to thematic roles on a crosslanguage basis:

Agent Goal Receiver Benefactor Instrument Location Time

As one proceeds from left to right, the possibility of subject and object assignment grows increasingly more restrictive, although languages will differ as to the exact cut-off point.[5] Hawkins' classification implies that case marking languages will have a cut-off point higher on the hierarchy, i.e., more to the left.

L2 data bearing on the question of whether adult learners despecify marked subject and object assignment possibilities suggest that they do choose a comfortable, high point on the hierarchy, even in those cases where the L1 would permit a grammatical function assignment to a lower thematic role (Jordens 1977; Kellerman 1978; Zydatiss 1974).

Extraction from nodes and Koster's (1978b) main projection rule. Emonds (1976) notes that French does not have wh-pronominalization of degree specifiers. This appears to pose problems for French learners with regard to the degree specifier 'how' in English. A typical error is illustrated below:

> I didn't realize $_{\bar{S}}$[$_{COMP}$ how $_S$[I was $_{AP}$[e comfortable]]]
> I didn't realize how comfortable I was

In Koster's framework (1978a, 1978b) all nodes are bounding in core grammar and only nodes immediately dominated by subject and verb--phrase may be empty. In the ungrammatical example, the degree specifier 'how' has been extracted from the adjectival phrase 'how comfortable', a clear departure from a putative core grammar constraint. Our deductive framework predicts that this kind of extraction should be absent from French-English interlanguage, as was the case with the extraction of 'combien' from the containing NP.

On a grammaticality judgement task low-level to advanced-level adult francophone ESL learners were presented with four open-ended discourses requiring completion with an embedded question in which the wh-word was the degree specifier 'how' (see Appendix 1). The indirect questions completing each discourse, and from which informants had to choose one, were grouped into two categories for the present analysis – extraction of the degree specifier from the adjectival phrase or fronting of the entire adjectival phrase. Table 2 displays the findings from this task. Judgements on the extractibility of 'how'/'*how much' are not uniform within levels although the acceptance of extraction versus non-extraction is fairly stable for some questions across the proficiency levels. Interestingly, it is the low-intermediate level which is most tolerant of extraction. One can only speculate whether at this level learners begin to notice that English is quite permissive with regard to extraction (e.g., preposition stranding) and that this in turn promotes the tolerance for it. Alternatively, it may also be the case that 'how'/'*how much' are initially categorized as a wh-pronominalization of a prepositional phrase, i.e., $_{AP}$[Adj. $_{PP}$[to wh-degree]], and the recategorization to a degree specifier does not occur until the high intermediate level. If the latter analysis is the correct one, then the tolerance for extraction would have its source in such Engish models as 'How much do you like her', with which they are certainly familiar.

Grammatical word order versus pragmatic word order. In the introductory

TABLE 2. Degree specifier extraction from Adj.P. in embedded wh-questions (cf. Appendix 1)

	Extraction How/*how much...X...$_{AP}$[e...Adj.]	No extraction How/*how much Adj....X...[e]
low-level (N = 14)		
No. 1	6	8
2	1	13
3	4	10
4	4	10
Extraction: 27%		
low-intermediate (N = 40)		
1	35	37
2	8	62
3	22	47
4	32	38
Extraction: 35%		
high-intermediate (N = 35)		
1	4	31
2	0	35
3	5	30
4	6	29
Extraction: 11%		
advanced (N = 31)		
1	4	27
2	2	35
3	2	30
4	0	29
Extraction: 6%		

* Informal observations had shown that lower-level learners employed *how much* + Adj. for the expression of degree. While this is ungrammatical, it was disregarded for purposes of the present analysis.

remarks to this section I advanced the view that pragmatic word-order prominence may represent a peripheral phenomenon. If we take pragmatic word-order prominence to refer to a word order which reflects more directly the information structure of an utterance context, we can note that this type of word order appears in the early multi-word combinations of child language (cf. Zobl 1983) and that it precedes the emergence of a level of autonomous syntax. Thus, while it is basic in a sense, this basicness resides in its being rooted in the extralinguistic reality. In contrast, the word-order properties discussed in the preceding section rest on abstract grammatical relations like subject and object and abstract schemata for expanding lexical heads (Lightfoot 1979). Therefore, it might be hypothesized that the crucial components of the acquisition device are not sensitive to pragmatic word-order. This assumption would account for Rutherford's (1983b) claim that there is little evidence for the transfer of grammatical word order in inter-language but that discourse/pragmatic word-order does indeed transfer.

Evidence for discourse/pragmatic word-order transfer is not hard to find (e.g., Schachter and Rutherford 1979; Rutherford 1983b; Huebner, to appear; Zydatiss 1974). German L1 interlanguage is particularly interesting in this regard. As I stated earlier, the verb-second constraint is dropped, a typologically defining feature of German. In contrast, object topicalization in German, which in many cases overlaps with the function of the passive in English (Kirkwood 1969), is transferred and used in that function (Zydatiss 1974).

Typological Inconsistency

Our model predicts that where an L2 is typologically inconsistent with respect to its core attributes and where the L1 is more consistent, then the auxiliary evaluation measure furnished by the L1 overrides the primary evaluation measure. It can be assumed that the projection procedure of the acquisition device projects the internally consistent correlated attribute. The projection is refuted by the incoming data but rather than moving on to a more marked assumption – as would be the case in L1 acquisition – the primary evaluation measure is supplanted by the auxiliary measure. Keller-man's (1983b) 'reasonable entity principle' is quite similar conceptually to the notion of a projection computed on internal consistency. I refer the reader to Zobl (in press b) for a discussion of one such case in French-English interlanguage where both nominal and pronominal possessive determiners are generated as prepositional phrases in posthead position. In this way, a possessed-possessor word order is achieved for both categories. Theoretical word-order studies (cf. Keenan 1979; Lehmann 1973; Venne-mann 1972) would seem to indicate that this is the word order that is harmonic with other verb-object properties of English. Since French is more consistent than English in this regard, our framework predicts that the L1 – qua auxiliary evaluation measure – impedes the French speaker's advance to the marked order possessor-possessed with nominals.

Typological Indeterminacy

The final peripheral phenomenon to be considered is typological fuzziness, a term I adopt from Vincent (1976). Theoretical word-order studies have repeatedly claimed that, as a verb-object language, adjectives in English would be positioned after the noun (e.g., Lehmann 1973) if English were typologically consistent. Yet it has also been demonstrated (Hawkins 1980; Vincent 1976) that certain word-order properties are not stringently con-trolled by the overall typology, one such property being the order of the descriptive adjective and noun. Vincent refers to it as a fuzzy criterion of word-order typology. How is this fuzziness reflected in interlanguages where the L1 and L2 contrast on adjective-noun order? In an interesting study in which an adult Spanish speaker was taught English conversationally over a period of several months, Hughes (1979) reports that correct adjective positioning appeared in the informant's speech after only several hours of exposure. Significantly, the possessor-possessed order with nominals was not acquired until much later. This difference not only bears out typological word order theory – which identifies the genitive construction as the more tightly controlled attribute – but it also supports the framework we have advanced in this paper, viz. that degree of typological control of an attribute is an external correlate of how crucially the acquisition device enters into its acquisition. In the case under discussion – the order of descriptive adjective and noun – we are dealing with a loosely controlled attribute. The evaluation measure moves on to the more marked adjective plus noun order with little difficulty. By the same token, the auxiliary evaluation measure furnished by the L1 interferes only minimally.

While the above account of the interaction of the L1 with this typologically fuzzy attribute is consonant with our deductive model, the same reasoning comes up short when we consider another indeterminate feature – the order of place and time adverbials relative to the verb. Here, too, purely theoretical considerations would indicate that place adverbials be positioned closer to the verb than time adverbials (Smith 1978) since the number of verbs which impose a subcategorization for place adverbials by far exceeds the verbs which impose a subcategorization for time. Yet languages appear to enjoy a great deal of leeway. As I stated earlier, two dialects of Hebrew exhibit contrasting word orders in this area. If this is possible within one and the same language, then the order of place and time adverbials can be looked on as a truly peripheral aspect. We have, here, a source of L1-L2 contrast whose cross-linguistic status is similar to that of the order of descriptive adjective and noun. Unfortunately, the explanatory framework we used to deal with the adjective-noun contrast in interlanguage patterning leads to incorrect results in the present case. The transfer of the native language order is not only well attested, but it seems to present a persistent source of difficulty in English L2 for speakers of Hebrew, Serbo-Croatian, French, Tagalog and German. If the primary evaluation measure is only minimally or not at all engaged by typologically indeterminate properties, then why do the findings fall out that differently? At this point it becomes obvious that our deductive model will have to be enriched with auxiliary hypotheses.

Contrastive Difficulty and the Competence-performance Distinction

We turn now to a brief examination of what advantage our deductive model holds for the third criticism raised against the contrastive analysis hypothesis – its failure to apply the competence-performance distinction to the notions of learning ease and learning difficulty.

It seems to be fairly well established that, for a given L2, learners of different L1 backgrounds can differ in the pace with which a target structure becomes productive in their speech (e.g., Keller-Cohen 1979; Jansen, Lallemann and Muysken 1981; Hakuta 1976; Zobl 1982). Are these differences to be ascribed to learning ease or difficulty at the level of competence, performance, or both? Slobin (1982), in a comparison of language acquisition across several languages, notes that the acquisition of Serbo-Croatian poses particular problems because the language exploits both word order and case inflections for underlying grammatical relations. The Serbo-Croatian child first evolves parsing routines based on word order which later have to be balanced out with parsing routines based on case inflection. In other words, parsing strategies have to be reorganized (Slobin 1982b, 158–9). Let us extrapolate from L1 acquisition to L2 acquisition and consider the problem of language distance in this light, e.g., a Swedish versus a Turkish learner of English. Parsing routines familiar from the L1 will go a long way for the Swedish speaker. But for the Turkish speaker the situation is radically different. As Meyer-Ingwersen (1977) points out, the agglutinative typology of Turkish, in which grammatical information is affixed to the verb, leads the Turkish speaker to apply 'local' parsing strategies to the L2. Clearly, these will not work, especially in the case of discontinuous constituents. Unlike the Swedish speaker, the Turkish speaker has to evolve new parsing routines. It should not be surprising that the former will make more rapid progress. Also, I think that the degree of initial success with which familiar parsing routines can be applied to the L2 may have a determining influence on how far down on the scale of language differentiation the complexification process begins.

Our deductive structure allows us to make some fairly specific claims about whether an instance of contrastive difficulty is due to parsing or production routines. Let us take the case of relative-clause difficulty discussed in Schachter (1974) and Hakuta (1976) in which L1 and L2 differ in basic word-order typology. It can be claimed that once a Japanese speaker has fixed verb-object and preposition-NP at the level of competence, then (s)he 'knows' that relative clauses must be in posthead position. This is a case of projected knowledge. In addition, intuitions into perceptual difficulty (Kuno 1974) would point to the same conclusion. Thus, it can be argued that where attributes are tightly controlled, and where a learner already shows evidence of possessing one or more control features, any delay in the emergence of a target structure is not indicative of a gap in competence. The same considerations apply to the problem of forward anaphora that English poses for speakers of Japanese (cf. Flynn 1981).

Conclusion

The theoretical position adopted in this paper assigns a rather restricted role to the L1 in interlanguage. Research into typological variation has accumulated an impressive body of evidence that typologies involve a clustering of attributes related to one another in an implicational or correlational manner. Such findings have to shape our views of the nature of the acquisition mechanism. On the assumption that this mechanism remains available for adult acquisition (see Clahsen and Muysken 1983 for provocative evidence to the contrary), there is scope for the L1 only in those instances where the device itself is relatively neutral (fuzzy properties) or where the auxiliary evaluation measure furnished by the L1 coincides with a projection which, however, is incompatible with the L2 data. I have also argued that considerations of language learnability add theoretical weight to the proposed restricted role of the L1.

Aside from the theoretical considerations indicating a restricted role for the L1, there are also research methodological gains connected with such a position. First, it allows us to pinpoint key areas for future investigation where empirical data will have a direct bearing on theories of adult acquisition. Obviously, if it can be shown that clusterings incompatible on typological grounds do co-occur in interlanguage, and that these incompatible co-occurrences are attributable to influence from the L1, then the acquisition mechanism we have assumed would not be applicable to interlanguage. There is yet another advantage. Throughout this paper it has been claimed that despecification of the L1 must take place in order for the projection procedure to operate. Yet what about cases of minimal L2 learning as with jargons or cases of L2 learning where interlanguage grammar formation begins at the [+specification] end of the scale? Our position forces us to entertain the possibility that L2 acquisition may not be a unitary phenomenon at all; not exactly a novel idea (cf. Wode 1979) but certainly one that has not received the scrutiny it deserves.

Notes

1) The terms 'centre' and 'periphery' are not to be identified with Chomsky and Lasnik's (1977) core-periphery distinction nor with Ross's (1974) centre-periphery distinction although there will be translations between my usage of the terms and the other two.

2) Eric Kellerman has pointed out to me that this example is infelicitous since in the corresponding German sentence *let* and *drive* are in fact adjacent, i.e., Die Bauern würden die Autos nicht über ihr Land *fahren lassen*. But this is only the case if the sentence is given a conditional reading. If *would* is given a habitual reading, *let* and *drive* are not adjacent.

3) Since writing this paper, I have come to the conclusion that pragmatic word-order prominence should not be considered a typological specialization. Its existence seems to depend on the presence of case marking or a system of cross-referencing, which fits with the notion of typological specialization. On the other hand, pragmatic word order does cut across the word-order types, occurring in SOV, SVO and VSO languages. The place of pragmatic word order in our framework clearly requires more careful investigation.

4) Eric Kellerman has drawn my attention to the occurrence of modal verb avoidance in Dutch L1 interlanguage.

5) Obviously, Agent has to be excluded from the hierarchy for object assignment.

Appendix 1. Grammaticality Judgement Task (cf. Table 2)

1) Mother: Your new boyfriend, Richard, is very nice.
   Daughter: Yes, Mother, I think he is wonderful!
   Mother: Tell me, . . . (fond of = épris de)
   a) How much are you fond of your boyfriend?
   b) How much fond are you of your boyfriend?
   c) How much fond of your boyfriend are you?
   d) How fond of your boyfriend are you?
   e) How fond are you of your boyfriend?
   f) How are you fond of your boyfriend?
   Daughter: Very much, Mother. We are going to get married.

2) Margaret: Mary won't come to Bill's party until very late. Bill is very angry
   with her. It will ruin his party.
   Anne: Why will it ruin the party? . . .
   a) How inconvenient that she will come late is it?
   b) How much inconvenient that she will come late is it?
   c) How much is it inconvenient that she will come late?
   d) How much inconvenient is it that she will come late?
   e) How inconvenient is it that she will come late?
   Margaret: It's very inconvenient. Mary promised to bring the food for Bill's
   party.

3) Mr Thompson has a new job in Ottawa. He is anxious to start.
   Mr Thompson: I am flying to Ottawa tomorrow morning. You stay here with
   the children and sell our house.
   Mrs Thompson: I know that you are excited about your new job but I had no
   idea . . .
   a) how anxious you were to leave.
   b) how anxious to leave you were.
   c) how much anxious to leave you were.
   d) how much anxious you were to leave.
   e) how much you were anxious to leave.
   f) how you were anxious to leave.

4) Paul: I played tennis from two o'clock until five o'clock. After the game I
   realized . . .
   a) how I was tired.
   b) how much I was tired.
   c) how much tired I was.
   d) how tired I was.

9. The Empirical Evidence for the
Influence of the L1 in Interlanguage

There is an irony present in being asked to discuss[1] the empirical evidence for first language (L1) influence on interlanguage, when at the same symposium there is also to be a paper on the theoretical implications of L1 influence. The irony lies in the fact that it is impossible to discuss, let alone assess, the evidence for such influence unless one already has a theory (hunch, model or hypothesis), however implicit, to guide one in the search for the evidence. Without at least a rudimentary theory, there can be no data, or at least no way of interpreting data, and when one looks at the mass of material that has been presented as evidence for L1 influence, and then the counter-evidence that is brought forward which contradicts it, it will be apparent that a theory of some sort is a necessity.

If one were to believe that native language influence is proven whenever the erroneous presence of features in the L2 which are reminiscent of the L1 is detected, then there are so many data in support of such a theory that my job at this symposium would be little more than to provide a boring taxonomy of taxonomies. A hypothesis like this would of course 'give transfer a boost' (Faerch 1984) since it would simply brush aside data from L1 acquisition and data from L2 learners whose L1s would have led to different expectations. However, the field turns out to be in some confusion and has not yet settled down to a concensus view on L1 influence. The subject still arouses partisan feelings, especially amongst those who do not believe in 'transfer'; in some cases the result has been a shrill rejection of its significance based on irresponsibly little evidence. In other cases, a more responsible attitude is revealed, as evidenced by research which seeks to determine what precisely constitutes L1 influence, and under what conditions, if any, it operates.

To illustrate how different theoretical stances can lead to different claims, take Schumann's attribution of 50 per cent of Alberto's errors to L1 influence, on the basis of a linguistic comparison by one of his students of adult Spanish and Alberto English (Schumann 1981). Meisel (1980, 29), operating from within a different perspective, is critical of Schumann's claim (what we might call 'giving transfer a boot'), since he argues against the pervasiveness of L1 influence, and, following in the wake of Dulay and Burt, seeks to show that mere linguistic of identity IL and L1 does not prove the existence of the process of transfer. Hence, in Meisel's view, Schumann overestimates the effects of L1 influence. Here, both Meisel and Schumann are operating at a product level of analysis. However, if one believes that L1 influence can be underdetermined by the product, then it is clear that Schumann's estimate of 50 per cent could be too low.

We now accept that 'Linguistics Across Cultures' fails because the specific cornerstones on which Lado's hypothesis rested did not work well enough – a description of the differences and similarities between L1 and L2 in tandem with a behaviouristic theory of transfer has been shown countless times to be an inadequate predictor of learner difficulty, as symbolized by L1-like error. Contrastive analyses made predictions that they couldn't keep; some expected difficulties didn't turn up, and some did that weren't expected at all – gatecrashers on a theory, you might say. But whereas it was clear that the L1 could not be invoked as the sole source of error even with the best will in the world, the true blow to 'transfer' did not come till the publication of Dulay and Burt's first paper on the topic in 1972, and the series that followed. The long-term effects of their work have been, I think, more apparent to the west of the Azores than in Europe, but have in any case proved to be a remarkable stimulant in their minimalization of the role of the L1 in L2 acquisition. Dulay and Burt brought with them a hypothesis which set out to stress the similarities between L1 and L2 acquisition, the irrelevance for language acquisition of behaviourism, and the inevitable association of transfer with behaviourist psychology – hence transfer did not exist, or at least played an entirely trivial role in the acquisition process. This meant that on them was placed the onus of interpreting what they called so poetically 'interference-like goofs'.

The rest is well known: Dulay and Burt re-analyse a number of L1-like errors in the only terms their hypothesis allows, namely as parallel to attested L1 acquisitional forms or as overgeneralizations of L2 material. Some of their analyses fail to convince because they fail to provide the critical supporting evidence for them (see the comments in e.g. Kellerman 1974, 1975), but the overall impact was enormous, and it was only a matter of time before the morpheme studies were underway. In the meantime, in Romania, Slama-Cazacu (1974) was coming to similar conclusions in a little-known but fascinating paper collecting together data from L1 and L2 (including L2 Romanian). The morpheme studies, a growth industry in the seventies, seemed to reveal not only a universal order of acquisition (or order of accuracy) irrespective of L1 background or age but even some similarities with L1 acquisition orders. Furthermore, despite various attempts to show that the morpheme orders were artefacts of the BSM or hid important individual variation, the creative construction hypothesis proved remarkably robust, and universal orders of acquisition in elements of syntax, such as negation and interrogation, begin to turn up everywhere.

Now Meisel, as we saw with regard to the Alberto data, was propounding an essentially anti-transfer line (since modified, Meisel 1983) Since, in this view, even L1-like errors cannot be taken as unambiguous evidence for L1 influence, it is unnecessary to consider the possibility of facilitatory effects from the L1, nor the existence of more subtle effects of the L1 on the learning and production of the L2 (such effects have been discussed in Kellerman 1983b). Consequently, there is very little value in claims made by scholars of different persuasions to show how important or unimportant L1 influence is in second language learning on the basis of error counts. We find recent statements like Dulay, Burt and Krashen's (Dulay, Burt and Krashen 1982, 102) that interlingual errors account for only 8–23 per cent of errors among adults, and that most of these are limited to word order, and not morphology. What can a statement like this mean? Judging by p.183 of their book, it is based on findings from just two studies (LoCoco 1975 and White 1977), both of which are small-scale and limited in scope. And yet Wode (1981, 56) quotes these same two studies, inter alia, as counter-evidence to Dulay and Burt's overly narrow view. One might well ask why errors that seem L1-based should be restricted to word order (where the evidence is mixed, to say the least). And the percentages just quoted in any case must also relate to the product level, not the process level, the only difference being that the basis for linguistic comparison has changed.

In the supposedly 'universal' morpheme acquisition orders, careful analysis reveals that the L1 does have a role to play. Usually the basis for ascription of a particular phenomenon to the L1 will be formed by some sort of comparison between performances in a common L2 domain by learners with different L1s. When differences in performance correspond to differences in language background, then it is reasonable to suppose, ceteris paribus, that the major reason for these differences is L1 influence. Patterns of L2 behaviour which can be strictly limited to a subset of L1s (and this subset may contain a single member) provide the best resource material for an investigation of L1 influence. Two morphemes to have been studied for evidence of L1 influence in their acquisition are the definite and indefinite articles.

Arabski's (1979) analysis of the English of Polish learners in Poland is based on a corpus of 4263 errors. His conclusion is that 'more than half the errors are caused by transfer' (101), pace the collected works of Dulay and Burt in his bibliography. Strangely enough, Arabski does not count the 974 article errors in his corpus as being due to Polish, even though Polish has no articles as such, his reasoning being that there can be no L1 influence when there is nothing to do the influencing. This is a very restricted view of the role of the L1. (Finnish learners of English, as reported in Granfors and Palmberg 1976 and Sajavaara 1981, also omit articles freely – Finnish having no article system either – and make considerably more errors in this respect than their compatriot Swedes, who, having an article system, tend not to omit them. See also Oller and Redding 1971.)

If we look carefully at Arabski's book we will see that advanced university learners perform very little better than school pupils with only two or three years English, though there are important qualitative differences. The more advanced learners tend to insert articles where none are required in English (39 per cent) and mix definite and indefinite up (26 per cent). Omission of articles accounts for 34 per cent of all errors. With the two school groups, omission accounts for 67 per cent and 63 per cent of errors respectively. The definite article is far less often omitted than the indefinite article, possibly due to the fact that Polish can use demonstrative adjectives in definite-article-like fashion. Thus 23 per cent of the corpus consist of article errors, which, if added to the errors which Arabski does count as due to Polish, leaves us with a massive count of over 70 per cent.[2] But of course an error count like this, and many of the others, I suspect, could be misleading if one does not keep in mind the distinction between type and token. L1-like article errors are frequent because articles are frequent, and the fact that Polish does not have an article system as we know it may contribute to the high frequency. As Larsen-Freeman (1978, 377) has shown, articles are the most frequent of the morpheme tokens in both her own L2 corpus and Brown's L1 corpus. And while articles do reasonably well among both adults and children in the L2 morpheme studies and occupy their reasonably consistent position in the acquisition/accuracy hierarchy, it is as well to remember that the initial studies tended to lump the articles into one category, ART, as Roger Brown did in response to the fact that:

> There were too many contexts of which one could only say that an article was required, and not whether the reference was specific or non-specific, let alone whether it was one variety of specificity rather than another. (Brown 1973, 264)

Rosansky (1976) and Andersen (1977, 1978) are exceptions, in that both keep the articles separate in their study of morphemes, and both claim that L1 interference (from Spanish) plays a significant role in their acquisition. It is interesting to note that, like Arabski's subjects, Andersen's and Rosansky's subjects make fewer errors with the definite article both the more proficient they are, and relative to the indefinite article. Hakuta (1976) also reports that his Japanese learner performed better on 'the' than on 'a'. The omission pattern for Arabski's Polish learners (decreasing with proficiency) certainly supports a Polish-based interpretation, but one can make no language-specific claims about the relative difficulty of definiteness over indefiniteness, especially when one also takes into account Sajavaara's report of the article errors made by Finns in English (Sajavaara 1981). He found that 85 per cent of all article errors were omissions, but whereas learners improved with regard to the definite article (fewer omissions and more correct instances), the error and omission rate stay fairly constant for the indefinite article over the four-year period reported. (see also Mace-Matluck 1979, 88).

This is the point at which to say something about terminology. The term 'transfer' has been used sparingly so far because of the difficulties this word still gives people. Thus Corder (1983a) pleads for the abandonment of the term and its replacement by 'mother tongue influence', on the grounds that 'transfer' belongs properly to behaviourist learning theory, and it is better to keep terms to their appropriate domains. But is there really a need to feel constrained by the use of the term any longer because of its outmoded laboratory connotations? 'Transfer' is a perfectly ordinary word which should be returned to the public domain, and not bound to an outmoded theory. Its use hardly leads to the kinds of confusion engendered by the cavalier use of the term 'markedness'.

There is a case for limiting the use of the term 'transfer', however, or at least defining its use more carefully. Let us say that it is a cover term for a number of unspecified processes which lead to L1-like behaviour in the L2. (For a description of various transfer processes see Faerch and Kasper, forthcoming.) We are then forced to find terms to cover the phenomenon of avoidance and the kinds of L1-based constraints on predicted L2 form studied by Kellerman (e.g. 1980) We also need a term to refer to the L2 influence on L1 (see, e.g. Py, forthcoming) – language loss is not an ideal term – and to refer to the role of L1 as catalyst or inhibitor (rather than structure provider) of the rate with which a second language is learned. What is needed is a theoretically neutral term under which all these phenomena may be subsumed without contortion: one solution is cross-linguistic influence (Kellerman and Sharwood Smith, forthcoming a.).

In the ensuing paragraphs I shall be looking at a number of linguistic domains where claims have been made for the existence of cross-linguistic influence. In some cases these claims have their matching counter-claims. I will not (with one partial exception) make any attempt to evaluate these various claims, because to do so will be to impinge on another speaker's territory. I shall not be dealing with IL phonology nor with pragmatics[3] and the possible role of the L1 in the development of IL rhetoric. And needless to say, I make no claims about completeness in any domain I do discuss. My aim is to give at least some indication as to the compass and character of the phenomenon of cross-linguistic influence. I begin with the discussion of the evidence for and against cross-linguistic influence in certain aspects of syntax. There then follows a discussion of the case for and against cross-linguistic influence in the acquisition of relative clauses, and pronominal reflexes in particular, where I will argue that the evidence is obscured by methodological fog. Following this I will look at a few studies of IL discourse, lexis and semantics, where the evidence seems clearer.

Syntax

a) Negation

Hyltenstam's (1977) is a well-known analysis of the acquisition of negation using implicational scaling, showing that learners with a wide variety of language backgrounds travel through the same stages with regard to the placement of the negative particle in Swedish in both main and subordinate clauses. A subsequent reanalysis by Hammarberg (1979) has suggested that learners with L1s not having preverbal negation, such as English, do not show evidence of the first stage where preverbal negation is the norm. English provides a leg up, so to speak, along the developmental ladder, because as far as negation is concerned, English is more like Swedish than the rest of the source languages studied by Hyltenstam. Thus those learners whose own L1s have preverbal negation will have a harder time making progress than those whose L1s do not. This view is consistent with Schumann (below).[4]

Wode (1976b) too presents evidence that shows that the universal pattern of negation acquisition may be disrupted, in albeit restricted fashion, by the L1 under specific conditions, i.e. where there is 'crucial similarity' between L1 and L2. He finds forms of negation in his Stages IIIa and b which also turn up in Ravem (1968), where Norwegian is L1, but are lacking in Milon (1974) – Japanese as L1, or Huang (1971) – Taiwanese as L1. Certainly to take a Romance language, Spanish, there is nothing like Wode's stage III in the data collected by Cancino, Rosansky and Schumann (1978). Thus a form like 'Marilyn like no sleeping', reminiscent of German postverbal negation, appears to be a structure unique to learners with a Germanic background. Schumann (e.g. 1978, 1982) has suggested that while preverbal negation may be found in the basic English of all acquirers, thus reducing the structural argument in favour of cross-linguistic influence, at the same time the fact that no + verb is the adult norm in certain L1s may delay the further acquisition of English negation.[5] In fact, if the L1 is not a preverbally negating language, then this L2 stage may be a relatively fleeting one. Certainly this is the implication from Hyltenstam's study where it is the Serbo-Croat learners who take the longest to acquire Swedish negation syntax, and the English speakers who show virtually no sign of preverbal negation. Interestingly, in Taeschner's (1983) study of the simultaneous acquisition of German and Italian by her two children, Neg + verb structures persist in their German, while verb + Neg forms are very rare in their Italian.

b) Word Order

As far as word-order errors are concerned, again there is some evidence of transfer, but equally well counter-evidence. While it is clear that subject-verb-object order is carried over into German by learners with Romance L1s, Clahsen and Muysken (1983), in their summary of research into untutored acquisition in adults, argue for a basic subject-verb-object strategy in initial stages, even in those cases where the L1 is not a subject-verb-object language. Thus Turkish learners, though apparently transferring subject-object-verb order to German (Dittmar 1981, quoted in Clahsen and

Muysken), are in fact only superficially doing so, via a complement pre-posing rule, which strands the verb in final position. Such forms as X-verb and X-subject-verb are also produced by learners with Romance L1s, where transfer cannot be an explanation, and where the most frequent word order is canonical subject-verb-object. Of course the interesting case here will be to see whether object preposing is employed significantly more by Turks than by Romance speakers in an effort to match Turkish word order. It is of course perfectly feasible that the subject-verb-object ordering of the initial stages of German is the result of transfer from L1 in some cases, i.e. in the case of Romance speakers, or equally possibly in the case of English speakers learning Dutch or German, where it may fossilize. Nevertheless, Clahsen and Muysken are right to emphasize that the presence of similar data from Turkish and Japanese learners of German does reduce the impact of the transfer argument and forces us to consider other possibilities. On the other hand, it would also be necessary to take the case of the learner with a subject-object-verb L1 learning another subject-object-verb language. Would such a learner acquire the L2 word order for free, so to speak? In this vein, Rutherford (1983) reports that Japanese learners, like Turks learning German, do not use their L1 order, subject-object-verb, in English. Clahsen and Muysken argue for an explanation of the preference for subject-verb-object order in terms of ease of processing via a 'neutral sentence type' (cf. McNeill 1979, who argues for subject-verb-object as a basic universal word order in first language acquisition). Needless to say, a subject-verb-object strategy will also meet with some success in both German and Dutch. However, in Jansen, Lalleman and Muysken (1981), the 'alternation hypo-thesis' proposed there suggests that when an L2 (like Dutch) offers two choices in word order, i.e. subject-verb-object and subject-object-verb, in e.g. main and subordinate clauses, then if the L1 is a subject-verb-object language, the subject-verb-object pattern will be generalized; if the L1 is subject-object-verb, then it is the subject-object-verb pattern which will be generalized. (The hypothesis is reminiscent of Levenston's 'overindulgence and underrepresentation', Levenston 1971). In main clauses it was found that Turks produced significantly more verbs in final position than Moroc-cans (subject-verb-object). In subordinate clauses (where Dutch is subject-object-verb), Turks produce more verb-final structures than Moroccans, but the sample of such clauses is small. There is some evidence in support of Zobl's claim that retardation may occur in the acquisition of the L2 when there is a developmental stage that resembles the adult L1 equivalent (Zobl 1980) in that the initial advantage that Moroccans have is to some extent cancelled out by their failure to break away from strict subject-verb order-ing, when there is a fronted constituent in initial position. Here Dutch would require subject-verb inversion, giving X-verb-subject, but Moroccans pro-duce less of these latter structures than Turks – a subtle example of cross-linguistic-influence, but by now familiar. Interestingly, in a study of Dutch foreigner talk addressed to non-Dutch speakers, Snow, van Eeden and Muysken found a large number of subject-verb-object orderings in subordinate clauses (1981).

c) Subject Pronoun Deletion

Similarly, the role of cross-linguistic influence in subject pronoun deletion is not entirely clear. Though there is plenty of evidence that such deletion takes place in the L2 of Romance speakers (putative transfer), it has also been argued that such deletion is not restricted to those speakers whose L1s experience pronoun-drop. Meisel (1980) has shown that in the L2, Romance speakers drop pronouns more in the third person than in the first person, which cannot be explained by transfer. And in case we should think the pronoun-drop is limited to speakers of Italian, Spanish or Portuguese, Zobl (forthcoming) reports some systematic subject pronoun deletion in L1 French learners of English. On the other hand, White (reported in White, forthcoming), investigating the pronoun-drop parameter, presumably in judgement tests, found that while Spaniards accepted that pronoun deletion was possible in English, French learners did not. Liceras studied performance on another aspect of the pronoun-drop parameter, namely the presence of an empty category immediately following a complementizer. That is to say, sentences of the kind 'who do you think that will come?' are grammatical in Spanish, but not in English. White noted that her Spanish subjects did not recognize the unacceptability of the above structure in English, and Liceras reports that with increasing proficiency her subjects stopped producing and accepting empty categories following complementizers, suggesting that claims that these apparently unrelated phenomena really do form part of a single parameter are well-founded (cf. Rutherford 1983).

d) Preposition Stranding

The arguments for transfer in English preposition-stranding also seem unclear. Mazurkewich (1983, quoted in White, forthcoming) showed that French learners moved from more pied-piped sentences in English (e.g. To whom did John give the book?) to more preposition-stranded ones (e.g. Who did John give the book to?). French does not have preposition-stranding (with certain minor exceptions), and so this looks like a clear case of initial interference, aided by the fact that pied-piping by no means violates English structural requirements. Although Mazurkewich claims that the development is apparent in Inuit learners of English (Inuit having no prepositions), that is to say there is a progression from unmarked pied-piping to marked preposition-stranding, and that therefore transfer cannot be an explanation alone, White observes that Inuit speakers use a higher percentage of preposition-stranded sentences irrespective of proficiency level when compared to the French subjects, and furthermore that the number of pied-piped constructions increases as proficiency grows, a fact that White attributes to the acquisition of more formal English. Liceras (1983), in her study of the acquisition of Spanish by speakers of English, finds that in judgement tasks, 43 per cent of her subjects accepted preposition-stranding in Spanish at the beginners' level, and also produced some in translation tasks (20 per cent). However, in the case of intermediate and advanced students, Liceras found, as she had already ascertained from her pilot studies (including free composition) that marked constructions are to all intents and purposes not accepted or produced in the IL. (White 1983 makes similar claims.)

e) Easy/Eager to Please

Bongaerts (1983), in a partial replication of L2 experiments based on the comprehension of complex structures in L1 acquisition, found that his Dutch subjects had far fewer problems with English 'easy to see'-type sentences than learners with French, Arabic and Hebrew backgrounds. This is most likely not only due to the fact that 'easy to see' structures are commonplace in Dutch (but not in the other languages studied), but also that Dutch speakers are used to making the semantic distinction between 'easy' and 'eager' sentences without the benefit of explicit syntactic marking, thus demonstrating that, although Bongaerts' subjects did make some errors in comprehension of these structures, the fact that they had prior experience of them via their L1s gave them a decided advantage over learners whose L1s did not have them.

f) Hypothetical Conditionals

I want to deal with one case from my own ongoing research, conducted with Herman Wekker (see e.g. Kellerman and Wekker 1982), into the development of the syntax of hypothetical conditionals in Dutch learners of English. A candidate for fossilization even among Dutch speakers of English who are otherwise virtually flawless is to use the model auxiliary 'would' in the protases of hypothetical conditionals, e.g. 'If it would rain tomorrow, the match would be cancelled'. While at first blush this looks like straightforward structure copying from Dutch (als het morgen zou regenen . . . – if it tomorrow would rain . . .), the story is not that simple. For although it is perfectly true that 'would'-insertion in hypothetical conditionals is a very common error in non-native English (it occurs in the English of at least Germans, Finns, Poles, Israelis, Czechs and Hungarians, for instance), it also occurs in the English of French learners (Trévise 1979). In European French, the conditional tense is not used in the protasis (except colloquially in 'si'-less clauses). Observation shows that English learners may use the conditional in French protases (though possibly under pressure from the requirement to use the future tense with the semantically linked 'quand'). What makes Dutch interesting is that in addition to the would + main verb the preterite or pluperfect are also possible, as in English, though probably specifically to indicate counterfactualness as distinct from non-committal hypotheticalness. The 'would'-protasis can also be used in counterfactual contexts, and is therefore the default mode. So there is a structural model in Dutch (of high frequency) which resembles the English target. Yet we find that it is the younger learners who use more correct past forms in the protasis (with modal meanings) while more proficient learners are more likely to use 'would'. Some of these latter learners may never arrive at the English target, while some clearly do. We cannot invoke a simple cross-linguistic inter- pretation of these findings to explain the shift in behaviour between less and more advanced learners. Nor can we make appeals to the presence of high-status American non-standard English in the input via popular forms of entertainment, where 'if . . . woulds' may be present, since we would then have to account for the fact that Dutch learners of French frequently use the conditional tense in hypothetical conditional protases. Furthermore, the tendency to insert 'would' or '-rais' forms in protases is certainly in accord- ance with general trends in Romance languages, where only the standard languages (plus Catalan) tend not to have structural parallelism in protasis and apodosis, usually, but not exclusively, of the '-rais/-rais' type (Posner 1976). Posner also argues that for these reasons it is not correct to ascribe the use of the conditional in Canadian French protases to the influence of English, in North African French to Spanish, or in Belgian French to Flemish. Nor for that matter, says Posner, should 'would'-intrusion in New York City English be ascribed to Yiddish.

In Buenos Aires Spanish, for instance, Lavandera (1975) has shown that the spoken, colloquial variant is undergoing a change towards parallel- ism, whereby the imperfect subjunctive required by Standard Spanish in the protasis is being replaced by the conditional tense in strictly non-counter- factual sentences, creating a distinction present in Dutch but not English, where context would be used to make the distinction. Thus it would appear that cross-linguistic influence cannot be invoked as the sole cause of the presence of intrusive 'would' in hypothetical conditionals, nor can it account for the fact that less proficient learners are less likely to make errors of this sort.

The Art in a State: the Case of the Pronominal Reflex

In recent years one of the most thoroughly researched areas of L2 grammar has been the relative clause. I think that here we have one area where there is surprisingly little disagreement amongst researchers as to precisely what may be ascribed to L1 influence and what to universals à la Keenan and Comrie. Such a measure of agreement is perhaps premature in view of the different methodologies and results obtained.

Schachter (1974), if not the first paper on L2 relative clauses, is now something of a classic because of its discussion of 'avoidance'. Schachter made use of then recent work by Keenan and Comrie (1972) on relative clauses and the noun phrase accessibility hierarchy, which showed that in the world's languages there was a general ordering of relative clause types according to the function of the relativized noun phrase head in the clause. To cut a long and familiar story short the accessibility hierarchy is Subject > Direct Object > Indirect Object > Object of Preposition > Possessive > Object of Comparative Particle. If a language can form a relative clause of a given function, then it will also be able to form relative clauses higher up the hierarchy, but not necessarily lower down. Also, if a language requires a pronominal reflex of the NP head in a given relative clause function, it will also require a pronominal reflex in every type of relative clause it can form lower down the hierarchy, but not necessarily higher up.

Schachter analysed the written performance of 50 learners of English with four different language backgrounds (and a native control group) and found that Persians and Arabs produce about as many English relative clauses as native Americans do, but between two and three times as many as Chinese and Japanese learners. In doing so, the Persians and the Arabs make the most errors (in 20–25 per cent of all relative clauses), but the Persians make many more errors due to illegal insertion of a pronominal reflex than Arabs (81 per cent versus 39 per cent of all errors). Schachter's point is that orthodox techniques of error analysis cannot deal with data of these kinds, because it is likely that Chinese and Japanese learners are producing considerably fewer relative clauses than Persians and Arabs since these are left-branching in the L1 rather than right-branching as in the L2. Hence Chinese and Japanese learners only risk relative clauses in English when they are sure of getting them right, making fewer errors in the process both absolutely and relatively (8 per cent and 12 per cent respectively). Schachter does not tell us how many of these very few errors are caused by the faulty insertion of a pronominal reflex, but such figures would be meaninglessly small anyway.

Secondly, when it comes to errors of pronominal-reflex insertion, Keenan and Comrie's data suggest that obligatory pronominal-reflex insertion is maximal in Persian relative-clause formation (with the possible exception of subject), while for Arabs, pronominal-reflex insertion is compulsory for all positions, with the possible exceptions of subject and direct object. Hence the higher proportion of pronominal-reflex errors amongst Persians is to be expected, if one accepts Schachter's account of the facts of pronominal-reflex insertion for the various L1s in her study. She makes use of Keenan and Comrie, as I have already indicated, but Keenan and Comrie (1972), which is crucially different from Keenan and Comrie (1977). What is more, according to the 1977 version, the Chinese should have more problems with pronominal-reflex retention than the Persians. That this is not evident can be accounted for by the much stronger force of avoidance of difficulty in relative-clause formation. Consequently, on the basis of the cross-linguistic data presented in Keenan and Comrie (1977), it is not at all clear that there is L1 influence in pronominal-reflex insertion, while relative-clause position may be an area of difficulty for Chinese and Japanese learners which is not experienced by Persians and Arabs.

Eckman (1977) is critical of Schachter in the sense that although her notion of avoidance is intuitively plausible, it should also be demonstrable in other ways, i.e. by the commission of forced errors (see also Kleinmann 1978). Eckman's own hypothesis, based on notions of markedness in universal grammar, and Keenan and Comrie (1972), offers different cross-linguistic predictions from Schachter based on error production rather than overall relative clause frequencies. However, as Kellerman (1979) points out, Eckman's predictions depend critically on the relativeclause data provided by Keenan and Comrie (1972). They are not supported by the data given in Keenan and Comrie (1977) nor, for that matter, in Gass (1980).[6] Schachter's follow-up work on relative clauses is harder to interpet (Schachter, Tyson and Diffley 1976). As far as pronominal-reflex insertion is concerned, Persian and Arab subjects were asked to judge the grammaticality of sentences with grammatical English relative clauses and 'English' relative clauses built on the L1 model with pronominal reflexes. Persian speakers accepted 87.5 per cent of the former category and 80 per cent of the latter, while Arabs accepted 82.4 per cent of the former, and, if they were not also Francophone bilinguals, 80 per cent of the latter. There appeared to be a tendency to behave randomly towards relative clauses based on the relative-clause patterns of other L1 groups (i.e. not based on pronominal-reflex insertion).

Consequently, one cannot be too confident about the validity of Ioup and Kruse (1977). Ioup and Kruse set out to determine whether cross-linguistic influence or inherent structural complexity (structural complexity corresponding to position on the accessibility hierarchy, with subject the least complex) was the conditioning factor in L2 performance in relative clauses. They too are critical of Schachter (1974) for postulating avoidance on the basis of production data, but they are right to point out that studying free performance alone can lead to the underdetermination of the learner's competence. Consequently they also used intuitional judgements as their data base with 'low' and 'middle' intermediate learners from five different language backgrounds (the four used by Schachter, plus Spanish, which reputedly has no pronominal reflex). As far as pronominal-reflex retention is concerned, Ioup and Kruse state that all groups seemed to have problems (even though they are only concerned with subject and direct object relative clauses), and that includes the Spanish group, who produced some 47 per cent incorrect judgements (as against the Arabs' 68.5 per cent at the one extreme, and the Japanese' 35 per cent on the other). The mean error rate for pronominal reflexes is higher than for any other category, a fact which clearly puzzles the authors. However, it is not at all surprising that pronominal-reflex sentences should not prove to be good discriminators by native language, given the elicitation format. It is unreasonable to expect that, just because a particular structure (in this case a pronominal reflex) is embedded in a relative clause, and then in a sentence, a learner will automatically be judging the sentence in terms of that structure let alone the presence or absence of a pronominal reflex. For instance, Ioup and Kruse offer 'The girl who she chased the bird fell down' as one of their malformed sentences to be judged. If this is to be judged for acceptability of pronominal reflex, then the first requirement is that 'girl' and 'she' should be seen as co-referential. Of 15 advanced Dutch learners of English I recently asked to judge, and if necessary, correct this sentence, 8 reformulated it by deleting the pronominal reflex. The remaining 7 each gave different responses suggesting that their problems lay elsewhere than with the pronominal reflex.

With some of the problems of previous research in mind, Gass (1979, 1980; Gass and Ard 1980, forthcoming) conducted a series of experiments on relative-clause performance. Gass used three tasks, a grammatical judgement task, a sentence-combining task and a free composition task. Gass shows that in the free composition task, the percentage of relative clauses used follows Keenan and Comrie's accessibility hierarchy. That is to say, the further down the hierarchy one goes the less frequent the relative clauses become. The sentence-combining task also yielded results which tallied well with the accessibility hierarchy (with one important exception, Possessive, where learners performed better than with all other relative-clause functions except Subject). In the judgement task, Gass noted a possible transfer effect in that subjects with L1s with pronominal reflexes were more likely to accept sentences with pronominal reflexes in them in the first three positions of the hierarchy than subjects with L1s without pronominal reflexes. By using both judgement and combination tasks, Gass increases the validity of her findings, compensating to some degree for the very low number (17) of subjects in her experiment.

Turning now to another story, Hyltenstam (1983) set out to examine the role of different elicitation instruments in L2 data production. He compared written compositions, picture identification (oral), imitation, and oral and written judgement tasks. Like Gass, Hyltenstam had (small numbers of) subjects divided according to whether their L1s were with or without pronominal reflexes. Hyltenstam's subjects had been in Sweden for two years or less, but were considered to be 'at a fairly advanced level'. The results are in some senses like Gass'. In the free composition task, the vast majority of relative clauses are Subject (c. 88 per cent). There were only 9 pronominal reflexes. Similarly a native speaker control group also only produced Subject and Object relative clauses. In the picture-identification task, regular implicational patterning was apparent in individuals in accordance with the accessibility hierarchy. Interestingly, all four L1 groups showed pronominal-reflex insertion, (though not in Subject position) – the Persians in 64 per cent of cases, the Greeks in 54 per cent (the two languages with pronominal reflexes), the Spaniards in 39 per cent, and the Finns in 12.5 per cent (the two languages without pronominal reflexes). In the judgement tasks, on the other hand, the results are very messy indeed, and no scaling is possible. Looking quickly at the data, all one can say is that some subjects tend to accept pronominal reflexes at least some of the time in all positions, the group with L1s with pronominal reflexes somewhat more than the group without. Even grouping the scores does not create order out of the chaos of individual variation. The imitation session produced little of interest, with only 11 pronominal reflexes counted. Hyltenstam's conclusion is that different elicitation tasks are not always equally suitable in gathering data. Only the oral production task produced patterned results and pronominal reflexes in interesting numbers. Hyltenstam also checked all his techniques with native speakers and reported extremely stable results. Once again, these results call into question the validity of other findings.

In a pilot study, Liceras (1983) found the sentence-combining task used by Gass unsatisfactory since the majority of sentences created produced subject relative clauses or no relative clauses at all. Like Gass and Hyltenstam, Liceras notes that the number of subject relative clauses produced in free compositions is very high relative to other relative-clause types. This was true for both native and non-native texts. Ultimately Liceras uses translation, grammatical judgements and a fill-in-the-blank task as her elicitation instruments. Liceras had four groups of subjects, 50 in all, of which 45 were Anglophone learners of Spanish at three levels of proficiency (beginners, intermediate and advanced), and 5 native speakers of Spanish.

Liceras' findings are as follows: pronominal reflexes are generally accepted by the beginners in the judgement task, and substantially so in the intermediate group. Her results do not confirm the hypothesis 'that resumptive pronouns would be more accepted in the most difficult positions' (194), and they were accepted in subject position. These results derive from grouped data. Advanced learners and the native speakers showed very little tendency to accept pronominal reflexes. One finding is that if the NP head is (+human), it is more likely to encourage the acceptance of a pronominal reflex in a judgement task. None of the other studies quoted have controlled for this variable (though Tarallo and Myhill 1983 note that [+animate] seems to favour a pronominal reflex). Another finding is that only the beginners produce responses in all three tasks that follow the accessibility hierarchy, and then with the exception of Subject and Direct Object. Once again, performance is worst on the judgement task.

The only conclusion possible at the moment is that the accessibility hierarchy seems to be a good predictor of frequency of pronominal-reflex functions in free composition. No satisfactory methodology has yet been evolved to study the role of the L1 in relative-clause formation. While it is

111

true that the bulk of the evidence suggests that pronominal-reflex insertion is more frequent among learners with L1s with pronominal reflexes, there is plenty of evidence to show that other learners also accept and produce them in a variety of tasks. (See also Trevisi 1978 for possible evidence of pronominal-reflex insertion in the French of Italian learners.) Since free compositions do not elicit a sufficient variety of relative-clause types, experimental techniques must be utilized. Quite the least reliable of these appears to be grammatical judgement tests. It is as well to remember the strictures of Snow and Meijer (1977) as far as syntactic judgements are concerned:

> ... testing even a relatively large group of (native speaker) subjects, all of them relatively intelligent and language-conscious, does not ensure internally consistent judgements concerning the relative acceptability of sentences. (174)

We also need data from learners with backgrounds of L1s without pronominal reflexes learning L2s where pronominal reflexes are the norm. Here we would be forced to predict no difficulty in learning to insert such pronouns, at least on the basis of Eckman's claims, and in view of Zobl's (1980a, b) claim that English has a tendency to insert pronominal reflexes, at least in some non-standard dialects (but see Tarallo and Myhill 1983).[7]

At this stage of research, it is quite impossible to state one way or the other that pronominal-reflex retention or insertion can uniquely be ascribed in the properties of a given L1. Methodologies need a great deal of tightening up in most respects, but most importantly of all, before we can even begin to study the phenomena in question, we have to establish the facts about the languages we are studying. Schachter's insight about avoidance still seems unassailed. As far as methodology is concerned, Bowerman's comments on the research on relative clauses in first-language acquisition (Bowerman 1979, 294) apply equally well to L2 research:

> ... it is unclear why different researchers have obtained different patterns of results, which in turn point to conflicting interpretations of how children process sentences containing relative clauses. It is possible that children have at their disposal more than one strategy for handling multiple-clause sentences; which strategy appears dominant in a given study may be a function of the exact nature of the task, the scoring procedures adopted, etc.

Some Discourse Studies

Let us now turn to some cases where cross-linguistic influence is not immediately apparent because it does not manifest itself in a surface structure echo of the L1 that can immediately be detected and ascribed to its source. A spectacular example is in Schachter and Rutherford (1979), who showed that what appears to be superficially a malformed passive in English produced by Mandarin and Japanese speakers tended on close analysis to be nothing of the sort. Instead, it is argued, such structures as 'most of food which is served in such restaurant have cooked already' or 'if I have finished these four jobs, I am confident that my company can list in the biggest 100 companies in the world' (Schachter and Rutherford 1979, 7–8) are actually attempts to transfer the topic-comment function to English form. Rutherford (1983) points out that the difficulty in recognizing this sort of transfer comes about through failure to look beyond syntax qua syntax and consider surface forms in terms of their function in discourse.

A similar phenomenon to the above exists in the English of advanced Dutch learners. A sentence such as 'In the so-called R.E.M. phase dreams occur' is usually adjudged by native speakers to be at least 'uncomfortable' and typical of the Dutchman's tendency to pile up adverbial phrases in front of the verb and subject (inverted in Dutch, but rarely in Dutch-English). Although they cannot usually say why such sentences are odd, it is because they violate the principle of 'endweight' (Quirk and Greenbaum 1973). Thus the usual correction offered is 'Dreams occur in the so-called R.E.M. phase', but the trick is to put this sentence back into its original context in discourse:

There then follows a period of rapid eye movements.
In the so-called R.E.M. phase dreams occur.

The native speaker correction with postposed prepositional phrase does not fit well with the requirements of discourse continuity here, and the appropriate correction would be in the form of a cleft sentence, viz.:

There then follows a period of rapid eye movements.
It is in the/this so-called R.E.M. phase that dreams occur.

In fact, our learner makes his error by following the discourse requirements of given-new, correctly applies local intrasentential syntactic rules (e.g. no inversion after a preposed element), but in so doing violates the principle of endweight only in those cases where sentence structure is X-subject-verb. This is a fairly subtle form of cross-linguistic influence, but one which is not infrequent in the written discourse of Dutch learners of English.

Another study which shows that errors which appear to be engendered by confusion between grammatical function and word order within the sentence are in fact to be interpreted within a discourse framework is Jordens (1983a, b, forthcoming), who examines the case-marking errors made by advanced Dutch and English learners of German (neither L1 being a case-marking language). Such errors occur when objects are incorrectly marked as nominatives, and subjects as accusatives, viz.

Jeder Republikaner betrachtete er als *sein* persönlich*er* Feind
(Jed*en* . . . sein*en* . . . persönlich*en*)
'Every Republican he considers a personal enemy of his'
*Dadürch entsteht *einen* Knall (*ein* Knall)
(Through that came into existence a bang)
'That caused a bang'

Jordens' argues that these errors are not caused simply by the failure to recognize the syntactic functions of subject and object, the sentence-initial NP being marked as nominative, and the sentence-final one as accusative. Rather these errors arise from L1-based semantic intuitions about the functions of the NPs within the overall discourse framework. Thus grammatical subjects are given accusative case-marking when they are the focus (and particularly when they are semantically patient), and grammatical objects will be marked as nominatives when they constitute the topic.

Another researcher to investigate cross-linguistic influence in discourse is Trévise (forthcoming), who looks at the range of topicalization devices available to and used by English learners of French, and French learners of English. Trévise shows that French learners do not transfer 'non-syntactic' or pragmatic forms of topicalization, but stick to more neutral syntactic devices permissible in 'le bon usage', such as 'canonical' subject-verb-object (not so canonical in spoken French) and extrapositional and identificational constructions (It's really great New York; Portugal it's very difficult to live there). Since Trévise's subjects were all learners of English in formal settings, it is quite possible that their unwillingness to transfer most of the topicalization devices of spoken French comes from a norm-oriented desire to avoid the worst excesses of colloquial speech. Even quite unexceptionable examples of thematic fronting found in English and French were never produced, so we cannot rule out the influence of the institutional setting. In the L2 French of English learners, subject-verb-object structures and anaphoric 'c'est' were frequently used (le groupe ici c'est très divisé). Trévise's conclusion is that learners tend to choose a few neutral topicalization devices, which generally do not lead to error (although they may not always be felicitous). Like the other studies mentioned here, Trévise's findings seem quite unambiguous.

Von Stutterheim's (forthcoming) studies of the German discourse of Turkish guest workers reveal patterns that do not appear in other L2 Germans. For instance, in the expression of temporality, Turks attempt to maintain in their German the two past tenses of Turkish. The remote past tense in Turkish is not relational (as the pluperfect in German or English would be), but strictly deictic. Before Turkish speakers develop tense marking in German, they express the distinction between remote and recent past via the use of gradable adverbs like 'ganz früher' – 'totally earlier', and thus remote, versus 'früher' – 'earlier', and thus recent. 'Ganz vorher' – 'totally previously' and 'voher' – 'previously' are similarly used. More advanced speakers will use the German pluperfect for the remote past.

Von Stutterheim also notes that Turkish speakers produce 'sein' ('to be') plus infinitive structures to maintain the imperfective/durative versus perfective/punctive distinction of their native language. Forms like 'Ich bin lesen/gehen' – 'I am read/go' – are, however, only used with verbs that are not inherently durative. Structures like 'Ich bin bleiben' – 'I am stay' are thus not attested. There is also a habitual use of this uniquely Turkish structure in L2 German, as in 'Ich bin immer busfahren' – 'I used to be a bus driver'. These durative structures are superficially akin to progressive structures in English (there is no equivalent in German), but in English, duration does not have to be marked by the progressive (they relaxed in the hot tub every Monday; he read the book over several years); interestingly enough, advanced Dutch learners use the English progressive duratively (and incorrectly), as in 'Day after day he was swotting for his exam' or 'It was raining for hours'.

Lexis

There are enormous quantities of evidence for the influence of the L1 on IL when it comes to lexis, yet such is our obsession with syntax, morphology and discourse that lexis tends to get overlooked. One language context which has provided an opportunity for close examination of how learners with typologically remote L1s learn a common L2 is that prevailing in Abo, in the south of Finland, where there is a Swedish-speaking enclave with their own university. Despite the existence of the two languages, their speakers live together harmoniously in one culture, though as one might expect, while Finnish is a second language for the Swedish-speaking Finns, for the Finns, Swedish is more of a foreign language. A long-term project has been under way for a number of years in which the English of Finnish- and Swedish-speaking Finns has been systematically analysed with a view to determining the differences in proficiency between the two groups. Both groups of speakers are bilingual to some extent, and the Finnish speakers are all receiving further education in a Swedish-speaking environment. This situation is an ideal one for studying the effects of the L1 on the learning of the L2, especially since Swedish is so clearly related to English and Finnish is not. A recent paper by Sjöholm (1983) will serve as illustration. He studied 723 learners of English (309 L1 Finnish and 414 L1 Swedish learners) at three different levels. Sjöholm's first test concerns prepositions, where Finns make many more mistakes than Swedes, especially where they themselves rate their responses to be completely correct (c. 36 per cent of responses for Swedes, and c. 56 per cent for Finns). It is almost superfluous to say that Swedish has prepositions and Finnish doesn't. The Finns use considerably fewer (15–20 per cent fewer) Swedish-based solutions, and, it is reported, 'did not have any great appetite for Finnish-based solutions, whereas Swedes clearly avoided them . . .' (182). So much, says Sjöholm, is true for prepositions, but it is not true necessarily for other elements in the L2. In a further study using idiomatic expressions and fixed collocations, it was found (as in Kellerman 1977 for L2 English, and Jordens 1977 for L2 German, both with Dutch as L1) that such expressions with Swedish equivalents were generally rejected by Swedes, and what acceptance there was tended to decline with proficiency. The Finns too tended to reject Finnish-like expressions, the more so as they became more proficient, whereas Swedes tended not to vary in their c. 60 per cent rejection of these idioms. Thus in conclusion we may say that while Swedish prepositions seem to be ripe for transfer as far as Swedes are concerned (and to a lesser extent the Finns), idiomatic expressions are not.

Ringbom (1978) examined the lexical errors made by Swedish and Finnish Finns, and found interesting patterns. Loan translations or extension of the semantic range of lexical items in English could be very clearly related to the L1 – the majority of errors could be attributed to the meanings of partial translation equivalents being transferred. Only two errors made by Finns could be attributed to a Swedish meaning being incorrectly transferred, while there were 14 attributable to Finnish amongst the Swedes. When it comes to formal morphological similarity, Swedish is the overwhelming source of error for both sets of learners. Language switch is uniquely from Swedish, and word blends of L1 and L2 are almost always Swedish-based. Anglicized nonce words are commonly based on Swedish and rarely on Finnish. And interlingual confusions also follow the predictable pattern. Thus on the formal level only, of the 187 errors collected by Ringbom from Finns, 162 are attributable to Swedish (c. 87 per cent); for Swedes, the figures are 315/322 (c. 98 per cent). Wikberg (1979) also reports that L3 interference (i.e. from Swedish) tends to be found more among Finns than among Swedes, but that Finns are more inventive in word-building, Finnish being very rich in derivational processes. However, since there are very few errors in Wikberg's corpus, no examples of the effect of this fact on L2 English are given.

Semantics

Some interesting directions are being pursued by those working with semantic cross-linguistic influence. We have already seen that a vast number of the errors reported by the Åbo team could be related to the attachment of meanings to English translation equivalents appropriate only to Finnish or Swedish, and the English is accordingly underdifferentiated (see also Arabski 1979). Kellerman, in various publications, has tried to show that cross-linguistic influence may have very subtle effects on learners' perceptions of the L2, at least in formal learning situations. These effects do not necessarily reveal themselves in the form of errors, however, and can only be explored by experimental means, since it is not possible to predict what may or may not be a candidate for transfer from the L1 simply by a linguistic comparison of L1 and L2. Instead, they are studied by tapping intuitions through a variety of strictly controlled elicitation techniques such as card sorting, translation, focused judgements, and paired comparison. Kellerman is careful not to claim to be able to predict spontaneous performance, since there are too many intervening variables to consider but also because of the enormous problems involved in collecting data about features of language likely to be absent in L2 performance. Nevertheless 'transfer-ability' is a probability measure that is one of the determinants of performance, and as such is viewed as a sine qua non in studies of cross-linguistic influence. The main problem with this sort of work resides in how it can be related directly to spontaneous performance, even though testing by various techniques suggests that the results obtained are robust. Furthermore, the phenomena described here may only be apparent in situations where learners may exercise maximum cognitive control.

In his study of 'break', Kellerman claimed that though the Dutch and English equivalents shared many of the meanings of this word, learners with a wide variety of experience were consistent in their judgements as to the relative transferability of the meanings. Furthermore, there was no differential effect due to L2. The intuitions of Dutch learners of German correlated significantly with those of learners of English. Translation tests confirmed the judgement tests – learners tended to avoid one-to-one correspondence between L1 and L2 where meanings were perceived as far from prototypical, even though this led them unwittingly to gratuitous error.

A further observation is that intuitions about transferability are prone to developmental change, not so much in qualitative terms as in quantitative ones. That is to say, the points at which learners will move from acceptance of equivalence to rejection (and possibly back again, see below) may change over time, but not the relative probabilities. Thus learners whose overall proficiency is lower than their peers may also be more tolerant of equivalence and thus appear to perform better. In fact, it is claimed they are making more use of their L1 than some more proficient learners. This observation led Kellerman to examine the responses by various proficiency groups in terms of acceptance and rejection of equivalence for the pair 'breken – break'. In particular a change in behaviour towards transitive and intransitive uses of 'break' was discernible amongst those learners in their last year at school and their first year at university, who rejected the intransitive much more than the transitive forms of prototypical 'break'. Thereafter, performance on intransitive 'break' began to pick-up again. Further evidence for such U-shaped behaviour (see e.g. Bowerman 1982; Karmiloff-Smith, forthcoming, for studies on this phenomenon in L1 development) has been reported elsewhere (Kellerman 1983b; Sharwood Smith and Kellerman, forthcoming). Such patterns give us one way of distinguishing between cross-linguistic influence and actual knowledge of the L2, where the product, not being erroneous but at the same time reflecting the structure of the L1, cannot be unambiguously interpreted as to its provenance. The existence of an intermediate developmental stage where there is no L1-L2 equivalence does indeed suggest that the earlier state of acceptance is not based on L2 knowledge but on the L1. The changing pattern of L2 conditional syntax discussed above is a further example.

Other studies which use the notion of semantic 'core' or 'prototype' are

Gass and Ard (forthcoming) and Flynn (1983). Gass and Ard discuss the notion of 'focal' meaning for certain English tense/aspect combinations such as the present progressive ('ongoing, witnessed activity which persists for an extended period of time' Gass and Ard forthcoming), where they note that an event which stresses ongoing activity in English is closer to the focus in English than an event which lacks this feature. They examine the L2 judgements of a large number of Japanese and Spanish learners as to the correctness of sentences using the present progressive (and other tenses) either in isolation or contextualized. In the case of the progressive, subjects were more likely to judge sentences as correct the closer the interpretation was to the focus (i.e. John is smoking American cigarettes now). The less focus-like the meaning (i.e. John is travelling to New York tomorrow), the less likely the sentence was to be accepted. In writing tasks, where learners were required to write sentences of their own choice based on uncontextualized sentences, there was a strong tendency to select only focus-like meanings. Similar results are reported for the simple present and 'will'-future. Thus 'I smoke cigars' is seen as more acceptable than 'PanAm flies to London tomorrow', and 'I will go to the library tomorrow' is more likely to be accepted than 'I will do it last night'. While there is a general similarity in performance between the two groups, there are some differences. For instance, Spanish learners perform differently from Japanese learners on the following progressive sentence pair:

> Dan is seeing better now
> John is travelling to New York tomorrow

Spanish speakers overwhelmingly judge the first as more acceptable than the second, while the Japanese tend to reject both (the first more heavily than the second). Since Gass and Ard claim that both sentences can be literally translated into Spanish,[8] they hypothesize that because of the greater similarity between Spanish and English verb semantics, judgements about English will be affected by intuitions about Spanish, and consequently the futurate use of the progressive, seen as non-focal in Spanish, is rejected in English. While we are not told what the facts of Japanese are, one assumes that they are very different from English. Consequently, and consonant with Kellerman's findings for the semantics of 'break', Japanese learners do not use the L1 as a source of predictions about English, and tend to accept only the focal meaning. Thus there are no cross-linguistic influence effects from Japanese to English, while they do seem to be apparent from Spanish. A possible difficulty for this research (apart from acceptability questions in Spanish) is that learners' judgements could be heavily biased by pedagogical strategies. One would expect the focus meanings to be the first to be taught, and so these results may equally well reflect teaching input.

K. Flynn (1983), in a similar study, looked at the use of the present perfect in the written work of Chinese, Arabic and Spanish learners of

English. She noted that although there were no significant differences in frequency of perfect use between the language groups, there were differences in use of the various functions of the perfect. Flynn uses an analysis of the perfect given by Comrie (1976), who divides up the perfect into (a) result/state perfect – 'Technology has produced changes in my country', (b) the experiential perfect – 'I have never seen a woman president in my country', (c) the perfect of persistent situation – 'Women having been working in those fields since the revolution in my country', and (d) the perfect of recent past – 'Recently women in my country have chosen to work out of the house' (all examples from Flynn 1983). Flynn shows that Spanish speakers use significantly more experiential perfects and considerably fewer recent past perfects than other groups, while Arabs used significantly fewer persistent situation perfects. These results are extremely interesting in that they again point to language-specific differences that only become apparent in comparative data. One major problem with this kind of research, to some extent obviated in Gass and Ard's more controlled framework, is that by using free production, Flynn leaves herself the arduous task of categorizing the L2 perfects, no easy matter when it comes to subtle distinctions of meaning contained within a single form (Herman Wekker, personal communication). However, it is felt that both this and the previous study take research into cross-linguistic influence into new and promising areas.

One recent study investigating lexicalization of the notions of movement, manner and direction in verbs is Harley (forthcoming), who looked at the written French composition of Anglophone students enrolled in an immersion programme and of native French-Canadians. She noted that the immersion students relied more heavily on prepositions than the native speakers, as they would in their L1, to express direction as a separate lexicalization outside the verb. English, as Talmy (1975) shows, tends to conflate movement and manner with the verb (She *danced* into the room), while Romance languages lexicalize movement and direction within the verb (Ella *entró* al cuarto *bailando* – She entered the room dancing). In French, unlike in English, the most common prepositions are neutral in terms of direction versus location (with exceptions, of course); in English direction and location are usually indicated by different prepositions (again with exceptions). To sum up Harley's results, immersion students tended to use more non-directional movement verbs and prepositions than native speakers, who, if they used such verbs, always did so with an explicitly directional preposition or prepositional phrase. Thus to take the relative uses of 'courir' (to run), a verb which conflates movement and manner, but not direction – a typically English pattern – the immersion students use this verb far more frequently than the native speakers, and where direction was involved, in conjunction with a preposition(al phrase) like 'à' unmarked for direction (le chat courait à la maison). Thus for native speakers, most prepositions drew their directional interpretation from the verb, while for immersion students, direction was frequently carried by the preposition alone. As Harley herself notes, we certainly need to know what Francophone learners of English will do in similar circumstances. We do know from Bowerman's research into L1 development (1982) that children make conflation errors in English, producing examples like 'I'm frowning out the door' and 'We crouched down the hill' (examples quoted in Weeks 1983), but among second-language learners one might expect to see the Romance pattern predominate (even though it is contrary to the general Indo-European trend) because it allows the expression of movement and direction in a single lexicalization, while manner, often a subsidiary requirement in communication, is lexicalized optionally.

Another study making use of comparative quantitative data is Wong (1983). She investigates the relatively greater number of 'make' constructions in the written compositions of Chinese learners of English than in the work of other learners. She claims that the predilection for 'make' structures is directly relatable to Chinese, where the relatively few lexicalized causative verbs are literary or technical, and the most frequent structure contains an explicit marker of causation (shi, 'make') + complement. Wong's claim is that the absence of lexicalization in Chinese will lead to under-lexicalization in English with resultant unidiomatic usage, such as 'They might make their friends get very upset about this', instead of, presumably, 'They might upset their friends very much about this', where 'to upset' in English is a lexicalized causative. Given that analytical 'make' + complement is well known in studies of L2 English as a means of circumventing lexical holes we see here a case where the structure of the L1 encourages a tendency towards grammaticalization already present in interlanguages in general which is probably of a greater order than in either L1 or L2 (see Haiman 1980 for the relationship between lexical roots and grammatical processes in language).

Envoi

The history of cross-linguistic influence in second-language learning is akin to the history of Poland in Europe, with ever-changing expansions and diminutions of its territory and even occasional disappearances off the map. At the moment, the study of cross-linguistic influence is undergoing a revival, and a theoretically responsible one at that. Yet there are still those who would wish to diminish its importance by reducing it to the status of a mere communication strategy or to generalize about its insignificance from limited instances where, had the learner only referred back to the structure of his L1, he would not have made the mistake he did. There is now evidence to suggest that cross-linguistic influence does not only operate as a source of surface form (thus leading to what used to be known as interference or positive transfer), but also serves to constrain the choice of surface forms in the learner's IL at levels smaller and larger than the sentence. Furthermore, where the adult L1 pattern is also consonant with a putatively universal developmental stage in L2 learning, the learner may proceed to that stage faster than those learners who do not have that pattern in their L1s. Conversely, possession of this L1 pattern may result in retardation or even fossilization. Cross-linguistic influence may operate at many levels of linguistic structure and perhaps via a variety of psycholinguistic processes, conscious and unconscious. (See the discussion in Faerch and Kasper, forthcoming.) It is misleading to say that it does not afflict the more advanced learner more than the less advanced: this hoary old chestnut should finally be squashed underfoot as an unwarranted overgeneralization based on very limited evidence. If one only looks at development in simple syntax, then such an observation is inevitable and trite. Advanced learners are affected by cross-linguistic influence in different ways from beginners, but simply because they know more and their knowledge opens up new susceptible areas.

One real problem in establishing the existence of cross-linguistic influence lies with the methodology we empty to make our claims. Often the methodology is determined by the sorts of linguistic structures we are looking at. We can collect plenty of data naturalistically as long as we restrict ourselves to subdomains where the tokens are easy to collect. Thus I find the arguments for and against cross-linguistic influence in basic syntax and morphology well informed by large quantities of data. In more complex syntax, discourse and semantics, the problems multiply due to the difficulty of interpreting the learner's intentions and the opportunities the learner has for ducking out of difficulties. Hence the need for 'tough' methods of elicitation. But such is our desire to make theoretical pronouncements that we often rush through our experimentation in the process. Or borrow someone else's pronouncements without checking their data collection techniques, as if the pronouncement was the proof itself. Never has the need for careful experimentation been more apparent, just as our field is once more beginning to enjoy the benefit of a cross-fertilization with theoretical linguistics. Any predictions, such as those made on the basis of some notion of markedness or universal grammar[9] about the course of second-language acquisition in general, and cross-linguistic influence in particular, must be subjected to the most careful scrutiny and rigorous testing procedures.

Notes

1) Thanks to Theo Bongaerts, Clive Perdue and Mike Sharwood Smith for their comments on this draft. Thanks, too, to my Discussant, Roger Andersen, whose critique I fully accept.

2) Terrell, Gomez and Marisal (1980, 159) probably claim the record with a 'possible' 89 per cent for their L2 Spanish data, collected in classroom.

3) Wenk's recent work on rhythm and cross-linguistic influence is worth at least a note, however (Wenk, forthcoming). And as Clive Perdue very properly reminds me, article use certainly is a matter of pragmatics.

4) It is also worth remembering that Hyltenstam's methodology, essentially gap-

filling, allows maximum monitoring, being a discrete-point test. In view of the critical remarks levelled at research using discrete-point testing, this fact has been surprisingly overlooked.

5) For a similar discussion, see Zobl (1980, 473). Also Andersen (1979) and Jordens (1977), and particularly Sharwood Smith (1983).

6) Tarallo and Myhill (1983) provided different data, claiming that pronominal reflex is restricted to Possessive in Chinese. Yet according to Comrie (personal communication), for Peking Mandarin, it is sometimes required on Direct Object and obligatory in all other positions except Subject.

7) It is not, however, immediately obvious how the fact that English is a crypto-pronominal-reflex language should contribute to pronominal-reflex insertion by learners of English with L1s with pronominal reflex. See, though, Visser (1963).

8) Native speakers do not always seem to agree with this claim, however.

9) E.g. Hyltenstam (1981), Comrie (forthcoming), White (forthcoming), to take three scholars who have recently invoked markedness as a predictor of cross-linguistic influence, and S. Flynn (1983) who has explored the effects of 'principal branching direction' on L2 performance.

10. Discussant

Before beginning, a short comment on terminology. Although I have used the term 'transfer' in the title of an earlier paper, I adhere to Kellerman's use of cross-language influence and Zobl's comparable use of 'cross-language generalization' in the discussion. I suspect that 'transfer' as a technical term for cross-language influence will soon become a marker of a particular period and disappear from current usage in interlanguage studies. My only regret is that the succinct phrasing of 'transfer to somewhere' around which I have developed my discussion here will now have to become 'cross-language influence to somewhere'. Something is lost in the translation.

Kellerman, Zobl, and I have all argued for cross-language influence playing a specific role in interlanguage development in conjunction with the natural developmental principles that guide interlanguage development without cross-language influence. I have called this the 'Transfer to Somewhere Principle' (Andersen 1983b; earlier versions in Andersen 1979b, 1980, 1982c), which is equivalent in many respects to Zobl's (1980b) three theses on 'the mechanisms underlying developmental and transfer errors' and Kellerman's (1983b) 'Reasonable Entity Principle'. I would not want to minimize differences among our respective views, since there certainly are differences and these differences may lead to productive future research, but for the purposes of this discussion I will assume that we are basically in agreement that cross-language influence operates essentially in conjunction with the natural principles of interlanguage construction that exist separate from any cross-language influence. As I have discussed in more detail elsewhere (Andersen 1979b, 1980, 1981a, 1982c, 1983a, in press), these natural developmental principles are identifiable as such because they are evident in a variety of language acquisition contexts (especially when studied within a cross-linguistic[1] perspective) – native-language acquisition as well as second-language acquisition and in pidgins, creoles, and situations of language loss and language death, as well as related cases of languages in contact. (I hasten to clarify that I do not intend to imply that these diverse developmental phenomena are identical. To the contrary, it is precisely because they are so different from each other in many respects that the emergence of common features in such different types of language development points to common principles behind all language acquisition and use.)

In their papers Zobl and Kellerman both argue for and provide evidence for cross-language influence having a well-defined role within the broader scope of interlanguage development. The intent of both writers is to establish empirically the mechanisms which govern cross-language influence and the limits on its operation. Zoble has realigned his earlier three theses in terms of a core-periphery distinction whereby cross-language influence operates only on the periphery. Kellerman tempers the extremes of advocates of an overly powerful role of cross-language influence as well as those who would minimize its role, by reviewing the evidence for it as well as certain counter-evidence. In many of the cases he reviews, the evidence is clear and irrefutable; in others the evidence is more ambivalent, in spite of certain unsupported claims to the contrary. At the risk of oversimplifying two quite different and complex discussions (and I *am* oversimplifying), I believe that the 'Transfer to Somewhere Principle' (do I have to say 'Cross-Linguistic Influence to Somewhere' now?) is amply documented in Zobl's theoretical framework and Kellerman's review of evidence in support of cross-language influence.

Zobl's position in his paper is consistent with his earlier position in most ways, but seems to constitute a major shift away from the general psycho-linguistic functional models that formed part of his earlier framework (e.g. Slobin 1982b; Bates, MacWhinney and Smith 1983) to the formal models of learnability theory associated with Chomsky's current generative theory (e.g. Wexler and Culicover 1980; Baker and McCarthy 1981; Tavakolian 1981). His intent is clear: research on cross-language influence has lacked an adequate theoretical framework and he hopes that learnability theory will provide that framework. As he states in his conclusion:

> the theoretical position adopted in this paper assigns a rather restricted role to the L1 in interlanguage.

He goes on to say that:

> there is scope for the L1 only in those instances where the [language acquisition] device itself is relatively neutral . . . or where the auxiliary evaluation measure furnished by the L1 coincides with a projection which is incompatible with the L2 data.

This position is based on Zobl's distinction between core and peripheral properties of language.

If I may be permitted the liberty of rather free paraphrasing, the total picture looks something like this: the learner will learn rapidly those features of the L2 that are defined by the core or implicationally predicted by the core if the L2 is typologically consistent. Moreover, very little input is needed for the learner to acquire such core properties and the learner can project implicationally-predictable features of the L2 without explicit L2 input that contains these features and acquire them 'free of charge'. The L1 will be involved only if the L2 has language-specific features not specified in the core or where an L2 feature is typologically inconsistent *and* the L1 feature matches the prediction made by the core or is consistent with the L2 feature.

It is thus in the periphery where the L1 seems to have its major influence. Zobl places three types of features in the periphery: (a) language-specific and thus non-core features, (b) features of the L2 that are typologically inconsistent, and (c) features not specified by the core and thus indeterminate and free to vary from language to language. (It is not clear how much overlap, if any, there is between the first and the third groups.)

With one exception this characterization of cross-language influence is similar to Zobl's earlier (1980b) theses that cross-language influence is activated by structural features of the L2 and/or natural developmental processes. The major difference is – and the difference is major – that he has gone much further in specifying the nature of the L2 features that activate transfer in formal abstract terms (those not in the core or underdetermined by the core) and has given the core-periphery distinction and projection from the core a central position, seemingly replacing his earlier and less-explicit 'natural developmental processes'.

I have three reservations about Zobl's proposal. First, there are too many missing bits of information in his exposition. What exactly is in the core and what is in the periphery? What is projected from or controlled by the core? I suspect that a reading of a number of the 'learnability theory' publications he cites would provide some of the answers, but I also suspect that a large part of the answer would be the well-known 'more research needed' response. Second, I found his earlier use of Slobin's (1973, 1984) operating principles to be an important link between empirical native-language acquisition and second-language acquisition research and I find that link missing or diminished here. I suspect that Zobl would still find cognitive operating principles to have an important role in explaining language acquisition (including cross-language influence), but that he would reply on such principles only where the language acquisition device fails to operate – the periphery. This takes us to the third reservation. I suspect that Zobl would also allocate all discourse-semantic and discourse-pragmatic features of language to the periphery and thus beyond the core. I then wonder whether the core is such a small core as to leave us with the same problems that now concern us within psycholinguistic and functional models of language acquisition and use. If this were to be the case, this would, of course, still be a major accomplishment. But I suspect Zobl expects more of his model than this.

This then brings us back to the first point: how much is specified in the core (by the language acquisition device) and how much – and what, specifically – is in the periphery. It would be interesting to use the evidence for cross-language influence in Kellerman's paper to test Zobl's model, but we are not provided with enough information about what corresponds to core and periphery features to conduct such a test. Zobl clearly means for his proposal to be tested and this is the most productive part of his proposal. He states that:

125

If it can be shown that clusterings incompatible on typological grounds do co-occur in interlanguage, and that these incompatible co-occurrences are attributable to influence from the L1, then the acquisition mechanism that we have assumed would not be applicable to interlanguage.

Zobl presents us with an interesting agenda for research.

Kellerman's paper is a valuable extension of an elaboration on his 1981 paper, 'Now You See It, Now You Don't' given at the University of Michigan conference on language transfer (Kellerman 1983b). 'Now You See It, Now You Don't' would be an appropriate title for this paper also, since it captures his continued concern for the two extremes of research and writing on cross-language influence. On the one hand there are those who wish to dismiss cross-language influence as insignificant, irrelevant, or simply not there. On the other are those who claim significant cross-language influence on second language interlanguage when, in fact, their evidence is ambivalent or even contradicts their conclusions. Within this framework Kellerman reviews an impressive array of evidence for cross-language influence (as well as inconclusive evidence and counterevidence) from both sides of the Atlantic and based on a variety of different languages. His discussion of evidence and counterevidence is fair and even. And his forceful message that advocates of cross-language influence and detractors alike had better pay closer attention to research methodology if they expect their pronouncements to hold up under careful scrutiny is exemplified in his critique of the nature of the evidence offered for or against cross-language influence as well as in his own research.

Rather than comment extensively on Kellerman's entire paper, I prefer to focus especially on a point I raised with regards to Zobl's proposal: that Slobin's operating principles and the discourse-semantic and discourse-pragmatic properties of language and interlanguage (as well as cross-language influence in these areas) are relegated to the periphery and, thus, in Zobl's model, the role of cross-language influence is still left largely undefined.

Within a transfer to somewhere framework for cross-language influence, I would interpret the 'natural developmental principles' portion of the framework as some integrated combination of cognitive operating principles and the discourse-semantic and discourse-pragmatic motivations for the choice of linguistic form and order of items to convey the speaker's intentions (his basic meaning and his perspective on this meaning). For me this is the motor of interlanguage construction and language use in general and the *somewhere* of the transfer to somewhere principle. Kellerman devotes a substantial portion of his discussion to 'some discourse studies' and 'semantics'. And a very lucid and convincing discussion at that. I am concerned, however, that by following the traditional division of linguistic areas into syntax, discourse, lexis, semantics, etc., we are carving up the object we are trying to study into some not totally relevant categories. I am uncomfortable with the treatment of 'discourse studies' as a self-contained linguistic area all by itself. As I see it, language *is* discourse. To make a rough analogy, if semantics is the battery, then discourse is the motor and sentence-level syntax the voltage regulator that makes the battery (semantics) and the motor (discourse) function within the constraints of a linear speech mechanism.

I would find it imperative to treat certain aspects of articles (discussed in his introduction) and almost all the areas Kellerman groups under syntax and semantics within a discourse-semantic and discourse-pragmatic framework. And I believe that Kellerman's discussion of most of these cases shows that he also assumes some such framework, at least in part. (Cf. Kellerman's discussion of the impossibility of evaluating evidence for cross-language influence without at least assuming some theoretical framework.) I will elaborate on this point with two areas from Kellerman's treatment of syntax: subject-pronoun deletion and word order.

Subject-pronoun deletion. As far as I can tell, all cases cited by Kellerman are restricted to sentence-level subject deletion. But for those languages with significant subject-pronoun deletion (or zero anaphora) the phenomenon is governed not by sentence-level syntax, but by discourse-pragmatics. Work by Silva (1982) on Spanish and Givón (1983) on topic continuity across languages, which includes zero anaphora, is revealing in this regard.

Meisel's (1983; see also Meisel, Clahsen and Pienemann 1981) position against a cross-language influence interpretation for subject-pronoun deletion was that such deletion constitutes a strategy used by individual learners to cope with the complexities in learning or using the L2. Even if this is true, then we would still predict that speakers of languages with subject-pronoun deletion (such as Spanish) would use this strategy more than speakers of languages with obligatory subjects (e.g. Dutch or English). (See Andersen (1983b, 190–1) for more discussion on this point.) But it is clear that it will simply not do to lump *all* types of subject-pronoun deletion together nor to operate solely on the sentence level.

Some case studies that a group of graduate students and I have done, following Silva (1982) and Givón (1983), show that in the English interlanguage of speakers of Spanish, Italian, and Korean zero anaphora is used for subjects with a high degree of topic continuity (i.e., continuous with the subject or object of the previous clause) and especially when (1) there is no competing referent for the zero subject and (2) there is also a high degree of action continuity (i.e., it is easy to retrieve from the information conveyed that the same agent is performing all actions in a series). These factors – (1) topic continuity, (2) lack of competing referents, and (3) a high degree of action continuity – seem to be the chief factors involved in subject-pronoun deletion in natural languages and interlanguage. But they operate *across* sentence boundaries (as well as within sentences). If this holds across

127

studies, then it would be another case of (1) discourse-pragmatic governed features of interlanguage and (2) the operation of cross-language influence in conjunction with natural processes of language acquisition and use.

Word order. I do not deny the strictly syntactic properties of certain aspects of word order. These are based on typological or language-specific characterics of language and languages. But it is not always so easy to separate discourse-governed properties of word order from others. In a very insightful longitudinal study of the German of Spanish speakers, Clahsen (in press) accounts for examples of pseudo-inversion in the Spanish-speakers' German, where all such cases involve utterance-final placement of the subject, by assuming that such inversion is strictly language-specific sentence-level syntax. He concludes that this pseudo-inversion is the learner's intermediate step towards eventually acquiring the native German rules for inversion. It could be, however, that the Spanish speaker is 'inverting' only in those cases where Spanish uses a verb-subject word order, which is governed by discourse-pragmatic principles (Silva 1982). There is thus a false congruence between German inversion and Spanish verb-subject order that causes the Spanish speaker to interpret German inversion in terms of his own native language procedures for ordering subject, verb, and object. If we assume ordering of subject, verb, and object to obey only sentence-level syntactic rules, we may be missing the real principles that guide the learner – and it is these principles, after all, that are the primary motivation for our research.

If many phenomena we have filed under syntactically-governed word order, deletion of sentence- or phrase-level constituents, morphology, semantics, etc. turn out to be much more discourse-governed than current interlanguage research leads us to believe, I think this would strengthen Kellerman's discussion and be consistent with the position he is taking in his paper. I also hope that such attention to the centrality of discourse-governed properties of language would help sharpen (for me, at least) our understanding of the relationship between core and peripheral properties of language in Zobl's model.

I congratulate Zobl and Kellerman on a stimulating, insightful and provocative treatment of the current state of our understanding of the role of cross-language influence in the development of interlanguage. As was to be expected from their previous work, the probable role of cross-language influence in interlanguage development is a lot clearer as a result of their discussion of the theoretical and empirical underpinnings of cross-language influence. And they have provided us with a stimulating research agenda for some time to come.

Note

1) I predict that 'cross-language' influence will now get confused with 'cross-linguistic' studies (which may or may not involve cross-language influence, and research on cross-language influence may or may not be carried out within a cross-linguistic design). But, then, I assume we can cope with this potential confusion.

11. Summary of Discussion

Neither Zobl nor Kellerman expressed serious disagreement with the comments made by the discussant and much of the following general discussion was devoted to the clarification of particular issues raised by Zobl's core-periphery model and its wider implications. Later, Kellerman indicated some disappointment, which was shared by other participants, that time had not been found to consider his extensive discussion on IL methodology.

While speakers in the open session welcomed the capacity of the Zobl model to provide testable predictions that language transfer was more likely to occur in peripheral areas than in the more tightly-knit clusterings of the core, some concern was expressed at the theoretical status of the model since it appeared to draw on two different theoretical sources (language typology and universal grammar) without a clear motivation for doing so, and that the possibility of establishing IL-specific universals had not been explored. Some participants were uneasy that syntax-led models in general not only tended to undervalue the function of other areas of language and language use, but also overvalued the notion of the norm at the expense of more detailed studies of language variation.

On a more general point, there was support for the view that the investigation of language transfer implied the development of models which incorporated cognitive principles that could provide definitions for concepts such as 'core', 'clustering', etc. in psychological terms instead of relying exclusively on categories of linguistic description.

PART THREE

THE ANALYSIS OF INTERLANGUAGE

12. Maturational Aspects of Universal Grammar

1. Introduction

It appears that, in the past, language acquisition has been studied under essentially two fundamental perspectives. The first of these is generally referred to as the *logical* problem of language acquisition and has, roughly speaking, to do with the question of why children can learn natural languages at all, i.e. what is it that makes language acquisition possible? The second perspective relates to the question of why natural languages are acquired the way they are, i.e. how can the regularities that have been observed in real-time acquisition processes be explained? I will call this problem the *developmental* problem of language acquisition.

In the past, the logical problem has been almost exclusively the concern of theoretical linguistics; in particular it has been a major motivating force in work on generative grammar (cf. Baker 1979; Wexler and Culicover 1980; White 1982; Lightfoot 1982; Chomsky 1976, 1981b). In contrast psycholinguists and language acquisition researchers have primarily dealt with the developmental problem (see Slobin 1973; Wode 1981; Clahsen 1982; Felix 1982a). This difference in focus is, I believe, mainly a matter of historical accident.[1] Nevertheless, the situation is somewhat unfortunate because, on a certain level of abstraction, both problems may be viewed as relating to essentially the same basic issue. Under such a perspective, it seems to be more promising to look simultaneously at *both* problems and to explore how linguistic and psycholinguistic evidence can contribute to a deeper understanding of the crucial mysteries of language acquisition. This is essentially the approach I wish to take in this paper.

The paper is organized as follows: in section 2 I will discuss some of the main issues in present-day acquisition research and illuminate a few basic problems which, I believe, most current proposals face. In particular, I will show that the question of why children restructure their grammars in an ordered sequence of stages has not received a satisfactory answer. In section 3 I will propose a model in which the transition from one developmental stage to the next is explained in terms of principles of Universal Grammar which are assumed to emerge in accordance with a genetically determined maturational schedule. Section 4 briefly discusses some of the empirical and theoretical consequences of this view.

2. The Developmental Problem of Language Acquisition

While the logical problem of language acquisition deals with the question of what enables children to acquire language at all, the developmental problem focuses on the question of why children acquire language the way they do.

In order to fully appreciate this difference in perspective it is necessary to recall that discussions about the logical problem have typically adopted an idealized view of language acquisition which abstracts away from the temporal dimension of the learning process. Under such an idealization language acquisition is taken to be an *instantaneous* process in which the only relevant factors to be considered are the child's linguistic experience and his biologically determined cognitive capacity (for a justification of this approach see Chomsky 1976, 3–35 and 118ff.). While the logical problem thus abstracts away from the temporal dimension of language acquisition, the developmental problem brings this aspect back into focus.

It seems that the developmental problem of language acquisition has been studied under essentially two aspects. Quite expectedly, it was found that many regularities of language acquisition appear to reflect the influence of a large number of external factors which relate to properties of the environment in which the individual learns his language (Snow and Ferguson 1977). In addition, there seem to be certain psychological variables, such as memory constraints, emotional and affective factors, attitudes, etc. which – particularly in second-language acquisition – may determine various aspects of the developmental process (Schumann 1975; Clahsen 1982).

Apart from such environment-dependent aspects, language-acquisition research has discovered developmental regularities which appear to be largely invariant across languages, across learners, and across acquisition types so that they resist an immediate interpretation in terms of environmental influence (McNeill 1970; Bloom 1970; Brown 1973; Wode 1977c). One of the most striking discoveries of developmental psycholinguistics has been that all instances of language acquisition seem to follow a certain basic structural pattern, commonly referred to as 'developmental sequence' or 'order of acquisition' (Brown 1973; Burt and Dulay 1980; Wode 1981; Felix 1982a; Clahsen et al. 1983).[2] The fundamental observation is that children acquire the structural properties of the language they are exposed to in a severely constrained temporal order. A given structure will emerge only after a specific set of other structures has previously been acquired. For illustration see Table 1 which shows some stages in the acquisition of English and German negation.

The following aspects of the data illustrated in Table 1 seem to be particularly significant with respect to the developmental problem of language acquisition:

1) the acquisition process is highly systematic in the sense that certain properties of this process hold across languages and across learners.

TABLE 1. Some early stages in the acquisition of negation
(Source: Bloom 1970, Klima and Bellugi 1971, Wode 1977, Felix 1978)

	English	German	
Stage I (Neg + S)	no the sun shining	nein hauen	(don't bang)
	no Daddy hungry	nein schaffe ich	(I can't manage)
	no see truck	nein spielen Katze	(I don't want to play with the cat)
Stage II (no/nein + VP)	Kathryn no like celery	ich nein schlafen	(I don't sleep)
	I no reach it	das nein aua	(that doesn't hurt)
	man go in there	ich nein hat eins	(I don't have one)
Stage III (not/nicht + V) (don't + V) (V + nicht)	Kathryn not go over here	ich nicht essen mehr	(I don't eat any more)
	I don't go sleep	Eric nicht schlafen	(Eric doesn't sleep)
	this one don't fits	Hennig braucht nicht Uni	(Hennig need not (go) to the university)

2) language acquisition proceeds in developmental stages, i.e. a given structure is used consistently and regularly for a certain period of time and is then replaced by some other structure.

3) the sequence of stages is ordered; i.e. the structure(s) characterizing any stage x emerge(s) only after the structure(s) characterizing stage $x - 1$ has/have been productively used.

4) children make regular use of constructions which are ungrammatical from the point of view of the adult language, i.e. they produce structures which do not reflect rules of the input language in any direct way.

Because of their largely invariant nature it has been widely assumed that the regularities expressed in the developmental sequences reflect properties of the human mind, rather than properties of the environment in which the individual grows up. More specifically, the basic developmental pattern illustrated in Table 1 is seen as something that specific properties of human mental organization impose on the acquisition process.

Keeping in mind such invariant developmental patterns we can now restate the developmental problem in a somewhat more precise way: why does language acquisition proceed by ordered sequences of stages? Why do developmental sequences look the way they do?

I believe that there are two fundamental aspects to the question of why the developmental process is structured in the way outlined above. First, we may ask where those of the child's constructions come from that do not exist in the adult language. Why is it that children use sentence-external negation, even though there are no such structures in the speech they hear? What motivates the child to create sentences such as 'Tommy no like milk' in the absence of any input forcing such a construction? The second aspect has to do with the fact that, at regular intervals, children move from one stage to the next. We may reasonably wonder why this is so. What is it that causes the child to give up a structure, e.g. 'NP no verb-phrase', which he has been perfectly happy with for an extended period of time?

As far as I know, most serious attempts to explain the developmental aspect of language acquisition have focused on the first question, presumably because most researchers felt that the answer to the second problem is fairly self-evident. However, I will attempt to show that it is the stage-transition phenomenon which, under current conceptions of language acquisition, is the most challenging aspect of the developmental problem.

To my knowledge there are two types of traditional answers to the question of why children move from one stage to another. The first has to do with what is commonly referred to as the communicative function of language. The child's linguistic progress, so the argument runs, is propelled by his deep-rooted desire to become a fully adequate member of the society in which he grows up. Since the ability to communicate effectively is an indispensible prerequisite for proper social functioning, the child will constantly strive to improve his communicative skills – i.e. move to the higher stages of language acquisition – so that eventually he will be accepted as an equal member of his society (for an explication of this view see Bates and MacWhinney 1982; Bates et al. 1983).

I believe that there are a number of problems with this view. If the acquisition of grammar is crucially motivated by each child's individual desire to function appropriately in society, then one should find significant variations in children's ultimate grammatical competence, since individual learners may obviously differ with respect to their inclination to adjust to social needs and requirements.

Moreover, if it is only his desire for effective communication that instigates aquisitional progress, then, of course, we should expect the child to be satisfied with much less than he actually attains. This fact was first pointed out by Lenneberg (1967, 1969). While aspects of communicative effectiveness might plausibly be addressed to explain the very early stages of language acquisition, they are certainly not a very convincing argument when it comes to later stages. From a point of view of communicative effectiveness, it is difficult to see why a child should learn all the intricate morphological, phonological and syntactic patterns that are a fundamental property of all natural languages.

Most importantly, however, the view that acquisitional progress is a function of the child's desire to communicate effectively seems to be difficult to reconcile with the fact that acquisition proceeds by developmental stages. Let us assume, for the sake of the argument, that the child's desire to improve his communicative skills is, in fact, the only crucial force behind language development. For illustration, consider once again the acquisition of negation outlined in Table 1. Suppose the child has used sentence-external negation for a couple of months after which he replaces this construction type by sentence-internal negation. Conceivably one might argue that this transition from Stage I to Stage II reflects the child's growing awareness that, in order to enhance his communicative skills, his language must be more 'adult-like'. But now the question arises why the child continuously used the same original structure for an extended period of time in the first place? Did he ignore his communicative needs for a couple of months, suddenly realizing that it would be communicatively more useful to produce a different type of structure? Or is it that his linguistic awareness develops in stages? But if this is the case, how can this phenomenon be explained in terms of communication? One might furthermore ask why the child uses sentence-internal negation – as an intermediate structure – at all? It is difficult to see in what sense 'Johnny no like milk' is communicatively more effective than 'no Johnny like milk'. And why does the child retain this new construction type again for an extended period of time? Does he suddenly disregard his communicative needs again? That is, why does the child's desire to be communicatively effective come in stages? From these considerations it seems fairly clear that aspects of communication, while obviously being influential, cannot fully and adequately account for the stage-transition problem of language acquisition.

There is another fairly popular view about children's linguistic progress which underlies much current work in language acquisition. In a very simplified version, the relevant argument goes something like this: on the basis of the available input the child formulates certain hypotheses about the structure of the language he is exposed to, i.e. he constructs a (fragmentary) grammar of that language in his own ways. The child will subsequently compare the utterances generated by his own grammar with those of the adult language and will thereby find out that – at least with respect to some structures – his grammar is in conflict with the adult grammar. He will then proceed to revise his grammar in such a way that it will be either identical or at least closer to the adult grammar.

I doubt very much that this story will turn out to be true. The view of language acquisition as nothing but a continuous process of simply testing hypotheses against adult output presupposes a satisfactory answer to a problem, for which, as far as I know, nobody has so far offered an adequate solution; namely, how does a child find out, in a principled way, if the rules of his own grammar are in conflict with those of the adult language.

I believe the reason nobody has given much serious attention to this question is simply that prima facie the answer is obvious: the child finds out that his grammar is in conflict with the adult grammar by comparing his own utterances with those produced in his environment. But upon closer examination it becomes clear that this answer cannot possibly be correct. The reason is essentially the same that has led researchers to reject the view that language acquisition is a process of inductive generalization. For ease of illustration let us consider again the negation data. How does the child find out that the type of sentence-external negation he uses at Stage I is not a grammatical structure in adult English? One might be inclined to answer that the child will come to know this simply because he never hears anybody in his environment use such construction. But for both empirical and logical reasons this answer turns out to be incorrect. Speakers are able to judge the grammaticality even of those structures that they never heard before. Recalling past experience or exposure cannot possibly be a basis for grammaticality judgements. Suppose the child were to accept as grammatical only those of his own structures that he hears other speakers in his environment use. In this case he could obviously acquire only a finite body of structures, thereby failing to achieve full competence of his language which encompasses knowledge of an infinite set of structures. Still worse, at least during the early stages the child could not accept any of his structures as grammatical since they are all in conflict with the adult language. Under such circumstances one might expect the child to revise his grammar continuously; however, as I have emphasized before, language development proceeds by stages, so that one might wonder what makes the child ignore the available conflicting evidence during the time within each stage. Finally, it is far from obvious in what sense comparing his own grammar with the adult language should force the child to move from sentence-external to sentence-internal negation rather than the other way around. Both construction types are totally unacceptable from the point of view of the adult language, so that the child will never be exposed to either one.

As far as I can see, there is only one type of evidence that would tell the child unambiguously that a given structure is ungrammatical; namely, if somebody came along and told him so, i.e. if the child had access to negative evidence. There are two problems with this story. First, there is little reason to suppose that children do have systematic access to negative evidence. Even though adults correct children's utterances once in a while, they do not do so regularly or consistently, in which case it would be a matter of pure chance whether or not the child found out the ungrammaticality of a given structure. More importantly, there are various reports in the literature (see Smith 1973; Brown 1973) showing that children tend to simply ignore adult's statements of correction. That is, even if the child did have regular access to negative evidence, apparently he could not care less.

A somewhat different solution is offered by White (1982). One of the central claims in White's work is that child grammars are *possible grammars*. That is, child grammars fall within the limits imposed by Universal Grammar in exactly the same way as adult grammars. The class of humanly accessible grammars does not only include all existing mature languages but also *all* grammars that characterize the child's linguistic knowledge at *any* stage of his development. This view implies that a child grammar will never violate any principle of Universal Grammar though, of course, individual parameters may still be undetermined.

White continues to argue that a grammar is obviously always a grammar of something and this something is a certain set of data. It is self-evident that the child does not construct an optimal grammar as such, but only an optimal grammar for a certain set of data. As soon as the data change, the one-time optimal grammar will no longer be optimal, but has to be replaced by a new grammar which, again, is optimal for the new set of data. This is White's central idea. Consequently, she argues, while the child constructs an optimal grammar at each stage, he will perceive the linguistic input differently at different stages. The child will construct an optimal grammar for the data he perceives, and as soon as his perception of the data changes he will construct a new, again optimal grammar for the new set of data. The fact that the child moves from one stage to the next is thus a matter of changing perception:

> The child at one stage will construct a grammar for the data of that stage; at another stage he will construct a different grammar. Both will be optimal representations of the child's linguistic knowledge at each stage. Therefore, one must assume that the child's perception of the data changes. Despite apparently similar *input* data at different stages, the child's *intake* actually varies (due to maturational factors, increasing memory, etc.). The child's perception of the data is different from the adult's. The grammar that he comes up with will be optimal for his own perception of the data, i.e. the relevant triggering experience, and the grammar that emerges at any given stage can provide us with a clue as to how he reacts to the data. (1981, 247–8)

Note, first of all, that White's view is a fairly specific proposal as to how to solve the stage-transition problem, i.e. to explain why children move from one stage to the next. According to White the temporal aspect of language development has nothing to do with principles of Universal Grammar, parameter-fixing and the like, but is strictly a matter of perception. It is only *after* perception has changed that Universal Grammar comes into play.

I believe that there are a number of serious problems with this story. In the absence of any specific proposals as to what the principles look like that cause perceptual changes, White's view remains largely mysterious and is essentially question-begging. By viewing language development largely as a restructuring process in which the child constructs optimal grammars for differently and independently perceived sets of data, White places the solution to the developmental problem, in particular the stage-transition aspect, outside the domain of the theory of grammar; more specifically, into the domain of the theory of perception.

Note, first of all, that White's theory of perceptual changes essentially amounts to claiming that there is some kind of perceptual mechanism that converts an adult utterance into the corresponding child structure. It is only *after* this conversion that principles of Universal Grammar (as well as any other mechanisms of structural analysis) begin to operate. That is, when an adult says something like 'Johnny doesn't like ice-cream' the child will *perceive* this utterance as 'no Johnny like ice-cream' and it is this latter structure that is the input to the language-acquisition device. While obviously not impossible in principle, it is difficult to see – considering what is generally known about perceptual mechanisms – how this type of structure-conversion should work in detail. Note furthermore that White's view is merely a logically necessary consequence of her claim that child grammars are possible grammars, a claim that is, I believe, independent of the parameter view of language acquisition as developed by Chomsky (1981c).

Let us suppose, for the sake of the argument, that there is, in fact a set of principles such that they determine the child's specific perception of the speech input. The crucial question is whether or not it can be shown that these principles are language-independent and must therefore be spelled out in the theory of (auditory) perception, rather than in the theory of grammar. There is little doubt that some such perceptual principles do exist. For example, there seems to be a principle of salience (cf. Smith 1973) which captures the fact that signals with certain acoustic properties are more easily perceivable than others. This principle is truly perceptual in the sense that it operates not only in language acquisition but also in many other kinds of auditory perception. It is thus a principle of the theory of perception which interacts with, but does not belong to the theory of grammar. I doubt very much if those principles that determine the child's early perception of linguistic structures along the line suggested by White are principles of the theory of perception in this sense. The reason is simply that the relevant principles must make crucial reference to grammatical facts. They must be able to distinguish between 'no' and 'not', between different syntactic positions, between syntactic categories such as subject or verb phrase, etc. If this is the case, however, then these principles are not principles of the theory of perception but rather principles of the theory of grammar (unless, of course, one assumes that the properties of language can be reduced to general properties of perception). Consequently they cannot simply be dismissed from considerations concerning the interaction of Universal Grammar and developmental phenomena.

While White attempts to remove the stage-transition problem from the domain of Universal Grammar by assigning it to the level of perception, it seems to me that this attempt is presumably misguided. In dealing with the child's (linguistic) knowledge at different developmental stages and how this knowledge changes we are concerned with genuinely linguistic questions and thus with the theory of grammar. It certainly doesn't come as a surprise that the child's grammatical knowledge determines his linguistic perception, rather than the other way around. Consequently White's view, too, fails to give a principled answer to the original question: what is it that makes the child realize that a given structure which served him nicely for an extended period of time, is inadequate, so that he will move to the next developmental stage?

I would like to emphasize again that the only reason for these problems in White's account is the initial assumption that child grammars must be possible grammars (in the technical sense), an assumption that may be true, but is by no means a logical necessity even under a parameter view of language acquisition. It seems that many aspects of language development make much more sense if we give up this assumption, an idea which I will explore in the following section.

3. The Maturational Schedule of Universal Grammar

In the preceding two sections I have argued that there are two fundamental problems with which any adequate explanatory theory of language (acquisition) has to deal: the *logical* problem of language acquisition which focuses on the question of why children are able to acquire language at all, and the *developmental* problem of language acquisition which relates to the question of why children acquire language the way they do. I have tried to demonstrate that one of the most interesting phenomena within the developmental problem concerns the stage-transition aspect of language acquisition: how do children manage to realize, in a principled way, that structures they have used productively for an extended period of time are ungrammatical in terms of the adult grammar? This insight is obviously a prerequisite to the formulation of a new set of rules and therefore to the emergence of a new developmental stage.

Of course, it is logically conceivable that two different and unrelated sets of principles need to be invoked to provide an adequate answer to each of the problems outlined above. That is, one might think of one set of principles (Universal Grammar) responding to the logical problem of language acquisition and a further independent set of principles which explains why children pass through an ordered sequence of developmental stages of the type illustrated and discussed in section 2. It seems to me that, in the past, most researchers have implicitly assumed that such a view is, in fact, the correct one. Discussions on the conceptual basis of Universal Grammar have usually focused on the logical problem (see Chomsky 1965, 1976, 1981c; Hornstein and Lightfoot 1981; Lightfoot 1982), while psycholinguists have, for the most part, tried to specify a different set of principles that were meant to account for the developmental aspect of language acquisition (see Slobin 1973; Clark and Haviland 1974; Marantz 1982; Clahsen 1982).

Under a somewhat different approach one might easily conceive of the possibility of handling both problem domains by the same set of principles. Note, first of all, that it is entirely a matter of empirical fact whether one or two sets of principles are needed to cope with the logical *and* the developmental aspect of language acquisition. On the other hand, it would clearly be preferable, on a priori grounds, to find a solution in which both aspects are adequately accounted for by one and the same set of principles. The reason for this a priori preference is simply the following: if we can show that the

141

principles of Universal Grammar are structured in such a way that also developmental regularities will follow from them, we thereby attribute more structure but less material to the child's genetic program. It is this option that I wish to explore in the present section.

The leading idea behind the proposal I wish to make is that the principles of Universal Grammar are themselves subject to an innately specified developmental process. While I retain the traditional idea that Universal Grammar constitutes the child's genetically determined a priori knowledge about the structure of humanly possible languages, I will suggest that during the developmental process the various principles of Universal Grammar will successively emerge and thus become operative in a specific temporal order. That is, although the set of universal principles is fully and exhaustively specified by the child's genetic program, each of these principles is somehow 'latent' up to a specific point in time after which it will start to operate and thus constrain the child's knowledge of what may be a humanly accessible language. Most crucially, I will suggest that the sequence in which the various principles of Universal Grammar emerge does not reflect any externally determined factors in the child's linguistic experience, but rather is itself an inherent part of the genetic program. Under this view the unfolding of the genetic program that characterizes the child's language faculty resembles very closely the genetic program determining the child's physical growth. While it is uncontroversial that the crucial physical properties of human organisms are genetically determined, it is, at the same time, clear that many of these properties do not emerge until a specific point in the child's bodily development. In this sense I wish to suggest that the genetic program which determines the child's language-related mental growth incorporates two facts: a set of constraints on possible mental representations and a maturational schedule for the emergence of these constraints.

Let us assume, in the spirit of this suggestion, that there is a set of principles $P_1, P_2, P_3 \ldots P_n$ – technically known as Universal Grammar – which constrains the class of humanly accessible languages. Let us furthermore assume that the relevant genetic program contains a maturational schedule which specifies a sequence of points in time $t_1, t_2, t_3 \ldots t_n$, where $j > i$ implies that t_j is later in real time than t_i. Under an appropriate idealization of this view[3] I will assume that there is a one-to-one correspondence between the principles of Universal Grammar and the sequence of points in time such that, for any i, t_i specifies the point in time at which the constraint expressed by P_i emerges and thus becomes available for the construction of grammar. This view crucially implies that at any stage t_i the child's grammar construction will be constrained by a set of principles bearing indices $\leq i$ while at the same time the structures which the child uses may violate principles bearing indices greater than i.

Ignoring details for the moment, the fundamental idea behind this view is that the various principles of Universal Grammar will successively emerge according to a specific maturational schedule so that at any stage of the development the child's grammar construction will be guided (or rather constrained) by a proper subset of universal principles; i.e. those that the maturational schedule has already made operative, while at the same time all those principles which are still 'latent' at that stage, may be violated. If this view is correct, in principle, then it becomes fairly obvious why and under what conditions the child will restructure his grammar and thus pass to the next higher stage. What makes the child realize that his grammar needs to be restructured is simply the emergence of a new principle, which his present grammar violates. Suppose that at some stage the child's grammar violates a principle P_i. According to the innately specified maturational schedule P_i will then emerge at some specific point in time making the child realize that his grammar is in conflict with a constraint of Universal Grammar. He will therefore have to restructure his grammar in such a way that it will henceforth meet the constraints expressed by P_i. That is to say, the observable sequence of developmental stages reflects the maturational schedule that brings in the principles of Universal Grammar one after the other.[4] What makes the child realize that something is wrong with his present grammar is neither a matter of perception nor of specific input data, but rather the emergence of a new principle of Universal Grammar, and it is this newly available principle which also tells the child which input data are relevant and which are not.

Whether or not this view of language development is, in fact, true, has to be regarded as an entirely empirical question. If the basic idea is correct, then it should be possible to show that at some early stage the child's grammar violates a specific principle of Universal Grammar, while the immediately following stage instantiates a restructuring process in which the child reorganizes his grammar in accordance with the principle as it has just become operative. In other words, we should find evidence in developmental data for the maturation of principles of Universal Grammar.

I will now look at some fairly well-known developmental data and try to show that the stage-transition aspect can, in fact, be regarded as reflecting the emergence of various principles of Universal Grammar. Note, however, that, in this attempt we are facing a problem of a predominately technical nature. Most of the principles of Universal Grammar that have been proposed in the literature relate to fairly complex structures which children do not use until relatively late stages in their development, while the majority of developmental studies have focused on the earlier stages of language acquisition. It is therefore far from obvious how some of the better established principles of Universal Grammar can be taken to account for the development of such early structures. In order to obtain a more precise understanding of how Universal Grammar and language development interact, it would be necessary to either have more detailed accounts of later developmental stages or to identify those principles of Universal Grammar that are relevant also for structures of very limited complexity.

In view of this problem the following account will be both highly selective and tentative. However, it seems to me that some of the basic notions in linguistic theory are already reflected in early child grammar and I will therefore try to demonstrate how the corresponding principles might account for the stage-transition aspect of language development.

Let us first of all look at some developmental data from the very earliest stages of language acquisition. It is customary in the psycholinguistic literature to refer to the early stage in which children produce the first multi-word utterances as the two-word stage or three-word stage, since children's sentences do not usually contain more than two or three words. Some such utterances taken from Miller and Ervin (1964), Bloom (1970, 1973), Brown and Fraser (1963), Braine (1963) are the following:

1) allgone shoe	11) see ball
2) allgone outside	12) want baby
3) bye bye man	13) want up
4) night-night hot	14) want bye bye car
5) night-night boat	15) there ball
6) more book	16) there high
7) more write	17) here more paper
8) other milk	18) hat off
9) no dirty	19) off bib
10) no down	20) that yellow

What is immediately striking about these utterances is that, from the point of view of the adult grammar, they do not seem to exhibit consistently any of the familiar syntactic patterns based on common grammatical notions such as subject, object, NP, verb phrase, etc. It appears that in forming these sentences children use construction principles of a fundamentally different nature from those of the adult language. It was Bloom (1970, 1973) who first suggested that children's early two-word and three-word utterances are not formed on the basis of *syntactic* rules, but encode *semantic* or rather *conceptual* relations; i.e. the child's first grammar maps directly from semantic relations to their surface expressions without any intervening grammatical level. One of the crucial observations is that in the earliest two-word stage every utterance obligatorily contains a function word such as *more, another, no, here, bye bye, allgone, want,* etc. which expresses an inherently relational concept; children combine anyone of these relational words with items out of a class of different words denoting objects, actions, properties and the like. The resulting phrase or sentence expresses the scope of the relation with respect to the non-relational word:

> Their [=the children's] early syntax, then, would appear to depend on the linguistic induction that such function words combine with other words in a direct and linear relation, and the meaning relation between the two words derives from the meaning of the function word. There is a linear one-to-one correspondence between the meaning of such words and the relational meanings between such words combined with other words. (Bloom 1973, 116)

144

In a comprehensive review of the then available literature Brown (1973, 178) concludes that 'learning to express a small set of semantic relations and their combination constitutes the principal work of Stage I'. Some such semantic relations that develop at Stage I are: agent-action; entity-locative; possessor-possession; etc. The child's earliest construction principles are thus semantic (or perhaps conceptual) in nature. The child forms semantic rather than syntactic categories, and the way in which words are combined to form more complex utterances is guided by semantic, not grammatical rules.

To my knowledge this view is fairly uncontroversial among psycholinguists, at least as far as the factual observations are concerned (see also Brown 1973; Bowerman 1973; Schlesinger 1974). I will therefore assume that it is essentially correct, i.e. the child's grammar during the two-word and three-word stage is based on a small set of semantic categories which enter into combinations that express semantic relations. We may formalize this view in something like the following way (for ease of exposition let us focus on utterances with function words as described by Bloom): Children form a lexical category R containing only words which inherently express a relation (no, more, here, want, etc.). R is thus semantically defined. Since R is the obligatory constituent in the relevant multi-word structures, we may assume that R forms the head of any construction in which it occurs. That is, R can take a certain range of complements which may be categories of different types that are again semantically defined (objects, actions, events, etc.). If this approach is correct then there will be a phrasal category RP (Relation Phrase) such that RP is some projection of R. (Whether or not RP is the maximal projection of R in the sense that there are 'intermediate' projections of R dominated by RP is an empirical question which need not concern us here.)

For a sentence such as 'here more paper' we thus obtain the following structure:

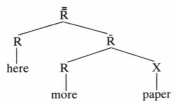

In a similar way we may look at other semantic relations, e.g. agent-action or entity-locative, as being projections of a semantically defined head category.

Let us assume that this view of early child grammar is correct, in essence. The interesting question is, of course, how things develop from here. Bloom is somewhat vague about this point. While she explicitly argues that 'cognitive categories do not develop in a one-to-one correspondence with mental linguistic categories' (1973, 121), she does not make any specific proposal as to how exactly syntactic categories and grammatical relations evolve from a rule system based on semantic notions. Nevertheless she does assume that children will have to replace the notion of semantic relation by the concept of grammatical relation in order to acquire full competence of the adult language.

A different approach is pursued by Schlesinger (1974). Since children start out with semantic relations, Schlesinger argues, and it is not conceivable how they could discover the concept of grammatical relation, we are forced to conclude that natural languages (adult grammars) are not really syntactic objects, but rather that what appear to be grammatical relations are reducible to semantic facts. I will not discuss Schlesinger's view any further, because I feel that it is fundamentally misconceived. While one might possibly argue that even later stages in child language development are semantically based I do not see how, in the face of three decades of extensive syntactic research, anyone could seriously maintain the view that (adult) grammars are purely semantic (for a detailed critique see also Marantz 1982).

We are thus facing the following situation. While the earliest child grammars are based on *semantic* categories and exclusively express *semantic* relations, adult grammars crucially contain *syntactic* categories and encode *grammatical* relations. Consequently the child has to discover at some stage that his original semantically based grammar is somehow misconceived, and that formal syntactic categories and grammatical relations are what needs to be encoded in his grammar. The question is: how does the child find this out?

It seems to me that this question cannot be adequately answered by appealing exclusively to the input that the child receives. Note first of all that many of the child's utterances are perfectly well-formed from the adult point of view or could be interpreted in terms of grammatical relations. If Bloom's story is correct, however, then a sentence such as 'want baby' does not represent a verb-object relation, but rather a R+Complement relation, where 'want' belongs to the same lexical category as 'more, allgone, here,' etc., but to a different category from 'write' or 'eat'. Thus the child's grammar will permit strings such as 'want up' or 'want hot' which are ungrammatical as a verb-object relation. As a consequence the child will discover that some of his utterances occur also in adult speech, while others do not. However, this discovery as such, should not affect the child's grammar construction, since, for reasons outlined in section 2, the non-occurrence of child structures in adult speech cannot be taken as disconfirming evidence for the child rules. Consequently there is nothing in the input that tells the child, in a principled way, that he is on the wrong track.

In the spirit of the ideas outlined above I would like to suggest that it is a principle of Universal Grammar emerging some time at the end of the two-word/three-word stage that tells the child that his present grammar is somehow misconceived. Once the principle has emerged in accordance with the maturational schedule the child's grammar will violate a principle of Universal Grammar and this is what forces the child to give up his original constructions and restructure his grammar. That is, restructuring is a process to bring the child's rule system in line with Universal Grammar.

Notice first of all that, in a very intuitive sense, early child grammars of the type outlined above do not appear to be possible grammars in White's sense. If it is an essential, i.e. biologically necessary property of human languages that they are syntactic rather than purely semantic objects then semantically based child grammars do not qualify as possible grammars, in an obvious sense.

The principle (or possibly set of principles) which, I would like to suggest, forces the child to restructure his grammar at the end of the two-word/three-word stage is the $\bar{X}$-schema. If it is true that the $\bar{X}$-schema specifies constraints in the class of humanly accessible grammars, then this schema will require any natural language to have – among other things – the following properties:

a) there are only four lexical categories that may enter into the projection of phrasal categories, namely noun, verb, adjective and preposition. That is, any phrasal category must have one of these and only these lexical categories as its head.

b) in the unmarked case, complements occur uniformly either to the right or to the left of the head (for details see Stowell 1981). That is, if in a language the complements of prepositions occur to the right, then the complements of *all* other lexical categories (noun, verb, adjective) will occur to the right. For left expansions the same holds respectively. In other words, constituents in a sentence cannot occur in random order.

Let us assume that as part of the genetic program's maturational schedule the $\bar{X}$-schema emerges some months after the onset of the two-word/three-word stage. Until that point in time the child has used a semantically-based grammar of the type outlined above. As soon as the $\bar{X}$-schema becomes operative, the child will realize that his current grammar is in conflict with constraints specifying the class of humanly accessible languages. First, the child's grammar contains – among other things – a lexical category R which enters into a phrasal projection RP. Such a projection, however, is ruled out by the $\bar{X}$-schema, since only noun, verb, adjective and preposition may be heads of phrasal categories. Furthermore the $\bar{X}$-schema requires a certain canonical order within each phrasal category, while the order in the child's grammar is free. This conflict between the child's grammar and the structural requirements imposed by principles of Universal Grammar initiates a process of re-structuring through which the child brings his rule system in line with a new set of constraints. In the case under discussion the child will abandon the rule(s) of RP-expansion and replace it/them by rules operating on 'permissible' phrasal categories such as NP, verb-phrase, adjectival-phrase and prepositional-phrase.[5] This restructur-

147

ing process will lead to a new developmental stage in which sentences encode grammatical relations as specified by the X̱-schema rather than purely semantic relations.

I would now like to turn to a set of data for which I hope to show how a number of successively emerging principles of Universal Grammar can explain an observable order of developmental stages. The phenomena I wish to examine concern the acquisition of word order in German. One interesting aspect of German word order is that main clauses have subject-verb-object, while embedded clauses have subject-object-verb, order. For reasons which are extensively discussed in the literature (see Ross 1970; Maling 1972; Koster 1975; Kohrt 1976; Bartsch et al. 1977; Thiersch 1978), it is generally assumed that the base-generated order corresponds to the one in embedded clauses, i.e. subject-object-verb. A transformational rule, commonly called Verb-Second, applies to main clauses and moves the finite verb into a 'second' position, yielding subject-verb-object (for details see Lenerz 1977; Thiersch 1978; Safir 1982; Sternefeld 1982). I will assume without further discussion that this story is essentially correct.

The question then arises: how do children learning German manage to acquire these facts? One of the crucial observations is that during the earliest developmental stage in which sentences contain subjects, verbs, and objects, children use a large variety of different word orders. There is some disagreement in the literature as to how extensive this variety is: Park (1974) presents evidence suggesting that *all* logically possible orders do, in fact, occur, while Clahsen (1982) argues that, even though there is no fixed linear order of constituents, verb-initial patterns do not occur.

Since it is difficult to decide between Clahsen's and Park's story without any further data, we have to leave the question unsettled at this point. What is crucial in the present context, however, is merely that, in simple declarative sentences, children use patterns other than subject-object-verb and subject-verb-object. Considering the input children receive, this variable word order does not seem surprising, since on the surface German does, in fact, exhibit (nearly) all logically possible patterns:

21) SVO main clauses
22) SOV embedded clauses
23) VSO yes/no questions
24) VOS marginal in yes/no questions
25) OSV object relative clauses
26) OVS object topicalization

If the child merely responded to the various surface word orders that occur in adult speech, he might conclude that German has random constituent order, and this is exactly what children seem to be doing during the earliest stage. The interesting aspect in this case is the child's further development which I will describe relying on Clahsen's (1982) and Clahsen and Muysken's (1983) account.

According to Clahsen the prominent feature of Stage II is that the children discontinue to produce free constituent order and use randomly subject-object-verb or subject-verb-object with finite verb forms and subject-object-verb with non-finite verb forms. At Stage III finite verb forms stabilize to subject-verb-object, while non-finite verb forms continue to occur only with subject-object-verb. This is essentially the correct adult situation, where complex verbals are 'split':

27) Hans trinkt ein Bier
    'John drinks a beer'
28) Hans hat ein Bier getrunken
    'John has a beer drunken'

Clahsen furthermore observes that children never make word order mistakes in embedded clauses, where they always place the verbal element(s) correctly in final position, so that the relevant rules seem to be firmly established by the time embedded clauses emerge.

Under a somewhat simplified perspective we are thus facing the following developmental situation: children learning German begin with variable constituent order; at the subsequent stage they restrict word orders to subject-object-verb and subject-verb-object which they partially use randomly. At the final stage they discover that subject-object-verb rather than subject-verb-object is the underlying word order, and simultaneously learn the rule of Verb-Second for main clauses. Once these rules are learned, we do not find any errors either in embedded clauses or in split verbals in main clauses. Given this development two questions call for an explanation: what makes the child select subject-object-verb and subject-verb-object as the correct order in simple declarative sentences (transition from Stage I to Stage II) and why does he subsequently choose subject-object-verb rather than subject-verb-object as the underlying word order?

As in the previous case I do not believe that these questions can be adequately answered by appealing alone to the child's input. As far as the word orders are concerned that the child actually hears, subject-object-verb and subject-verb-object have no privileged status; consequently there is nothing in the data that should *force* the child to restrict word orders to subject-object-verb and subject-verb-object at Stage II. In much the same way the input itself does not tell the child that subject-object-verb rather than subject-verb-object is the underlying word order (transition from Stage II to Stage III). In fact, logically the child has two options: either subject-verb-object is the underlying order in which case a rule of Verb-Final applies in embedded clauses and in split verbals; or subject-object-verb is the underlying order with a rule of Verb-Second applying in main clauses. As the developmental data indicate, children consistently choose the latter option.

I would like to suggest that the restriction of word orders at Stage II

149

reflects the maturational emergence of the X̄-schema (or rather one specific aspect thereof), while the choice of underlying subject-object-verb over subject-verb-object can be explained in terms of the notion *government* and of Emonds' (1976) Structure Preserving Principle which emerge some time after the X̄-schema becomes operative.

As already outlined in the previous case the X̄-schema incorporates – among other things – two restrictions: the first limits the choice of lexical categories that may enter categorial projections (i.e. noun, verb, adjective and preposition), while the second concerns possible word orders. It is this latter constraint of the X̄-schema which, I will suggest, explains the transition from Stage I to Stage II. Recall that the X̄-schema constrains constituent order through the notion of 'maximal projection'. Each maximal projection constitutes some kind of a 'closed' domain consisting of a head and its complement, such that complements appear either to the left or to the right of their lexical heads. In other words, the order of lexical heads and their complements is constrained in some specific way, so that base rules generating random word order are excluded in principle. It thus follows from the X̄-schema that in the case of the verb phrase as the maximal projection of the verb the object must occur either directly to the left or directly to the right of the verbal head and cannot be separated from the verb by material which does not belong to the verb phrase. I would therefore like to suggest that, with the maturational emergence of the X̄-schema, the child will know that the base-generated order of constituents must be in some way constrained. To put it differently, the child receiving input from a language such as German which permits a wide range of different surface orders will be forced to conclude that some of the orders are base-generated, while others are the result of movement. More specifically, the X̄-schema will 'tell' the child that base-generated word orders can be only those in which the object is directly adjacent to the verb.[6] That is, all orders in which the subject separates the object from its verb must be derived via movement.

Returning to the six different word orders that the child used at Stage I, the maturational emergence of the X̄-schema will thus rule out verb-subject-object and object-subject-verb as base-generated strings. We may also conjecture that, due to its marginal status, the child will not consider verb-object-subject as a possible base-generated word order. Consequently, the X̄-schema constrains the number of possible underlying word orders to three combinations of subject, verb, and object: subject-verb-object, subject-object-verb, and object-verb-subject. As the developmental data indicate the child does, in fact, limit his use of word orders to subject-verb-object and subject-object-verb at Stage II. Under the present reasoning we would also expect object-verb-subject to occur, which, however, is not the case. At present I have no explanation for this fact; one might, however, speculate on why the child also rejects object-verb-subject as an underlying word order. Since both subject-verb-object and subject-object-verb show subject-initial position whereas object-verb-subject has the subject in final position the child may be led to conclude, on the basis of some kind of majority consideration, that the subject initial-position is the correct one. We may also conjecture that, by some principle of Universal Grammar, object-verb-subject is simply not a possible base-generated word order of human languages.[7] Whatever the correct solution may be, it is clear that the X̄-schema constrains the number of possible underlying word orders in natural languages. Since the developmental data indicate that children move from a stage of nearly random word order to a stage of more restricted word order we may account for this fact by assuming that the X̄-schema, as a principle of Universal Grammar, emerges at some time after the onset of language development and thus tells the child that languages simply do not permit random constituent order in the phrase-structure component.

Let us look at the same facts from a somewhat different perspective. It is well-known that in natural languages word order and morphological case correlate in a specific way. Languages with relatively fixed word order such as English, French, Italian, etc. usually do not have a well-developed system of morphological case-marking, whereas languages with an overt case system such as German, Russian, Japanese, etc. generally show relatively unconstrained word order combinations. Let us assume that this distribution is non-accidental. Suppose furthermore that abstract Case can only be assigned under some very strict condition of adjacency in the spirit of Stowell (1981). If a language does not simultaneously mark cases morphologically, then the order of constituents under which abstract Case is assigned must, in principle, be preserved at sentence-structure because otherwise case relations could not be properly identified. If, in contrast, cases are morphologically marked, then some kind of scrambling rule can freely re-arrange constituents without destroying proper case-identification. It may be reasonable to assume that the principle specifying the correlation between word order and overt case-marking is part of Case Theory and thus of Universal Grammar.

If this view is correct in essence, then we may explain the children's development in the following way. Free word order is only possible if cases are morphologically marked, otherwise fixed word order is obligatory. At Stage I children use free word order even though NPs are not morphologically marked for case. By the relevant principles of Case Theory such a grammar does not qualify as a possible human language. If we assume that Case Theory maturationally emerges at some specific point in time, we will predict that at exactly this point the child will realize that his current grammar which permits free word order without morphological case-marking violates principles of Universal Grammar. As a consequence, the child will, in the absence of morphological case, constrain the number of possible underlying word orders in such a way that objects are always adjacent to the verb from which they receive (abstract) Case. Under this

151

view, subject-verb-object, subject-object-verb and object-verb-subject will again qualify as the only possible underlying word orders.

To summarize, after the maturational emergence of the X̄-schema and, possibly, Case Theory the child will have to restructure his grammar in such a way that only subject-verb-object and subject-object-verb will be base-generated, since all other orders would violate principles of Universal Grammar. We will now have to explain the transition from Stage II to Stage III, i.e. why the child eventually opts for subject-object-verb rather than subject-verb-object as the underlying word order, deriving the main clause order by a movement rule. Note that there are actually two aspects involved in the transition from Stage II to Stage III. First, the child has to realize that it is not possible to have two different base-generated word orders, but rather that only one order can be base-generated with the other order derived through movement. Secondly, the child has to find out which is which.

It seems to be a tacit assumption in generative grammar – rarely stated explicitly – that the base component of a grammar generates only *one* underlying order so that all other orders which may appear on the surface are the result of movement rules. If this is correct, then it seems clear that a grammar base-generating two different word orders does not qualify as a humanly accessible grammar, in an intuitively obvious sense. The question is whether or not this assumption can be related to some principle of Universal Grammar. I believe that the relevant principle is the notion of Government. It can be shown that the government relation works always into one and only one direction. Consider the following German structures which G. Fanselow called to my attention:

29) ein hübsches Mädchen
    a pretty girl
30) ein Mädchen hübsch
    a girl pretty

(29) represents the standard article-adjective-noun sequence in German. Crucially the adjective *hübsches* carries the inflectional ending *-es* through which the adjective agrees in gender and number with the noun *Mädchen*. Following standard assumptions we may say that the noun governs the adjective thereby assigning an agreement marker to it. Now observe the contrast in (30), a structure which has a definitely archaic and/or poetic flavour. Here the adjective occurs to right of the noun and crucially carries no agreement marker. If we assume that government works only into one direction, this contrast can be readily explained. Since government goes to the left in German the adjective in (29) receives its agreement marker, while in (30) the adjective appears in a neutral form.

Returning to the word order case, it is clear that the notion of government as specified above, predicts that a grammar cannot base-generate two different word orders. If the object NP is governed by the verb and if government goes only into one direction, then only one of the word orders, subject-verb-object or subject-object-verb, is base-generated, while the other is derived via movement. Let us assume, in the spirit of the leading idea outlined at the beginning of this section, that the notion of government emerges some time towards the end of Stage II. The child will then know that only one of the two word orders can be base-generated and he will then have to find out whether subject-object-verb or subject-verb-object is in fact the underlying order. Let us now turn to the question of what may determine the child's choice in this respect. Recall that logically there are two options available to the child. First, he may choose subject-verb-object as the underlying word order, in which case the correct position of the verb in embedded clauses and in split verbals will result from a movement rule which we may call 'Verb-final'. Alternatively, he could opt for subject-object-verb as the base-generated word order so that a movement rule of Verb-Second will account for the correct position of finite verb forms in main clauses. Adopting an idea first expressed by Roeper (1972) I would like to suggest that children's consistent choice of the latter alternative, i.e. subject-object-verb, again reflects the emergence of a principle of Universal Grammar, namely Emonds' (1976) Structure-Preserving Constraint. To put it in a somewhat simplified version, Emonds' constraint requires that all non-local transformations either apply to root sentences or be structure-preserving in the sense that a constituent can only move to a position which bears the same categorial label as the constituent itself, i.e. NPs can only be moved to NP positions, verbs only to verb positions, etc. It is easy to see that a Verb-final rule operating on base-generated subject-verb-object and moving the finite verb form to the final position in *embedded* clauses would clearly violate the Structure-Preserving Constraint, since there is no base-generated final verb-position to which the verb could move. In contrast, a Verb-Second rule operating on base-generated subject-object-verb and moving the finite verb form to a 'second' position in *main* clauses does not violate the Structure-Preserving Constraint, since root transformations, i.e. those applying to the highest sentence-structure, need not be structure-preserving.[8]

If we assume again that, as a reflection of a biologically determined maturational schedule, the Structure-Preserving Constraint emerges at a specific point in time, then the explanation for the transition from Stage II to Stage III is obvious. As soon as the Structure-Preserving Constraint becomes available the child will know that it is the word order of the embedded clause that must be base-generated because otherwise a rule violating the constraint would need to be invoked.

If this view is correct, then an important prediction will be made. Assuming that the child takes subject-object-verb as the base-generated word order and then acquires a rule of Verb-Second applying in main clauses, one would expect to find erroneous subject-object-verb in main clauses, but never erroneous subject-verb-object in embedded clauses. That is, the child might have problems with the rule of Verb-Second, sometimes forgetting to apply it; however, there is no possibility for word order errors in embedded clauses, because these have the simple base-generated subject-object-verb. Notice that this is exactly what Clahsen (1982) found. Children never make mistakes with respect to subject-object-verb in embedded clauses, but once in a while they do make mistakes in main clauses where they sometimes use erroneous subject-object-verb.

To summarize, I have suggested that the development of word order in children learning German can be explained with reference to the interaction of a number of principles of Universal Grammar which emerge maturationally in a specific order. The X̄-schema in conjunction with Case Theory leads the child to constrain the number of underlying word orders that he will consider. The choice among the remaining word orders is subsequently determined by the emergence of the notion of government and the Structure-Preserving Constraint proposed on independent grounds by Emonds (1976).

I would now like to discuss the developmental data on negation as shown in Table 1. In particular, I would like to propose an explanation for the transition from Stage I to Stage II, i.e. how children come to realize at a certain point in time that 'negator + sentence' is not the correct structure for sentential negation, so that they will move to the next developmental stage in which the negator is placed between the subject NP and the verb phrase.

Notice first of all that – perhaps somewhat unexpectedly – natural languages do not seem to express sentential negation by means of placing the negator in pre-sentential position, i.e. the structure 'negator + sentence' does not seem to occur in natural (adult) languages. In his survey of sentence negation in 240 languages representing some 40 language families and genetically isolated languages Dahl (1979, 93) observes: 'the only examples of sentence-initial Neg placement that I have found are verb-initial languages, where this position is identical to immediate pre-FE [finite element] position'. Dahl furthermore observes that inflected negators tend to behave exactly like other auxiliaries, while uninflected negators tend to occur before the finite verb form of the sentence.

If Dahl's observations are correct and the phenomenon itself is non-accidental, then it seems reasonable to assume that there is a principle (or possibly set of principles) of Universal Grammar that rules out the possibility of 'negator + sentence' structures in natural languages. If this is the case, then, of course, the structures produced by children at Stage I do not qualify as a possible grammar. Let us assume, again in the spirit of the previous proposals, that the relevant principle(s) emerge(s) at some specific point in time during the child's development; then it is clear that he will have to restructure his grammar once the principle becomes operative, and thus move to Stage II where the negator henceforth appears in pre-verb-phrase position.

I am not aware of any particular principle proposed in the literature that would specifically rule out pre-sentential negator-placement; so let us speculate on what such a principle may look like. If the negator appears as the leftmost element in a sentence, then, logically, there are three possibilities with respect to the position where it could be base-generated:

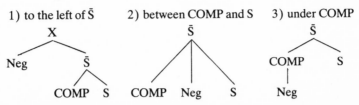

The first possibility is ruled out if we follow the standard assumption that S̄ is the highest node, i.e. the initial symbol of the phrase structure component. The second possibility would imply the claim that there is a categorial node between COMP (complementizer) and S under which Neg could be generated. However, it is again standardly assumed that S̄ expands only into COMP and S, so that there is, in fact, no such node. This leaves us with the third possibility. Note, however, that according to Chomsky (1981c, 23ff.) COMP is either [±wh] or *for,* i.e. only wh-phrases or complementizers may occur in COMP. It is clear that the negator is neither a wh-phrase nor a complementizer, so that also the third possibility is ruled out. Admittedly, all the assumptions on which the present argument is based are essentially stipulations and do not follow from any known principle of grammar. Note, however, that these stipulations seem to be necessary on independent grounds and do not directly relate to any specific properties of negation.

Since the negator can thus not be base-generated in pre-sentential position, we still have to examine the possibility of this position being the result of movement. However, this does not seem to be an attractive solution either. First of all the question arises: if Neg moves into COMP, where does it originate? Secondly, in negative questions, both the wh-phrase and Neg would be in COMP, in which case neither element can bind its trace for reasons analogous to the *that-t* effect. Finally, if we assume that the scope of the negator is the entire sentence, then at some point the sentence would have to move into its own COMP, a somewhat exotic idea.

It thus seems that the impossibility of pre-sentential negator-placement follows from independent properties of the theory of grammar and need not be stipulated. We may thus assume that, if the COMP position and the initial rule S̄→COMP+S are universal properties of natural languages, the emergence of these properties will automatically rule out pre-sentential negator-placement.

Let us finally turn to a set of data which appear to be characterized by a specific type of deletion. It is a standard observation in the psycholinguistic literature that during the early two-word and three-word stage children frequently produce utterances in which two nouns occur in juxtaposition. These utterances are commonly referred to as N + N constructions. Consider the following sentences taken from Bloom (1970):

31) mommy sock
32) mommy cottage cheese
33) baby milk
34) mommy pig tale
35) girl dress
36) sweater chair
37) Wendy elevator
38) bean bag horse
39) sheep ear
40) baby raisin

What makes these constructions interesting is the fact that they exhibit a certain range of different relations between the two nouns. On the basis of contextual clues Bloom determines the following relationships:

a) *attributive constructions*: the first noun modifies the second noun;

b) *conjunction constructions*: the two nouns are conjoined without any overt conjunctor *and* or *or*;

c) *identity constructions,* corresponding to adult NP – *is* – NP patterns;

d) *subject-object constructions*;

e) *subject-locative constructions.*

In the following discussion I will be exclusively concerned with the construction types (d) and (e) in which the first noun represents the subject and the second noun represents the object of an unexpressed action or event or, in the case of locative constructions the place at which a certain action or event occurs. Bloom (1970, 51ff.) observes that subject-object constructions are by far the most frequent pattern.

Superficially, the crucial difference between the child's utterances and the corresponding adult constructions is the lack of a verb form in the case of the child's utterances. Consequently the question arises: why do children leave out the verb in these constructions?

It has frequently been suggested that the lack of the verb in subject-object sentences is a performance phenomenon and reflects certain memory constraints. That is, the child's processing capacity is limited to producing no more than two words per utterance and this is why the verb is deleted. If this view is correct, then we may assume that the child's grammatical knowledge does contain rules expanding S into NP + verb + NP; however, processing limitations require an additional rule of verb deletion. Alternatively, one could assume that the child's grammar contains a rule that does not exist in the adult language, namely $S \rightarrow NP_1 + NP_2$, where NP_1 is the subject and NP_2 is the object. I will consider both possibilities in turn.

Bloom argues for the first alternative, i.e. even at the early two- and three-word stage the child 'knows' the subject-verb-object pattern, but is unable to produce all three constituents in a single utterance. The crucial evidence that Bloom presents comes from a number of sentences in which the verb is, in fact, present:

41) me show mommy
42) machine make noise
43) man ride a bus

On the basis of utterances such as (41)–(43) Bloom argues that the subject-object-verb pattern must be available to the child, in principle; however, the child's grammar contains a rule which optionally deletes the verb and thus facilitates sentence processing. We are therefore facing the following situation: at Stage I children may optionally delete verbs between subjects and objects whereas at some following stage they have to realize that such subject-object constructions are ungrammatical, because the verb cannot be deleted. The crucial question is again: how does the child find out that the deletion of verbs is ungrammatical in the context of simple subject-object patterns?

Notice again that this question cannot be satisfactorily answered by merely pointing to the input that the child receives. Many utterances that children hear do, in fact, have deleted verbs as e.g. in Gapping or Right Node Raising constructions (see Maling 1972). So what the child has to find out is not that the deletion of verbs is generally incorrect, but rather that it is ungrammatical in certain configurations such as simple subject-object constructions. If the child were to rely merely on the input he receives he might just as well be led to the conclusion that the deletion of verbs in subject-object constructions is a perfectly grammatical option which, only by co-incidence, does not occur in the utterances he happens to hear.

Another point may be added. Intuitively, we would not expect to find a natural language in which the type of subject-object construction typical of early child language constitutes a regular and permissible syntactic pattern. That is, natural languages do not seem to allow free deletion of verbs in simple sentence structures. If this observation is correct, then early child grammars do not qualify as possible human languages in White's sense in the domain exemplified by (31)–(40). If the lack of free verb deletion is a non-accidental property of human language, we would expect some principle(s) of Universal Grammar to account for this fact and it is clear that the child's grammar at Stage I obviously violates this principle.

I would like to suggest that the principle that explains the problems under discussion is the well-known constraint on the recoverability of deletion, i.e. a lexical item may be deleted if and only if it can be *syntactically* recovered. In other words, there must be syntactic clues which unambiguously indicate which item exactly has been deleted (for details see Katz and Postal 1964; Back 1974, 100, 101, 241; Chomsky and Lasnik 1977; Radford 1981, 257ff.). While it is true that in many cases the verb missing in the child's utterance can be reconstructed from the general contextual background, there is no syntactic way of recovering the deleted verb. Consequently, constructions such as Gapping or Right Node Raising are permissible whereas verb deletions in simple sentences are ungrammatical.

Let us assume again that the constraint on the recoverability of deletion is a principle of Universal Grammar whose emergence at a specific point in time is determined by the maturational schedule which is part of our genetic program. I will assume that this principle emerges and becomes operative some time at the end of Stage I during which the child has used N + N constructions of the type outlined above. As soon as the child 'realizes' that only those lexical items can be deleted which are syntactically recoverable, he will automatically know that his own N + N constructions are ungrammatical because they violate a principle of Universal Grammar. He will also know that Gapping constructions are possible since they do not violate the Recoverability Constraint. In other words, the child will discontinue to use his original N + N constructions and thus move to the next developmental stage.

Let us now consider the alternative idea explicitly dismissed by Bloom, but defended by other psycholinguistic researchers, namely that the child does not delete the verb, but rather that at Stage I the child has a rule $S \rightarrow N(P) + N(P)$ which encodes subject-object relations. Again it seems intuitively clear that such a rule does not occur in natural languages, i.e. one is inclined to think that subject-object relations are always tied to the presence of a verb or some kind of predicate. I suggest that this fact follows from the θ-Criterion which according to Chomsky (1981c, 36) states that

> each argument bears one and only one θ-role, and each θ-role is assigned to one and only one argument.

In constructions containing two arguments where one is the subject and the other the object, θ-roles are assigned by the verb or some other predicate. If, however, a verb or predicate is not present, the two arguments will not receive their respective θ-roles, thereby violating the θ-Criterion. Obviously, neither one of the two NPs could have the status of a predicate since this would exclude the grammatical function of subject or object. As a consequence the θ-Criterion as a principle of Universal Grammar rules out a base-generated NP + NP structure encoding a subject-object relation. Following the spirit of the previous proposals we may assume that the θ-Criterion emerges at some time at the end of Stage I, thereby forcing the child to abandon the original $N(P) + N(P)$ constructions and to restructure his grammar in accordance with the newly available principle of Universal Grammar.

4. Conclusion

In this paper I have tried to show that linguistic theory conceived of as a theory about the biologically determined properties of natural languages cannot only successfully deal with the logical problem of language acquisi tion, but may be extended to explain, at the same time, certain developmental aspects of real-time language growth. This extension involves one additional (non-standard) assumption, namely that man's genetic program does not only specify the principles of Universal Grammar, but also contains a concomitant maturational schedule which determines a specific temporal order in which these universal principles emerge during the developmental process. This assumption was defended on both conceptual and empirical grounds.

If the ideas developed in this paper are not totally misconceived, then two rather exciting consequences seem to follow. First, by successfully extending the theory of Universal Grammar to also cover developmental aspects of language acquisition, the theory receives empirical support from a domain for which – quite explicitly – it was never designed. This, it seems, is one of the strongest kinds of support any theory could hope for. Second, we may begin to see some glimmerings of how developmental data may become potentially relevant for dealing with problems which – for well-known reasons – have so far been adequately treated only by syntactic theory proper. Recall that Chomsky (1981c, 9) observes that 'such evidence [evidence from acquisition studies] is, for the time being, insufficient to provide much insight concerning these problems'. It appears that Chomsky's scepticism derives primarily from the fact that, in the past, it was mostly far from obvious how psycholinguistic evidence could contribute to our understanding of matters concerning linguistic competence and principles of Universal Grammar.

Let us speculate on how developmental data might profitably be used to explore problems of linguistic theory (as a theory of the human mind) – given the assumptions defended in this paper. Suppose there are two successive stages A and B such that the transition from A to B can be adequately explained in terms of the emergence of, say, principles of Case assignment. Suppose, furthermore, that there are two later stages D and E where the transition to E can be accounted for by the emergence of the notion of government. Such explanations are obviously in conflict with standard assumptions in linguistic theory according to which Case assignment presupposes the notion of government. Consequently, either the developmental explanation is incorrect or the relationship between Case and government is different from what is standardly assumed – clearly an empirical question. To take a further example, what is frequently referred to as a principle of Universal Grammar may be nothing else than a convenient cover term for a set of essentially unrelated universal properties. Take e.g. the X̄-schema which unites statements about properties as different as lexical categories, phrasal projections and constituent order. It would be interesting to know whether or not all these properties reflect a uniform phenomenon, in which case one would expect all these universal properties to emerge at roughly the same time within the process of language growth.

In much the same way one might wonder whether or not the principles A, B, and C of the Binding Theory emerge at the same time, indicating that they do, in fact, belong to the 'same' theory.

How do the ideas developed in this paper relate to the view that language acquisition is essentially a process of fixing parameters of Universal Grammar? I believe that the notions of 'parameter' and 'maturational schedule' bear upon two different aspects of the same fundamental problem and thus express complementary rather than alternative views. The notion 'parameter' in conjunction with the theory of markedness accounts for the way in which children choose among various language-specific options once they have realized that their present grammar needs to be restructured, while the notion 'maturational schedule' is meant to explain how children come to realize that their grammar is inadequate in the first place.

It thus appears that various questions relating to the logical and to the developmental aspect of language acquisition can be fruitfully explored under a common set of assumptions, a certainly exciting idea for future research.

Acknowledgements. I am greatly indebted to many colleagues and friends for helpful criticism and stimulating comments, in particular to Gisbert Fanselow, Peter Staudacher, Lydia White, Tom Roeper, Arnim von Stechow and Günther Grewendorf.

Notes

1) In the early and mid-60s much influential work was carried out by researchers who were psychologists rather than linguists by education. Psychology, at that time, was seen as the science dealing with cognitive *processes* rather than with systems of mental representation.

2) Strictly speaking, 'developmental sequence' and 'order of acquisition' refer to different concepts. While 'order of acquisition' refer to different concepts. While 'order of acquisition' concerns the order in which different structures are fully *mastered,* 'developmental sequence' refers to the sequence of developmental stages through which children pass before they master a given structure completely (see Felix 1982).

3) This view is idealized in the sense that possibly clusters of principles may emerge at a given point in time, i.e. it is conceivable that the maturational schedule specifies fewer points of emergence than there are principles of Universal Grammar.

4) See note 3; it is also conceivable that certain very fundamental principles are operative from the very start, while only 'highly-order' principles emerge maturationally. These questions are, of course, empirical in nature.

5) Of course, I am not claiming that all permissible phrasal categories are acquired at the same time.

6) Stowell (1981, 113) proposes the following Adjacency Principle:
In the configuration $[\alpha\beta \ldots]$ or $[\ldots \beta\alpha]$ α Case-marks β, where
  i) α governs β and
  ii) α is adjacent to β and
  iii) α is $[-N]$

7) In his survey of languages Greenberg (1963) did not find any object-verb-subject language arguing that object-verb-subject is not a possible word order. Mallinson and

Blake (1982) found a single language with object-verb-subject which may be, how-ever, an 'ergative' language.

8) A similar idea has been developed by Roeper (1972) who at that time, of course, did not invoke the notion of government. In much the same way, Clahsen and Muysken (1983) rely on Emonds' Principle to explain certain differences between first- and second-language development.

13. Some Theoretical Implications of L2 Acquisition Research and the Grammar of Interlanguages

Purpose

The past 10–12 years of L2 research have been extremely exciting and fruitful. Although many controversies and unresolved problems remain, there can be no doubt at all that great advances have been made, the most important probably being that the field of language acquisition is no longer regarded as being restricted to young L1 children. For a proper understanding of how languages are learned, all types of language acquisition and all age ranges have to be included (Wode 1974, 1983a). This re-orientation has important implications. For one thing, foreign-language teaching can no longer be regarded as a type of language learning which is completely unrelated to the mastery of the language in non-teaching situations (cf., e.g., Wode 1974, 1978a, 1981; Dulay and Burt 1972, 1973, 1974a–c; Felix 1977a–b, 1982a; Krashen 1977, 1981; Schröder 1979; Lightbown 1980, 1983; Hahn 1982, etc.). The attempts so far to characterize language learning from such a comprehensive point of view are quite encouraging. It appears from such studies that learners do not proceed in totally different and wholly unrelated ways. Rather, they seem to learn languages in much the same way, although there is a good deal of individual variation as a function of the acquisitional types and the individual speakers (cf., e.g., Fillmore 1976; Wode 1979, 1981; Felix 1982a; Clahsen et al. 1983). Moreover, it seems to be accepted now that transfer is an integral part of how L2s are learned and how they are used in actual communication (cf., e.g., Wode 1977, 1981a; Kellerman 1979; Zobl 1983b; Meisel 1982, etc.). Other areas in which L2 research has greatly advanced our overall understanding of how languages are learned include issues like the relevancy of age; general cognition; situational, pragmatic, and numerous other variables (summaries in McLaughlin 1978; Wode 1981; Felix 1982; Dulay et al. 1982; Clahsen et al. 1983).

However, it seems that this comprehensive perspective should be further enlarged by relating the insights about language acquisition to the general functioning of natural human languages. The insights summarized above involve only language learning. It is a commonplace within linguistics to argue that it is not possible to fully understand the design and the functioning of natural languages unless it is known how they are learned. But the reverse also holds, namely, that we will not be able to appreciate properly all the many facts and insights collected about language learning unless this is integrated with what is known about the functioning of natural human languages in non-learning domains.

The purpose of this paper is to raise some pertinent issues and to explore some of their implications. Eventually they will extend into various disciplines, such as psychology, sociology, education, neurology, brain research, and, of course, linguistics. This paper will be limited primarily to linguistics, because this discipline seems to be affected much more directly than any of the other disciplines mentioned above. The following questions appear to be central:

1) How does language learning in general, and how do interlanguages in particular, relate to language typology, language universals, and markedness hierarchies?

2) How does language learning in general, and how do interlanguages in particular, relate to language change? Recall that many researchers assume that children are chiefly responsible for diachronic changes of a language. Children are thought to recapitulate developmentally the diachronic development of a language. Another view is that children can only simplify a language or add low-level rules to it. Yet another view is that children are the chief propagators of language change. (See Baron 1977 for a survey of such ideas.)

3) To what extent will linguists be required to re-conceptualize their theoretical constructs and assumptions, for example, the learnability assumption? Recall that natural languages can be structured only in such a way that they are learnable by the human brain and the processing systems associated with it. Recall further that Chomsky made this a cornerstone of his theory, although for him learnability relates primarily to the L1 child. The best grammar is the one that mirrors how the L1 child learns a language (Chomsky 1965, 1973, 1976, and elsewhere). But do adults not learn languages? How about adolescents? It is argued that Chomsky's claim is completely arbitrary. The learnability assumption must be re-conceptualized in the sense that it cannot be based on a specific age group; it must be related to the language-learning capacity of people in general, irrespective of any arbitrary age restrictions.

4) The fourth question is the crucial one: Can linguistic universals be explained psycholinguistically? The issue is not to detect and describe universals and universal restrictions on natural human languages, as is traditionally done within language typology. The issue is to explain why these universals and the various typological constraints are as they are. If linguistic universals can be explained by recourse to some other domain, we will be in a position to state why natural human languages and their linguistic structures are structured the way they are; why languages change only the way they do; why learner languages take the form they do; and the re-

conceptualization of the learnability assumption would follow naturally from such an argument.

Theoretically, the answer to the above issues is easy and obvious: natural human languages are as they are because they must be processible by the processing system(s) of the human brain. Linguistic universals, therefore, are determined by the functioning of the human brain. Languages can only change in such a way that they remain learnable. Language change, consequently, must stay within the limits set by the brain's processing system(s). Learner languages, as well as the structure of marginal languages, like pidgins, must be subject to the same restrictions irrespective of the age of the speakers. And, lastly, language variation must also follow the same constraints.

This would be a neat argument if only more was known about the functioning of the language processing system(s) of the human brain. Unfortunately, we are far from this goal. The best that can be done, at present, is to look for empirical evidence that would at least encourage researchers to pursue such questions without being dependent exclusively on speculation. This, it seems, can now be done, thanks primarily to the advances in L2 research. And, by placing the study of interlanguages and language learning in such a context provides it with the kind of theoretical significance the field deserves.

It would, of course, be presumptuous and premature to expect a fully satisfactory solution, particularly concerning psycholinguistic explanations of language universals. In the long run, all types of universals need to be explained, i.e. substantive universals, formal universals, implicational universals, etc. Moreover, in a certain sense every detail of language structure can be regarded as being constrained by the functioning of the human brain. Therefore, in order to make the task manageable the whole problem can be thought of as involving two extremes. One end of the spectrum is marked by various 'low-level' details; the other end constitutes the 'upper bound', i.e. the total range of options open to natural languages. The focus in this paper is on the 'upper bound'.

The remainder of this paper contains two major parts. In section 1 I review empirical evidence primarily from grammatical areas and which can be brought to bear on the issues raised above. The procedure is to see whether the various types of language varieties lend support to the idea that the same set of constraints underlie all of them. The starting point is the data on language acquisition, because this material provided the original challenge for the re-conceptualization proposed in this paper. Section 2 is devoted to speculations about some theoretical issues. Throughout the entire paper the term interlanguage is used to refer to learner languages of not fully competent speakers of any acquisitional types, i.e. L1, L2, re-learning, or others.

TABLE 1. Some early stages in the L1 and L2 acquisition of the negation systems of German and English by children aged up to 10 (adapted from Wode 1977a)

L1-German	L2-German/L1-English

I   nein
     no
	I-II nein
	      no

II nein, Milch no, (I would like some) milk	nein, da no, (it is) there

III nein hauen
     no bang (on the table)
	III nein helfen
	     no help (me)

IV Heiko nicht essen
     Heiko (is) not (to) eat (this)
	IV Katze nein schlafen
	     (the) cat no sleep

die nicht kaputt these (are) not broken	Milch nicht da (the) milk (is) not there

L1-English	L2-English/L1-German
I no	I-II no
II no, Mom	no, you
III no close	III no play baseball

IV Katherine no like celery	IV that's no good
	     Marilyn like no sleepy
	     lunch is no ready
	     me no close the window

Katherine not quite through	John go not to school me and Jennifer not play

1. Some Data: the Nature of Learner Languages

Language Learning and Language Typology

L1- and L2-acquisition. Table 1 summarizes the major developmental structures and the developmental sequences for the L1 and L2 acquisition of German and English.[1] That is, L1 German is matched by L2 German acquired by speakers with English as L1; and L1 English is matched by L2 English acquired by speakers with German as L1. The material comes from chidren aged up to 10. The roman numerals indicate the major developmental stages during the early phases of acquiring the particular language. The developmental structures characteristic of the various stages are listed under the respective roman numerals.

The important points about Table 1 are: there is a regular progression from less to complex structures in the development of the learner languages. Some of the developmental structures cannot be related to the structure of the target language in any direct way. Note, in particular, stages III–IV. Utterances like 'no close' (don't shut (the door)), 'no play baseball' ((we) don't (want to) play baseball) or the German structures of III tend not to be provided by the linguistic environment to which children are normally exposed. Likewise, utterances like 'Katherine no like celery' (Katherine doesn't like celery), 'Marilyn like no sleepy' (Marilyn doesn't want to go to sleep), 'me no close the window' (I don't want to shut the window), 'John go not to the school' (John is not going to school), as well as the German structures of IV are not regularly used in discourse directed to foreign learners nor in talk not directed at learners.[2] Where then do negation structures such as neg-X, subject-neg-verb phrase or subject-verb-neg (X) come from? If they are not taught and if they are not picked up directly from the input addressed to the learner, they can only be the learner's own contribution. To be more precise, the morphological items can be traced to the respective target languages. But where do the word order patterns originate from? They must be contributed by the learner. But then the question is, where does the learner's ability to produce such structures come from, and why do they show the kind of constraints that can be observed? Why, for example, is a negator not simply inserted after the first, second or third word? It is suggested below that these peculiarities result from universal constraints governing the possible form of natural human languages.[3]

Another important point to note about Table 1 is the relationship of such learner data to language typology. Notice that all the developmental structures summarized in Table 1 are typologically possible. That is to say, one way or another the structural options utilized in these learner data are well evidenced in typological surveys of the negation systems of natural human languages (see, in particular, Dahl 1979). In fact, pre-verbal negation, as in the structural type subject-neg-verb phrase of stage IV, is one of the most frequent negation structures in the languages of the world. Preposed external placement of neg is also typologically possible, although it is less frequently attested than the type subject-neg-verb phrase. In addition, the post-verbal placement of neg is quite familiar from, for example, German and Norwegian.

Although the data reviewed so far came from children aged 4–10, such developmental structures are by no means restricted to these age ranges nor to the acquisitional types surveyed in Table 1. The same developmental structures also occur with adult L2 learners, and the same negation structures have also been found in foreign-language classroom situations. Wode (1981a) reports such data for adult migrants learning L2 German in a naturalistic environment and for 10–12-year-old German secondary-school students who were taught English. Furthermore, Hyltenstam (1978b) observed the same developmental negation structures with a large number of adult L2 learners of Swedish who spoke various immigrant languages from all over the world. And more data of this sort are presently being analysed by Hakuta for over 50 Spanish-speaking adults learning English (personal communication).

TABLE 2. Negation structures neg X-X neg and subject-neg-verb phrase in several types of language acquisition, pidgins, and early creoles (adapted from Wode 1981)

	Non-anaphoric neg X-X neg		Subject-neg-verb phrase
L1 monolingualism			
English (Bloom 1970)	no close		I no want envelope
German	nein schaff ich no make I	Kaffee nein coffee no	hier nicht wohnen here not live
Swedish	nej kossa		Embla inte na täcket
(Lange and Larsson 1973)	no cow		Embla not have blanket
Latvian (Wode and	nē minimi	gib nē	ipupu nē ita
Ruke-Dravina 1977)	no pencil	want no	bathroom no go
L1 trilingualism			
(Kadar-Hoffmann 1977)			
German	Nein Hanno kann no John can		das nein geht that no works
Hungarian	nem jó no good		itt nem jön atró from here no the metro come
French	non Hanno aime no John like		après Daniel non ouvre afterwards Daniel no open
Naturalistic L2			
L2-English/L1-German	no play baseball		me no close the window
L2-English/L1-Spanish	no like coffee		I can no see
(Schumann 1975)			
L2-English/L1-Norwegian	no like it		I no like that
(Ravem 1974)			
L2-German/L1-English	nein meine		ich nein hat eins
(Felix 1978)	no mine		I no have one
L2-English/L1-French			you no under the bed
(Tiphine 1983)			
Re-learning of L2			
L2-English/L1-German	no sit here		I no want to play
Pidgins and creoles			
Ewondo Populaire	ke bo		me ke bo
(Todd 1974)	don't do		I don't do
Freetown Krio	no do		a no do
(Todd 1974)	don't do		I don't do
Hawaian Pidgin	my father, no take care me		baby name, me no like
(Carr 1972)			
Chinese Pidgin	can do? no can do?		he no belong handsome
(Bauer 1974)			he no is handsome
Jamaican Creole	no sliip pan da bed		nobody no gaan a puos yet
(Bailey 1966)	no sleep on this bed		nobody no went to the post-office yet

Individual variation in language learning and typology. The systematicity and the uniformity of the data summarized in Tables 1 and 2 is misleading in that it suggests that all learners proceed exactly alike. This is not true. There is individual variation among learners in various respects, notably in terms of speed of acquisition, ultimate level of achievement, differences in task-specific behaviour, and, also, variation in the linguistic structure of the developmental learner structures.[4] The last type of individual variation is important with respect to the basic question of this paper. If the structure of learner utterances and learner languages is constrained by the universal constraints on the structure of natural human languages, then one would expect that the range of individual variation in learner languages should be finite and it should not go counter to the constraints familiar from typological surveys. Table 3 is intended to illustrate this point. The data is provided by the same children that were the subjects for L1 German and L2 English/L1 German in Table 1. Table 3 lists the majority of the developmental structures observed with these four children when they acquired English. The date of first occurrence of the respective developmental type is given on the right. Note that not all developmental structures occurred with every child. The nature of the relationship can be illustrated via the developmental structures subject-neg-verb phrase, auxiliary-neg-X, and subject-verb-neg-X. For subject-verb-neg-X, each child had the variant with 'no' or 'not' as the morphological marker of negation. In the type subject-neg-verb phrase, three children used only 'not' as a negative marker; whereas the youngest child had both 'no' and 'not'. For post-auxiliary negation the type can-no-verb phrase occurs with two children; the types cannot-verb phrase and can't-verb phrase occur with all four of them.[5] Moreover, none of the developmental structures conflicts with negation structures familiar from typological surveys.

In summary then, from Tables 1–3 it is clear that learner languages and the structure of learner utterances do not go counter to typological constraints on the structure of natural human languages as observable in fully-fledged languages; and these restrictions also constrain the possible form that individual variation in learner languages can take. (For a similar view see Gass (this volume).)

Marginal Languages and Language Typology: Pidgins

Pidgins are included in Table 2 for two reasons. First, in terms of origin, pidgins are a special case of naturalistic L2 acquisition (Bickerton 1981; Wode 1983c). From this point of view it is not at all surprising to find that the kind of negation structures characteristic of early pidgin languages should parallel those observable in naturalistic L2 acquisition. Second, pidgins are included to show that such marginal languages also conform to the universal constraints on the structure of natural human languages. Of course, this conclusion already follows from the insight that pidginization is a variety of

TABLE 3. Developmental negation structures in the naturalistic L2 acquisition of English by four German children. Optional elements in ( ) (adapted from Wode 1981)

Structural type	Illustrative example	Hei	Bi	La	Ig
		Date of first occurrence for			
anaphoric no	no	1;9	—	1;1	1;0
anaphoric no X	no, Tiff	1;18	0;10	1;18	2;6
non-anaphoric neg X					
no Adj	no cold	0;24	—	1;17	1;17
no V	no sleep	0;27	0;28	0;28	—
no N(P)	no bread	0;28	0;28	0;28	2;21
no VP	no catch it	0;27	1;13	2;1	3;4
X (be) neg Y					
... no Y	that's no right	1;19	—	(1;15) 1;20	3;12 (1;22)
... not Y	you not dummy	1;13	1;13	2;3	1;24
subj V neg X					
... V no X	everybody catch no the fish	1;24	3;29	1;23	3;18
... V not X	John go not to the school	1;13	2;5	1;26	4;6
subj					
Subj V pron neg (X)					
... V Pron not	I catch that not	2;7	3;22	—	4;1
... V Pron not X	you got me not out	—	1;24	—	5;19
Subj V a neg N					
... a not N	you have not a fish	1;12	—	1;20	—
... a no N	you have a no snag	1;30	—	1;30	—
Subj neg VP					
... no VP	me no close the window	—	—	—	3;16
... not Vp	you not shut up	1;13	3;1	1;18	4;20
Subj Aux Neg x					
... can no VP	you can not have it	—	3;27	—	3;21
... cannot VP	he cannot hit the ball	2;2	2;19	1;24	4;3
... can't VP	I can't get him out	2;15	4;19	1;27	3;21
imperative don't VP	don't broke don't break it	1;12	2;19	2;13	3;19
imperative V(pron) neg (X)					
... V Pron not (X)	hit it not over the fence	1;13	—	—	5;3
... V not (X)	shut not your mouth	2;0	2;3	—	—
eliptical not	not inside	1;22	1;25	1;24	2;6
pre-nominal no N	Birgit catch no fish	1;23	—	(1;26) 4;0	3;16
pronominal nothing	I see nothing	1;22	1;24	2;18	2;15
pre-nominal nothing N	I go nothing shoe	—	3;18	—	4;20
Subj don't know	I don't know	1;24	1;24	1;24	2;19
suppletive don't/didn't	no don't	1;25	—	2;0	3;21
	no, you don't	1;30	3;11	2;21	3;30
Subj don't/didn't VP	I didn't see	(1;13) 2;12	3;11	2;18	(4;15) 5;8
Subj don't/didn't Aux VP	I didn't can closed it	2;12	5;15	2;20	—
negative any	I saw any wheels	3;14	4;26	3;4	—

169

naturalistic L2 acquisition. In any event, the two negation structures are well attested in pidgins (and early creoles) all over the world. (See survey of some 30 pidgins and creoles in Hoffmann and Rudeloff 1982). That is to say, the two negation types occur not only in pidgins involving European or Indo-European languages, but also in cases where non-Indo-European languages are involved.

The above observations are extremely important, because they further support the previous insights, namely, that the two negation structures seem to be universal; that the relationships observed between learner languages proper and language typology carry over to pidginization; and that age must be ruled out as the variable that determines the structure of such utterances, because pidginization is not, in general, carried out by children, but by people from the adolescent and adult age-ranges.

Language Learning and Language Change

The relationship between language learning, pidginization, language typology, and language change is illustrated in Table 4. It summarizes the major developments in the history of the negation systems of French, German and English. At one time or another each of these three languages had pre-verbal negation, post-verbal negation, and double negation. Table 4 clearly suggests that there is no justification for those traditional claims concerning the relationship between child language and language change as summarized in the first section, namely, that language learning recapitulates the history of the respective language, that children are the chief innovators of language change, and that children propagate it.

It is obvious from the data of Table 4 that the developmental sequences of language learners do not necessarily recapitulate the diachronic development of a language. For example, in the course of its history English once had post-verbal negation.[6] On the other hand, there is no L1 learner of English on record who went through a developmental stage marked by post-verbal negation. Similarly, English once had a variation between post-verbal negation and pre-verbal negation as in the writings of Shakespeare. Again, no L1 learner of English is on record who went through a developmental stage characterized by a variation between post-verbal and pre-verbal negation. Lastly, L1 learners of English go through a stage of double negation where the two negators may be morphophonologically the same. However, this developmental stage is not such as can be illustrated from middle English where the two negative markers are different.

Perhaps the most conclusive evidence concerning the issue of whether children recapitulate the history of a language is available for the acquisition of inflectional systems. Such evidence can be related to the notion of the linguistic cycle (recently made popular again by Hodge 1970). Languages are said to go through diachronic cycles such that, for example, an analytic language changes into a synthetic one, then back into an analytic one, and so forth. Egyptian is said to be a language which can be documented as having gone through this cycle twice. On the other hand, there is no single learner on record who went through such cycles as often as the target language did during its history.

TABLE 4. History of sentence negation of English, German and French (adapted from Jespersen 1917; Behagel 1924)

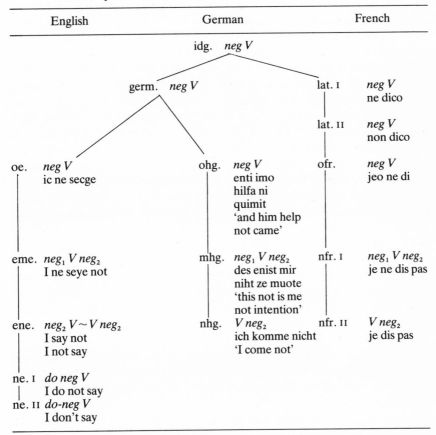

The question of who creates innovations cannot be decided at all. In the discussion on the various tables presented so far it has been amply demonstrated that age is not a crucial variable in determining the linguistic structure of learner utterances, including pidgin languages. If adults and children can be expected to produce the same type of developmental structures then it is impossible, in principle, to determine whether a given change in a language is due to children or to adults. For various reasons children cannot be regarded as the main propagators of language change. As pointed out above, speakers from the non-child age-ranges may create the same innovations as children. Second, detailed socio-linguistic investigations show that it is primarily the non-child age groups that propagate changes in the language, notably, middle-aged people (for example, Labov 1963, 1966; Trudgill 1974).

The above arguments concerning the re-assessment of the impact of children on language change were based on empirical observations. These conclusions can be strengthened by speculations relating to the survival and the evolution of the human species. Such speculations, it seems, lead to two points. First, it should be the adult population rather than children who are chiefly responsible for the propagation of linguistic changes; second, age should not be a crucial variable in the sense that it causes the language-learning abilities of children to deteriorate as assumed in the critical period hypothesis of language learning (notably, Lenneberg 1967) or in other views to the effect that adults lose the ability to learn a language like children do or that this ability deteriorates (for example, Krashen 1981). At the times when the early humans still roamed around in small bands rather than living in larger societies, let alone in large ones familiar from modern-day man, it was essential that the adult, i.e. the fighting population, should be able to quickly learn at least the rudiments of the language of another band. Such groups would have quickly exterminated each other over quarrels concerning privileges to territories, which, in turn, implies privileges to hunt, to gather food, and so on. To prevent such fatal consequences, nature had to develop an ability in homo sapiens that allows for inter-band communication. This ability would have been useless if adults did not have it, if they lost it after puberty or even earlier, or if it allowed them to learn the language of other bands only after long troublesome periods of contact with the language. Moreover, those bands conquered by others would be doomed to perish and they could not be integrated into the new band unless they had the ability to – quickly – learn the language of the dominant band.

What, then, is the relationship between language learning and language change? It seems that both are constrained by the same set of restrictions. Moreover, since it has already been shown that such restrictions also hold between language learning, the structure of marginal languages like pidgins (and creoles), and language typology, it follows that the whole range of the manifestations of natural languages and language structures is constrained by the same set of restrictions. That is to say, they are truly universal. Parallels between language learning and language change, therefore, are due to the super-imposed universal constraints on the structure of natural languages. It is these constraints which seem to have misled previous scholars to – erroneously – propose that children innovate language change, propagate it, or even recapitulate the history of a language. Of course, the traditional views about the role of children in language change are based on L1 children and monolingual situations. In a later section I discuss transfer and borrowing as two phenomena of language change in language-contact situations.

Language Learning and Markedness

The elements, structures, and subsystems of a language can be regarded as inherently more or less complex than others. This assumption is captured by the linguistic notion of markedness. It has become of central importance recently. The idea originated within Prague linguistics. The notion referred to two members of a phonological opposition one of which contained a feature lacking in the other. The phoneme carrying the feature was called 'merkmalhaltig', i.e. marked, the other 'merkmallos', i.e. unmarked (Trubetzkoy 1936a, 1936b). The idea was quickly carried over to inflectional morphology by Jakobson (reprinted 1971) and was later revived within transformational generative grammar (Chomsky and Halle 1968; Lakoff 1970).

The notion of markedness is also extremely attractive for the study of language acquisition, whatever the type of acquisition to be studied. The developmental sequences seem to reflect the internal complexity of the structure or the structural system to be learned, hence the degree of markedness. It seems that the unmarked or the less marked items are learned early, the more marked ones later. And it appears further that items with a very low degree of markedness may appear in developmental sequences even if they are not present in any of the other languages involved, i.e. in cases where neither the target language nor, as in the non-L1 acquisitional types, the other languages learned previously contain them. The negation structure subject-neg-verb phrase is a highly illuminating case in point.

When languages are learned which code negation morphologically, there is a very early stage in the developmental sequence where the negative item is placed after the subject and before the predicate, i.e. subject-neg-verb phrase irrespective of whether the target language has this word order, as in Spanish, or whether it does not, as in German, English, or French. Furthermore the same regularity is found irrespective of whether the negative item of the target language is a free form, as in German 'nein', English 'no', French 'non', or Spanish 'no', or a bound form, as in Russian 'ne-' or Latvian 'ne-'. This is not only so in L1 acquisition. The situation is similar for L2 acquisition. Subject-neg-verb phrase is found in cases where the target language or the prior L1 has pre-verbal negation, as in L2 English/L1 Spanish, but also if none of the languages involved has this word order for negation, as in L2 English/L1 German, L2 English/L1 French, or L2 English/L1 Norwegian (recall Table 2).

As for markedness, it appears that subject-neg-verb phrase is unmarked, at least its degree of markedness is extremely low. As pointed out, Dahl (1979) showed that subject-neg-verb phrase is one of the most frequent and geographically most widespread devices to code negation.

The most important issue with respect to the occurrence of such structures is whether the case of negation can be generalized, and in particular whether or not there are any constraints that govern the appearance of such unmarked structures in developmental sequences. Certainly, negation is not the only such case. Hyltenstam (1983a) reports similar observations with respect to the appearance of pronominal copies in restricted relative clauses in the speech of adult L2 learners of Swedish with Spanish, Finnish, Greek, or Persian as their L1 background. Only Greek and Persian have pronominal copies in – some – relative clauses. Hyltenstam reports that pronominal copies occurred in the interlanguages for all four language backgrounds. In addition, Hyltenstam (1983b) summarizes additional data relating to the acquisition of the lexical differentiation for verbs of sense perception. Mazurkiewich (1980) studied the use of the dative coded as double objects or as object plus prepositional object for L2 English. And Wode (1977b, 1981) reports comparable findings for the acquisition of phonology, namely, the acquisition of the various kinds of /r/. (See also the material discussed in Gass in this volume.)

In addition I know of at least one structural area for which empirical evidence is available on the issue of whether or not there are restrictions on the occurrence of unmarked or less marked items in developmental sequences. This concerns the acquisition of interrogative systems. According to Ultan (1978) the least marked way to code questions is via intonation without any concomitant word order changes or the use of morphological markers; slightly more marked is the use of morphological markers, i.e. interrogative pronouns without concomitant word order changes; next in degree of markedness are word-order permutations; and probably more marked still is the use of affixes. The rise and the development of questions follows this markedness hierarchy in L1 and in L2 acquisition. Intonation questions without inversion are the first to appear; next are pronominal questions without inversion; and only after that do inversion and/or affixal questions arise (Wode 1976a, 1978b; Ufert 1980. Table 5 gives some illustrative examples).

However, the case of interrogation differs from the evidence reviewed for negation in one important respect. As far as I am aware, the use of intonation questions in language acquisition is reported only for those cases where the target language actually has this device. For example, Bowerman (1973) did not find intonation questions when she studied two children learning Finnish as their L1. Finnish does not have intonation questions. Unfortunately there are no L2 studies involving Finnish so that we do not know whether such restrictions also apply to non-L1 types of acquisition if only one of the languages involved has intonation questions. But, nevertheless, the case of L1 Finnish clearly indicates that there may be some constraints on the appearance of unmarked structures in developmental sequences, whatever the details. Clearly, this problem urgently needs clarification.

TABLE 5. Non-inverted yes/no questions and pronominal questions in various acquisitional types

	Subj-VP	wh-Subj-VP	Source
L1 English	mom pinch finger?	where me sleep?	Bellugi 1967
L1 German	du Uni warst? you University been?	wo Bjorn wohnt? where Bjorn lives?	Wode 1976
L2-English/ L1-German	you catch me here?	where they drove?	Ufert 1980
L2-English/ L1-Spanish	I got it there?	where the gallenas live?	Ufert 1980
L2-English/ L1-French	you see this sun?	how we get Concord?	Tiphine 1983

Transfer, Borrowing, Typology, and Markedness

The thinking of L2 researchers about transfer has changed drastically, over the last years. Before the rise of research on naturalistic L2 acquisition, transfer was regarded as all pervasive. The evidence was derived from foreign language teaching (cf. such classics as Fries 1945; Weinrich 1953; Lado 1957). Then Dulay and Burt (1972, 1973, 1974a–c) claimed that transfer was non-existent or at best unimportant in L2 acquisition. This view was not widely accepted in Europe, where the opposite suggestion was upheld, namely, that transfer is an integral part of how L2s are acquired (Wode 1977a, 1978c, 1981; Kellerman 1979). It was noted that transfer was not random but systematic, that it occurs in developmental sequences only under specific conditions, and that the structure to be transferred from the L1 into the target L2 had to be crucially similar to the respective L2 structure before the L1 structure could be transferred to the L2.

Although the terms transfer and borrowing are generally used to refer to different domains of language functioning – transfer to language learning situations; borrowing to language change and, less commonly, to code-switching – there is no convincing evidence that I know of to suggest that transfer and borrowing are two entirely different phenomena. In terms of underlying processes they appear to be the same. Table 6 is to illustrate this via the comparison between various types of L2 Englishes and Pennsylvania German. In this case English lexical material is 'borrowed' into the Pennsylvania variety of German. The phonological adaptations that occur are those familiar from Germans learning English.

As for transfer and typology it appears that transfer-based structures are typologically possible structures. The data summarized on negation in Tables 1–3 clearly illustrates this. That post-verbal negation is due to transfer is obvious from the fact that it has so far been observed only in those

L2 combinations of English where the L1 learned previously has this structure, as in L2 English based on L1 German, Norwegian, or French; whereas post-verbal negation is not yet reported, e.g., for L2 English/L1 Spanish (Schumann 1975, 1978; Fillmore 1976; overviews in Schumann 1978; Wode 1981). Of course, post-verbal negation is typologically possible, as in German or Norwegian. Moreover, negation is not an isolated example. To my knowledge, no empirical evidence is available to contradict the conclusion that transfer is also subject to the same 'upper bound' constraints as language typology, language change, pidginization, and language learning, with respect to the non-transfer regularities.

However, to suggest that transfer is 'upper bounded' by the same constraints as language typology provides very little information on the details of transfer. It appears that the concept of markedness may help us to understand some problems that could not be solved satisfactorily in the past. Why are only some L1 structures transferred into the target L2 and why not every L1 structure in cases where the L1 and the L2 differ? As summarized above, the traditional explanation was to assume that the structures involved had to be sufficiently similar for transfer to occur. This assumption is still adequate. However, the notion of markedness may help us to understand what happens in cases where such similarities are not involved. A number of studies are available which indicate that there is at least the following tendency: less marked L1 structures tend to get transferred to the L2 if the L2 structures are more marked than the corresponding L1 structures (cf, e.g., Eckmann 1977; Kellerman 1978b; Hyltenstam 1981, 1983; Rutherford 1982). As pointed out before, the use of subject-neg-verb phrase in the acquisition of negation is an instance where a less marked structure appears in the developmental sequence in place of the more marked one, for example, post-verbal negation in L2 English/L1 German (recall Table 1).

Transfer in conjunction with markedness may also help to explain why in some situations negation structures like subject-neg-verb phrase are more frequent and more resistant to further development than in others. Such structures tend to occur more frequently in the speech of non-L1 learners, if the target language or the other languages involved have pre-verbal negation; if none of the languages involved has subject-neg-verb phrase then such structures tend to occur less frequently and they tend to be used for shorter periods of time. Consider L2 English. German children have been observed to produce structures like subject-no-verb phrase, but they apparently do so much less frequently and for a much shorter period than Spanish-speaking children learning English (Schumann 1979). As suggested above the rise of the word order pattern can be explained via its low degree of markedness. The use of 'no' instead of English '(do)n't', 'not', or other negative markers is very likely due to the fact that 'no' is the least marked negative item in English at least in terms of its morpho-syntactic properties. Spanish has pre-verbal negation; and it also uses a highly unmarked negative marker 'no' in that position. The parallels with the developmental structure subject-no-verb phrase plus, perhaps, the phonological parallels between English 'no' and Spanish 'no' probably have a reinforcing kind of transfer affect leading Spanish learners of English to use subject-no-verb phrase much more than, for example, Germans or Norwegians. It appears then, that, in general, developmental structures tend to be used longer and more frequently in L2 acquisition if they are backed by structures of the L1 paralleling the respective developmental structure(s) in terms of the degree of markedness. If the degree of markedness does not match then the appearance of unmarked or little marked developmental structures may, but need not, be short and fleeting (recall Table 3 and see Wode 1981a for details on the frequency of such developmental structures and on the range of individual variation among L2 learners).

To summarize section 1, the major variables which determine the grammar of interlanguages seem to be these: the upper bound is set by typology and universal constraints on the structure of natural languages, i.e. in terms of both the overall structural options and the range of variability. The developmental sequences mirror the markedness hierarchy and the typological implications inherent in the structures of the target language as reflected in the input which the learner is exposed to and which he processes as he builds up his competence. Markedness considerations and transfer operate in close interdependence with each other (see Zobl in this volume for some very suggestive proposals). In addition, there seem to be restrictions on the occurrence of developmental structures in a developmental sequence of a sort illustrated by the acquisition of interrogation (recall Table 5). At present it is unclear whether these restrictions are due to genuine incompatibilities between the structures involved or whether these restrictions are triggered by the presence or absence of certain structures in the input which the learner receives. The latter solution appears to be correct, because Latvian has intonational, pronominal, and affixal questions. Intonation questions are learned first, then pronominal ones, and the affixal type is the last to be acquired (Ruke-Dravina 1963; Wode 1976).

It should be noted that the ideas above have been developed from the inspection of grammatical aspects of interlanguages. Nevertheless, the essential points seem to carry over to other structural areas, for example, to phonology. Table 6 summarizes some L2 phonological data. Note that transfer occurs, but that not all target phonological items are subject to transfer to the same degree. For example, the English diphthongs /$\epsilon\iota$, oω/ tend to be monophthongized in any type of L2 English if the L1 learned previously does not have such diphthongs. On the other hand the English diphthongs /aι, oι, aω/ are much less subject to transfer even if the L1 does not have such diphthongs. For example, French learners do not have any notable difficulties in producing recognizable diphthongs like /aω, aι, oι/ although French does not have such diphthongs. On the other hand, the

English diphthongs /ɛι, oω/ tend to be monophthongized in L2 English/L1 French (for details, cf. Wode 1980).

2. Discussion: Some Theoretical Implications

The data presented in section 1 can be regarded as an empirical paradigm spanning central and less central manifestations of the design of natural languages and their functioning. The paradigm leads to the identification of parallels which cut across all these different areas and which consequently unite the latter. What are the implications?

TABLE 6. Vowel substitutions in English-based pidgins and in borrowings from English; ? = unclear cases

English vowels	i	ι	ɛ	æ	u	U	Λ	aι	eι	ɔι	aU	əU	
Melanesian Pidgin English	i	i	ɛ/e	ɛ	u	U	a	aι	e	ɔι	aU	o	(Hall 1943)
Hawaian Pidgin English (Korean speaker)	i	i	e	ɛ/a	u	u	a	aι	eι/e	?	aU	o	(Carr 1972)
Westafrican Pidgin English (bilingual Yoruba-Isoko speaker)	i	i	ɛ	ɛ/a	u	u	ɔ	aι/α	e	ɔι	aU	o	(Mafeni 1971)
Pennsylvania German	i	ι	ɛ	æ	u	U	?	aι	e	ɔι	aU	o	(Kelz 1971)

The most important point seems to be that it is extremely challenging and rewarding to take such a comprehensive perspective. So far linguists have not met the challenge yet. They have analysed languages synchronically, diachronically, and in many other ways. But all this remains merely descriptive and preliminary in the sense that it does not tell us why what we describe is as it is. That is, linguists must go beyond descriptions and attempt to answer the most fundamental question, namely, why are languages and their structures structured the way they are.[7] (Note Givón 1979 and Bickerton 1981 for similar pleas.)

This point of view contrasts sharply with the current division of labour among the various branches of linguistics. The comprehensive approach taken in this paper, it is hoped, will eventually help to develop a unified view about natural languages. This will require a revision of a number of views concerning very basic assumptions about languages and linguistics, notably: language structure and cognition; the learnability assumption; synchronic mechanisms for language change; marginal languages; markedness theory; and contrastive analysis.

Language and Cognition

What needs to be explained, first and foremost, are the parallels between the various manifestations of the design of natural languages and the origins of the parallels. In particular, where do the parallels with language learning and the developmental structures in learner languages originate from? The data reviewed in section 1 clearly suggests that the respective negation structures cannot be taken directly from the input to which the learner is exposed. Factors external to the learner, such as differences in the cultural environment, technological changes in the world around us, etc. will not account for the parallels either. Neither will personality variables, like IQ, motivation, or the like. Such factors vary enormously over any given population, let alone across different societies and cultures. This means that these variables constitute a great range of variation. On the other hand, learner languages show a great amount of invariance. Obviously, invariance cannot be explained by variation. So the explanation of the invariance can only be based on other types of factors. The only option left, so it seems, is the functioning of the human brain and the cognitive processing system(s) associated with it. The crucial problem then is to determine the nature of these systems and whether they can be equated with general cognition. The kind of cognition required to be able to learn languages must be different from general cognition or those capacities underlying problem solving or the kind of operations crucial in Piagetian types of developmental psychology. A number of arguments can be brought to bear on this issue.

Chomsky, for example, has developed a type of reasoning that is more theoretical in nature. It is based on speculations about language learning, primarily by L1 children. In essence, Chomsky's procedure is to develop principles of language structure and then to inquire whether they can be learned from the input the child is exposed to or whether the ability to detect such formal properties in the target language pre-supposes knowledge about the nature of these properties. Chomsky invariably opts for the latter solution. He argues that the input the child is exposed to is so chaotic and unsystematic that principles of language structure(s), most of them being highly abstract, cannot possibly be extracted from such raw material. But since children do learn languages nonetheless, they must have the requisite knowledge beforehand. This means, Chomsky suggests, that the formal principles of language structure must be genetically pre-programmed and that they constitute a special type of cognitive capacities (Chomsky 1965, 1973, 1976, and elsewhere). Three remarks are in order concerning Chomsky's proposals. First, the issue of what is genetically endowed can be separated from the question of whether the cognitive capacities prerequisite for the processing of language data are, or are not, of the same kind as general cognition. It may well be the case that the cognitive capacities needed for language processing are built up from other types of capacities not yet known. This issue needs much more research before a firm stand can be taken on it. Second, Chomsky's view about the chaotic nature of learner input is counterfactual.[8] Third, the idea that the processing of language data requires specific cognitive abilities different from general cognition, need not be decided on by relying only on Chomskyan types of speculations. Other kinds or arguments derived from detailed empirical investigations of language learning can be brought to bear on this issue. This evidence, as reviewed in section 1, strongly points in the same direction as Chomsky's conclusions.

Probably the most telling argument based on insights into language acquisition derives from a very simple observation. If it is claimed that general cognition determines the structure of learner languages, then it must also be explained why children as well as adults produce (much) the same developmental structures. If cognitive deficits are assumed to explain the non-targetlike nature of child L1 acquisition then this type of argument does not carry over to adult learners producing the same developmental structures. Adults and adolescents can be credited with having at their disposal concepts of cause, time, direction, instrumentality, negativity, and so forth. If adult L2 learners and young L1 children produce the same developmental negation structures then this cannot be due to the fact that the adult has a full-fledged negativity concept whereas the child does not. It follows that the capacities which enable human beings to learn natural languages are of a different kind than those which underly the ability of human beings to cognize their environment in terms of concepts and logical operations of whatever sort. This argument from language learning, then, leads to the same conclusion as Chomsky's argument, namely, that what is required to handle natural languages is a special type of cognition. It is termed linguo-cognition (in Wode 1981).[9] Next to nothing is presently known about the nature and the functioning of these linguo-cognitive systems. (Some suggestions are presented in Wode 1979, 1981, building on Slobin 1973.) Nonetheless, it seems appropriate to enlarge on the original proposal and to suggest that, apparently, it is these linguo-cognitive processing systems that ultimately constrain the design and the functioning of all types of natural languages. These constraints constitute the 'upper bound' of structural options.

A Re-conceptualization of the Learnability Axiom

The above discussion concerning language learning and cognition clearly shows that it is impossible to continue to base the learnability assumption on L1 acquisition and on young children. Natural languages do not function exclusively in monolingual societies. Bilingualism and other types of contact situations are much more common throughout the world and they are not restricted to child populations. There is no need to go back to the contingencies of the evolution of the human species to be able to suggest that a re-conceptualization of the learnability assumption is required. The original restriction to L1 children was completely arbitrary. Why not have a different learnability assumption for every age group or every learning situation? Why not base the assumption on adults?

No restriction in terms of age ranges or acquisitional types and situations is warranted. The learnability assumption must be based on people's overall ability to learn languages. After all, the human brain is a powerful but finite mechanism. What would the biological basis be if numerous learnability assumptions were introduced, say, as a function of age, number of languages learned, learning situations, etc.? It makes very good sense, indeed, to find, upon careful empirical observation, all these many parallels across age groups and acquisitional types as reviewed in section 1. These findings indicate that the brain is equipped with a single mechanism for learning languages. It has two vital properties: it is, apparently, flexible enough to cope with various differences in the external setting of the learning situation; and the mechanism does not change, let alone deteriorate (drastically) as a function of age, as implied in many preconceived views current not only among laymen. Linguistic theoreticians will have to adjust their thinking accordingly.

Moreover, it makes even better sense to find the sort of parallels between language learning and other areas of language structure and language functioning, namely, to see them all constrained in highly similar ways. What else would one expect, given the finite character of the human brain?

The Notion of Markedness

It may still be difficult at the present state of affairs to identify, in each given instance, which item is to be regarded as marked, unmarked or more/less marked. It should be possible to resolve these difficulties in the long run. After all, the learner data reviewed in section 1 and other material available elsewhere are extremely uniform. Consequently there must be a psycholinguistic basis to markedness. However, in line with the point of view adopted in this paper, markedness also needs to be explained. Why does it take the form it does? What constrains it? Obviously, markedness is one aspect of the universal restrictions governing natural languages. To be more precise, markedness hierarchies seem to be a reflex of the linguo-cognitive processing constraints, although globally delimited by the 'upper bound' but more geared to 'lower-level' types of organization (in terms of the distinction introduced in the first section).

Linguistic Theories and Language Transfer

Another area in which a re-conceptualization is urgently required is language transfer. One of the outstanding characteristics of natural languages is that they are quickly adaptable to changes in the world around us. This requires a built-in synchronic mechanism for language change. It is this mechanism that makes languages such a useful instrument for communication. One extremely important component within this flexibility mechanism relates to the ability to transfer from one language into the other. Consequently, any linguistic theory that does not adequately provide for transfer or that is not suitable for handling transfer cannot possibly qualify as an adequate description of a language or as a theoretical framework for describing natural languages. As far as can be made out, no presently available linguistic theory comes anywhere near meeting this requirement. It seems, then, that linguists so far have failed to incorporate, and to give proper consideration to, one of the most important aspects of natural human languages (for details cf. Wode 1982).

Marginal Languages

Furthermore it seems obvious that linguists must give much more attention to marginal languages. Such varieties no longer belong in a linguistic curiosity shop. Learner languages, pidgins, creoles, bilingualism, and other marginal areas, are of central importance to linguistics and to theories provided by this discipline. In fact, it is these marginal areas of language functioning and language manifestation that provide the most challenging incentive for the kind of comprehensive view adopted here (see similar pleas by Bailey 1973; Givón 1979; or Bickerton 1981).

Contrastive Analysis and Language Teaching

Contrastive analysis has recently been criticized heavily for being unable to handle learner data (for example, Wardaugh 1970; Richards 1971). Some scholars have suggested we disregard contrastive analysis in our dealings with L2 problems altogether (for example, Dulay and Burt 1973, 1974a–c). This view is certainly unjustified. Contrastive analysis basically deals with comparing languages or language systems. It is thus at the very heart of linguistic methodology. The major misunderstanding, it seems, relates to the implication that contrastive analysis should be a language-learning theory. This is exactly what it is not. Contrastive analysis describes different linguistic structures and, if handled well, this methodology allows linguists to relate different language systems to each other. As for language learning, such a comparison will not do. The data reviewed in section 1 clearly show that clashes between two linguistic systems are resolved by learners not ad hoc or in completely random ways. Rather, different learners resolve such clashes in much the same way. The important point is that contrastive analysis does not allow for any kind of prediction on how the learner will resolve such a clash. That is why contrastive analysis is not a language learning theory. However, this does not mean that contrastive analysis is useless for L2 problems. On the contrary, it is an indispensible part of any attempt to devise a theory of language acquisition in general or of naturalistic L2 acquisition in particular.

Contrastive analysis specifies the nature of the structural clash. A language learning component needs to be added to determine and predict how learners will resolve such clashes and it is this kind of information that is needed by language teachers (details in Wode 1983b).

As for linguistics, contrastive analysis is just as indispensible. The psycholinguistic approach basic to this paper might provide guide-lines on how to set up such a contrastive analysis. This is to say, in the various approaches to contrastive analysis the problem of the tertium comparationis is notoriously difficult to solve. Why not let psycholinguistic data decide such issues?

Notes

1) For details about the framework, cf. Wode (1981).

2) Except in child-child interaction, or in those cases where the respective languages employ such structures, as in Black English, or in pidgins and creoles.

3) A detailed account of how these (and other) developmental negation structures relate to the structure of the target language(s) is given in Wode (1977b) for L1 acquisition and in Wode (1981) for L2 acquisition. These details are not immediately relevant to the discussion in the present paper.

4) Individual variation in the linguistic structure of learner utterances is a well documented phenomenon for L1 acquisition. Studies on this type of structural variation are still few in number for the other acquisitional types, notably the non-simultaneous types of acquisition (cf. Fillmore 1976; Bahns 1976; Burmeister 1977; Clahsen 1980; Pienemann 1980; Ufert 1980; Allendorff 1980; Wode 1981).

5) There is much more evidence available than referred to in Table 3. This is particularly true with respect to the L1 acquisition of negation (overview in Wode 1977b). For more details on naturalistic L2 acquisition see Wode (1981a). In particular the L2 combinations involving English as a target can be extended further to include other L1s, like Japanese (Milon 1974), French (Tiphine 1980), Taiwanese (Huang 1971), etc. The re-learning of a language has been studied only very rarely. The only extensive data that seems to be presently available concerns L2 English/L1 German (Allendorff 1980).

6) Most handbooks give the impression that post-verbal negation occurred in English only in variation with pre-verbal negation, as in early modern English (for example, Jespersen 1917; Traugott 1972). This does not seem to be fully correct. Schwarze (1982) reports that certain parts of the Wycliffe Bible have post-verbal negation only.

7) Although Chomsky introduced various levels of adequacy including explanatory adequacy (1964, 1965, and elsewhere), this notion of explanation is still essentially descriptive as I use the term here (following Givón 1979b). Chomsky's notion of explanatory adequacy refers to the explanatory power of a linguistic theory, i.e. its predictive capacity. Such a notion is not adequate to explain the nature of a range of phenomena from a domain X by recourse to a domain Y, like the psychology of vision/sight explained by the physiology and the bio-chemistry of the organs and the nervous apparatus involved.

8) Detailed investigations of the speech used in various exposure situations, such as adult-child, adolescent-child, native-foreigner, clearly show that the more competent speakers can, and mostly do, adapt their speech in remarkable ways to the level of their addressee's. Such learner talk tends to be less marked by errors and other inconsistencies than normal discourse. For L1 acquisition see, for example, the

articles in Snow and Ferguson (1977); for L2 acquisition note Hatch (1978a); Peck (1978); van der Geest and Heckhausen (1978) (summary in Wode 1981). However, the effect that such adaptations have on the learning process is still very much an open question.

9) Other types of observations from language learning can also be brought to bear on the issue of whether or not general cognition can be equated with linguo-cognition. An argument from the acquisition of L1 bilingualism is developed in Slobin (1973), for L1 monolingualism see Wode (1974, 1976a). A detailed review of the issue of language specific cognition with particular reference to the inadequacy of Piagetian psychology to explain language learning and language structures is Felix (1982a). However, the whole debate is focused too much on cognitive schemata, representations and cognitive capacities underlying them. More attention needs to be given to the actual processing of speech.

14. Discussant

The field of interlanguage studies now has a history of about fifteen years. During that time, as Henning Wode stated, our goal has been to describe the origin, structure and development of IL. This effort has proceeded up until the present in the absence of any overall theory of IL. Even the most well-known theory of second language acquisition, the Monitor Model, has very little to say, in terms of specific hypotheses, about how IL develops. This discussion of the papers by Wode and Felix will focus on their contribution to a theory of IL.

Wode in outlining some theoretical implications of second language acquisition research and the grammar of interlanguages makes two claims:

1) The cognitive abilities underlying the acquisition of language are different from those which underlie 'the ability of human beings to cognize their environment in terms of concepts and logical operations of whatever sort' (p.180).

2) The brain is equipped with a single language-learning mechanism that does not change with age and which is responsible for first-language acquisition and child, adolescent and adult second-language acquisition.

The basis for his argument is the view that developmental sequences produced by child L1 learners and older L2 learners are essentially the same. Therefore, child L1 acquisition sequences cannot be explained by general cognitive development. Instead, Wode argues that all language acquisition is controlled by a special type of cognition called linguo-cognition which constitutes the genetically preprogrammed formal principles of language structure as described by Chomsky and others.

Wode views both transfer and markedness as playing important roles in SLA. He argues that markedness constraints are a result of linguo-cognitive processing and are applicable to L1 and L2 acquisition and that a linguistic theory to be adequate must be able to account for transfer. He also claims that developmentally, less marked structures will appear before more marked structures and that less marked L1 forms will be transferred to the L2 if the L2 structures are more marked than the corresponding L1 forms.

These positions offer interesting hypotheses about IL development and should continue to motivate research, but as Wode points out, there are difficulties in determining which items are to be regarded as marked, unmarked or more/less marked. Since it is claimed that less marked structures are acquired early and more marked structures later, what has to be avoided is the potential circularity in identifying as unmarked those forms which appear first in language development. In fact, a consensus on the definition of markedness would be of great value to Wode's paradigm.

The aim of Wode's paper, however, is not simply to develop a theoretical perspective on second language acquisition, but to develop 'a unified view about natural languages'. He offers the above as a step toward that goal and we will look forward to his subsequent efforts in this area.

Felix's paper calls our attention to the current perspective of generative grammar. Indeed he presents us with what I consider a most interesting view of first language acquisition, namely, the Maturational Schedule of Universal Grammar. Focusing specifically on stage-transition phenomena in language development he argues that

> the principles of Universal Grammar . . . are subject to an innately specified developmental process. . . . Although the set of universal principles is fully and exhaustively specified by the child's genetic program, each of these principles is somehow 'latent' up to a specific point in time after which it will start to operate and thus constrain the child's knowledge of what may be humanly accessible language. . . . Under this view the unfolding off the genetic program that characterizes the child's language faculty resembles very closely the genetic program determining the child's physical growth.

Felix makes an analogy between the genetically programmed principles of language and any genetically programmed capacitty such as growing teeth. His position allows him to view language acquisition as a maturationally based process in which the innately determined program specifies when each principle will become operational.

Whereas this formulation is a particularly elegant account of first-language acquisition, it seems to me that it fails to explain or even address the origin and development of IL. That is, it does not account for second-language acquisition. If the onset of the principles of Universal Grammar is a maturationally controlled process, it would appear that, like the growth of teeth, once the process is completed it cannot be recapitulated. If, on the other hand, such recapitulation is possible, how and why it would take place is not at all obvious, and Felix attempts no explanation in this paper.

The original title of his presentation was 'Two problems of language acquisition: the relevance of grammatical studies to the theory of interlanguage'. If we assume the generally accepted notion that IL is the speech of a second-language learner, then we have to conclude that whereas Felix's formulation may be an interesting account of first-language acquisition, he has not shown it to be of any relevance to SLA and therefore a theory of IL. But the account which Felix rejects, that of White (see also Hyams 1983), offers possibilities. Felix objects to this position because it maintains that child grammars at any stage in development fall within Universal Grammar. Therefore utterances that deviate from the target must be seen as reflections of the learners' perception of the target, and movement from one stage to another must result from changes in perception. Felix argues that this position places the problem of language development outside the domain of a theory of grammar and into the domain of a theory of perception. My feeling is that this problem of perception makes White's and Hyam's formulations somewhat less elegant than Felix's, but nevertheless, they are at least relevant to the issue of IL development. Thus whereas Felix's position leaves us with nothing, White's and Hyam's position provide us with a set of very specific hypotheses about the sequence of forms that should appear in IL, if L2 is constrained by the same factors that constrain L1. (For example, that a + pro-drop IL will become − pro-drop with the onset of expletives and modals.) Of course, IL is more than syntax, and a purely syntactic theory of IL would of necessity be incomplete. However, as Susan Foster (personal communication) has suggested, if the theory provides a reasonable account of syntactic development, it then helps to define which areas of language acquisition can best be handled by a complementary theory of discourse pragmatics.

In sum, Wode sees first- and second-language acquisition as controlled by the same language-learning mechanism. He suggests that examining transfer, markedness and their interaction may provide an understanding of the origin, structure and development of IL. Felix presents a maturational perspective on Universal Grammar which may be plausible for first-language acquisition, and which perhaps could also be valuable for a theory of IL if he would demonstrate how that schedule applies to SLA.

Acknowledgement. I want to thank Sharon Melrose, a doctoral student in Applied Linguistics at UCLA, for her valuable comments on an earlier draft of this paper.

15. Summary of Discussion

Neither Felix nor Wode found much to disagree with in the discussant's remarks. On the SLA issue, however, Felix commented that, in spite of the present lack of evidence, the grammar-restructuring processes outlined in the maturational schedule might be expected to operate for second languages at least until puberty, though probably not thereafter. Wode re-emphasized his interest in a comprehensive definition of IL which would include both first- and second-language acquisition as well as other examples of learner language, and expressed some doubt at the relevance of assigning a special significance to puberty in accounting for variation in language acquisition. The subsequent open discussion explored a range of issues provoked by the clear contrast between the rigorously specified approach of the maturational model and the comprehensive views adopted by Wode. Most of the comments, however, clustered round two particular themes to which the seminar addressed itself on a number of occasions.

The first of these concerned the identification of IL as an autonomous field of enquiry and the consequent need for a definition of its domain of study. A range of definitions had emerged during the symposium (one speaker claimed to have identified at least four), but none had succeeded in attracting a consensus. The core issue remained the legitimacy of recognizing a fundamental distinction between first- and second-language acquisition. If the former were defined as the maturational schedule implied (it was described by one participant as so circumscribed as to suggest that child language acquisition was a kind of 'criterion-referenced activity with a discrete beginning and end'), then SLA could be held to refer to any other form of language learning activity. If, however, such a sharp distinction were rejected, then IL was free to adopt the same principles and procedures of enquiry for all instances of learner language. On the methodology issue, it was pointed out that one serious problem with the universal grammar approach adopted by the maturational schedule was that it forced the model into a dualism which distinguished between the stage-by-stage 'unfolding' of knowledge on the one hand, and the separate development of processing mechanisms for handling this knowledge in real situations of language use on the other. A simpler and more flexible view would allow for a loosely related set of developmental orders to operate at the same time (cf. the creative construction approach). Such an approach might account better for performance variation, particularly in SLA where there was little evidence for a strictly defined sequence of discrete stages of development.

In response to these and similar comments, it was claimed that, although a focus on grammatical knowledge in the universal grammar tradition implied an approach to theory-construction that required the identification of idealized 'sub-components' (syntax, lexis, etc.), it was nevertheless a valid procedure provided the relationships between components were accounted for at a later stage of analysis. The objection was raised, however, that a methodology of this kind failed to address the crucial problem, namely whether the idealization procedures of the analyst, which typically employed established categories of linguistic description, adequately reflected the processes of IL development, which might require special language-user categories of a different order altogether. The core of the argument was summarized as a 'conundrum' in which components could not be related until they were understood in their own right, and they could not be understood unless the relationships between them were known.

Towards the end of the discussion at least one speaker wondered whether the interests of workers in the IL field were always best served by revisiting traditional preoccupations which tended to distract attention from the practical realities of IL studies.

16. Theoretical Review of Discourse and Interlanguage

Discourse analysis has had a powerful influence on the study of second language acquisition. But the direction that interlanguage research has taken under this influence is not what one might have predicted five to eight years ago. In this paper I hope to show that we have learned a great deal about interlanguage from 'discourse based' studies in three major areas, yet know surprisingly little about discourse as a linguistic level of interlanguage.

1. Interactive Discourse

Communication theorists proposed a set of system universals which govern the *form* of interactive discourse. In addition, a set of language-specific ritual constraints protect the 'face' of interactants in conversations. E.g. Goffman's (1976) System Universals were:

1) Contact signals (openings, closings, etc.)
2) Turn-over signals (turn taking system)
3) Acoustically adequate and interpretable messages
4) Backchannel reception signals (feedback signals)
5) Signals for message rerun (repair)
6) Gricean norms of conversation
7) Framing of asides
8) Non-participant constraints.

The most thoroughly researched universals are *two-way acoustically adequate and interpretable messages* and the importance of the *rerun system* in obtaining message clarity. Voluminous research documents the characteristics of foreigner talk (language addressed to learners) which aid the learner to interpret messages and the modifications which make it easier for the learner to carry a role in conversation (for reviews, see Hatch 1983; Long 1983b). The negotiation of meaning by L2 learners through message rerun and *repair* has been described (cf. Schwartz 1980; Gaskill 1980) and an interesting related issue has been the ongoing theoretical argumentation of Tarone (1980b) and Faerch and Kasper (1983c) regarding communication strategies. Krashen (1980) has drawn heavily on the input/interaction research, expanding the claims on the importance of interactions and the resulting 'comprehensible input' for language acquisition. Whether such input is 'necessary and/or sufficient' to second-language acquisition is the focus of much discussion in our field.

190

Interestingly, we know that (given appropriate feedback signals) conversations can continue unabated even when messages are not truly interpreted by either parties. Only later examination of the data or questioning of participants (cf. Hatch et al 1978; Hawkins 1983) show how little of each message was interpreted. (Nevertheless, the messages and the exchange may be perfectly comprehensible to persons hearing the exchange.) This emphasizes the role *feedback signals* have in maintaining smooth interaction. We'll consider this further in a moment.

Other important elements of the discourse system are *openings* and *preclosing/closing sequences* and the systematics of *turn taking*. How these are realized vary across languages for they must meet 'face' constraints of the cultural system as well. Scarcella (1983) investigated L2 conversation skills in taped interview situations (native speakers interviewed learners). She found successful openings and closings; learners were less successful in responses to preclosers. Interviews can be taped, but it is difficult to tape spontaneous conversations. While it is difficult to reliably log preclosing moves in casual conversations, openings are easily observed. In a month-long tally of observed conversation openers between university students on campus, native-speakers more frequently included 'noticings' following or within their greetings than did foreign students. Examples of noticings incorporated in openings were:

Native Speaker:	Hi-ayy, you're lookin' great in that suit!
	Hi, m'god what happened t'you?
	Hi, great haircut!
	Hiya, gorgeous!
Non-native Speakers:	Good morning, M.
	Hi, teacher.
	Hello, C., how are you?

Noticings during openings may be more common in accidental encounters where the interactants have not recently met. Yet, some talk must fill the gap between a recognition greeting and the anchor for the first topic. This space typically serves the ritual face concerns before getting to the topics at hand even in informal office meetings or more formal business meetings. A conventional method of doing this is to ask after the addressee's health. Students in one of my classes tallied responses of native and non-native speakers' replies to their own marked responses to 'how are you'. The marked responses were 'fantastic' or 'don't ask'. In this very informal experiment, the responses of foreign students included inappropriate neutral responses to 'fantastic' while native-speakers usually requested an explanation. They also gave more expressions of concern than guesses as to what was wrong in the 'don't ask' condition. Examples of replies to marked responses:

'Fantastic'	'Don't ask'
Native Speaker:	Native Speaker:
What's up?	Oh, the exam, huh.
Hey, tell me about it!	Ya gotta get that car fixed!
Non-native Speaker:	Non-native Speaker:
Good.	Oh, I'm so sorry.

Just as in the opening segment, ritual concerns may have a special place in pre-closing moves. Wolfson's (1983) famous invitations ('Let's get together for lunch sometime soon') frequently occur in this space, often as ritual bonding statements rather than actual invitations. Personal noticings can also occur as last-minute comments before closing begins. The openings and closings do provide a frame for the conversation but they also serve as a place in which to express the concerns of the ritual system. While we know L2 learners quickly acquire (or are taught) standard greetings, we do not know what a developmental interlanguage sequence of pre-closings and opening extenders might be.

The *turn-taking system* includes turn allocation and the timing of exchanges in turns at talk. Again, the system is universal but must be responsive to ritual constraints. In American English, overlaps in turns do occur but they are relatively rare, occur at predictable points (such as at a tag question boundary), or have power bid functions. People generally speak one at a time, and the timing of turns is precise. The exchange is in rhythm so that a conversation flows like an orchestrated event. To cut the pause too short is rushing things (being pushy or aggressive). Allowing the pause to exceed 3 to 5 beats may be interpreted as an expression of disapproval or a refusal to claim the turn. ESL students who use long pauses typical of interactions in their first languages are labelled slow or inattentive.

More seriously, a slow response disrupts the flow of interactive discourse. Silence gives the turn back to the first speaker and invites *repair*. If a native speaker does not respond during his pause period, we assume the listener disagrees. If a non-native speaker does not respond, we assume lack of understanding. In both cases, the result is a repair. In one case, the repair will be a clarification and, in the other, we may back down or revise the strength of our claim. An example of pause length inviting repair was given by Pomerantz (1978):

B: . . . an' that's an awful lotta fruitcake.
A: (1.0)
B: Course it is. A little piece goes a long way,
A: W'll that's right.

While differences in pause length have often been noted, we are only beginning to collect hard data on pause length in interlanguage conversations. Will we find that inappropriate pause length is always accounted for as L1 transfer, or are long pauses a feature of early IL in general? Speakers can, of course, capture and keep turns. In order to hold a turn while formulating an idea, we often employ fillers such as 'mmmm' or 'ahhh', with level or slightly rising intonation. These fillers prevent a turn exchange. However, we seldom use fillers in utterance-initial position, and especially not with falling intonation. To do so would signal willingness to give up a turn. According to Scarcella (1983), Spanish speakers use fillers in this position. An American would hear these as backchannel signals, not the preliminary to a complete turn. So the American takes up the turn and the Spanish speaker feels rudely interrupted. The Spanish speaker, hearing no such fillers in the speech of Americans, sees them as curt or brusque.

Backchannel signals are given during interaction to show that the message is being received. While most feedback is stereotyped ('umhmm', 'I know whatcha mean', 'yeah', etc.), the feedback may become ritualized in more formal discourse (e.g., 'amens' in church services, 'gritos' to music performances, even the audience responses reported by Day (1983) during showings of the *Rocky Horror Show*).

Again, types of feedback vary and carry different meanings in different language groups. Smiles and nods do not always signal comprehension. They may be 'yes, I'm listening' rather than 'yes, I understand' signals. Repetition is commonly used as an appropriate feedback signal in some linguistic groups, but when transferred to English, may be interpreted as a signal of sarcasm or disbelief. Examples noted in informal experiments suggest that differences in feedback signals can best be accounted for as L1 transfer. However, we have no information on the frequency of inappropriate signals, nor tests of claims of L1 transfer versus development of feedback as part of the interlanguage discourse system.

Gricean constraints assume that conversation is a cooperative venture with participants making *relevant* contributions to what they perceive to be the *goals* of the conversation. These contributions will be regulated by the 'politeness principle' which protects 'face'. Comprehension of conversation, in a psycholinguistic sense, is the identification of these goals – goals which may be explicitly stated, kept deliberately ambiguous, or even be, in certain cases, hidden. Several goals may co-occur or overlap. And all must be negotiated, preserving the social worth of speaker and hearer.

Many conversations have no goal other than 'sociability'.

Much of what passes for communication is rather the equivalent of a handclasp or an embrace; its purpose is sociability. (Bolinger 1975, 524)
A: Hi, Jean.
B: Hi, gee, y'gotcher hair cut.
A: No, that's weeks ago.
B: I'm so observant, but it's good t'see ya. We gotta get t'gether after exams.
A: Yeah.
B: I'll give ya a call.
A: Great. Good luck on exams.
B: You too.

193

Conversations with phatic goals may be very common for adults in immersion situations. Economides (personal communication) gives an example of a Japanese scholar who – presumably after many such interactions – gave all his answers for the interaction before questions were even asked – his name, his home university, field of expertise, arrival date, and a statement of pleasure at being in the US. One might wish that the goals of all interactions be transparent, but, given the fragile nature of cross-cultural communication, more likely they will be quite opaque. Since goals and intentionality are so difficult to define, many researchers have turned to speech-act theory (or notional/functional categories) for a guiding framework. In these studies, speech acts or speech events such as invitations, complaints, and direction requests have been extracted from the discourse for analysis. The comparison of findings on L1 and interlanguage performance is a rapidly expanding field of inquiry. For the first collection of such studies, outlining how such functions as inviting, complaining, complimenting are accomplished, see Wolfson and Judd (1983).

As can be seen in these few examples, discourse analysis is rapidly enlarging our information on interlanguage; but it also shows that the *linguistic* discourse system, the *sociolinguistic* variation, and the *cross-cultural* value systems are tightly interwoven. We would like to be able to separate that which is purely linguistic. The description of interlanguage discourse as a separate *linguistic* subsystem is difficult. Should it consist of description of system universals proposed by Goffman, or would some alternative framework be more revealing? Since research on discourse structure is still in its infancy, it is not clear what features should be considered. Scarcella's (1983) study is the first to even consider what a developmental order might look like for interlanguage conversational skills. Some researchers have opted for a totally ethnographic approach (or a sociolinguistic or cross-cultural approach), deliberately rejecting the separation of linguistic form and ritual systems. In the end, this may turn out to be the most informative procedure for applied linguistics.

Since all parts of the interlanguage system are separate yet overlap, a second question has been the relationship of interactive discourse to syntax, lexicon, morphology and phonology.

Peck (1978) investigated this question by studying child–child interactions. In addition to extensive phonology play (play with the sounds of the language), she found the children participated in stereotyped game interactions which featured formulaic utterances (e.g., 'my turn', 'throw it to him'). Wong-Fillmore (1976) documented the large number of routines, formulaic patterns in the schooltime interactions of child L2 learners. These routines, she suggested, formed the basis for syntactic development (hence, 'syntax out of discourse' through interaction formulas).

Adult learners report constructing their own learning syllabi by repeating specific interactions (e.g., identical service encounters, asking directions to the same place from many people, etc.) until mastering each. Schmidt (1983) suggests that Wes, an adult Japanese, acquired menu-ordering skills after many such exchanges. As in the Economides example, Wes took away the waiter's part and, with more natural results, recited his choices: 'Yes, I'd like teriyaki steak, medium rare, rice, salad, thousand, coffee.' (Others are not so successful. For example, an Italian visiting professor at UCLA, on leaving a party, said to his host, 'See ya at the pole'. This was a leave-taking formula of two professors in a nearby office who always met later at the university flagpole to share a ride home.)

The acquisition of large numbers of appropriate formulas shows success in attending to parts of interactive discourse. However, these formulas present a problem in the analysis of interlanguage syntax. If they must be excluded from the data for syntactic analysis, do they at least form a basis for development of syntactic structures? The limited research in this area suggests they may for the child learner. The evidence is much less persuasive for adults. Learners such as Zoila (Shapira 1978), Armando (Lynch 1983) and Wes (Schmidt 1983) show good to excellent discourse abilities but little evidence that discourse skills lead to progress in syntax. Syntax in these studies has, however, meant primarily morphosyntax. The development of syntax not related to bound morphology may eventually be shown to be more directly connected to discourse than these studies suggest.

It may be that the effect of discourse will be clearer in the development of lexical rules and the suprasegmental system, and through them only indirectly on the morphophonemic and phonological systems. This may be difficult to establish. We know that learners often supply correct morphology in formulaic utterances but not elsewhere. Similarly, learners may be able to perform chants, poems, even songs with native-like suprasegmentals and phonology and not transfer this to their interlanguage systems. The measurement of appropriate suprasegmentals along with development of the discourse level has yet to be attempted.

To summarize this section, the analysis of the structure of conversation should be a central issue of interlanguage discourse analysis. Research on the formal system has, however, quickly branched out in many directions – from input/interaction to speculations on the importance of comprehensible input to acquisition, from repair systems to communication strategies, from Gricean constraints to performance of speech-act functions. The results are of immense value, and document the impact of discourse analysis on our field. It is only unfortunate that we still know very little about the linguistic-discourse system of interlanguage conversations.

2. Discourse of Text Types

For many L2 learners, comprehension and production of written discourse is even more important than are oral-discourse skills. There are, of course, many similarities between oral and written discourse. Both have opening and closing segments, topics are nominated, topic continuity maintained, asides are marked, and topic shifts nicely touched off or bridged. Repairs occur in the composing process (and somewhat differently in the reading process), resulting in text more tightly organized in terms of discourse and syntax.

For those who advocate a top-down model of reading comprehension, discourse structure is promoted to a guiding rule. The reader is assumed to internalize the discourse structure of various text types and, once these are acquired, to use them to guide efficient reading as well as writing. For example, in English narratives, we expect an orientation section to give us the setting, place, time, and introduce us to the major characters (at least, the hero/heroine). This is followed by a set of temporally ordered clauses (and possibly less central, background clauses), the climax of the story, perhaps an evaluative segment, and a coda to bring us back to present time. Rumelhart (1975) claims that comprehension of such narratives is guided not so much by the discourse form as by what we know about narratives. First, he says, we search for the hero/heroine and the problem (e.g., the detective must solve the crime). Once these are located, we look for the steps taken to solve the problem, and the final solution. While it may be that the general form of the narrative is universal, the language/cultural values immediately surface when we look at narratives across languages. What constitutes a problem, the attributes of heroes/heroines, what motivates characters, the kinds of steps taken, what constitutes a satisfactory solution, and the meaning of the solution to the culture will differ. The overlap of the linguistic organization of discourse and the ritual/cultural system in the discourse is again an issue. (Cf. Carrell's (1981) study of the comprehensibility of translated narratives.)

Argumentative prose (where the goal is persuasion to the author's point of view) is another text type where we would expect differences. While there is no single comprehensive description of this text type, Winterowd (1975) describes the 'classical organization'. This includes an introduction, followed by an explanation of the case under consideration, an outline of the argument, the proof, the refutation, and the conclusion.

Maccoun (1983), however, found eight different formats in the reading materials presented to an advanced ESL class. Her students experienced a variety of problems in dealing with such text. On the basis of test data and follow-up interviews, she hypothesized a developmental set of stages for the concepts needed to solve argumentation prose.

1) Views all discussion as neutral.
2) Mistakes opposition's arguments for author's.
3) Correctly locates local author bias.
4) Correctly identifies global argument and refutation.
5) Correctly interprets concession.
6) Correctly identifies global and local bias, direct refutation, and concession.
7) Correctly interprets sarcastically marked disagreement.

During interviews, some students claimed not to understand why a writer would present arguments of the other side. When the text was arranged so that the opposition argument was first, some students argued that what comes first must show the author's point of view. While arguments for the other side are often presented in argumentative text, there are formulaic as well as more subtle ways of showing that this is not the view of the writer. There is little evidence to show that L2 learners find these formulas as easy to acquire as those of oral discourse. I suspect it is not easy for the learner to identify such formulas as 'One commonly held (= but wrong/inappropriate) belief' or 'A standard view (= which I now ask you to reject)'.

Unfortunately, we still do not have comprehensive descriptions of most text types. We assume most languages have narrative, descriptive, procedural, and, perhaps, hortatory text, but we really do not know which are truly universal or at least valued by most language groups. Certainly, English has highly developed text types for scientific writing (e.g., the APA format for reports of experiments) – types which are neither universal nor universally valued. Since so much of reading and composing relies on 'background knowledge' (topic information *and* text type information), the description of text types is an important area of ongoing research. The acquisition of text types as discourse should become part of our description of interlanguage competence.

Discovery of the overall discourse framework within which text is displayed and the acquisition of text type frames is important, but it is not the central question of present research. Rather, the focus has turned to the linguistic devices which either promote or are the result of coherent text. Thus, the central question is how discourse uses linguistic devices to *explicitly* show relationships between sentences and/or across paragraphs of text. Extensive work, of course, has been done on coherence and cohesion. Some of the studies examine structural markers and lexical cohesion primarily in inter-sentential relationships (e.g., Halliday and Hassan 1976). Others emphasize semantic unity and propositional relationships (e.g., van Dijk 1977). Still others include discourse organization as part of the taxonomy of cohesive elements. Givon's extensive investigation of topic-continuity is also relevant to the issue of linguistic ways of typing text into a coherent whole. Types of cohesive elements include:

Phonology: Repetition of sounds (alliteration); intonation
Lexis: Lexical conjugation, collocation, reiteration
Structure: Ellipsis, substitution, repetition, chaining, Givon's topic-continuity scale, nominalization
Speech act: Repetition, flow of old to new information
Discourse: Opening, closing, topic nomination, topic shift

For a comprehensive review of much of this research, see Scarcella (1984).

While much effort has been spent on the identification of cohesive ties, we know little about their distribution, scope or frequency, for English, let alone the languages of the world. Some languages (for example, Arabic) are said to set high value on lexical cohesion. It may be that languages which favour strong lexical cohesion (for example, Navajo, according to Bartelt (1983)) also use more chaining or repetition of large segments to promote coherence. Wonderly shows this is the case for Mayan. Writers of English avoid such repetition, using conjunctive ties and ellipsis instead. Overall repetition, however, is promoted by teachers of English composition. Students are taught to 'say what you will say, say it, and in summary, say it again'. Such repetition is strictly avoided in many language groups (cf. Kachru 1983).

If these differences across languages are substantial, we would expect that different learners would show real differences in achieving coherence in L2 composition. That is, no interlanguage continuum would be found. These differences ought to show up most clearly in text types other than narrative, descriptive and procedural. In these three, the discourse organization is strong enough to allow for coherence with few structural cohesion markers. That is, temporal or spatial organization of the discourse alone can create coherence. However, even here, Canale et al. (1980) suggest that there are subtle differences in organization, and that mastery of similar narrative structure in L1 will not transfer smoothly to L2.

Some L2 writers are able to create coherent text without explicit cohesive ties. Hottel-Burkhart (1983) showed that advanced ESL students use no more cohesive ties than less proficient students (though more proficient students used a wider variety of cohesive ties). Error analyses are beginning to reveal the difficulties even very advanced students have in proper use of conjunctive ties (cf. Beebe 1979; Jisa and Scarcella 1981) and reference (cf. Johns 1979). Scarcella (1984) suggests that there may be developmental patterns to be discovered across learners – 'for example, in reference, the establishment of explicit, unambiguous ties; in conjunction, the appropriate use of ties'.

Jisa and Scarcella's study is especially interesting since it highlights 'register' errors in cohesion (e.g., 'But 10 years ago *ya know* we still a developing nation') as well as conjunction cohesion errors like 'on the other hand' with no 'first hand'. This points up, I believe, the formulaic nature of many cohesion markers. Learners appear to find them salient and sprinkle them about, often without any clear intuition of their function. Somehow the 'native-like' formulas acquired in spoken discourse appear to be more successfully matched to function, and perhaps for this reason also show up in written text.

Interest in comparing the use of cohesive markers in the writing of native speakers and L2 learners is strong. The many theses and dissertations in preparation at the moment assure us of new insights on interlanguage discourse. It is already clear that ESL students show differential abilities in organizing text (discourse) and in grammar. The linguistic subsystems are distinct, yet overlap. Once again, however, research has moved away from the acquisition of discourse text types (in reading and composing) to the study of the linguistic signals used to make relationships among the parts of text explicit.

3. Form/Function to Parameter Setting

Working from child second-language data, Gough (1975) pointed out a flaw in the then-current morpheme research. It was, she said, quite possible for second-language learners to acquire forms without having acquired the function of the forms. Her observation was confirmed in subsequent research (cf. Plann 1979; Olshtain 1979). Conversely, second-language data also showed evidence of acquisition of function without acquisition of form. The study of acquisition of linguistic forms should not, Gough argued, be divorced from study of the appropriate use of form in context. The emphasis on function continues in the work of Andersen, Lightbown and Pfaff, all of whom have taken a functional approach to second-language research.

Form/function analysis has been especially helpful in explaining data of learners whose languages (i.e., topic-comment languages) are organized to show pragmatic relationships more clearly than in English. English, of course, does have ways of maintaining its strict word order and grammatical organization to accomplish pragmatic goals – the use of articles, dummy subjects, passives, cleft, and topicalized sentences, for example. So researchers have looked at these particular structures in data of ESL learners from topic-comment languages (or mixed subject-prominent/topic-comment). With a functional analysis, Schachter and Rutherford (1978) showed that errors of Chinese learners of English could be identified as transfer of topic-comment organization from Chinese to English. Huebner (1979) demonstrated that straight analysis of form showed little about the progress of English-language acquisition of his Hmong speaker. A functional analysis, however, revealed a gradual process of change in use of articles from more topic-comment-like structures to more subject-prominent structures.

Watabe and Brown (1983) also used a form/function approach in analysing the composition errors of ESL and Japanese-as-a-second-language students. In their study, Americans learning Japanese formed passives quite accurately. However, they used them for the topicalization function that passives have in English. Passives in Japanese do topicalize, but, in addition, they can have an 'adversative' function. In English, we might say 'America was discovered by Columbus' in order to focus on Columbus as the discoverer. The sentence in Japanese is, however, inappropriate when it takes on the adversity meaning:

1492 nen Korombusu ni hakkens-are-te kara samazamana
1492 year Colombus by discover-PASS-Past since various

kuni no hito-tati ga Amerika tairiku ni watatte
countries GEN people SUBJ America continent to come
ki-mati-ta.
over-POL-Past
= After it was unfortunate enough to be discovered by Columbus in 1492. . . .

In form/function analysis, L2 researchers, including Andersen, Rutherford, Schumann, and their students, also turned to look at how well the rudimentary syntax evidenced in early interlanguage accomplishes discourse functions. A wide variety of discourse-related questions can be addressed in this approach; for example: How do L2 learners mark topics? Do they begin with simple presyntactic forms or non-verbal deixis? How do they manage topic continuity? How do they mark foreground and background information? Which discourse functions are syntactically signalled in interlanguage and which are not? Can an order of presyntactic to syntactic structures be identified for various functions?

While much will be learned if such questions are successfully addressed, most researchers are rapidly moving away from the *discourse* basis of these questions. The discourse – usually the narrative – has become a 'given', simply a way of eliciting usable data to comb for examples of paratactic or syntactic structures. The questions are also changing so that the focus is on the organization of syntactic functions rather than discourse functions. These syntactic functions, taken from L1 research, usually include: gender (categorizing objects into classes), reference (marking of non-specific versus known, and the NP continuity scale), locative (markings of spatial relationships), tense-aspect (marking events as to when or how they are experienced), and causative (causal relations among people, objects and/or events). Certainly such work is well within the form/function framework, but, without sustained care, runs the risk of being separated from its discourse base.

The examination of discourse function along with form, then, is a third major contribution of discourse analysis to L2 research. One focus has been to contrast language typologies and the organization of discourse pragmatics, and to relate that information to interlanguage data. The second focus began with an examination of how discourse carries out its functions via syntax. That focus seems to be shifting towards an examination of the syntacticization of linguistic functions such as temporality, reference, etc. in interlanguage. Since the analysis is becoming more tangentially related to discourse, it is only natural that explanations of findings should be sought not in closer examination of the discourse itself but rather in speculations regarding the internal system (e.g., the parameters of Universal Grammar).

The move from discourse (analysis of external data for its system of organization) to parameter setting (speculations about the internal system) is now in motion. One positive point is that much of what we have learned from the analysis of the external data – through Greenberg's (1968) descriptions of language universals, typology work of Keenan (1976) and Comrie (1981), and from Li and Thompson's (1976) work on topic-comment languages – has been incorporated into speculations about the internal system this time around. And, whether in the guise of 'naturalness' or 'markedness', information on perceptual/conceptual saliency, scope and the degree of variation in forms, ease/difficulty of articulation, etc., and frequency of forms – most of which have been determined by examination of L1 and L2 acquisition data – is now included in various dependency statements. Thus, what has been discovered from the external evidence of L1 and L2 acquisition has also become part of that speculation. All of this information can now be considered when we think about what the language faculty must look like.

Chomsky has suggested that the principles of Universal Grammar must involve a set of properties with certain parameters. These parameters remain 'open' until they are set by experience. The setting of the parameter of any principle allows the learner to construct the grammar of the language being learned. In relation to markedness, some parameters should be set before others. The move from core rules to periphery rules should also be 'governed' by markedness (as an internal theory rather than as a cover term for a set of findings related to external discourse data). The parameters will, of course, be set differently for different languages.

> In our idealized theory of language acquisition, we assume that the child approaches the task equipped with UG and an associated theory of markedness that serves two functions: it imposes a preference structure on the parameters of UG and it permits the extension of core grammar to a marked periphery. Experience is necessary to fix the parameters of core grammar. In the absence of evidence to the contrary, unmarked options are selected. (Chomsky 1981, 8)

For example, one rubric of language acquisition (dating back at least to Wundt's writings in the 1880s) is that the learner should be sensitive to the principal word order of the language (Slobin's principle of paying attention to word order). Bartsch and Venneman (1972) called this a principle of 'natural serialization'. We know from language typology research that subject-verb-object languages show this organization in one way and subject-object-verb languages in another:

VO Languages:	OV Languages:
V obj	Obj V
Aux main V	Main V Aux
V Adv	Adv V
V infin.	Infin. V
Prep N	N prep
N Rel Cl.	Rel Cl. N
N poss.	Poss. N
N Adj.	Adj. N
N demonstr.	Demonstr. N

Sensitivity to branching direction should give the learner a natural principle for organizing a wide range of grammatical structures. Setting the direction of natural serialization is a powerful discovery since so much follows from it.

A question for L2 acquisition is whether one can again begin with Universal Grammar, or whether the parameters once set for L1 must be reset or readjusted for L2. It is not difficult to see that speculations about the internal system of parameters and parameter-setting allows us to return to our favourite topics of contrastive analysis and language transfer with a whole new set of terms to play with.

The relationship of L1 and L2 parameters and markedness predictions has been discussed by White (1983). In her research, she suggested that the setting of the pro-drop parameter in L1 would give learners a special sensitivity to this parameter if the second language corresponded to that of the L1. Flynn (in press), noting that the direction of grammatical anaphora accords with the principle branching order of a language, hypothesized that sensitivity to subject-verb-object order would facilitate comprehension of anaphora for ESL students. She hypothesized that second-language learners from other right-branching languages (e.g., Spanish) would perform better in an English imitation task which included examples of zero and pronoun anaphora than would students from left-branching languages (e.g., Japanese). In both cases, the researchers suggest that parameter-setting is an active guiding process in L2 acquisition as well as in first.

The form/function research involving learners from object-verb or topic-comment languages would fit neatly into this 'parameter-setting' frame of reference. In the terminology of this approach, such research shows the difficulty students have in first discovering relevant parameters and then resetting them for their second language.

The change of focus away from external discourse to internal parameter setting is undoubtedly being welcomed by many. The danger, I believe, is that we will once again centre all our attention on syntax separated from discourse. What began as an attempt to move the field to considerations of larger discourse contexts has too quickly curled back again to speculations about the internal system (with emphasis on syntax).

One reason for the quick move away from the analysis of discourse as a linguistic subsystem in its own right (while still stressing the importance of a discourse basis in findings) is that discourse is not an easily defined subsystem. Since it has been so difficult to get a handle on it, many have been wary (if not disdainful) from the start. If we cannot fit the analysis to current linguistic models, many would argue that it is better to preserve the models than waste our efforts examining real text or interactions. This, however, does not mean throwing away the baby until someone else finds a new bathtub that fits. Rather, it means spending more time with the baby. After all, the present model contains insights on universals and markedness that formerly were ignored. Linguists now agree that discourse constraints govern the operations of certain transformational rules, and so are willing to

202

work on ways to expand linguistic models to include such information. Form/function analyses may also one day be included in linguistic models. For now, many see discourse analysis as either sociolinguistics or psycholinguistics, and therefore 'not linguistics'. But they may well change their minds once we present them with adequate information on the structure of discourse.

In fact, this is already written into the model. Throughout this literature, you will find the small phrase 'experience is necessary'. Discourse analysis is the definition of that experience. It is precisely through analysis of experience (interactive face-to-face communication or interaction with written text) that we define the discourse level, understand how that experience facilitates learning, obtain a clearer definition of markedness theory, and demonstrate stages of acquisition. So, through our definitions of experience, we have the opportunity to understand what and how discourse contributes to all levels of interlanguage, thereby meeting the requirements Corder (1978) set for us. Surely that was our aim when we began to consider the importance of discourse in interlanguage research. An adequate model must (Corder 1978) reconcile the following relevant findings:

1) The variability of the occurrence of 'interference phenomena' in differing learning conditions.
2) The considerable similarity of the sequential development of different mother tongues when acquiring certain aspects of some particular second language.
3) The relative different magnitudes of the task of learning different second languages in relation to different tongues of learners.

17. The Analysis of Discourse in Interlanguage Studies: the Pedagogical Evidence

1. Introduction

The general issue addressed by this paper is that of the possible contribution of a discoursal perspective to interlanguage studies. Hatch (this volume) has reviewed the non-pedagogic literature on the topic, and so this paper will restrict itself to the domain of pedagogy, and more specifically to the possible contribution of a discoursal perspective to studies of language learning (or 'acquisition', no technical distinction is intended) in the classroom.

It should be clear that we are not concerned, here, with the classroom development of discoursal skills, important as this topic undoubtedly is,[1] but only with a discoursal *perspective* on *linguistic* development. Interlanguage studies involve two separate enterprises. The first of these is descriptive, an attempt to find the best ways to characterize second-language development. Early work (Selinker 1971, for example) focused on the possible *extent* of development, under the heading of 'fossilization', while others with a directly pedagogical interest focused on the *rate* of development to see if development was faster for instructed learners (see Upshur 1968 and Long 1983a for a recent review). Most descriptive work, however, has focused on the *course* of second-language development, and much of it has been associated with an attempt to establish what seems now quite widely accepted as the 'natural order' of acquisition (Krashen 1977) for at least the few linguistic phenomena that have been extensively studied. Such descriptive work, however, is of relatively little interest in isolation from the second enterprise in interlanguage studies, that of characterizing the factors responsible for the descriptive findings, and the processes whereby such factors have their effects. This is explanatory work, trying to identify causal variables and the processes associated with them. There is no need, here, for a review of the relevant literature on possible causal variables, all that needs to be done is to locate the concerns of this paper within this explanatory enterprise. One question is: can the discoursal characteristics of classroom language learning experiences contribute to our understanding of second-language development in the classroom?

The next question is: how could they, in principle? We could be looking upon discoursal characteristics as directly causal in themselves, somehow directly creating the patterns of development the descriptive work has revealed, or, perhaps more likely, we could be looking at discoursal characteristics as mediating variables, mediating between some other causal variables and the actual processes that constitute acquisition. For example, the work of Gardner and colleagues (see Gardner et al. 1976) suggests that a causal variable such as motivation may have its effects because it influences classroom behaviour, which in turn results in differential progress. Gardner and his colleagues do not work within the framework and terminology of 'interlanguage studies', but the example should suffice to introduce the potential contribution of the discoursal characteristics of the language classroom, as mediating variables, if not as directly causal ones.

This brings us to the question of how the discoursal characteristics of any particular setting could be expected to affect linguistic development. There are three main areas to be considered in this respect (see Allwright 1984 for more background to what follows). *First*, the discourse constitutes the *input*. It may not constitute the only input in a classroom setting, given the probable use of a textbook, but it is likely to be a major source of input to the learners. Classroom discourse offers not only samples of the target language (both of native-speaker and of interlanguage forms), it also offers input in the form of deliberate attempts to draw learners' attention to what are to be held to be criterial features of target-language forms, and in the form of information feedback (as when the teacher corrects a learner, or congratulates one, in reaction to a learner utterance). Classroom discourse also, at least sometimes, offers input concerning not just the target language but concerning the process of learning itself, and how it can best be managed. This input also occurs in the three forms noted for input concerning the target language. *Secondly*, the discourse constitutes the *practice opportunities* available to the learner (apart from private study, presumably). Again there is a distinction worth making between practice opportunities as concerned with target-language phenomena, and as concerned with learning itself. Hearing a native-speaker talk offers opportunities for practising listening as a skill, but it also offers opportunities for practising the skill of using listening for the purpose of learning (the distinction may be more clearly captured in the following two questions: How good are you at listening? How good are you at learning from listening?). *Thirdly*, although 'constitutes' is no longer the appropriate term perhaps, the discourse is the local expression of the relationship between people that could be summed up, for our purposes, using Stevick's (1976) term: receptivity – the state of willingness, or otherwise, to make progress in the target language, to use the opportunities afforded in terms of input and practice opportunities (see also the 'affective filter' notion, Krashen 1982). Again this must be related both to the language itself and to the learning process – the willingness to learn language X and the willingness to be a learner, per se.

To sum up so far, we might expect the discoursal characteristics of a setting to relate closely to *input, practice opportunities,* and *receptivity.* If these three can themselves be expected to influence the extent, rate, or especially the course of linguistic development, then we have a case for studying those discoursal characteristics as potentially contributing to our understanding of the phenomena of linguistic development.

We can now turn to the special case of the *pedagogic* setting in the language classroom. Before looking in any detail at its discoursal characteristics, however, we need to attempt, at least, to clear up some of the problems associated with defining what we mean by 'the language classroom'. Essentially we are concerned here with distinguishing between formal and informal learning (or acquisition) environments. When Krashen and Seliger first approached this issue (1975) they concluded that:

> the universal and presumably crucial ingredients of formal instruction are (1) the isolation of rules and lexical items of the target language, and (2) the possibility of error detection or correction. (Krashen and Seliger 1975, 173)

These conclusions were based mainly on an 'armchair' study of current (in 1975) teaching methods, using an eight-point features analysis, not on extended observation of methods in use. They were associated, at the time, with a claim for the essential superiority of 'formal instruction' over the 'informal' alternative, and the two 'ingredients' referred to above were held to be the likely causal variables for that superiority. Interestingly, counter-evidence (of adult learners progressing well without the benefits of classroom instruction) was accounted for by the suggestion that successful 'free' learners might really be using 'formal instruction' (approaching items in the target language 'one at a time, . . . and . . . also getting feedback', Krashen and Seliger 1975, 181). This was an early recognition of the possibility that it might prove difficult to separate 'formal' from 'informal' language learning (or acquisition) processes (see Krashen and Terrell 1983). To add to this problem of 'pollution' between environments there is the probability, in the classroom, that the isolation of rules and words, and the possibility of error detection or correction, even if they are the distinguishing characteristics, do not constitute the major ways in which classroom time is spent. Any account of classroom second-language development that bases itself on the discoursal characteristics of the setting is going to have to deal with its non-criterial as well as its criterial attributes as identified by Krashen and Seliger in 1975.

An alternative approach to the 'formal'/'informal' distinction, though equally 'armchair', could be based on the commonsense understanding that we have of pedagogy that pre-supposes the existence of someone in the role of teacher. We might then argue that 'formal' environments are those for which there is a teacher – someone whose role it is to take deliberate and planned steps to promote learning. 'Informal' environments would then be those where no-one occupies the 'teacher' role. Krashen and Seliger's 'anomolous' cases of successful out-of-class learners could then be regarded (potentially) as cases of self-instruction, where the learners take deliberate and planned steps to promote their own learning. This alternative view of the formal/informal distinction does not eliminate the problem of 'pollution', but it does throw new light on the whole issue. It gives us three categories to consider. First there is 'natural' or unrestricted learning, in which no-one takes any deliberate or planned steps to promote learning – it just happens. Pure cases may be extremely rare in practice, it is very difficult to say, but entirely natural learning is at least a logical possibility. Second, there is self-instruction, where the learners do take deliberate and planned steps to promote their own learning. Again we must expect 'pure' cases to be rare. Third, there is 'instruction' as commonly conceived – formal classroom instruction – where the learners have their learning managed by someone acting as their teacher. What is especially interesting about this third case, for our purposes, is that when learners have a teacher to take charge of the management of their learning, then they typically delegate to that teacher the management of classroom discourse itself, since it is by managing the discourse that the teacher exercises control over the management of classroom learning.

The analysis of discourse in a classroom setting, then, if we are interested in using it to help account for classroom second-language development, must be responsive to this complication that the discourse both constitutes the *input* and the *practice opportunities*, and locally determines *receptivity*, and also constitutes the means by which one participant (the teacher) seeks to manage the language-learning behaviour of the others. Put more simply, classroom discourse, or pedagogic discourse in general, is distinguished by the control of discourse by one participant for the purpose of promoting learning on the part of all the others. Before we look in more detail at what we know about classroom discourse, however, we should perhaps look at what we know about the nature of the phenomenon under discussion – classroom language development.

2. Classroom Language Development: is there a 'Natural Order'?

In this section we are concerned with the nature of the phenomenon we hope later to explain (partially at least) by reference to the discoursal characteristics of the language classroom. An exhaustive survey would be extremely useful but beyond present possibilities. An illustrative survey will have to suffice.

We can again make use of the three dependent variables already referred to – the *extent* of development, the *rate* of development, and the *course* of development. The first one of these, the *extent* of development, seems to be an empty category for our purposes, there being no substantial body of findings to refer to for an overall picture of classroom language development from this point of view. The second, *rate* of development, has been the subject of a good number of studies, recently reviewed (as noted earlier) in Long (1983a) as a response to the question 'Does Second Language Instruction Make a Difference?'. The question itself is a severely practical one, given the public and professional doubts about the answer, and the implied worry that perhaps instruction has nothing to offer learners for whom 'natural exposure' (presumably with or without self-instruction as defined above) is equally available. The question would appear irrelevant to a context where natural exposure outside the classroom is just not possible, but if it could be shown that classroom instruction (as characterized by typical teaching methods that embody rule and word isolation, and error detection and correction) really cannot even match the rate of development under 'informal' conditions, let alone accelerate, then that would suggest that, as in the Bangalore/Madras 'Communicational Language Teaching Project' (Prabhu 1980), classroom teachers should perhaps be striving to find ways of promoting 'natural' processes in the classroom (see again Krashen and Terrill 1983). Fortunately, perhaps, for the second language teaching profession, Long feels able to give what he calls a 'not-so-tentative "Yes" ' (p.380) as his answer to his original question 'Does second language instruction make a difference?', by which he means he feels he has been able to show that, in the majority of cases at least, research studies can best be interpreted as demonstrating superiority for 'instruction' over 'exposure'. He hastens to add, however, that his answer is 'obviously not as clearcut or as "positive" as most TESOL professionals would like' (p.380). This caution is wellfounded, clearly, and it leaves open the question of whether instruction should seek to maximize the efficiency of its 'formal' elements, or take the Bangalore/Madras route and seek to maximize the potential of the classroom as an environment for 'natural' language development. For the purpose of this paper the issue is not central, in any case, There is no clearcut overall picture of the rate of acquisition in some absolute sense, nothing special for the analysis of discourse in the classroom to try to account for.

Another view on the *rate* of development has recently been put forward however (Swain and Wong-Fillmore 1984), one that calls for an explanation. Swain and Wong-Fillmore draw attention to the fact that, for children, at least, the rate of second-language development is subject to very considerable individual differences, differences far greater than those that would be considered within the normal range for first-language development. Unfortunately, for our purposes here, Swain and Wong-Fillmore do not propose that these large individual differences are characteristic of classroom-bound learners, indeed they do not differentiate but appear to have in mind the youngest learners rather than adolescents, and learners in an English medium environment receiving English medium instruction that may (but may not) include specific English-language instruction. Again, then, there is nothing special for the analysis of discourse in the classroom to try to account for.

The picture is different, fortunately, when we turn to the *course* of linguistic (specifically 'morpheme') development as our dependent variable. The main interest here lies in trying to establish whether or not the proposed 'natural order' of acquisition is context-sensitive. Corder raised this issue in 1967 when he wrote about the learner's 'built-in syllabus' and the probable need for the teaching to adapt to the learner, rather than the converse (Richards 1974, 27). It would have been entirely reasonable at that time to suppose that standard language teaching practice, with its typical emphasis on the taught syllabus as an imposed and fixed sequence of discrete language items, could only frustrate the natural course of development, since only by chance would the two coincide. It would have seemed equally reasonable at the time, no doubt, to expect that frustration to be effective, in the sense that the investigation of classroom language development could be expected to reveal disturbed natural orders, orders that reflected the taught rather than the presumed 'built-in' one. Increasingly, however, the pedagogical evidence seems to support the somewhat surprising conclusion that the 'natural order' is remarkably independent of context, that classroom learners somehow find ways of preserving the 'natural order', in spite of the constraints that one would imagine are represented by the imposition of a fixed sequence on the teaching. Since this 'fixed sequence' is manifested in classroom discourse, however, we have at last a clear reason for investigating the discourse, as a way of throwing light on this rather surprising phenomenon of linguistic development in the language classroom – learner independence of the taught syllabus. First, however, we must look at the phenomenon itself, to establish that there really is a case to answer. Is it really the case that classroom learners conform to the 'natural order' established for uninstructed learners?

Immediately one addresses this question one comes up against the problem of the *origins* of the putative 'natural order'. A review of the studies cited by Krashen (1977) in establishing the claim for a 'natural order' reveals that in many of them, particularly those with 'grouped cross-sectional' design, the majority (e.g., Dulay and Burt 1974) or even all (e.g., Krashen et al. 1977) of the subjects were receiving or had received specific ESL instruction. Indeed the studies themselves are at pains to point out that they find no significant difference between instructed and uninstructed learners. The question would appear to have been answered before it was asked, therefore. We can hardly be very surprised if we later find a good correlation between the 'natural order' and the results of studies of formal learners, if the 'natural order' is itself to a large extent the product of such studies, and thus might just as aptly have been labelled the 'instructed order'. What we do not have, it seems, is a comprehensive statement of a 'natural order' based exclusively on uninstructed learners. That would presumably be the proper point of comparison for any classroom studies. Unfortunately any such statement would have to be based on relatively few subjects, and the number would have to drop even more if a reasonably strict definition of 'uninstructed' were applied. For example, in Dulay and Burt's (1973) study all the 151 children were in schools where English was the medium of instruction for at least half the curriculum, and, as Pica (1983) points out in relation to a later study by Fathman (1978), it is probably unwise to view school exposure as 'totally naturalistic' (Pica 1983, 468).[2] If we excluded all subjects with school exposure we would probably be left with little more than the handful of studies of individual L2 development, and not even all of those (we would probably wish to exclude Jorge, Marta, Juan and Cheo, for example, see Schumann (1980), for brief biodata).

Given such problems it may be better to make do with a somewhat 'unnatural' 'natural order', because it is still an interesting phenomenon, however mixed its origins. It still suggests that the course of morpheme development in second language acquisition is insensitive to context, since there is no doubt a considerable difference between, for example, exposure in formal ESL classes and exposure in the rest of the curriculum, and yet the 'same order' appears with considerable regularity. There are exceptions, of course. Pica, in her recent review (1983), cites two such studies (Krashen et al. 1976,[3] and Fuller 1978[4]) showing a disturbed order, but the finding appears to relate more closely to the oral/written elicitation mode distinction, than to the uninstructed/instructed one. Pica goes on to raise the interesting issue, for present purposes, of disturbance in the 'natural order' 'for students in foreign-language contexts with little or no access to naturalistic input' (p.471). Almost all studies involving comparisons between instructed and uninstructed learners have only looked at contexts where both sets of learners were at least attending an English medium school, if not actually living in a generally Anglophone environment. In such contexts it should not be too surprising if the impact of specific language instruction is less than that of the rest of the learner's life. Fathman, however, in her 1978 study, looked at English-as-a-foreign-language classes in Germany, where the input provided 'was, in general, formal, structured, grammatically simplified, and limited in both content and context' (p.215). Using the SLOPE test she compared these English-as-a-foreign-language learners with ESL learners in US public schools 'where no or very minimal special English instruction was offered' (p.215), and where 'the English input available to these ESL students was unsimplified, constant, meaningful and varied' (p.215). Fathman made no comparisons with Krashen's putative 'natural order' but instead simply compared SLOPE scores across the two groups, finding a positive correlation (Spearman Rank Order: $r = 0.62$, $p = 0.05$). She, it must be added, talks of *difficulty* order rather than order of *acquisition,* and she does point to potentially interesting differences between the groups, but against a general background of a positive correlation overall. Also in Germany, Felix (1981) looked at English-as-a-foreign-language learners and found similarities with data from naturalistic L2 acquisition. Like Fathman, however, Felix made no explicit comparisons with Krashen's putative 'natural order', in this case because he was more concerned with developmental sequences within subsystems of English (specifically negation, interrogation, sentence types, and pronouns). There is unfortunately a problem of comparability with his English-as-a-foreign-language data base however, at least for anyone wishing to make comparisons with morpheme accuracy studies, since Felix studied only classroom talk, and, in his own words 'there was hardly any room for spontaneous utterances: in their verbal productions students were expected to strictly conform to the type of pattern presented by the teacher' (p.90). He had no data comparable, therefore, to that obtained by the elicitation measures typically used elsewhere. Even in such restricted classroom circumstances, however, Felix felt that his data showed that 'at least some of the principles that govern naturalistic language acquisition also determine the processes by which students learn a foreign language under classroom conditions' (p.108).

Lightbown et al. (1981) studied 'French-speaking children and adolescents . . . learning English principally through classroom exposure to the language' (p.163). 'Classroom exposure' apparently refers to exclusively to standard ESL instruction, since these students were in French language public schools near Montreal, Canada. Lightbown's grammaticality judgement task and communication game both produced results consistent with Krashen's 'natural order', but she noted:

> We do not consider the fact that the relative accuracy scores for our subjects are similar to those reported in previous research is strong supportive evidence for a 'natural order' of morpheme acquisition (p.168).

The 'task did not provide', she added 'a sufficiently large number of examples of any single structure to make strong conclusions about accuracy orders possible' (p.168).

Pica (1983) found two other studies to cite in relation to the possibility of a disturbance to the 'natural order' for students of English-as-a-foreign-language. Makino (1979) studied 777 subjects in Japanese secondary schools, and analysed their written responses to twenty test questions (related to three pictures) giving three to four expected contexts for each of the nine morphemes studied (p.428). Using what one might have expected to be a highly monitorable elicitation procedure Makino nevertheless was able to conclude:

> The order of morphemes for all subjects was significantly correlated with orders obtained by Dulay and Burt, and also most other L2 studies including Bailey, Madden, and Krashen (1974), the speaking and imitating tasks of Larsen-Freeman (1975), and Rosansky (1976), but not the one given by Hakuta (1974) (p.428).[5]

Makino also reported (but without giving significance figures) 'a similar acquisition hierarchy to the one discovered by Dulay and Burt and to the "natural order" proposed by Krashen (1977)'.

Pica's other example is a study by Sajavaara (1981), unfortunately not currently available to the present author, who employed a spontaneous speech elicitation procedure on Finnish English-as-a-foreign-language students and found a disturbed 'natural order'. This unusual result is all the more interesting, Pica points out (p.471), because both Finnish and Japanese differ from English in their lack of an article system, and yet only on the Finnish data was the rank order for 'article' significantly different from the 'natural order'.

Pica's own study, following her review, compared three groups of six subjects, one of which consisted of English-as-a-foreign-language attending specific English instruction classes in Mexico City, with only 'minimal input from films, television, music, newspapers, and magazines' (p.472) outside the classroom. Using hour-long conversational data she then compared these six with a 'Naturalistic' and a 'Mixed' group, both in Philadelphia. The 'Mixed' group were attending an intensive English programme while the 'Naturalistic' group were simply resident locally, not in class and not, as far as could be ascertained, involved in 'self-instruction' (as outlined above). Using percentage of suppliance in obligatory contexts as the measure, Pica found very high correlations between all three groups on the eight morphemes under consideration, and between the three groups and Krashen's 'natural order'. The correlation between the 'natural order' and the Instruction Only group was, at $p < 0.001$ ($r_s = 0.93$, Spearman), the highest of them all.

The picture is forming, then, of a surprisingly reliable order, whether it is 'natural' or not, that seems largely impervious to context. The pedagogical question is going to have to be: 'Why is pedagogy so incapable of making any impact (pace Sajavaara), in spite of all the effort that goes into teaching syllabuses that would appear to impose a fixed and non-natural sequence?' Before addressing that question, however, there are two more relevant studies that have appeared since Pica's, and both deserve attention here.

Lightbown (1983, 221), in further work in Francophone Canada, reports her earlier cross-sectional work as showing a disturbed 'natural order' in that:

> 1) accuracy on the plural was considerably worse than accuracy on the auxiliary: and 2), except for the grade 6 group, accuracy on *-ing* was extremely low relative to the -s morphemes.

Her 1983 study pursues the issue longitudinally, and with very considerable attention to the characteristics of classroom discourse, as we shall see later. She concludes:

> While we are convinced there are predictable sequences in the acquisition of English as a second language, this paper is not meant to support the 'natural sequence' hypothesis in any strict sense of a specific order of acquisition of six grammatical morphemes or even groups of morphemes (Krashen 1977; Dulay and Burt 1978). . . . On the other hand, we cannot argue that our results disconfirm the 'natural sequence' hypothesis. (p.240).

Some problems exist then, with the 'natural order' but nothing that casts major doubt on the general reliability of the phenomenon's independence of context.

The most recent investigation available to the present author is Ellis's (1984) study of the acquisition of wh-questions by thirteen 11 to 15-year-old children receiving three separate hours of 'audiolingual' type formal instruction precisely on wh-questions. These were children in ESL classes in London, and so did not represent a clear case of 'instruction only'. However the limited focus of the investigation and the specificity of the instruction might be held to constitute a good situation in which to expect the effects of formal instruction to make themselves felt. In his conclusion Ellis addresses both 'rate' and 'route' variables. On 'rate' he concludes (with interesting further discussion not cited here):

> It has been shown that some of the children made conspicious improvement, but this improvement does not appear to be related to the amount of direct teaching specifically addressed to the children. (p.146)

On 'route' he concludes (also with interesting further discussion) that 'the results of the three hours of teaching of wh-questions show that there were no effects on the route' (p.146). And he notes 'that the teaching did not completely follow the "natural" order of development' (p.146) established by longitudinal work. Later he also writes that the study 'indicated that for all the children the teaching did not subvert the "natural" order of development' (p.151).

To summarize this section, it appears that there is indeed a phenomenon to investigate concerning the notion of a stable and reliable (if not absolutely invariant) sequence for those aspects of second-language linguistic development that have been studied extensively. With the possible exception of Sajavaara's, all the studies cited point to stability rather than variation, and thus to a phenomenon that appears to be surprisingly insensitive to context, given that the studies have looked at subjects from five-year-old children to adults, in 'naturalistic', 'mixed' and 'instruction only' settings. It is important that the strongest counter-evidence should come from an 'instruction only' setting (Finland, for Sajavaara) but equally important that strong supporting evidence should come from a very large sample (777) in another 'instruction only' setting (Japan, for Makino).

There is then, something to account for, even if its origins do not lie in a 'natural order' derived exclusively from 'naturalistic' cases, a phenomenon that is apparently so impervious to context that it probably deserves the 'natural order' label anyway.[6] What remains to be seen is whether or not a discoursal perspective on the phenomenon can help in any way.

3. The Discoursal Characteristics of the Language Classroom.

The problem for this section is a rather curious one. When Corder wrote in 1967 about the learners' 'built-in syllabus' he might well have expected that by now we would be looking at the discoursal characteristics of the language classroom as a way of accounting, in detail, for the wholesale frustration of learners' 'built-in syllabuses' by the imposition of fixed and un-natural teaching syllabuses. Instead we are in the strange position of having to account for the converse phenomenon – the apparent powerlessness of classroom discourse to subvert (to use Ellis's 1984 term) the natural course of morpheme development. How can it be that our instructional efforts have so little impact?

It is, of course, possible to argue that the natural order of development is simply the stronger phenomenon, but merely calling it 'stronger' does not explain how it can avoid being affected by the skewed provision of learning opportunities that formal instruction, one would expect, represents. One possible hypothesis must be that, somehow or other, classroom discourse just is not significantly different, in its provision of learning opportunities, from the discourse of any other setting – that classroom discourse, no matter how hard it tries, does not succeed, for example, in providing for 'the isolation of rules and lexical items of the target language' or for 'the possibility of error detection or correction' (Karshen and Seliger 1975, 173), at least not to an extent that would distinguish it from any other sort of discoursal setting. It may be that these two aspects are not in fact criterial, of course, but, given the amount of professional and academic work that has gone into language teaching, it would surely be surprising if language classroom discourse were in no way different from any other in its provision of opportunities for linguistic development.

It is clear, of course, that in some respects, language classroom discourse *is* special. We know, for example, that classroom discourse in general exhibits an 'initiation', response, 'feedback' pattern not commonly observed in other settings, and that language classroom discourse is no exception (see Sinclair and Coulthard 1975). What is special about classroom discourse is the provision of a feedback move, which would appear to relate directly to Krashen and Seliger's second characteristic of formal instruction – 'the possibility of error detection and correction' (1975, 173).

Another general finding about classroom discourse concerns the absolute distribution of talk. Typically, it seems, teachers talk for about two-thirds of classroom talking time, leaving the one-third to be distributed among the learners (Flanders 1963). Again this finding does not distinguish the language classroom from other pedagogic settings, but it is held to distinguish pedagogic discourse from non-pedagogic varieties (although it must be admitted that it is assumed, rather than empirically established). From our point of view it is not difficult to see why this finding should have an impact on linguistic development, since it would appear to support the suggestion made earlier, that instructed learners delegate responsibility for the management of discourse to their teachers, and it seems only reasonable to infer that teachers who produce two-thirds of classroom talk are in a good position to influence very strongly the learning opportunities that become available to their learners. And yet whatever influence this confers does not apparently suffice to 'subvert the natural order', as we have seen.

Classroom discourse is also held to be special in the absolute frequency and relative distribution of question-types in teacher-talk. Long and Sato (1983) found that 'compared with NSs (native-speakers) in informal NS-NNS (native-speaker/non-native-speaker) conversations, the ESL teachers asked more display questions and fewer referential questions' (p.283). They also found that 'the distribution of questions, statements, and imperatives in time-units in the instructional talk also differed significantly from that in the speech of the thirty-six NSs outside the classroom' (p.283). More evidence, then, for language classroom discourse being special, but it is difficult to see what effect such differences could be expected to have on any 'natural' order for linguistic development, unless it can be shown that these differences influence the learning opportunities for the linguistic phenomenon involved.

If we consider 'learning opportunities' as being related to frequency of occurrence, as seems reasonable, then we have a reason to look at frequency as a possible distinguishing feature of language classroom discourse. Long and Sato, however, found that:

> The rank order of the relevant frequence of nine grammatical morphemes in the teachers' speech was significantly positively correlated with the frequency order for those items in the NSs' speech to NNSs outside classrooms (p.283)

They add 'but nonsignificantly related to an accuracy order for those items' (p.283), and then:

> The correlation between ESL teachers' input frequency order and the accuracy order was lower than that between the NS frequency order outside classrooms and the accuracy order (p.283).

It must be added that they were investigating ESL instruction in primarily Anglophone environments, but the findings are still noteworthy. Long and Sato relate their results particularly to work by Larsen-Freeman (1976) who reported 'mostly significant positive correlations between teachers' input frequency and a student accuracy order' (Long and Sato, p.282) and to suggest that their own surprising result may be related to the fact that their six teachers were working with beginners, whereas Larsen-Freeman's two teachers had intermediate students. It appears, however, that in neither study was the student accuracy order established with reference to the actual learners involved, but taken from the general literature instead.

More detailed studies of input frequency have been conducted in circumstances where it has been possible to relate input frequencies to learner performance data. Hamayan and Tucker (1980), studying nine structures in French (not the 'classical' set of morphemes of most other studies reported in the paper), found a strong correlation in the frequency of occurrence of these structures across grade levels and across French immersion and regular French school classes (note: specific French language instruction was not involved in either setting). They also found that the frequency of occurrence of the nine structures in teacher speech correlated significantly with the frequency of their occurrence in learner performance on a story-telling task. Any easy inference of a direct casual relationship was disturbed, however, by the additional finding of 'no significant relationship between production and input' (p.461) for a group of English-speaking children who happened to be attending a regular French-medium school rather than a French immersion one. They suggest that perhaps age-peer input from native-speakers might be more influential than that of a teacher, although that possibility has not been empirically investigated.

Lightbown (1983b) also pursued the possible significance of input frequency in her longitudinal study of English learners in the Montreal area. Lightbown went well beyond other studies to investigate frequency not only in the teachers' speech, but also in the textbooks used, and in learners' classroom utterances. Within teacher speech she even differentiated between 'textbook-based' and 'spontaneous' occurrences. She found a nearly perfect (p.234) correlation with Larsen-Freeman's (1976) rank ordering of morphemes, but nevertheless concludes:

> The results of this study . . . suggest that there is no direct relationship between the frequency with which certain forms appear in the classroom and the frequency and accuracy of these forms in the learners' language at the same point in time (p.239).

It seems, then, that frequency of occurrence is not a strong candidate in our search either for factors reliably distinguishing language classroom discourse from that of other contexts, nor for casual factors generally.

Ellis took the problem somewhat further in his 1984 study, where he, as reported above, investigated the development, under specific instruction, of wh-questions. He looked in detail at the classroom interaction involved in the three lessons, to investigate the three possibilities that quantity of practice, consistency and accuracy of teacher feedback, and quality of interaction, might be more important than overall input frequency. In contrast to Seliger's earlier work (1977) he found a negative correlation between quantity of classroom practice and improvement: 'It was the slow developers who typically engaged in high interaction, and the fast developers who were low interactors' (p.146). In attempting to account for this result he looked first at 'the consistency and accuracy of feedback' to particular learners but concludes:

> There are clear cases of pupils who were submitted to rigorous correction but who registered no improvement, and also of pupils who were allowed to get away with incorrect questions but who showed substantial development (p.147).

He interprets 'quality of interaction' in terms of the possibility that 'com-

216

municatively rich interaction which affords opportunities for the negotiation meaning may aid development' (p.147). He points out that there were 'relatively few communicatively rich exchanges' (p.148) (a point echoed in virtually all the classroom studies mentioned in this paper) but notes that 'a number of occasions for more spontaneous conversation did arise and these always involved a pupil from the group that showed some development' (p.148). Clearly such observations are, at present, very little more than suggestions for further study, but they do offer some small hope that the detailed study of language classroom discourse,[7] going far beyond frequency studies, will eventually be able to contribute to our understanding of linguistic development in the classroom.

The foregoing discussion, however, does not immediately suggest a way of accounting for the imperviousness of learners to instruction which is implied in the regular appearance of a 'natural order' in morpheme studies. We have established that classroom discourse differs in a variety of ways from other sorts of discourse, and we have found, perhaps surprisingly, that frequency of occurrence is not one of these ways, and yet this prime candidate for key factor status does not itself relate reliably to learner performance data when these have been studied together. What other factors might account for learners' apparent imperviousness to instruction in the area of morpheme development (whether or not expressed in frequency terms)?

One possibility quite outside the normal range of interlanguage studies, is raised by Cohen (1983) who stopped classes to enquire what was on learners' minds at the time of being stopped. He found 'that only about fifty per cent of the students are attending to the content of the lesson at the moment we stop the class' (p.143). Informally, at least, this figure does not seem to surprise language teaching professionals, and it fits in well with observations. For example, in my own work on inconsistency in the treatment of error (Allwright 1975) it always has seemed reasonable to suppose that the only thing that saves learners from utter confusion in class is their relative lack of attention to the potentially confusing features of classroom interaction. Chaudron's work may also be relevant here where he draws attention to language teachers' difficulties with producing the sorts of simplifications that will in fact make their teaching more, rather than less, comprehensible (1983). There is more, still all too informal and as yet unpublished, evidence in learners' relative inability, in questionnaires completed immediately after a lesson, to accurately identify the main teaching points involved. Research in progress at Lancaster may soon provide better documented evidence, but this is not an area where conclusive results are likely.

Failure to secure and maintain learner attention, however, is a general education problem, and it could, at least in principle, help account for the apparent ineffectiveness of language instruction at subverting the 'natural order' raised in the first section of this paper, where it was argued that discoursal characteristics might be sensibly related to 'input' and to 'practice

217

opportunities', as well as to 'receptivity' – the willingness to receive instruction. In this present section we have looked now at all three, without being able to reach more than the most general of conclusions – that the detailed study of classroom interaction might help us understand how it is that teaching and linguistic development are so curiously independent.

4. Conclusions and Caveats.

This paper has deliberately focused on just one aspect, though arguably a major one, of the general topic. It has made no attempt to deal with the development of discoursal skills, and has largely accepted the limitations imposed by the preponderance of studies dealing with morphemes in obligatory contexts. These are severe limitations, but useful if they help limit discursive speculation about uncharted areas. This paper has also limited itself to pedagogical evidence, and that in relation to just one issue, the apparent reliability and stability of 'natural' development sequences in greatly varying contexts. This has raised the much more general educational issue of the problematic relationship between language teaching and language learning, and it is to be hoped that the current interest in the topic will spread to more researchers and be rewarded with increasing insights into classroom language development. What seems abundantly clear from this present review is that crude measures such as input frequency are not going to suffice to account for our findings, but it is not so obvious what measures *will* be helpful. Ellis's suggestion for 'quality of interaction' as an important variable is well documented in his doctoral work and clearly relates well to general thinking in the language teaching profession about the potential value of a communicative approach. 'Quality of interaction' is a difficult variable to quantify, by definition, however, and very laborious to study. It suggests investigations at the individual case-study level, and that predicts slow progress for the foreseeable future. Slow progress in useful directions is preferable to quick dashes up blind alleys, however.

To return, finally, to the origins of this paper, Corder's suggestion of a 'built-in syllabus' for language learners. I hope I have shown that the idea of a 'built-in' syllabus of some sort has been increasingly supported by the pedagogical evidence. It does appear to be a viable object of investigation, and one of very substantial pedagogic significance, the more we investigate it. We may hope that our investigations will eventually, to paraphrase Corder 1967, help us learn to adapt ourselves to our learners' needs, rather than try to impose upon them our preconceptions of how they ought to learn, what they ought to learn, and when they ought to learn it.

Notes

1) For work in this area see Faerch and Kasper (forthcoming c).

2) Pica had adolescent schooling in mind and referred specifically to the importance of language arts instruction in the American education system. It seems worth extending her worry to the lower age ranges, however, where teachers may also put

their learner through what Pica calls 'formal experiences in the reading, writing, and spelling of English' (1983, 468).

3) It is difficult to interpret Pica's reference, however, as she relates it to SLOPE test results and Krashen et al. make no mention of this particular measure.

4) Not available to the present author.

5) Hakuta's subject was noted as a counter-example by Krashen (1977, 49).

6) This section has, for reasons of space, omitted some of the points that might cast doubt on the wisdom of paying so much attention to the 'natural order' question. Chief among these is probably Lightbown et al.'s (1981) point that the methodology of 'supplied in obligatory contexts' analyses necessarily leaves a great amount of interesting data totally unaccounted for (p.168). (For a detailed critique see Long and Sato, this volume.)

7) For a brief survey see Gaies (1983).

18. Discussant

Professor Candlin was originally scheduled to present his comments on Hatch and Allwright. Since he was not able to be present I was asked to substitute for him, a task I was pleased to take on. Since all of this happened at the last minute, however, I may not have been able to do justice to the papers nor present a commentary as precise and provocative as that of the other commenters. Here are the issues as I see them.

For Hatch, the central issue in interlanguage research is *and should be* the study of discourse, i.e. the study of communicative acts between participants and how the participants display this structure and achieve the goals of the communication. I think that, for her, discourse is central because the study of the structure of communication is valuable in its own right but also, although she does not explicitly claim this in her paper, she views syntactic development of the learner as arising out of discourse, i.e., if the researcher wants to see how one learns the syntax of the target language, at least in a naturalistic environment, the researcher must necessarily look at the discourse that the learner participates in over time.

Hatch has chosen three areas to focus on. First, the study of the universals which govern the form of interactive discourse, the constraints which govern all communicative acts: the contact signals, the turn over signals, backchannel reception signals, signals for message reruns, etc. Second, studies leading to the characterization of specific text types, both oral and written: types such as narratives, descriptions, procedures, etc. Third, form/function analyses, the area which most closely relates the use of specific syntactic and morphological forms to their functions in the discourse.

What Hatch does is give overviews of interesting developments in these areas over the last few years, ending each section with what I take to be a statement of her concern that in each area we seem to have strayed somewhat from the straight and narrow path, and with a gentle suggestion that we would do better to get back on it.

Regarding the first area, she claims that the analysis of the structure of conversation should be *the* central issue of interlanguage discourse analysis but that what we seem to have done is discover bits and pieces about that structure and taken these bits and pieces to use as arguments about what is or is not *crucial* to language development – is input the crucial variable or is interaction?; is comprehensible input necessary and sufficient for acquisition?; how important are repair systems?, etc.

In the second area, the study of text types, she argues that what seems to have developed is not that we have pursued the goals of the characterization of text type frames, and how learners acquire them, but rather that we have turned our attention, in English at least, to the linguistic devices which make text types explicit. She points out that we know little about cohesion and coherence devices in other languages of the world and even less about how L2 learners of English go about creating coherent and cohesive text.

But it is for the third area, the study of form/function relationships that Hatch expresses most concern, because what she perceives as happening is that researchers are currently using discourse as a basis for collecting a data base for their *true* interests, the study of syntactic structures rather than the discourse types these structures are used in. She sees a move from the discourse analysis of external data for its system of organization toward speculations about the internal syntactic system, a move represented by those who are currently taking up the now popular government and binding model within syntactic theory construction and trying to make a case for its usefulness in second-language acquisition study.

It is in this last area that I think her concerns are not well founded in that from my perspective those who are working within the framework of universal grammar, with its associated principles and parameters, are simply not concerned with the communicative act at all. Their concern starts with the question of what language is, and for them language is *not* communication, but rather a formal system of internalized rules that allows us to understand and produce an infinite number of sentences with a finite set of rules, independent of any use we might make of this system to interact in a communicative setting. Their concern is not with form/function analysis but rather with the questions of *learnability* and how a child can, with limited input, a short period of time and no negative data, master that system. Whether this model is applicable in the second-language acquisition case is open to debate, but I suspect that it will not in any way deter second language researchers from continuing the form/function analysis that Hatch sees as so valuable. There have always been descriptively oriented researchers – and I know that Hatch considers herself to be one – and there have always been model-oriented linguists, and I have yet to see either side convince the other that what they are doing is wrong.

Allwright's paper is a little harder for me to comment on, no doubt because I have had so little time to think about it. What he addresses in his paper is the question of the possible contribution of a discourse perspective to the study of language learning in the classroom.

Allwright points out at the beginning that his concern, at least in this paper, is not with the classroom development of discoursal skills (an enterprise that Hatch argues is crucial, I might add) but rather with what he calls a discoursal perspective in linguistic development and the major question to which he addresses himself is: can the discoursal characteristics of classroom language learning experiences contribute to our understanding of second-language development in the classroom?

Allwright poses two questions that must be addressed prior to a consideration of the major question. First, how could the discourse characteristics of any setting be expected to affect linguistic development? And second, what are the special characteristics of classroom discourse?

Regarding the first question, he points out that the classroom discourse constitutes the major input to many learners. It also provides their main source of practice opportunities. And furthermore, it provides what he calls the setting for receptivity on the part of the learner.

Concerning the second question, the discourse characteristics of the classroom that make it differ from those of other settings, he notes three major differences. One is that classroom discourse in general exhibits an 'initiation, response, feedback' pattern not commonly observed in other settings, and that the language classroom is no exception, with the feedback move being the obvious differentiation between classroom and non-classroom settings. Another is the absolute distribution of talk, with the teacher taking the dominant role and using up about two-thirds of the available talk time. And last is the absolute frequency and relative distribution of question types in teacher talk, with teachers asking more display questions and fewer referential questions than native speakers do in informal interactions with non-natives.

There is every reason to expect, then, that the discourse characteristics of the classroom should affect the linguistic development of the learner in the classroom setting. The question is, do they? And Allwright's answer is a resounding 'No'.

Using to a large extent the by-now-vast literature on morpheme acquisition studies and to a smaller extent studies of other structures, he argues that the 'natural' order he sees substantiated over and over again in a variety of settings, classroom and non-classroom, shows that the linguistic development of the learner is impervious to the discourse setting in which it occurs and presumably (although he does not say so explicitly) that the learner is responding more to an internal 'built in' syllabus than to the structure of the input itself.

What we have here then, are two specialists in second-language acquisition research, both knowledgeable about the area of discourse analysis, coming to opposite conclusions regarding the impact of the discourse setting the learner participates in – an interesting point from which to begin the discussion.

19. Summary of Discussion

In responding to the discussant, Hatch and Allwright confined their comments to points of emphasis. Hatch expressed her concern at the tendency of form/function analysts at the present time to favour system-making at the expense of 'continuing reconnection' with the characteristics of discourse patterning. Allwright pointed out that his views on the stability of the 'natural order of acquisition' were limited only to those input conditions stated in his paper and were not intended as a general statement.

The general discussion was noteworthy for a contribution from Pit Corder towards the end of the session in which he provided an historical perspective on the development of IL studies since 1967. In the early years the people who interested themselves in what later became known as interlanguage were, he said, applied linguists with experience of language teaching who thought that their investigations might guide them in their pedagogic practice in various ways. Over the years, however, it came to be realized that the study of interlanguage could make a wider contribution to the study of human language in terms of a more general framework of linguistic theory. These developments were very welcome, but it was, nevertheless, important not to lose sight of the original motivation for IL research in education.

Corder's remarks came in the context of a debate which had returned to a recurrent theme of the seminar, namely the definition of interlanguage, its relationship to neighbouring disciplines, and the specification of an appropriate research methodology. In the view of some speakers, there was a danger that IL might adopt a theoretical framework derived from universal grammar without a sufficiently stringent examination of the implications of doing so, notably whether there was a reasoned basis for assuming that the criterion of learnability in first-language acquisition as normally defined in universal grammar was compatible with the investigation of second-language acquisition. Others pointed out, however, that the absence of a generally agreed consensus on the central focus of IL studies made the issue difficult to resolve. If there was indeed a trend among IL specialists towards incorporating universal grammar, the principal practical effect might be a gradual loss of interest in discourse-based studies and the re-establishment of syntax-led IL research which would, in the eyes of some participants, be a retrograde step. There was in any case some confusion as to the proper role of discourse in interlanguage: was it merely one among many approaches to the study of syntax, or was it central to the definition of interlanguage itself? In the latter case it assumed a general significance for all engaged in the field.

The debate on the discourse versus universal grammar question emerged from specific issues contained in the contributors' papers, in particular the sensitivity of the 'natural order of acquisition' to variations in input conditions, including those originating in the classroom. The apparent imperviousness of the natural order to conditions such as those reported by Allwright was disputed by other participants whose data showed extensive evidence that variations in learner output (for example, fluctuations in the distribution of error-types and disturbances in the supposed 'natural' order) derived from both input variation and from differences traceable to features of the mother tongue.

20. The Study of Lexis in Interlanguage

Interlanguage theory has traditionally had very little to say about the lexical behaviour of non-native speakers. None of the main sources discuss learners' lexical problems in any depth, and most of them ignore the question completely, or treat it in a very superficial fashion. There are, in fact, only a handful of high-quality studies which have attempted to consider the implications of how learners handle words, and even these have generally taken a very restricted view of what their proper field of enquiry was.

This paper falls into two main sections. Section 1 provides a brief survey of what I consider to be the most important papers in the interlanguage tradition that have studied the way learners handle lexis. These papers are mainly concerned with lexical errors in one form or another. I will argue that this concern with errors is actually rather cramping where lexical behaviour is concerned, because a lot of the interesting differences between learners and native speakers do not result in errors. These differences are nonetheless very real, and the inability of classical interlanguage techniques to handle them is a problem which should be taken seriously. Section 2 provides a short account of some of the work currently under way at Birkbeck College. Superficially this work does not bear much resemblance to a classical interlanguage study, but I shall argue that these differences are not serious, and that the experimental methods we rely on are an important tool for the investigation of interlanguage.

1. Studies of Lexis in Interlanguage

This section will briefly consider a number of papers which report analyses of learners' lexical errors, and then pass on to a more detailed consideration of work by Kellerman and by Levenston.

1.1. Error Analyses

As in most work on interlanguage, the classic research tool in the study of lexical interlanguage has been the analysis of learners' errors. A number of examples of this genre exist, for example, Myint Su (1971), Obanya (1974), Ludwig (1977), Ringbom (1978) and Wickberg (1979). The best of these papers go to some length to set up taxonomies of the errors collected, and so up to a point they describe the data in a reasonably coherent and concise form.

The problem with taxonomies, however, is that they are essentially post hoc analyses, and have little predictive or explanatory power. Consider, for example, an outstanding example of a taxonomy of errors (from Ringbom 1978), one of the most thorough of the analyses listed above.

TABLE 1. A taxonomy of lexical errors from Ringbom 1978

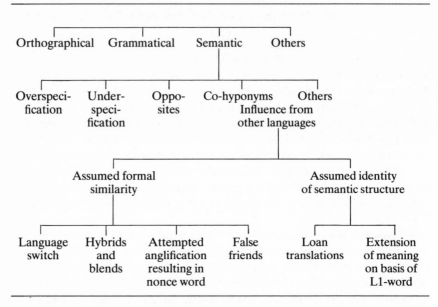

Ringbom's paper differs from most of the others listed because the taxonomy is not the high point of the paper. He uses the taxonomy not as an end in itself, but as a tool in the analysis of the errors made by 577 Swedish and an equal number of Finnish learners of English. This analysis shows that the two groups of learners make quite different types of errors and that these differences can be explained by the close relationship between English and Swedish, and the lack of such a relationship between English and Finnish. Within the framework of a single language, however, which is the prevailing pattern among analyses of lexical errors, the potential of a taxonomy, even a detailed one, is rather limited. Even with a taxonomy as fully developed as Ringbom's, it is difficult to see what else you could use it for other than to classify yet more errors. The taxonomy does not in itself predict which types of errors will occur, or explain why certain types of errors should occur in preference to other possible error types. It does not even suggest any obvious way of providing instruction which could eliminate the more dramatic errors. Nor, unlike some of the best interlanguage work, does it manage to suggest that such errors as do occur form part of a coherent developmental pattern. Clearly, then, though these error analyses may provide us with some useful preliminary data, they do not on the whole take us very far.

1.2. Kellerman's Work

A rather more interesting approach to the lexical errors of learners, in that it tries to establish an explanatory principle for certain types of errors, is to be found in the work of Kellerman (especially Kellerman 1978a). This paper reports a series of experiments investigating learners' use of a set of idiomatic expressions. These experiments show that learners can easily identify the core meanings of a word, for example the English word 'break', when it is used in idioms, and it is also easy for learners to identify metaphorical uses of the same verb in other expressions. Further experiments indicated that learners assume idioms in their L1 will transfer to their L2 if these idioms involve core meanings. If the idioms involve more peripheral, metaphorical meanings, then learners seem to assume that the idiom will not transfer, and tend to avoid using it in the L2. These ideas are obviously of considerable interest. They provide a plausible explanation for the way learners treat certain types of idioms, and they raise some interesting questions about how learners learn to handle new idioms. The work is, however, rather limited in scope in that, in the 1978 paper at least, only a single set of idioms based on one verb are discussed, and only three languages are considered – English, Dutch and German. It is not clear whether the same sort of principles would apply in the case of languages which were culturally or linguistically remote, say English and Chinese, for example. It is also not clear how far this technique could be extended to other areas of the lexicon. This last point is slightly unfair, in that it criticizes Kellerman for failing to do something which was clearly outside his remit. Nevertheless, it is also an important point in the more general context. Kellerman's work is justifiably well known and often cited as a good example of a good study on the area of lexical interlanguage. Yet it is slightly surprising to find that a study whose scope is as tightly constrained as this one should be one of the best studies that interlanguage has been able to produce in the area under review. Idioms make up only a small part of our daily use of language – indeed, in many types of discourse, they play no part at all. The vast majority of the words we use are not used idiomatically, but literally, and it is unfortunately not clear how this particular technique could be used to throw light on the difficulties which many learners have even with the literal use of words.

1.3. Levenston's Work

The most substantial body of work on lexis within the interlanguage framework is undoubtedly that of Levenston (Levenston 1979; Levenston and Blum 1977, 1978; Blum and Levenston 1977, 1978a, 1978b. See also Bialystok and Frolich 1980 for a similar approach).

Levenston is principally concerned with the idea of lexical simplification, by which he means how learners cope with situations where they want to avoid certain types of words when they are operating in their L2. Levenston's main argument is that when learners choose to avoid a word in the L2 that would be an obvious choice for an L1 speaker, the covert principles behind this choice are basically the same as the more overt principles used in the simplification of texts by publishers, in caretaker talk with children, and in certain types of foreigner talk. Frequent words tend to be used in preference to infrequent ones; words for which no direct translation in the L2 exists also tend to be avoided; morphologically simple words are used in preference to morphologically complex ones. In addition, L2 learners, like children, tend to overgeneralize in their use of words, particularly where relationships of antonymy are concerned. Surprisingly, perhaps, Levenston's work does not provide any support for the widely held view that phonological difficulty is a major cause of avoidance behaviour.

Most of Levenston's work is based on a discourse completion task. In this task, learners are required to fill in gaps in a text which has been specially constructed so that only one item can satisfactorily appear in the blank. This technique is thus one that induces errors, rather than relying on errors produced in a 'natural setting', but errors are still the basis of the analysis.

Levenston's 1979 paper is important in that it goes beyond the data reported in his other studies to a considered statement of why lexical behaviour needs to be studied, and how we might go about this. He lists five 'fundamental issues' about which we know next to nothing:

a) how far is the acquisition of vocabulary the same in an L1 and L2?

b) by what stages, influenced by what factors, does a learner's lexical stock expand and grow?

c) what personality factors affect vocabulary learning and vocabulary use?

d) what is the relationship between active/productive and passive/receptive knowledge of vocabulary? and

e) more generally, what kinds of research in lexical acquisition are required?

Each of these questions, especially the last, is considered in some detail in the paper. In the context of this conference, these questions that Levenston raises are important because they stress how limited interlanguage is when it is faced with data that does not fit easily into the traditional mould. Levenston himself is securely rooted in the interlanguage tradition, and very much concerned with accounting for the differences between the output of a learner and the output of a native speaker. However, the questions raised by his work are not strictly in line with the classical idea of interlanguage. Some of them range much wider than this, and take us into areas that would not normally be considered within the realm of interlanguage at all. This is an important point, and will be taken up again in section 2.

1.4. Discussion

It should be obvious from this very cursory survey, that studies of lexical interlanguage are not very numerous, and by no stretch of the imagination could the field be considered as forming a single comprehensive body of knowledge. There is, of course, a fair amount of other research which has considered the learner's L2 lexicon from a wide variety of different angles – see Meara (1980) and Meara (1983) for reviews of this work – but very few of these studies would claim any formal links with the interlanguage tradition.

And yet, if interlanguage theory is really in the business of accounting for all the important phenomena in L2 acquisition, then this state of affairs is one which ought to cause us some embarrassment. Lexical problems of one sort or another play a very important part in determining how learners behave in their L2 – a far more important part than the extent of the research reviewed here would lead a casual onlooker to believe. Learners themselves, for instance, are very quick to identify lexical problems as their greatest single source of difficulty in the L2, and this self-assessment is borne out by the fact that large collections of errors – such as the Utrecht corpus – consistently show lexical errors outnumbering grammatical errors by three or four to one (Blaas 1982). Furthermore, native speakers faced with learner errors normally rate lexical errors as more disruptive and more serious than grammatical errors (Johannson 1978). Any one of these findings alone would be sufficient to justify a serious, large-scale research project on vocabulary acquisition. Taken together, they seem to present an irresistible challenge which applied linguists can scarcely ignore. It is clear, however, that this work has not been undertaken.

Why should this be? There are, I think, two main factors which account for this unjustified neglect of the lexical problem. The first factor is one that stems from the way applied linguists have consistently seen themselves as deriving their legitimacy from using contemporary linguistic theory in language teaching. One of the side effects of this dependency has been that we have tended to concentrate our efforts on the same sorts of phenomena that had previously been the focus of attention in theoretical linguistics, rather than deciding for ourselves what our own priorities were, and developing tools to deal with them. Vocabulary acquisition is one of the areas that has suffered because of this policy. Everyone knows that linguists have not had a great deal to say about semantics, and even less to say about how the words we know might be incorporated into some sort of performance grammar. This has meant that there is no tradition of models in this area which could be applied to solve practical problems, or even to suggest interesting lines of pure research. True, some of the work on structural semantics which was produced in the 1970s is now beginning to find its way into teaching handbooks (Rudska et al. 1982), but this work is not really part of the interlanguage tradition, however. It provides a useful framework for handling contrasts between the L1 and the L2, but it does not really help us to describe what it is that learners learn when they acquire new words in the L2, or why it is that this learning sometimes goes awry. More recent work on semantics has concentrated on the semantics of sentences and larger texts, and so fails

229

to provide a model which can be used to handle the problems learners have at the level of individual words.

The second factor which has contributed to the neglect of lexis in interlanguage goes rather deeper than this lack of an obviously applicable model. Among linguists there seems to be a firm belief that the lexicon, unlike our knowledge of syntax and phonology, is an inherently messy part of our linguistic competence, and that it cannot be handled conveniently using the sorts of rules which have been used to describe the more manageable parts of a language. Syntax and phonology are both basically concerned with ordering relationships among a small set of primitives, and the rules we use are designed to state these relationships economically and concisely. It is difficult to see, however, how this idea could be extended and applied to the lexicon. Certain types of collocations can perhaps be described by rules, but these necessarily apply at a very specific level, and come nowhere near to describing adequately the full complexity of the speaker-hearer's lexical system. In any case, though one could imagine writing some sort of rule system that would adequately describe a vocabulary of a couple of hundred words, it is much more difficult to see how to describe in this way large vocabularies of twenty, thirty or even forty thousand words such as one might expect to find in an educated native speaker.

Now, rules, particularly generative rules, have always played an important role in interlanguage, and the best studies have always used plausible sets of rules as a way of explaining the discrepancies between learner performance and native speaker performance. In fact, it could be said that this use of rules is what really distinguishes interlanguage from other less rigorous branches of error analysis. Here again, then, we have another reason for the neglect of lexis. Lexical problems do not readily lend themselves to solution by a rule-based framework, and the sorts of abstract questions which can be asked about learners' use of lexis also tend to be ones where the preferred tools of interlanguage do not apply. Is it really any wonder, then, that interlanguage has had so little to say about lexis?

2. A Broader Approach

At this point, it might seem as though I have succeeded in arguing myself into a corner. On the one hand, interlanguage has not had much to say about lexis, but lexis is far too important a subject to be ignored in this way. On the other hand, there is no way that lexis can be sensibly handled using the tools and methods which have been traditionally associated with interlanguage studies, and for interlanguage to attempt to study lexis would result in turning it into something else. This dilemma is, of course, more apparent than real, however. It rests on an underlying assumption that the current tools and methods of interlanguage form a definitive canon, and not just a collection of utilities. At bottom, the problem is a simple confusion between aims and methods.

The original idea behind interlanguage was the idea that it might be possible to explain the way learners behaved in their L2 as a result of a faulty and incomplete representation of their L2. For historical reasons, most of the early work concentrated on syntactic phenomena, and these were easily described, indeed imaginatively described, in terms of a set of rules which differed critically from the rules internalized by the native speaker. The important point here, however, is that what we are interested in is the difference between the learners' internalized description of his L2 and the internalized descriptions that native speakers have. The tools used to characterize these differences are of only secondary importance, and cannot be definitive in any important sense.

If we adopt this more fundamentalist account of what interlanguage is all about, then, obviously, there is very much that can be said about lexis. Obviously, learners have an internalized L2 lexicon, just as native speakers have an internalized L1 lexicon, and in any full account of a learners' knowledge of his L2, an account of this lexicon, its structure and its peculiarities, is going to play a significant part. Equally obviously, there are good reasons for believing that there might be significant differences between the lexicon of a learner and that of a native speaker.

Now let us consider a very crude model of what a lexicon might look like, and use this to ask some simple questions about learners' lexicons. Probably the simplest model of the lexicon which one could imagine is one in which each lexical entry looks something like a classical dictionary entry. It comes in two parts, a phonological (or orthographical) code which identifies the basic form of a word, and a semantic entry which specifies the meaning of the word in so far as it is known. It is, of course, possible that one half of the entry could be blank, as in the frequent case of a learner who knows he knows a word but also knows that he no longer knows what it means. Even with this singularly unpromising and oversimplified start, we can ask a number of interesting questions. What do the phonological representations look like? Are they fully spelled out or not, and if not, what features of the remaining fragmentary representations are intact? What do the semantic representations look like? Can they be adequately described in terms of semantic trees, feature matrices, pointers to clusters of related entries, or what? Less obviously, we can ask how the items are ordered relative to one another. Obviously alphabetical ordering is not likely to be the organizing principle behind the mental lexicon, but it is not difficult to think of a number of other plausible ways of ordering a dictionary – some sort of semantic-based system as in a thesaurus, for instance, or a system based on length, on frequency of use, on recency, or even on the order of acquisition. We can also ask questions about how the entries in the lexicon are accessed in the course of normal language behaviour. When we recognize a word, for instance, do we start at the beginning of the file and work through each entry until we find a match? Do we home in on likely candidates and then use a close matching technique? The list of possible search types and storage methods is enormous, limited principally by your own imagination.

Readers familiar with the psycholinguistic research literature will undoubtedly recognize many of these questions as being the staples of psycholinguistic research on reading, word recognition and word storage. Indeed, they are far from new questions, and yet, surprisingly, the relevance of this psycholinguistic work for our understanding of second language acquisition does not seem to have been widely appreciated.

A couple of years ago, I started a modest project on vocabulary acquisition which aimed to ask of learners some of the questions that psycholinguistics had been asking of native speakers. Most of this work started off in the form of experimental projects carried out by students as part of their course work, and because of this, the picture that emerges from what we have done is a rather coarse grained one, suggestive rather than conclusive. Nevertheless, it is quite clear that some important differences between native speakers and learners of the same language can be easily identified.

The project began with a series of studies of learners' word associations, which I felt at the time would be a good way of gaining some insights into the semantic organization of the L2 lexicon. Native speakers tend to produce a majority of responses which show there are close semantic links between words. The early work that we did confirmed some previous suggestions that despite the small size of their vocabularies, learners produce responses which are far more varied and unpredictable than the responses made by native speakers. They also produce a surprisingly large number of responses which were not semantically motivated at all, but depended on some sort of phonological link with the stimulus word. There was also a large number of responses which were best explained by appealing to some sort of phonological or orthographic confusion. For example, a common response to 'prêtre' was 'argent' – not the anticlerical response it appears to be at first sight, but rather a simple confusion between 'prêtre' and 'prêter', for which 'argent' would be a reasonable associate. Other examples of this sort of phenomenon will be found in Table 2.

Our subsequent work in this area has concentrated on the stability of the associations made by learners. Native speakers are typically very stable in the responses they provide, changing very little from one week to another. Learners, in contrast, appear to be very unstable, and this makes it very difficult to use word associations as an index of development, or to link change in association patterns with progress in other areas. This instability is particularly marked in the case of words which have recently been learned, though here there are some indications that the instability is due to a gradual movement towards more native-like response patterns. Our recent work in this field has concentrated on small networks of words which one would expect to form a closely linked cluster in the lexicon of the native speaker. 'Top', 'snow', 'hill', 'valley', 'goat' and 'high', for example, are all com-

PAUL MEARA

TABLE 2. Associations made by native English speakers to French stimulus words. All these associations illustrate some sort of phonological or orthographic confusion

Stimulus	Response	Source of confusion
béton	animal	bête
béton	stupide	bête
béton	conducteur	bâton
béton	orchestre	bâton
béton	téléphoner	jeton
béton	Normandie	breton
fendre	permettre	défendre
naguère	eau	nager
caque	poulet	cackle (?)
caque	rigoler	cackle
caque	gateaux	cake
semelle	dessert	semolina (?)
semelle	odeur	smell
traire	essayer	try
cruche	important	crucial
émail	lettre	mail
émail	chevalier	mail
dru	dessiner	drew
toupie	argent	2p (?)
toupie	cheveux	toupé
risible	lavable	rinsable (?)
risible	incre	rinsable (?)
jeter	hurler	hurl
mou	vache	!!!
etc. . . .		

monly associated to 'mountain' by native speakers. Consequently, it is not surprising to find that these words tend to elicit each other as well. It is possible to draw networks that map these interrelationships between the set of words, and make some general claims about the resulting structures – which words are likely to elicit which others, the average density of the native speaker network, the structure of subgroups within the overall field, and so on. Preliminary work using this technique suggests that there are very great differences between native speakers and learners in the way their networks are structured. Learners come out worse than native speakers on all the features we have looked at, though the main distinguishing feature is that the learner networks are often so tenuous that they are practically non-existent, even when the words tested are very common ones.

What seems to emerge here, then, is a picture in which it is obvious that there are clear differences between native speakers and learners on a whole series of word-association tasks. If we assume that word associations do provide some insight into the semantic organization of the lexicon, then it seems a learner's lexicon looks quite different from that of the native

233

speaker. It is more loosely organized, and the semantic factors are frequently overridden by extraneous phonological factors, such as the chance resemblance between a form in the L1 and another in the L2.

The second area that the project has investigated concerns the nature of the phonological entries for words in an L2 lexicon. Earlier we noted that learners' word associations are often unduly influenced by phonologically related words, and a similar sort of effect can be found in other types of behaviour where learners frequently produce malapropisms and similar mistakes. What is striking about these errors is that they bear a close resemblance to the errors reported by Brown and McNeill (1966) in a paper on the speech errors of native speakers. In errors of this sort, certain features of the target word tend to be preserved in the error. Initial segments are relatively immune to change, and consonants and consonant clusters tend to be preserved. The place and nature of vowel segments is much less reliable, however. Some instances of this can be seen in Table 2. Now it seems very unlikely that Brown and McNeill's feature hierarchy is a universal one. Word structure seems to be one area where the differences between languages are very great, and one might expect these differences to produce widely different strategies of word-handling in speakers of different languages. Tone, for example, is a major factor in the recognition of Chinese words, but plays no part in a native English speaker's lexicon. Stress is crucial for identifying English words, but is almost entirely predictable in French, for instance. Brown and McNeill use their data to argue that the phonological representations of words in the mental lexicon are only partially sketched in, and that lexical errors arise because of this. However, if different languages do give rise to widely differing word-handling strategies, then it is possible that learners will continue to use these strategies for handling words in their L2, even if the strategies are not particularly well adapted. This would lead to L2 words being stored with completely inappropriate entries if the L1 and L2 were ill-matched, and could account for much of the difficulty learners find with 'hard' languages such as Chinese and Arabic.

The work we have done in this area so far has concentrated mainly on very gross differences between languages. In particular, we have looked at Chinese-speaking learners of English, and found that they, in common with other learners who are unfamiliar with the roman alphabet, have an unexpectedly great difficulty with long words. They also seem to pay more attention to the ends of words than native English speakers do, which suggests that they have to construct words out of their parts, instead of using sequential redundancies to enable them to read words as wholes. We have also found a group of Chinese speakers who behave rather like surface dyslexics, in that they can read words they know, but are unable to guess at the pronunciation of words they are unfamiliar with. Nearer to home, we have also carried out some studies on Spanish speakers, and these suggest that there may be some unexpected and interesting differences between the way native speakers of English and Spanish handle words. At the moment we are working on the idea that syllables play a much more important role in the representation of words for Spanish speakers than is the case for English.

Although much of this work is very exploratory in nature, it all points to there being major differences between native speakers and learners of a language in the way they store and handle words, and some of these differences are likely to have important consequences for the learner's ability to perform fluently in his or her L2. None of the work I have reported looks much like a classical interlanguage study, however. It uses a variety of experimental techniques, and relies on very accurate measurements of reaction times, tachistoscopes, sophisticated computer programs, and specially built equipment. Nevertheless, what lies behind the work we are doing is very much what lay behind the early work on interlanguage. We know that learners do not behave like native speakers, and we think we can explain these discrepancies by looking for differences in the way linguistic knowledge is stored in an L1 and an L2. So far we have not been able to show that the differences we have found are transient, or that they form part of any sort of developmental transition between ignorance and a full working knowledge of the L2. My hunch is that this will undoubtedly emerge in the end, however.

In the meantime, I hope that this summary of the work we have been doing at Birkbeck will have convinced some of our readers at least that it is worthwhile adopting a much broader definition of interlanguage than has perhaps been common in the past. Doing this opens up areas which are of considerable importance, both practically and theoretically, and reaches parts of the learner's L2 which more restricted and narrower definitions cannot reach. There are, of course, some disadvantages in doing this. It may in the short run reduce the superficial coherence of interlanguage studies as a field of research, and it may force us into using models and techniques which are unfamiliar and strange to those of us who were trained primarily in the skills of linguistic analysis. These disadvantages do not seem very great to me, however.

Earlier, I noted that most collections of learner errors showed that lexical errors outnumber grammatical ones by something like three or four to one, and I argued that this figure still represents only the visible tip of an enormous iceberg of lexical deficiencies that do not result in overt errors. It would take a lot to convince me that we have a right to turn our backs on a problem of this magnitude simply because it does not fit our preconceived ideas of what a problem in interlanguage ought to look like.

Acknowledgements. Some of the work reported in this paper was carried out by Martyn Coles, Annette Capel, Linda Wright, John Hughes, Raila Morrison, Jane Woolfenden, Rob Kennedy and Judith Beck, and I am very grateful for their help.

21. Discussant

Preliminaries

Paul Meara reviews the research done within what he calls 'classical inter-language studies' and finds it reflects to a regrettable extent the focus on rules, and on syntax and morphology generally, which he says has marked modern linguistics up to now. This is part of his general plea that much more should be done on lexis, echoing a complaint made by Levenston some years ago (Levenston 1979), and more specifically that more attention should be paid to applying the tools and techniques of psycholinguistics to the study of how learners acquire what has been recently called 'knowledge' and 'control' of the target lexicon (cf. Bialystok and Sharwood Smith 1984); he concludes with a brief illustration drawn from research being carried out at Birkbeck College, London.

Since I think that the study of lexis should be an important part of interlanguage studies, or whatever this area might be called, and that more use should indeed be made of more theoretical and fundamentalist research, I shall not quarrel with this major theme in Meara's discussion. I shall however attempt to extend and sometimes qualify his claims, and finally identify some risks in the wholesale adoption of fundamentalist research strategies from just one source discipline.

Description and Explanation

Firstly, I think that the two flaws of the classical approach that Meara refers to, namely an obsession with syntax and rule-writing and especially a tendency to develop taxonomies rather than explanations were, and to a lesser degree, are still a consequence of the pre-scientific period our discipline has gone through. The programmatic papers that marked the beginning of interlanguage (IL) studies, notably Corder 1967, Nemser 1971 and Selinker 1972 can hardly be blamed for shirking explanation. And, if ever labels like 'transfer' and 'overgeneralization' were purely taxonomic and linguistic, the early work of Dulay and Burt soon drew attention to the folly of confusing product with process (cf. Dulay and Burt 1972). It is also quite clear by now that writing rule systems to describe data is only a first step to getting to grips with how the 'mental grammars' develop, i.e. not the rules that reveal systematicity in a given corpus of learner language so much as the organizing principles in the learner's 'head' that this *observed* systematicity reflects. Since describing with any degree of comprehensiveness the current IL of a given learner or set of learners is a practical impossibility, one is more or less forced to keep the explanatory goal of such studies in mind. The only other option is to fall back to a teacher's viewpoint which sees learner performance as reflecting either an accurate grasp of the target system or simply ignorance. The major body of IL research to date shows this leap from zero to complete acquisition without any intervening stage or stages to be a complete fallacy. The controversy involves how these transitional stages should be accounted for. I would like to return to this point later.

Lexical Studies

I think, rather than deal with lexis as a unitary area, it is useful to distinguish a whole range of sub-areas which should be considered, one of which will inevitably be lexical storage in the developing bilingual, and another, the control mechanisms whereby 'words' are assembled for reception and production in real time. But there are a whole number of aspects to lexis that also need to be considered, i.e. their morphology, their semantics, their phonology and last but not least the syntactic and pragmatic coding that is essential for their proper use. If this is taken into account, then a little more research into IL has touched on lexical matters than Meara seems to imply. The work on learning and communicating strategies (see readings in Faerch and Kasper 1983, for example), is a case in point. Much has been said about word coinage, lexical borrowings and paraphrase in this regard. Also, I think Kellerman's work has been given short shrift by being characterized as having to do with a more peripheral aspect of lexical behaviour, namely idioms. Apart from the fact that they appear to be equally or even more 'processible' than non-idiomatic speech as researchers like Canter, Cutler, Lancker and Swinney have shown (see Cutler 1978), Kellerman's research has covered much more than this (see Kellerman in this volume): his work on polysemy can hardly be called peripheral to the important features of everyday communication. Also, if one takes 'post-classical' studies into consideration I think there is already a growing interest in lexis (cf. Adjémian 1983a, Bartelt 1983, and Faerch and Kasper op. cit., not to speak of Meara's own investigations). This is even more true of linguistics nowadays. Linguists can no longer be accused of ignoring lexical aspects of language. Even generative grammar has become much more lexically oriented and much more economical in its reliance on transformational rules, which now form a simpler, more modest version of a once central component in the theory of grammar. Hence the budding lexical interlinguist would be making a big mistake by turning exclusively to the psycholinguistic literature and ignoring the linguistic work on matters lexical (e.g. Farkas et al. 1978, Hoekstra et al. 1981 and IL research by Adjémian op. cit.). Finally, psycholinguists, as Meara points out, have much to offer here and it is relevant to refer to the work of people like Miller and Johnson-Laird as also work pioneered by Eve Clark and Eleanor Rosch in developmental psycholinguistics, not to mention work specifically on the bilingual lexicon (see Albert and Obler 1978, and Kerkman 1981 on second-language learners). There is clearly a truly enormous field of investigation for anyone concerned with conducting research into the IL lexicon with a reasonable degree of theoretical and experimental sophistication.

Transitional Stages in the Learner's Lexicon

I would like to return to the notion that learners go through transitional stages in their acquisition of the target lexicon and turn Meara's overmodest 'hunch', that such stages might indeed turn out to exist, into a (working) assumption because, in fact, it seems quite implausible that learners should switch from alpha to omega in their lexical abilities, just as implausible as the possibility that learners might leap from no syntax to target syntax in one go.

The Birkbeck research that Meara mentions clearly shows that, in some sense of the term, there *are* transitional states in the lexicon. The trend in his argumentation would seem to be that these transitional states do not as yet show any developmental pattern and are simply messy, although the implication behind some of his comments is that there is some evidence that these systems have there own characteristics in that learners studied by Meara pay attention to certain aspects of words more than others, mostly, it would seem under the influence of the native language lexical system, in this case Chinese or Spanish. It seems to me there will be certain organizational aspects of the lexicon where a single new lexical acquisition will not necessarily have any direct impact, and there will be other ways in which every new item acquired will indeed involve a change, namely one of a simple, *quantitative* nature. The organizational aspects, whether they are describable by means of features, networks or rules, are surely those which may indeed show evidence of various kinds of interesting and developmental patterning whereas the other, more *idiosyncratic* aspects are relatively trivial – at least from a psycholinguistic point of view: it is of no great psycholinguistic interest that the target word for snow is learnt before the target word for dog unless there are implications for the way the learner has to represent them using his or her current representational system. Even then, I would claim that searching for some common (or 'universal') predictable developmental sequence that learners go through is less important than revealing the *qualitative* ways in which a learner lexicon at a given time differs from a native lexicon. Once you have established a recognizable, definable difference in kind you have established a type of lexicon; it may of course be transitional and it may imply a staging post in a particular sequence but it is sufficient first to judge it according to the canons of traditional IL studies *on its own merits* and not just as a quantitatively reduced version vis-à-vis some target norm. Whether this stage is related to other stages in a fixed sequence is a separate issue although perhaps IL studies have been too mesmerized by the need to find such sequences and less involved in seeing how different parts of a given learner system relate to one another.

To sum up, there are a number of points here. The first is that the focus should be on how second language learners structure and restructure their mental lexica as a result of being exposed to the target language using whatever building principles they have at their disposal (that is, either as a result of their biological inheritance or as a result of their prior experience learning their native lexical system). The second point is that those aspects of a learner lexicon that show it to be merely an inadequately specified native-speaker lexicon are the least significant ones. Differences are not of themselves interesting. The third point is that the internal structure of a learner lexicon is interesting in itself whether or not developmental sequences in the direction of some target norm or set of norms can or cannot be discovered. A final point is that access and retrieval behaviour in second language learners, i.e. lexical control, which is a special psycholinguistic area of interest, should be kept theoretically and methodologically distinct from the form in which lexical structures are stored in long term memory, i.e. lexical knowledge: this latter topic crucially involves problems of a theoretical linguistic nature as well as strictly psychological ones.

Closing Remarks

The kind of advances in IL research that Meara is rightly looking for are both theoretical and technical in nature. His paper makes more of the latter: IL research has been, for various obvious reasons, fairly unsophisticated on the whole. I would argue that a move to make research more fundamentalist by adopting the methods and techniques of experimental psycholinguistics will only be worthwhile if accompanied by a serious consideration of the theoretical underpinnings. Since experimental data cannot of themselves inform us about the nature of the learner's current mental lexicon the more rigorous approach to designing a framework that can contribute to explaining experimental data, and of course to eliciting that body of data in the first place, cannot be imported from just one field of study. We have to exploit linguistics as well as psycholinguistics. Only by drawing on a variety of available ways of investigating lexis can the study of the IL lexicon get beyond measurement and description and fulfil the explanatory goal that Meara wants for it. Put another way, linguistic studies of the lexicon have a crucial role to play and it is not completely clear to me, as an outsider, that by buying an experimental psycholinguistic framework, we would have everything we need to answer the questions that Levenston and others have been asking.

22. Summary of Discussion

Meara accepted the discussant's comment that IL research had shown more interest in lexis-related studies than it had been credited with in his paper. However, he re-asserted his position on the non-separability of lexical knowledge from lexical accessing systems on the grounds that the distinction was mistaken in principle and impossible to apply in practice. In response to a further question, he outlined his research interest as the investigation of differences in lexical processing between native and second-language speakers, and expressed concern at the absence of a sound theoretical model which could provide clear and testable hypotheses.

Much of the open discussion concentrated on the contrast between dualistic lexical models which distinguished between alternative access systems (e.g. direct lexical access versus phonological recoding), and unitary models which did not posit different orthography-dependent systems (e.g. for Chinese and Spanish) but sought to account for variations in accessing in terms of differing conditions and experience of use. Other topics included the value of word-association studies in mapping semantic fields which, it was felt, were worth doing even though they tended to produce unmanageable quantities of data and some of the cross-linguistic research suffered from inappropriate words-lists which contained too many high frequency items while much of the research interest lay in studying the acquisition of (less frequent) new words.

There was also a brief mention of the lexical component in some forms of language pathology, including the observation that differences in the reported incidence of dyslexia among readers of different languages may be more apparent than real in the sense that the ability to cope with a 'phonetically regular' orthography such as Spanish may mask an underlying dyslexic condition which only shows up when the subject attempts to learn an 'irregular' system such as English. It was noted that the implications of this finding were of some importance to the teaching of English as a second/ foreign language.

23. The Relationship Between Theory and Method
in Second-Language-Acquisition Research

Language acquisition is the quintessential human activity and, as such, it takes place in the context of a wide variety of external factors. Second-language acquisition contexts are even more subject to variation than those of first-language acquisition. It is unlikely that researchers will ever be able to abstract language acquisition from the complex of related variables, and findings from stripped-down laboratory-based 'pure research' are not likely to answer satisfactorily questions about how language is learned in situ. On the other hand, our understanding of the processes which underlie second-language acquisition will not be significantly advanced by research which consists principally of making lists of observations and anecdotes – no matter how interesting or true these are.

I will examine some SLA theories and the research methods which tend to be used in related research, and I will then discuss some general concerns regarding research methodology, emphasizing the need to avoid over-interpretation of results.

Theories and Methods

Virtually all SLA researchers profess to have an interest in the development of a theoretical framework which can explain and predict the observed phenomena of SLA, but they differ in the kind of theory they seek to develop. The first point of divergence is that some seek a 'scientific' theory while others seek a 'pedagogical' or 'educational' theory (see Kerlinger 1977; Sampson 1984 for relevant discussions). Furthermore, there is considerable diversity within each of these two broad categories. It is in part this diversity of theories which accounts for and, to a certain extent, justifies a wide diversity in methodologies.

Concentrating on the ongoing search for a scientific theory is not meant to suggest that scientific theory development should be the principal objective of all SLA research. The development of pedagogical theories is of great importance. In addition, there is great value in pedagogical research which is not aimed at theory development but at the investigation of specific pedagogical issues in specific settings. What is crucial, however, is to distinguish one kind of research from another and to avoid inappropriate generalizations. A good example of such specific pedagogical research is the very important and well-designed research on French-immersion programs for

Canadian anglophones (see Swain and Lapkin 1982 and Genesee 1982 for reviews). Because this research was carried out within a very specific peda-gogical (and social) context, it would be inappropriate – without further research – to use it as the basis for specific recommendations for other language teaching and learning settings (see Swain 1983).

Researchers whose aim is to develop a scientific theory of SLA differ with regard to the discipline(s) from which they draw their hypotheses: linguistics, social psychology, sociolinguistics (including discourse analysis), psychological learning theory, and neurolinguistics. In addition, the past fifteen years have seen the development of theories of SLA which cross traditional disciplinary lines. Naturally the methods used – or preferred – by these researchers differ widely.

Many researchers working within *linguistic* theory seek to relate SLA to theories about adult linguistic competence and language universals and to support the hypothesis that at least some aspects of SLA are determined less by individual circumstances of acquisition than by universal characteristics of language and/or human beings' language-learning capacities. Within this group would be those whose SLA research centres around some version of Chomsky's linguistic theory, specifically the hypothesis that there exists an innate language-acquisition device which serves to limit the hypotheses a language acquirer can make about the specific structures of the language he is acquiring (see Cook, in press, for review). Some SLA researchers work-ing within this framework, hypothesize that this language-acquisition device functions for SLA as well as for first-language acquisition (see e.g., Dulay, Burt and Krashen 1982). The focus of these researchers tends to be the formal characteristics of language – particularly syntax. For some, the influence of previously learned languages is not considered an important factor limiting interlanguage hypotheses (e.g., Felix 1982a; Mazurkewich, in press). For others, the nature of first language influence on L2 acquisition is a major area of investigation (Gass 1984; White 1983; Zobl 1980b).

Two preferred research procedures for researchers with this linguistic-theory orientation are grammaticality judgement tasks and comprehension tasks. Such tasks place the emphasis on the language itself, assuring the researcher that the relevant linguistic structure has been the basis for judge-ment or comprehension because the sentence has been removed from any non-linguistic context which might affect its interpretation. These methods are both more credible than structured elicited imitation production tasks in which the learners' production may be seen as task-determined, and they are more reliable than anecdotal examples taken from conversation or from free writing tasks in which learners may simply avoid a particular linguistic structure by using a paraphrase.

Other researchers seek a theory which grows out of *social psychology*. These researchers, usually concerned with such aspects of language acquisi-tion as rate of acquisition and eventual levels of proficiency, usually measure and compare the performance of learners in groups rather than as individuals, seeking to account for differences in outcome by relating them to differences in learning contexts and opportunities. In addition to examining learning environments, these researchers focus on learners' attitudes, intellectual abilities, personalities or learning styles and seek to identify the variable or variables which might explain the differences.

Social psychological studies often use structured interviews or questionnaires to characterize the acquisition environment(s) and paper and pencil tests to measure language proficiency. The methods developed for this kind of research must be appropriate for use with large groups of subjects because the role of social psychological variables can only be assessed when it can be determined that they account for a substantial proportion of variance, and such analyses can only be carried out with large groups and using properly-selected statistical procedures (see e.g., Genesee and Hamayan 1980; d'Anglejan and Renaud 1981; also McLaughlin 1980 for an interesting discussion).

Closely related to the social-psychological research is the research based on *sociolinguistic* theory and discourse analysis. Researchers in this group predict systematic variation not only in the final levels of proficiency by learners with different learning opportunities and environments but also systematic variation in the interlanguage itself. This systematic variation is seen as related to the contexts of language acquisition (Klein and Dittmar 1979; Schumann 1978a) and the contexts in which it is observed (Tarone 1979; Beebe 1983). The aim is a theory of language acquisition which will account for the variation in learners' performance and, apparently, in their competence as well. What distinguishes the social psychological from the sociolinguistic research is the tendency of the latter to emphasize detailed qualitative analyses of individual learners' interlanguage while the former emphasizes group phenomena and rarely investigates details of the interlanguage of individuals.

Other SLA researchers who seek a scientific theory anticipate that the only satisfactory theory will come from *neurolinguistics* or, indeed, from medical research on the brain and its role in language acquisition and use (e.g., Obler 1980; Lamendella 1977; Whitaker 1978). The methods used for this research include dichotic listening tests, tachistoscopic tests, and what may seem to be an exotic collection of procedures such as finger tapping and eye movements observations. More credible methods are those which are strictly neuro-*medical* (see Genesee 1982 for review). Needless to say, such research can be carried out only within very narrow limits. Most neuro-*linguistic* research depends on opportunities to investigate linguistic phenomena in individuals whose neurological health has been somehow threatened or impaired. For this reason, progress is likely to be slow and generalizations to normal populations will not be easy to make. Surprisingly, this distance of neurological research from normal SLA has not prevented some

243

researchers from making recommendations for pedagogical practice (see Whitaker 1978 for an example).

Another group of researchers aiming for a scientific theory are those who work within *psychological* theory, particularly in cognitive psychology where the emphasis is on memory and information processing, which are the broader headings under which *learning* could be classified (e.g., Favreau and Segalowitz 1982; Masny 1983). This work is not generally seen as being part of the mainstream in SLA research, and there are probably two reasons for this. First, it is usually reported in psychology or psycholinguistics journals rather than in linguistics or applied linguistics journals. The second reason is that the researchers, to their credit, rarely refer to language teaching in their 'conclusions' section. They focus, as a rule, on very narrowly-defined research questions which they – quite rightly – would perceive as being far removed from pedagogical concerns (see Kerlinger 1977).

Many theoretical linguists and applied linguists tend to reject psychological theory as an important source of knowledge regarding language learning. Theoretical linguists, at least those working within Chomsky's theory, are more concerned with discovering what the language learner already knows which makes language acquisition possible in the context of limited primary input data and little or no 'negative evidence'. Of course, Chomsky himself has referred to linguistics and language acquisition as being branches of cognitive psychology (1972), but the emphasis is on the learner's innate biological contribution to acquisition rather than on details of the learner's interaction with the environment. (See the Chomsky-Piaget debate in Piatelli-Palmarini 1980 and a valuable discussion by Hebb, Lambert and Tucker 1971.)

Applied linguists or language teachers have rejected psychological theories for historical reasons related to the 'bad old days' when some hasty interpretations and applications of behaviourist psychology influenced audio-lingual approaches to teaching languages.

The first research which identified itself as being specifically SLA research was inspired largely by the observation that second-language learners' difficulties – errors – were in some ways similar to those of children learning their first language (Corder 1967; Dulay and Burt 1972). For a certain period many SLA researchers rejected both linguistic theory and psychological theory as possible sources of hypotheses or research questions, claiming instead that SLA research and language teaching needed to develop independently, creating their own paradigms and theories. From this perspective, the first order of business was a series of descriptive studies to determine what second-language learners actually do (see Hakuta and Cancino 1977). It seems to me that such an approach was a useful, and perhaps even a necessary developmental stage in SLA research. The result of this, however, is that we have now passed through a period of nearly two decades during which a large proportion of SLA studies were simply descriptive and most of the analyses were of a pre-theoretical or an a-theoretical nature.

We have now scores of descriptive studies covering many odds and ends, bits and pieces of learners' language chosen for analysis because they caught the researcher's eye, seemed to exhibit some systematicity, confirmed some intuition one had about SLA, or had been found interesting in L1 acquisition. Such research has, in fact, confirmed that there are patterns of regularity in learners' developing interlanguage. So far, however, most of these observations are reported with 'shot-in-the-dark' post hoc interpretive guesses which pass for explanations. As other studies follow, it is as if the researchers hope that an accumulation of descriptions will eventually add up to answers to larger questions about SLA, indeed, to a theory of SLA. In many studies, however, there is little control over the basis for the description. Furthermore, it seems that generalizations which have been made on the basis of descriptions and post hoc explanations have not always taken into account the limitations of observational research. I would count the morpheme acquisition studies in this category of descriptive studies whose cumulative results have been over-interpreted. They constitute a set of observations on a large number of second-language learners, and they clearly show some regularity in learners' behaviours. However, subsequent research has shown that some of the generalizations were premature. For example, there is growing evidence that even for grammatical morphology, input and L1 factors play a role in determining acquisition sequences (see further discussion below).

Ochsner (1979) rejects the notion that descriptive and/or introspective research can be used only as a kind of 'trail-blazing' for the 'real' research, that is, research of an 'experimental' nature, yet many researchers working within such a framework find it difficult to get beyond making lists of observations. This must be done if we are to organize our future research in terms of testable hypotheses which derive from a theoretical framework, however tentative. Without such a framework – or series of them – we cannot expect research to move forward toward clearer understanding of SLA.

Up to this point I have tended to use the term 'theory' in the broadest sense, referring to linguistic, social psychological, sociolinguistic, psychological, and neurological theories as general frameworks within which a theory or theories of SLA might be developed. Relatively few theories have emerged which are based specifically on SLA itself. Long (in press) suggests there are as many as '15 to 20 "theories", "models", "metaphors", and "perspectives" in the current literature', but few of them are well known. Fewer still have been developed through a programme of research. Undoubtedly the best known and the one which has probably induced the most research is Krashen's Monitor Model (Krashen 1976, 1981). One of the things which has made it interesting and intriguing is that it reflects the complex nature of SLA, taking into account concerns of a linguistic theory (through its 'natural order' hypothesis), social psychological theory (through its 'affective filter' hypothesis), psychological learning theory (through its acquisition-learning hypothesis), discourse analysis and socio-linguistic theory (through both the comprehensible input hypothesis and the 'monitor' hypothesis).

Many researchers have criticized the Monitor Model, arguing that it is based largely on introspection and the morpheme acquisition studies and that, contrary to Krashen's claims, he has proposed no testable hypotheses (McLaughlin 1978). However, while these criticisms have some substance, there seem to be plenty of opportunities for other researchers to operationalize some of Krashen's hypotheses or to develop related ones. Indeed, Bialystok (1979) has had some success in examining what she calls the explicit/implicit knowledge distinction in SLA use. Long (in press) and Wesche and Ready (in press) have worked on testing the comprehensible input hypothesis. The natural order hypothesis has been found, in some research, to be over-specified for morpheme acquisition because of its failure to take L1 influence into account (Mace-Matluck 1979), but there is still much evidence that learning stages or sequences do exist and tend to be impervious to instructional change (Pica 1983; Pienemann 1982). The exception to this has been learners in a restricted, instruction-*only,* environment (Pica 1984; Lightbown 1983a). In such a context, it may be argued that learners are not proceeding in 'natural orders' toward the target language because they have never been exposed to the target language but only to a limited and distorted version of it – so distorted that it may be said to constitute a different 'target language'.

Questions, Methodology and Conclusions in SLA Research

In a 1979 article, Bialystok and Swain suggested that, in SLA as in other fields of research, the formulation of research questions is often 'a function of available methodologies rather than . . . a function of theoretical motivations' (p.137). As noted above, a survey of SLA research over the past fifteen years certainly reveals a very large number of studies which reflect the tendency to use 'available' methodology instead of proceeding through a series of theory-based hypotheses. Some SLA researchers essentially replicated early research from first-language acquisition, carrying out observational/descriptive studies and seeking to explain the findings post hoc. SLA research is maturing, however, and more researchers are approaching their investigations with better-defined research questions and testable hypotheses and, as a consequence, with more sophisticated research methodologies.

The specific objectives of any single research project will differ from those of others, of course. And the global objectives are also different. Hatch and Farhady (1982), Bialystok and Swain (1978) as well as others have pointed out the distinction between research which generates hypotheses and research which tests them. Different research questions which grow out of different theoretical orientations require different methodological procedures. For example, questions about variability at a given time and the evolution over time in the use of specific linguistic structures cannot be answered in large cross-sectional studies which simply measure accuracy in target-like performance in a test setting. Social psychological questions about the role of a learner's intelligence or level of education cannot be answered with single-subject longitudinal case studies.

These two examples of research questions and research methods are useful ones, however, for two reasons. First, while the specified questions cannot be *answered* using the methods mentioned, these methods are valuable for generating hypotheses for which subsequent research can provide appropriate tests. Second, if the two proposed methods were reversed and attached to the other question, they *would* become appropriate, that is, assuming careful design, large cross-sectional studies *are* appropriate for answering questions about education and language learning (see, e.g., Painchaud, d'Anglejan and Vincent 1982), and longitudinal case studies can be used to test hypotheses about the evolution of linguistic structures (see, e.g., Huebner 1979). In other words, no research method is always and only appropriate for hypothesis-generating research while another is always and only suitable for hypothesis-testing research. The problem lies in mistaking the *results* of one type of research for the results of the other.

As Evelyn Hatch emphasized in her 1978 paper, 'the only question a researcher should answer is the one he asks'. A good example of failure to follow this rule was the dismissal by certain SLA researchers during the 1970s of any significant influence of L1 knowledge on L2 development. To disconfirm an oversimplified version of the 'contrastive analysis hypothesis' (that all non-target-like aspects of interlanguage could be traced directly to L1), it was sufficient to demonstrate that many L2 errors were not explainable by L1 and that some interlanguage errors in fact contradicted predictions of the contrastive analysis hypothesis. But this disconfirmation was not – is not – sufficient to make the opposite claim: that little if any influence of L1 can be found in interlanguage (see Dulay, Burt and Krashen 1982).

Researchers working within the current version of Chomsky's linguistic theory or within a 'creative construction' model, are looking for that which they consider fundamental in language acquisition – evidence that there are some characteristics of language which are the same for all languages – whether full natural languages or developing interlanguages. For this reason, they tend to use methods which focus on the details of language itself and which ignore, insofar as it is possible to do so, external factors which differentiate learners from each other. Indeed, some researchers working within this framework may even deny any influence of differentiating variables such as prior knowledge of other specific languages, input variation, intelligence, etc. on the form of the interlanguage. Such variables, they suggest, may affect rate of acquisition or final achievement of native-like skills or even pronunciation, but do not affect the unfolding of the knowledge of linguistic structure.

As support for this view, researchers cite evidence from a number of studies showing that the acquisition of some linguistic structures does not vary according to external variables but seems instead to follow universal patterns of development or to conform to a hypothetical 'universal grammar' at every stage of development. Some examples of research leading to such conclusions include studies of grammatical morphemes (e.g., Dulay and Burt 1974), question formation (e.g., Ravem 1974) or the markedness or accessibility hierarchy of, for example, relative clauses (Ioup and Kruse 1977) and dative alternation (Mazurkewich 1984). Where the data from different learners do differ, differences may be considered irrelevant because they are based on 'conscious communication strategies' or on knowledge gained through formal instruction and therefore considered to lie outside the speaker's actual interlanguage system (see Dulay, Burt and Krashen 1982).

This research has been very persuasive, but it can be shown to be limited in its generalizability. For every one of the examples given above, there are other studies which provide counter-evidence, usually related to the influence of the first language on SLA, but also to variation in input or even in the degree of social integration. Specifically, Mace-Matluck (1979) and Hakuta (1976) have reported on research which suggests that important L1 factors influence the sequence of acquisition of grammatical morphemes in English, and Lightbown (1983a) has found evidence that both L1 and input variations influence the sequence – or at least the accuracy of use – of some grammatical morphemes. Meisel, Clahsen and Pienemann (1981) have reported that variability in the use or deletion of the copula was correlated with learners' degree of social integration, while other aspects of the acquisition of German appeared to develop in the same sequence for all learners. Lightbown (1980) has shown that question formation (specifically subject-auxiliary inversion) for French SLA need not be interpreted in terms of linguistic universals or language acquisition universals since it largely conforms to the input learners experience. Schachter (1974) has reported evidence for L1 influence in relative clause formation. Mazurkewich's results on dative alternation can also be interpreted as showing L1 influence (see White 1983).

The methodological implication in all this is that the counter-evidence should serve to draw attention to the necessity, in linguistically oriented research, to *control for* and eventually to *manipulate* – rather than to *ignore* – certain variables such as L1, conditions of exposure to L2, social or instructional context. If this is done, then it will be possible to expand generalizability step by step and to *demonstrate* the validity of certain assumptions rather than leaving them as, just that, assumptions.

248

Some Problems in SLA Research Methodology

Some methodological problems cross a number of boundaries – applying to many different kinds of research. Indeed, there are some methodological weaknesses which are frequently seen in SLA research, regardless of the theoretical-orientation or lack of one. The list below is not exhaustive, but it reflects the kind of methodological problems which make other researchers dismiss studies which may otherwise be both sound and interesting. The choices for inclusion in the list are probably attributable to my graduate students who balk at taking seriously the results of studies which exemplify one or more of these errors.

One serious methodological problem is the difficulty of carrying out appropriate *replication* studies. Expanding generalizability is surely a major objective in SLA research as it is in other research. Each research project is necessarily (and intentionally) limited with regard to a number of variables. Every study, whether hypothesis-generating or hypothesis-testing, whether linguistically, psycholinguistically or sociolinguistically oriented, is limited in terms of the characteristics of the subject population (age, L1, instructional history, etc.), data collection procedures (natural language samples versus specific elicitation instruments, oral versus written data, etc.), level of language analysed (word or morpheme level versus sentence level or discourse level) analytical framework (obligatory contexts, contrastive analysis, language universals, etc.), etc. The generalizability of any single study's results and conclusions may thus also be limited to subjects with the same characteristics performing the same type of task. Replication studies, each systematically changing a critical variable, make an extremely valuable contribution to our knowledge in the field.

The principal difficulty with replication studies is that of changing one variable at a time when the report of the research to be replicated is insufficiently precise and detailed. The potential replicator may not be able to determine with certainty that factors, other than the one to be investigated, have been held constant. Results may thus be interpreted as reflecting, for example, age differences, when they reflect instead some combination of factors including age, task, input, analytical technique, etc.

A second methodological problem is the failure, in many studies, to consider – if not to actually investigate – relevant and sufficient *input data* when interpreting second language learners' behaviour. Such data are crucial because apparent deviations from target-like behaviour may be abundantly modelled in the input to which learners are exposed. If this is the case, then it seems inappropriate to attribute learners' behaviours to complex unobservable mechanisms until it can be shown that learners who do not get the same input exhibit the same behaviour.

A third general methodological problem is the use of a *single context or procedure* for collecting interlanguage data – especially when the learners have had both formal instruction and informal exposure to the language. This problem has frequently been pointed out (see Tarone 1979; Larsen-Freeman 1975a; Beebe 1977; Corder 1973). Learners may perform differently in different settings, and it is important to document those differences and account for them. One example of this which has been frequently cited is that learners perform differently on 'communicative' and 'linguistic manipulation' tasks. This has been documented in a number of studies. On the other hand, it is not appropriate to label a task as one or the other after the results have been obtained. For example, the SLOPE test (Fathman 1975) and the 'wug' test (Berko 1958) do not become communicative *tasks* simply because learners' performance on them (in terms of grammatical morphology) resembles their performance in free conversation.

Another problem is the use of data collection *procedures which are inappropriate* for one or more of the groups being tested – because of, for example, age, education, or instructional history. Differences in results should not be interpreted as due to external factors when in fact the procedures may have tested different things in different learners – e.g., grammaticality judgement tasks may measure metalinguistic skills in adults and short-term memory or attention span in young children. This is a very serious problem for those who are concerned specifying the crucial variables distinguishing among groups who are different from each other in several respects.

Another troubling problem is the use of *anecdotes* rather than quantitative analyses in what purports to be hypothesis-testing research. This is particularly troubling when it is used by researchers who have access to large corpora but choose to report only selected anecdotes as support for their views. Observational studies of large groups, diary studies or case studies which have collected many hours of tape or notes are particularly plagued by this problem – losing sight of the forest because each tree is so interesting.

Another methodological problem which plagues many studies is the *failure to validate data collection instruments* in pilot studies or to obtain appropriate baseline data, including – in some cases – data from target-language native speakers and from L1 speakers of the same language as the L2 learners. Such validation and baseline data are crucial if patterns of interlanguage are to be properly interpreted.

There are other problems, of course, many of them. Every researcher has learned from experience – or should have learned – that every research design involves trade-offs: large sample versus in-depth analysis of fewer subjects; tasks designed to elicit specific linguistic structures versus natural language; 'uncontaminated' subjects versus environmental manipulation, etc. In addition, there are always the unforseen variables which interfere with all research involving human subjects. Instead of inappropriately generalizing from the research we *have* done, we should acknowledge the limitations, making them clear and explicit, restrict our conclusions accordingly, and in light of this, propose future research that systematically builds on previous work to expand our knowledge further.

Conclusion

Long (in press) using Reynolds' (1971) terminology, has observed with some regret that most SLA research is of the 'research-then-theory' rather than 'theory-then-research' type. It seems to me that the error lies neither in a research-then-theory nor in a theory-then-research approach. Both of these approaches are essential to the advancement of the field and must be seen as interactive, not mutually exclusive. The real threat to progress in the field lies in the approaches which might be called: 'research-then-research and theory-then-theory'.

At one extreme are those who continue eternally to gather data, amassing such a volume of information that the original research questions get buried under the avalanche. At best, the outcome of such research is a detailed description of an *example* of SLA. At the other extreme are those whose SLA theories are derived from linguistic theories which are in turn derived not from empirical research but from introspection. Thinkers (one wonders whether to call them 'researchers') adhering most strongly to a theory-then-theory approach never allow themselves to be distracted by contradictory evidence and are, when they notice them at all, disdainful of researchers who are engaged in empirical research.

Fortunately, many investigators continue to pursue their research in a cycle of research-then-theory-then-research, different individuals showing different preferences for the entry point (theory or research) but never losing sight of the need to have one informed by the other. I am convinced that this cyclical approach will advance our understanding of the processes underlying language acquisition and use in a great variety of contexts for acquisition and learning. New issues will always emerge and will require some 'brush clearing' before adequate hypothesis-testing research can begin. This is not to say that every individual researcher will complete the cycle in investigating every research question, but both language and SLA are too complex for a single line of cumulative research.

Researchers should see themselves as a cooperative network, each one with lines of communication coming in and going out. Progress in SLA research will be enhanced by such communication – either directly, through cooperative research or seminars such as this one, or indirectly, by keeping up-to-date on existing published research. In this way, we can convert the research 'cycle' into a research 'spiral', with researchers always seeking to make clear how their new research *adds to* that which precedes it.

One limiting factor in realizing this objective is the increasing difficulty many of us have in keeping up-to-date with the relevant literature. Thus we find, often *after* the publication of a research paper, that we have failed to link our research to relevant existing research. When our work confirms or extends existing research, this may not be so serious, but when our findings differ from those of other researchers, our failure to call attention to this, to acknowledge it, seek explanations for it, and adapt our future research accordingly, limits its usefulness to other researchers.

There is a great need in the field for review papers which summarize and critique the research in a given area. Some good examples of this are Cook's (in press) article on the role of 'universal grammar' in SLA research, Long's (1981) review of research related to the role(s) of modified input and modified interaction in SLA as well as some state-of-the-art papers presented at recent TESOL conventions and in the Cambridge Language Teaching Surveys and CILT/ETIC Language Teaching and Linguistics Surveys. Such review articles need to do more than summarize *results,* they need to *evaluate* the appropriateness of the methodology and the soundness of the interpretations of results as well.

I'll close with a modest proposal. Perhaps we would do ourselves, our colleagues and our students a great service by declaring an International SLA Reading Year – a moratorium on new research and publications – while we all catch up on our reading and seek to determine the state-of-the-art in those aspects of SLA research in which we wish to work, then strike out again, with a much better set of research questions and hypotheses.

MICHAEL H. LONG AND CHARLENE J.SATO

24. Methodological Issues in Interlanguage Studies: An Interactionist Perspective

1. Introduction

To take a field of scientific inquiry and to critique its research methodology in isolation would be an artificial exercise. Researchers do not, after all, select their procedures for collecting and analysing data in a vacuum. Their choices are influenced by the kinds of data they look at and the purpose behind the looking. In other words, the motivation for a study, the data collected and the way the data are analysed are determined by the researchers' theoretical orientation, implicit though this may be. Interlanguage (IL) research is no exception. In our view, methodological issues have always reflected changes in theoretical orientation in the field. When one critiques the methodology, therefore, one implicitly evaluates the underlying theory.

In this paper, we consider four issues which have a major impact on the way IL studies are conducted. We make no claim that they are the only important methodological issues confronting the field today. For some, they may not even be *the* most important ones. We argue, nevertheless, that IL research has been limited by a tendency to focus on (1) product rather than process, (2) form rather than function, (3) single rather than multiple levels of linguistic analysis, and (4) IL in isolation rather than in its linguistic and conversational context. An explanatory theory of IL development, we think, will have to consider interactions between and among all four.

2. Process and Product in IL Studies
2.1. Contrastive Analysis

Most SLA research in the 1960s was conducted within the framework of contrastive analysis. As noted by a recent reviewer (James 1980, 27):

> Contrastivists see it as their goal to explain certain aspects of L2 learning. Their means are descriptive accounts of the learner's L1 and the L2 to be learnt, and techniques for the comparison of these descriptions. In other words, the *goal* belongs to psychology while the *means* are derived from linguistic science.

While contrastive analysis has a useful and respected tradition in comparative linguistics, its adoption as the only tool necessary to explicate language *learning* is an example of 'linguistics applied'. In this (less celebrated) tradition, it is assumed that a problem of language in social life can be solved by applying what is known about language(s) alone, ignoring everything else – in this case, the learner and the learning context. Even those who accepted contrastive analysis as theoretically adequate for the task soon encountered serious difficulties in practice. Comparisons of languages were frequently hampered by the partiality of linguistic descriptions, by the fact that most such descriptions were of surface structure only, and because the analyses had often been produced by linguists working within different theoretical frameworks.

Despite these problems, *differences* between pairs of languages were isolated and converted into predictions concerning some kind of *difficulty* a speaker would have in learning the other (the 'strong' or predictive version of the contrastive analysis hypothesis), as reflected, for example, in the frequency or tenacity of errors that would occur. The most sophisticated contrastive analysis predictions took into account not just the existence of difference, but the types of difference revealed by a comparison. Thus, Stockwell, Bowen and Martin (1965) proposed a hierarchy of difficulty for certain L1/L2 contrasts, depending on whether movement from L1 to L2 involved acquiring new distinctions, refining existing ones (divergence), merging existing ones into a simpler set (convergence), abandoning distinctions altogether, or recognizing isomorphism.

As is well known by now, however, differences between languages alone were found to be inadequate as an explanation of learning outcomes. The contrastive analysis hypothesis *over*predicts, identifying difficulties which do not in fact arise, as demonstrated, for example, by Whitman and Jackson (1972) in their study of 2,500 Japanese students learning ESL. In that study, *similarities* between Japanese and English were found to cause the greatest problems, a finding confirmed by subsequent researchers and stated as a principle of SLA by Wode (1978d):

> Only if L1 and L2 have structures meeting a crucial similarity measure will there be interference, i.e. reliance on prior L1 knowledge.

Contrastive analysis also *under*predicts, failing to identify difficulties which do occur, such as initial production of pre-verbal negation strings in Swedish L2, not just by learners with pre- or mid-verbal L1 negation (e.g. Spanish and English speakers, respectively), but also by (e.g. Turkish) learners with the same post-verbal system they encounter in the L2 (Hyltenstam 1977). Finally, contrastive analysis says nothing at all about many other frequently occurring errors and error types in the ILs of speakers of widely differing L1s, such as

> He doesn't like*s* movies, and
> He go*ed* to his house.

As Richards (1971) pointed out, such errors have fairly obvious causes if factors other than linguistic differences between the L1 and L2, such as general learning strategies, are admissible as potential sources of error.

Facts like these led some (e.g. Wardaugh 1970) to propose that the strong version of the hypothesis be withdrawn, and that contrastive analysis be used a posteriori as an 'explanation' of (some of) those errors that actually occurred, i.e. those that could be attributed to negative transfer. However, this was really to admit that contrastive analysis had no true explanatory (i.e. predictive) power, that it was theoretically bankrupt. It was not, of course, to deny that a learner's native language has an important influence on SLA (see Zobl and Kellerman, this volume), but simply to reject contrastive analysis as a method of predicting when that influence would be felt.

Even if its predictions had been borne out, however, contrastive analysis could at best have explained what was learned, and when. It could not have explained how and could not have said anything about all that was learned which did not conform to target language norms. This is to ignore SLA by the majority of the world's learners, who never attain target-like performance. It is also to ignore everything that happens *before* the target is reached both by the majority of learners and by the successful minority who do achieve native-like proficiency.

Contrastive analysis, in other words, was flawed from the outset by its static, *product* orientation. It sought to explain a psycholinguistic phenomenon (SLA) by exclusively linguistic means (description and comparison of languages). In doing so, it focused upon the full forms of two existing languages as spoken by native speakers of each, and ignored languages in the process of creation (ILs) and their speakers, second-language learners.

2.2. The Study of Interlanguage

IL studies: Error analysis. The theoretical reorientation in SLA research proposed by Corder, Nemser and Selinker in the late 1960s and early 1970s was a reaction not only to contrastive analysis, but also to the prevailing neo-behaviourist learning theory of the day, and to methods of language teaching (such as the Audio-Lingual Method) based on both. Common to the notions of 'idiosyncratic dialects' (Corder 1971), 'approximative systems' (Nemser 1971) and 'interlanguages' (Selinker 1972), was the idea that second-language learners actively and continually revised their underlying grammatical systems as they moved towards the target language. Each formulation of the idea, that is, involved positing a powerful *cognitive* contribution to SLA on the part of the learner.

It followed that ILs – to use what has become the most widely accepted term – merit recognition as systems in themselves, which can be analysed without constant reference to the native language or target language involved. Of interest are the learner's efforts to restructure an abstract system of rules that ultimately, given favourable environmental circumstances, will approximate that of the target system. All three proposals stressed the *uniqueness* of each IL. It was claimed, however, that resources available to all learners, such as language transfer, transfer of training, generalization, and various forms of simplification/complexification, could account for the *systematicity* of particular ILs, and also explain common patterns of development *across* ILs, patterns reflected in common errors, common error types, and common sequences in the emergence of such linguistic subsystems as interrogatives, negation, and relative clause formation.

The new 'IL' paradigm was cognitivist, as already noted, and also somewhat more process-oriented. It viewed ILs as languages in their own right, legitimate objects of study whose evolution owed much to factors other than the shape of the target language. Consequently, adoption of the paradigm entailed development of data-analysis procedures which would capture the dynamic qualities of language change within an individual. In a very real sense, therefore, both the recognition of ILs and the development of suitable methodologies for their study exemplify the emergence of 'applied linguistics' as an autonomous discipline (for discussion, see Corder 1973). As many before us have commented, it is ironic that the name by which it has become known, 'applied linguistics', conceals the fact that it was precisely the inadequacy of narrowly conceived 'linguistics' which made the new discipline's independent development so necessary.

Initially, the methodology most often employed by researchers was, of course, error analysis. IL data from learners of different native languages were analysed for evidence of both the systematicity in development and the common processes posited to explain development. This work, in turn, sometimes generated new hypotheses as to the nature of these processes, as shown, e.g. by Richards' (1971) work on intralingual and developmental errors, and the four causes for them he suggested: overgeneralization, ignorance of rule restrictions, incomplete application of rules, and false concepts being hypothesized by the learner. Other researchers looked at sequences in the development of grammatical subsystems, identifying common stages, for example, in the acquisition of English negation: *no* V, *don't* V, aux-neg., and analysed *don't* (Cazden, Cancino, Rosansky and Schumann 1975).

While the advent of error analysis undoubtedly signified an important advance in IL studies, and brought learner performance *prior* to target-like behaviour into focus, the approach was not without its critics. Schachter and Celce-Murcia (1977) identified six weaknesses:

1) Due to its focus on errors, error analysis produced only partial accounts of ILs, saying little about what the learner was doing that was correct.

2) Analysts often classified errors subjectively, sometimes underestimating the L1 as a source of error because of lack of familiarity with the range of native languages represented in their sample.

3) Analyses were often unquantified. Of those that *were* quantified, many addressed the controversy over the relative contribution of negative transfer and natural developmental processes as sources of error through a mislead-

ing comparison of the *absolute* frequencies of errors attributable to either source. Yet transfer often operates over larger linguistic domains (e.g. word order), thereby reducing the potential number of contexts for errors of that type, so leading analysts to underestimate its influence on IL development.

4) Explanations of errors were often impressionistic and vague. Two or more sources of error were often plausible, yet analysts sometimes opted for just one. This is a criticism taken up by Burt, Dulay and Krashen (1982), who see the root of the problem as researchers' attempts to describe *and* classify errors simultaneously. Burt et al. argue for a two-stage analysis. First, errors should be described, e.g. by reference to linguistic domain (word order, morphology, lexis, etc.) or 'surface strategy' (omission, addition, misformation or misordering). Only then should causes, such as overgeneralization or interference, be attributed.

5) Error analysis studies suffered from biased samples, with over-representation of certain L1s, certain types of subjects, and certain types of (performance) data precluding valid generalizations.

6) By focusing on what the learner *did* (wrongly), error analysis ignored avoidance (Kleinmann 1977; Schachter 1974). Speakers of a particular L1 might not even attempt L2 constructions which were difficult for them, thereby making fewer errors than an L1 group for whom the constructions were in fact easier, and so apparently having less difficulty with those constructions. Again, this was to underestimate the importance of negative transfer.

On the basis of these often cogent criticisms, Schachter and Celce-Murcia came close to calling for a return to contrastive analysis, although nowhere addressing its weaknesses. In her earlier paper, in fact, Schachter (1974) explicitly advocated a combination of (1) error analysis, which she credited with leading her to recognize the avoidance phenomenon, (2) the original 'strong'/predictive version of contrastive analysis, for syntax (but not for phonology since it was impossible for learners to avoid phonological constructions, in the way they could syntactic ones), and (3) comprehension testing, the last in an attempt to tap more directly into the true object of IL studies, learners' (transitional) competence. While Schachter's motivations for this proposal are clear and understandable, the proposal itself involves attempting to account for IL development using two methodologies with competing theoretical assumptions and claims. In addition, problems with error analysis do not make readoption of contrastive analysis, with its problems, any more attractive.

Criticisms (2) through (5) are really criticisms of particular studies conducted within the error analysis framework, not of error analysis itself. There is a further problem, not discussed by Schachter and Celce-Murcia, which *is* inherent in error analysis, however. This is the fact that, while ostensibly directed at explicating the SLA process, error analysis is still target-oriented. To say, after all, that a piece of IL behaviour is an 'error' is to say that it is a(systematic, rule-governed) deviation from standard target usage. In this respect, error analysis, like contrastive analysis, treats a given IL form in terms of the status of that form in the full, native speaker version of the target language. To this extent, therefore, it diverts attention away from the possibly quite different function of the form at a particular stage of IL development, and so away from process issues, or the way a second language is acquired.

IL studies: Performance analysis. A second line of research on IL, begun a little later than error analysis studies, but which came temporarily to dominate North American SLA research in the 1970s, was performance analysis, initially represented by the so-called 'morpheme studies'. As has so often been the case, the morpheme studies reflected a reaction by SLA researchers to a development in research on *first* language acquisition – a reaction which, with the advantage of hindsight, can now be seen to have been somewhat over-enthusiastic.

A common order of appearance of a set of English grammatical morphemes accurately supplied in obligatory contexts was first reported by Brown (1973) on the basis of a longitudinal study of three American children acquiring English as their mother tongue. The finding was soon confirmed cross-sectionally in a second study of 24 more children by de Villiers and de Villiers (1973).

Similar analyses of L2 performance followed, the earliest being cross-sectional studies of children (Dulay and Burt 1974b) and adults (Bailey, Madden and Krashen 1974; Larsen-Freeman 1975a) from a variety of L1 backgrounds. While there *were* differences according both to subjects' NL and the types of tasks they were engaged on (Larsen-Freeman 1975a), the differences were *genrally* insufficient to obscure the common pattern in the order statistically.

While different from the child L1 order (presumably due to the greater cognitive maturity of the older L2 learners, be they children or adults), the English L2 order showed up in subjects of different ages and different language backgrounds, and in both instructed and naturalistic acquirers. Further, despite earlier claims to the contrary (e.g. Porter 1977), the order was not an artifact of the Bilingual Syntax Measure, the elicitation instrument used in some of the early research, as shown by studies (e.g. Krashen, Houck, Giunchi, Bode, Birnbaum and Strei 1977) which obtained the same order without the measure. And while group means inevitably conceal a certain amount of variation at the level of the individual (Rosansky 1976), longitudinally obtained accuracy orders for individuals generally did not differ significantly from orders obtained cross-sectionally for groups (with the notable exception of 'Uguisu', a Japanese child studied by Hakuta (1976)), provided researchers adhered to the criterion of ten or more obligatory contexts for use in their corpora (Andersen 1977, 1978; Krashen 1977).

Thus, when Krashen (1977) reviewed the findings of 21 longitudinal and cross-sectional L1 and L2 studies of normal and abnormal child and adult populations, he found few counter-examples (less than 10 per cent) to what he termed the 'natural order' for second language: [-ing/plural/cop.]→ [aux./article]→[irregular past]→[regular past/third person singular/ possessive]. Following Burt, Dulay and others, he claimed that evidence now existed of a common underlying learning process (which he termed *acquisition*), perhaps not unlike the built-in 'learner syllabus' posited by Corder (1967) a decade earlier. The 'natural order' has since been confirmed by at least 20 subsequent studies (for review, see Larsen-Freeman and Long, forthcoming).

In one sense, performance analysis satisfied Schachter and Celce-Murcia's first criticism of error analysis, namely, that its focus on error tended to result in partial accounts of ILs, which ignored what the learner did that was correct. As the name implies, after all, performance analysis looked at second-language performance, not just at erroneous performance. In several other respects, however, the morpheme studies were equally limited.

The following are ten problems associated with performance analysis as exemplified by the morpheme studies:

1) 'Supplied in obligatory contexts' analysis overestimates learners' level of development. The analysis credited a learner with having mastered a form (to the level of accuracy observed) if that form appeared where a native speaker would use it in obligatory contexts. Yet provision of the form in those contexts often concealed lack of mastery shown elsewhere in *non*-obligatory contexts in an IL sample (see Pica 1984 for a detailed explication of this problem). A native speaker of Polish, for example, might omit all articles in English, and thereby obtain credit for non-suppliance in obligatory contexts for zero article. Alternatively, Spanish speakers might supply English definite article not only in obligatory contexts for 'the', but also before abstract and generic NPs, thereby revealing that they were in fact effectively transferring their Spanish article system. They would receive credit for suppliance of 'the' in obligatory contexts (scoring 100 per cent for these), and not be penalized for the other errors since these occurred in non-obligatory contexts, which fell outside the scope of the analysis. Again, a child L2 learner, a native speaker of English studied by Andersen (1982b), would have scored approximately 50 per cent for gender marking on Spanish definite and indefinite articles on 'supplied in obligatory contexts' analysis (had Andersen used this) by virtue of having just one definite article (feminine *la*) and one indefinite article (masculine *un*), which he used in *all* contexts. The child thus marked 100 per cent of the contexts for the feminine definite article correctly, but none of those of the masculine form, and 100 per cent of the contexts for masculine indefinite article correctly, but none of those for the feminine form. What meaning would there have been in saying

that this learner had mastered this aspect of English grammar at (an average of) 50 per cent accuracy?

2) Accurate suppliance of a target language form does not necessarily mean the learner knows its function(s). Wagner-Gough's five-year-old Farsi-speaker, 'Homer', for example, produced many instances of -ing, but often did so in utterances such as 'Sitting down like that', used as a command (Wagner-Gough 1978, 159), which revealed anything *but* mastery of the functions of -ing in English.

3) The analysis is goal-oriented, and so misses transitional stages of development. It looks at the order in which morphemes 'cross the finishing line', which may not be the order in which they first appear and/or develop prior to that moment (Brown 1983).

4) The analysis obscures developmental patterns by lumping together different contexts/functions/uses of a given morpheme (Pica 1983). For example, a particular use of a morpheme (such as the anaphoric use of the English definite article) may be easy for some learners, and be supplied at the 100 per cent accuracy level. Simultaneously, however, another use of the same morpheme may be hard for those learners, and be performed at 0 per cent. A finding of (say) 50 per cent accuracy in obligatory contexts *of both kinds* obscures what are really two separate developmental sequences.

5) The analysis, like contrastive analysis, misses avoidance. A particular use of a morpheme, e.g. possessive apostrophe 's' after proper nouns (John's book) in English, may be easy, and a learner appear to do well with the English possessive. Yet harder uses, as in complex NPs (the metal's temperature), may be being avoided through use of the periphrastic construction (the temperature of the metal). This would not be noted in 'supplied in obligatory contexts' analysis since contexts in which the periphrastic construction is acceptable will not be obligatory contexts for the inflectional form.

6) The analysis misses 'premature forms' (Wode, Bahns, Bedey and Frank 1978). For example, as is the case with some children acquiring English as L1, the initial appearance of (high frequency) lexical past forms (*went, took,* etc.) can be mistaken for target-like attainment when, in fact, they subsequently give way to forms like *goed* and *taked,* as the distinction between lexical and inflectional past forms begins to be internalized.

7) The Spearman rank-order correlation coefficient, the statistic used in most studies to measure the strength of association between two rank orders of accurate suppliance of a set of forms, is weak. As shown by Brown (1983), quite substantial differences need to exist before statistically non-significant results are obtained. Hence, findings of statistically significant commonalities in rank orders tend to overestimate the extent of actual similarities.

8) The morpheme studies look at a trivial portion of the whole language, and therefore do not constitute a valid basis for generalizations about how that language is acquired. Clearly, they are especially unrevealing of insights into the acquisition of morphologically 'poor' languages.

9) Related to (8), above, the morpheme studies preclude cross-linguistic generalizations. Even if they tell us something about the acquisition of English as a second language, they say nothing about other languages. Direct comparisons of forms are obviously ruled out. Comparisons of types of marking are also next to impossible since even languages which make use of the same semantic distinctions (number, gender, case, etc.) may not mark them morphologically or, if so, rarely in ways which would make cross-linguistic generalizations possible. Some may use a bound, not a free morpheme, a prefix, not a suffix, etc.

10) The morpheme studies are not motivated by any linguistic theory, the particular forms investigated being a miscellany of bound and free, NP and verb phrase items, which are in fact more revealing of developmental patterns when analysed in subsets (Andersen 1978; Brown 1983; Krashen 1977). This, of course, is the result of replicating L1 studies, where choice of the forms was related to issues in cognitive development. A strong form of this criticism is to claim that whatever order of appearance is observed in IL development is uninterpretable (because theoretically unmotivated) and so uninteresting (Gregg 1984). A less controversial expression of the idea is to recognize that accuracy orders are facts about SLA (assuming one agrees that they *are* facts) which need to be explained. They do not themselves help us understand how a second language is acquired, but do tell us something about what is acquired, and in what order.

Criticisms such as these (rarely made of L1 studies, incidentally), have led some to dismiss the second-language morpheme studies and/or theoretical claims based upon them. The sheer popularity of the studies themselves in the 1970s (occasionally referred to as 'morpheme addiction'), perhaps coupled with reservations about methodological issues, seems to have led others to want to distance themselves from the research and from its (disputed) findings. Fortunately, still others have taken a more constructive (if less fashionable) attitude, and have instead tried to develop more sophisticated analytical procedures. They argue that the commonalities across orders established by numerous researchers demand attention (and explanation) unless it can be shown that they are *entirely* an artifact of the methodology employed in the original studies – and, in our estimation, no one has been able to do this.

One attempt to improve upon the early performance analysis methodology is now known as 'target-like use' analysis, although not always called this by its users (see, e.g. Hakuta 1976; Lightbown, Spada and Wallace 1980; Pica 1983, 1984; Stauble 1981; Stauble and Schumann 1983). Briefly, the standard formula used for calculating percentage suppliance in obligatory contexts was:

$$\frac{(\text{n correct suppliance in obligatory contexts} \times 2) + (\text{n misformations in obligatory contexts})}{(\text{n obligatory contexts} \times 2)} \times 100$$

Percentage target-like use is calculated:

$$\frac{\text{n correct suppliance in obligatory contexts}}{(\text{n obligatory contexts}) + \begin{array}{c}(\text{n non-obligatory contexts}\\ \text{with inappropriate suppliance})\end{array}} \times 100$$

Although crude, this measure of target-like use goes some way towards giving a more accurate (de-inflated) estimate of subjects' ability, thereby responding to criticism (1) and, in part, criticism (2), above. This is shown by Pica (1984) through a comparison of the analyses applied to the same (constructed) IL sample:

> Yesterday I *speaked*[(a)] with a few *friends*[(b)] and my two *teacher*[(c)] about a grammar *tests*[(d)] I *took*[(e)] last week. They *gived*[(f)] me much help. They *telled*[(g)] me *answers*[(h)] to my *questions*[(i)]. I *studied*[(j)] last night. Now I *understood*[(k)] better.

Target-like use	*Suppliance in obligatory contexts*

Past Irregular

correct suppliance: 1 (e)
non-obligatory contexts with in-appropriate suppliance: 1 (k)
obligatory contexts: 4 (a, e, f, g)
TLU = 1/(4) + (1) = $^1/_5$ = 20%

correct suppliance: 1 (e)
misformation: 3 (a, f, g)
obligatory contexts: 4 (a, e, f, g)
SOC = (2) + (3)/(4) × (2) = $^5/_8$ = 63%

Past Regular

correct suppliance: 1 (j)
non-obligatory contexts with in-appropriate suppliance: 3 (a, f, g)
obligatory contexts: 1 (j)
TLU = 1/(1) + (3) = $^1/_4$ = 25%

correct suppliance: 4 (a, f, g, j)
misformation: 0
obligatory contexts: 4 (a, f, g, j)
SOC = (4) × (2)/(4) × (2) = $^8/_8$ = 100%

Plural -s

correct suppliance: 3 (b, h, i)
non-obligatory contexts with in-appropriate suppliance: 1 (d)
obligatory contexts: 4 (b, c, h, i)
TLU = 3/(4) + (1) = $^3/_5$ = 60%

correct suppliance: 3 (b, h, i)
misformation: 0
obligatory contexts: 4 (b, c, h, i)
SOC = (3) × (2)/(4) × (2) = $^6/_8$ = 75%

Pica (1984) also goes on to propose several improvements to this standard target-like use analysis, which, for limitations of space, we will not detail here.

Of the other criticisms of performance analysis, (4) and (5) are remediable, not by changes in the analysis itself, but by making finer distinctions in what is analysed, i.e. by distinguishing different contexts/uses of the forms. Criticisms (3) and (6) relate to issues in sampling procedures, and more generally, to the limitations of cross-sectional studies using any (not just 'suppliance in obligatory contexts') analysis. They can be dealt with, at least in part, through use of several samples of IL performance at different global proficiency levels, i.e. with proficiency being determined by any means which does not involve testing mastery of the items in question. Alternatively, of course, they can be handled through longitudinal studies. Criticism (7) seems legitimate. One solution adopted by increasing numbers of researchers, however (see, e.g. Andersen 1978; Hyltenstam 1977; Lamotte, Pearson-Joseph and Zupko 1982), is use of the more powerful procedures of implicational scaling and its accompanying statistics (see Hatch and Farhady 1982).

More problematic are criticisms (8), (9) and (10), concerning the narrow scope, lack of cross-linguistic generalizability, and 'uninterpretability' of the morpheme studies. Note, however, that (8) and (9) concern limitations to the generalizability of the studies' findings, not to threats to their internal validity. And even the strong form of criticism (10), that the results are uninterpretable, does not preclude use of one or more forms of performance analysis on items which *are* linguistically related or theoretically motivated in some other way.

Even if one accepts these as actual or potential defences of the morpheme studies against the ten criticisms of them outlined above, performance analysis is arguably still flawed. Like contrastive and error analysis before it, it is target-oriented. What performance analysis looks at are target language forms, and the way it assesses their suppliance is always in terms of their suppliance by native speakers of that target language. In this respect, therefore, it, too, inherently focuses the analyst on the second language, and away from the IL as a system in its own right.

At a very practical level, the limitations of such an approach are obvious to anyone who has studied *early* stages of IL development, especially that of naturalistic acquirers, for many of the target linguistic forms do not figure in these learners' output at all. One can, of course, report zero suppliance of all these items, but this hardly provides a very revealing account of what *is* in (and happening in) an IL. The focus on target-like production of a few forms yields virtually no knowledge about how learners entered the L2 system or about the repertoire of strategies they accessed or developed to do so. As Hatch and Wagner-Gough (1976, 53) put it:

> We [are] so prone to think about linguistic description that we are blind to the psycholinguistic processes; we pay little attention to what the learner really does.

At a very basic level, in other words, performance analysis underestimates what learners may be able to do with the admittedly limited, undeniably non-target-like, means at their disposal. Its target orientation, that is, like that of contrastive and error analysis, makes it an inadequate method, not just of explaining the processes by which target-like use of target-language forms is attained, but of describing a learner's transitional *communicative* competence.

Fortunately, while pervasive in the three approaches to IL we have considered thus far, a target orientation is not one that has distracted creolists, for the simple reason that there is no target for creolization. In our view, it is creolinguistics that has provided the impetus for the first genuine process orientation in IL studies.

IL studies: The influence of creolinguistics. Although the 'cross-fertilization' of SLA and creolinguistics has become most explicit in the last few years (see, e.g. Andersen 1981b, 1983c collections; Schumann and Stauble 1983; Stauble 1981), serious discussion among researchers was initiated during the mid-1970s following Schumann's (1975) pioneering, if controversial, analogy between early SLA and pidginization. Since then, what pidgin-creole studies have contributed to IL research, in our view, is a theoretical framework for the study of linguistic variation and language change, a framework primarily shaped by the work of Bailey (1971, 1973); Bickerton (1971, 1973, 1975, 1976); Labov (1966, 1969); and Labov, Cohen, Robins and Lewis (1968).

While each scholar has pursued a different course within the framework, all recognize as central to a valid theory of language the proposition that language is inherently variable (Bailey 1971; Bickerton 1971; Labov 1969), and that this variability is systematic. In an early statement of this position Weinreich, Labov and Herzog (1968, 100) argued:

> Long before predictive theories of language change can be attempted, it will be necessary to see language – whether from a diachronic *or* [italics in original] a synchronic vantage – as an object possessing orderly heterogeneity.

In Bailey's (1973, 21) terms, the two central aspects of a variationist perspective are a 'conceptualist' orientation 'which accepts as real and worthy of study both the flux of variation in data . . . and also the reality and suitability for study of abstract relations among data variants'; and, second, a 'dynamic paradigm, which, in contrast with the static paradigm of both structuralism and transformationalism, includes time as a fundamental dimension of all analysis'.

Bickerton (1973, 643) provides further elaboration of the radical nature of the new paradigm:

> Language is then seen as a dynamic process evolving through space and time; 'leaky' grammars, variants that fit no system, conflicting native-speaker intuitions – all the problems that vexed previous formulations are now seen as the inevitable consequences of spatial or temporal segmentation of what is really a seamless whole. It follows that to speak of 'dialects' or even perhaps 'languages' may be misleading; these terms merely seek to freeze at an arbitrary moment, and to coalesce into an arbitrary whole, phenomena which in nature are ongoing and heterogeneous.

By definition, then, the variationist perspective is process-oriented. Because linguistic systems are seen to change through time and space, linguistic description and explanation must capture diachrony within synchronic 'snapshots' of any given language. Bickerton and Givón (1976, 13–14) argue that

> diachronic change in a language must show itself synchronically in terms of variation. It does not follow from this assumption that *all* variation necessarily reflects ongoing change. However, if, in any given area of variation, we find

elements of categoriality (a rule that is optional in some environments either *must* or *must not* be applied in others), of hierarchy (an optional rule is *consistently* applied more in some environments than in others), or of implicational relationship (application of an optional rule in one environment implies its application in others), then we may reasonably assume that an on-going change is reflected, and that the synchronic hierarchy of environments for the change (ranging from that wherein the new rule is oftenest applied to that wherein it is least often applied) will likewise reflect the diachronic hierarchy of environments (i.e., that wherein the new rule is oftenest applied will represent the first environment in which it was acquired, that wherein it is least often applied will represent the most recent environment in which it was acquired, and so on).

Because pidgin-creole communities are characterized by multilingual and highly heterogenous sociolinguistic contact, and because linguistic change is usually accelerated in such contexts, they have served as a major proving ground for the variationist framework. Following Schumann's (1978) extension of the pidginization process to describe the early stages of the English IL of a native Spanish speaker, subsequent work has foregrounded the broader language-acquisition context of pidginization and creolization. Both the Heidelberger Forschungsprojekt 'Pidgin Deutsch' and the Zweitsprachewerb italinerischer und spanischer Arbeiter (ZISA) project, for example, originated as sociolinguistic studies of the acqusition of German by migrant workers. However,

> increased concern with external factors was correlated with an increased need to describe the variation between learners and the varieties of the second language that they use, and the need to distinguish between developmental sequences and inter-subject variation. (Nicholas and Meisel 1983, 71)

The ZISA group has proposed a theory which views SLA as a 'multidimensional process" (Meisel, Clahsen and Pienemann 1981). Their model attempts to treat both developmental sequences/stages and variation within each stage of SLA, the ultimate aim being to determine 'how socio-psychological factors . . . influence a learner's position in the two other dimensions: development towards the target variety and use of a more or less restricted variety within each stage' (Meisel et al. 1981, 128). Whatever one's stance on the relationship between sociopsychological and linguistic aspects of SL development, the value of this approach is that it assigns a central role to process-based analyses in IL studies. Its non-target orientation also raises new methodological problems concerning the status of L2 forms in analyses that are not target-oriented, however, and it is to these that we now turn.

3. Form and Function in IL Studies

The shift from a focus on product to a focus on process in IL development has resulted in the replacement of what might be called a 'form only' analysis of IL data to a 'form-to-function' mode of analysis. While the former aims to measure increasing target-like production of particular forms, the latter attempts a comprehensive analysis of the functional distribution of a particular form in a learner's IL. A third type of analysis, which we refer to as 'function-to-form' analysis, begins with a functional domain, such as the expression of temporality, and documents the evolution of grammatical encoding of that functional domain. In this section, we will discuss each of these modes of analysis, focusing on the strengths and weaknesses of form-to-function and function-to-form analysis.

3.1. Form-only Analysis

Form-only analysis is best exemplified by the morpheme studies, constrained as they were by an exclusively target language orientation, and in which the relevant data were perceived as being derived from a subset of all instances of a form in the entire corpus of speech obtained from learners. Omitted from consideration, therefore, was (1) the possible functional variation of a form, and (2) all occasions where other forms in learners' ILs may have covered roughly the same functional/semantic scope as the forms actually analysed. Both points of weakness of form-only analysis have since been addressed by two alternative modes of analysis: form-to-function and function-to-form analysis, respectively.

3.2. Form-to-Function Analysis

In an analysis of the functional distribution of -ing in Homer's English IL, Wagner-Gough (1975, 1978) demonstrated that the acquisition of this form does not necessarily entail the simultaneous acquisition of its target-language function as a progressive aspect marker. In fact, -ing appeared in four different temporal contexts: immediate intention, intentions of the distant future, past, and process-state – as well as in imperatives. Moreover, -ing alternated with unmarked verb stems in the same kinds of temporal and imperative contexts. Wagner-Gough thus argued convincingly for detailed longitudinal analyses of learners' ILs in order to trace variation in form-to-function mapping.

Another advocate of form-to-function analysis is Bickerton (1981a), who takes the position that a true understanding of SL development can only emerge from consideration of how a SL is acquired rather than simply of what structural features or rules are acquired:

> the acquisition of a target feature *qua* feature – a given morphological shape – and the acquisition of an accurate range of target meaning/function are two completely different things. (Bickerton 1981a, 204)

In Bickerton's view, SLA is 'targeted' language change in which

> the surface forms of features are borrowed from the target language and incorporated into the semantic and syntactic structure of the acquirer's language at whatever stage this has currently reached; only subsequently, and often only by gradual changes, do these features reassume the range of meanings and functions that they had in their language of origin. (op. cit., 204)

Support for this position is derived from his extensive cross-sectional work on language change in pidgin/creole settings.

A recent longitudinal SLA study which adopts Bickerton's 'dynamic' approach to form-to-function acquisition is Huebner's (1983) investigation of the acquisition of English by an uninstructed Hmong-speaking adult. In keeping with the notion of a 'dynamic paradigm', Huebner (1983, 26–7) questions the assumption

> that it is possible to determine obligatory Standard English contexts for morphemes which resemble Standard English only in their forms (sometimes) and are used in distinctly non-English ways in an interlanguage rather far removed from Standard English. An attempt to do so is based on the assumption that one can find morpheme-for-morpheme correspondences between a given language and an interlanguage. It has been long since established in linguistics that this is not possible between languages. There is no evidence to support the assumption that it is possible between a standard language and an interlanguage.

In his study, Huebner focuses on the learner's 'changing [but non-random] use of the form 'is(a)', of the article 'da', and of the anaphoric devices of pronouns and zero' in order to characterize the general shift in information organization from 'topic-comment-like structures to more subject-predicate-like structures' (1983, 53). As an illustration of form-to-function analysis, we present here a summary of Huebner's 'da' analysis.

Included in the analysis are not only all instances of 'da', target-like and non-target-like, but all pre-noun phrase positions as well. All 'da' contexts are defined along semantico-pragamatic dimensions, expressed as 'the two binary features [+ Information Assumed Known to the Hearer] and [+ Specific Referent] (op. cit., 130). Examination of the frequency distribution of 'da' in these contexts over time ultimately reveals that the learner's 'use of the article *da* shift[s] from an almost SE one, but one which is dominated by the notion of topic, to one in which the form marks virtually all noun phrases. From that point, Ge's use of *da* is first phased out of environments which share no common feature values with SE definite noun phrases, followed by those environments that share one of the two feature values with SE definite noun phrases' (op. cit., 130). Huebner concludes that the learner's use of 'da' manifested non-random variation prior to its appearance in more target-like contexts.

Clearly, the insights afforded by analyses such as this one are valuable. The hypothesis that learner IL is systematic beneath its superficial chaos receives strong confirmation, and the analysis comfortably accommodates the dynamism of IL development.

Despite its strengths, form-to-function analysis is limited in at least one important respect. When the analytical procedure dictates that one starts with a form and then traces its functional distribution in the data over time, only forms that exist at the time analysis is undertaken can be studied. In the early stages of SLA, a vast array of forms does not appear, and is, therefore, not susceptible to analysis, with the result that the picture of IL development provided is necessarily incomplete. Put another way, form-to-function analysis, by itself, does not allow a comprehensive analysis of the development of communicative competence in SLA because it precludes analysis of meanings and functions which a learner has not yet encoded in particular surface forms.

A clear example of this problem comes from Huebner's (1983) study. Although he had originally intended to analyse the development of the tense-aspect system in this learner's IL, Huebner found very little evidence of any growth in this area. He thus decided to examine the linguistic organization of information instead. Given the goal of describing the *linguistic structure* of the IL, Huebner's decision to abandon analysis of tense-aspect development is understandable. However, given the goal of describing and, ultimately, explaining how SLA proceeds from a psycholinguistic perspective, it is less easy to justify neglect of a particular IL subsystem.

Perhaps the problem is due to an uncritical acceptance of the notion that units of linguistic analysis, e.g. morphemes and words, are equatable with a learner's units of acquisition. A few researchers in L1 acquisition (e.g. Peters 1980, 1983) and SLA (Hakuta 1981) have argued strongly that the traditional units of linguistic analysis cannot be assumed to be the learner's units of acquisition. Morphemes, words, or even sentences, that is, may not represent units either of perception or production at all stages of acquisition.

In light of this argument, what seems advisable is a more 'liberal' view of behaviours that could be serving as units of acquisition and, hence, units of analysis. To return to the particular subsystem which Huebner found to show minimal development, the domain of tense-aspect, the question becomes, how are tense-aspect distinctions expressed, given a lack of the usual target-language morphological devices? The answer to this kind of question directs researchers towards a consideration of the role of discourse-pragmatics in the communication of meaning in the absence of overt linguistic encoding. Such a direction has been taken in some of the recent work exemplifying 'function-to-form' analysis.

3.3. Function-to-Form Analysis

One kind of function-to-form analysis has been proposed by Kumpf (1981, 1983), who derives concepts for the 'discourse-functional' approach from work by Bickerton (1981a), Givón (1979a and b, 1982) and Hopper (1979). Kumpf (1983, 179) proposes that linguistic forms are motivated by particular discourse functions, i.e. that the use of a form 'is indexed to a particular context in discourse'. With respect to IL data, this kind of analysis yields evidence that 'interlanguages reflect discourse structure in ways which are characteristic of native languages, and that their grammar can be seen as a function of discourse'.

The analysis involves, first, the identification of discourse modes in the data, e.g. narration, conversation and exposition. The internal structure of a mode is then analysed through identification and quantification of coding points. Function is thus dealt with initially at the genre level. Beyond this level, internal structure is delineated in terms of a variety of linguistic coding devices. In the case of Kumpf's (1983) analysis of conversational narratives in the English IL of a single speaker, the devices include clause types and modes, tense-aspect categories, verb types and verb forms.

While this analysis yields interesting insights into (in particular) narrative structure and the functional distribution of coding devices, a problematic result is that ϕ-forms of verbs, i.e. unmarked stem forms, are reported to express various tense or aspect meanings. Subsequent applications of this analysis to a sample of English IL from a native speaker of Russian (Flashner 1983) and a native speaker of Spanish (Lynch 1983) also call attention to this problem. Flashner (1983, 89) notes:

> It was found that the base form of verbs is used for stative verbs with perfective meaning, for all the imperfective forms including the habitual, the continuous, the perfect, the anterior, irrealis forms, negatives and questions.

Lynch (1983, 224) acknowledges that 'a description of the subject's tense-aspect system [is] difficult because of the overuse of the base form'. Such statements indicate, as Kumpf (1981) observes, that this kind of analysis 'does not say much by itself . . . about a language . . . which basically has no morphological TAM system'. It is less interesting to report how tense-aspect is *not* marked than to be able to account for such lack of morphological coding in terms of features of the discourse or interactional context.

What is valuable about Kumpf's discourse-functional approach is that it treats function beyond the clause level. Recall that the analytical procedure first separates different discourse modes in the data, and then goes on to examine the marking of a semantic/functional domain, such as tense-aspect-modality. While the studies employing this analytical procedure have to date been limited to single samples of speech collected at one point in time, the analysis could very easily be extended to longitudinal data. Kumpf (1981, 26–7) suggests:

> With a *range* of speakers – both those in the process of acquiring TAM systems, sampled at different points in time *and* those whose TAM systems have fossilized at various points – analysed according to this method, the development of tense, aspect and modality can be shown as it elaborates morphologically. . . . These TAM analyses would combine with other approaches which would, for example, log changes in word order as the learners' systems grammaticize, show the emergence of the subsystems for reference/definiteness, demonstrate the progressive changes in conjunction/subordination as the syntax tightens, and so on. With these features of the systems described, light would be shed on the interpretations of processes of acquisition relative to the learners' input circumstances and the first language involved.

Another recent line of function-to-form analysis has moved in just this direction, and addresses the problem of 'non-development' in morphology. A number of researchers (e.g. Andersen 1982; Dittmar 1981; Klein 1981; Meisel 1982; Sato 1982, 1984; Schumann 1983) have taken as a point of departure the functional domain of temporality and focused on past time reference in particular. Their analyses consist of mapping out the linguistic and discourse-pragmatic means by which past time is established in ILs.

What is important about such analyses is their inclusion of an array of linguistic devices beyond verb morphology (walked, was going, etc.). These include (data from Sato 1984):

1) Temporal adverbials: 'yesterday', 'last night', 'in two months'.

2) Locative adverbials: 'in Vietnam', 'at work', 'over there'.

3) Calendaric expressions: 'January', 'Tuesday'.

as well as features of the discourse and pragmatic contexts:

4) Clause sequencing: 'I go to school Vietnam. I come U.S.' (= I went to school in Vietnam. Then I came to the U.S.).

5) Interlocutor scaffolding: NS: Yeah, tell me about your goal. How did you make it? Learner: Left foot. I shoot left foot. (= With the left foot. I shot with my left foot.)

6) Implicit reference (in narrative context): (Learner is recounting soccer game) Learner: I don't know what he (imitates whistle blowing). NS: The referee? The referee. Learner: He unfair. (= He was unfair.)

7) Implicit reference (in descriptive context): (Describing snapshots) Learner: She walk across. (= She walked across.)

The focus on alternative means of establishing past time reference was motivated precisely because IL data from beginning learners yielded very little in the way of morphological markers. All of the studies find that learners rely heavily on the various discourse-pragmatic devices or strategies while developing control over lexical and morphological forms. Given the goal of a comprehensive account of IL development, it is important to note that such findings would not have been obtained had target-language forms been adopted as the units of analysis.

A few details of the procedures followed in these analyses merit further comment. Andersen (1982), for example, is careful to begin with the selection of narrative excerpts from conversational data and to identify topic units in these excerpts before coding the data for past time markers and discourse strategies. This kind of hierarchical analysis provides for a more explicit account of what level of situated communication contributes to the establishment of temporal reference, i.e. speech event or topic. Similarly, in a longitudinal study of two Vietnamese speakers' acquisition of English, Sato (1984) further specifies the category most studies have called 'implicit reference' in terms of conversational units: self's immediately preceding utterance, other's immediately preceding utterance, and non-immediately preceding utterance. Thus, for a given learner utterance without linguistic encoding of past time, it is possible tentatively to identify the locus of contextual inference in real-time discourse. Both of these procedural points illustrate modifications made in function-to-form analysis which have contributed to much finer-grained, and more comprehensive, descriptions of IL development in one domain.

In our view, function-to-form analysis is highly productive, but it would be limited if undertaken without complementary form-to-function analysis. One or the other, alone, provides an incomplete account of IL development. Function-to-form analysis has the advantage of being able to describe prelinguistic means of communicating meaning. However, the complexities of form/meaning mapping in language development require microanalyses of particular forms as they acquire new functions, lose old ones, and shift from old to new functions. Of particular interest, of course, is the process through which meanings or functional domains originally expressed by discourse-pragmatic strategies come to be lexicalized or grammaticized, i.e. encoded in linguistic form (see Givón 1979; and, for a longitudinal second-language study of this process, Sato 1984).

Our discussion of form and function in IL studies raises the question of what should be considered the appropriate linguistic levels at which to undertake IL analyses. By now it must be clear that function-to-form analysis, at least, automatically commits one to *multi*-level analysis, since the entire repertoire of strategies and devices used by the learner must be examined. In the following section, we elaborate upon this issue, illustrating how the traditional levels of phonology, morphology, lexis and syntax interact with one another and with discourse-pragmatics in IL development.

4. The Interdependence of Linguistic Levels in SLA

Because of the broad scope of his proposed model of language change, Givón's (1979a, b, 1981, forthcoming) functional-typological syntactic analysis has received increasing attention from SLA researchers (Andersen 1983; Gass 1983; Pfaff 1982; Rutherford 1983; Sato 1984; Schumann 1981, forthcoming). In Givón's view, the linguistic coding devices of word order, intonation, and morphology contribute differentially to the marking of functional domains (e.g. topic continuity, temporality) of language. A different division of labour obtains among these devices, depending on the stage of development a communication system has reached, whether in the context of language change, pidginization, creolization, or first or second language acquisition.

An important methodological correlate of this model is that devices from more than one linguistic 'level' are simultaneously examined in the analysis of a functional domain, as illustrated by the most recent formulation of Givón's (1983, 17) cross-linguistic scale of topic accessibility:

Most continuous / accessible topic
zero anaphora
unstressed / bound pronouns or grammatical agreement
stressed / independent pronouns
R-dislocated DEF-NPs
neutral-ordered DEF-NPs
L-dislocated DEF-NPs
Y-moved NPs ('contrastive topicalization')
cleft / focus constructions
referential indefinite NPs
Most discontinuous / inaccessible topic

In this example, it can be seen that relevant coding devices in this domain operate at the level of discourse (zero anaphora and pronominalization), word order variation (e.g. R-dislocated DEF-NPs), and morphology (pronouns, and determiners in definite and indefinite NPs). The inclusion of the phonological level can be seen in prosodic features, such as stress (on pronouns) and intonation (in dislocations and cleft / focus constructions). New configurations of devices from different linguistic levels are created in the analysis of other domains.

As noted earlier, Givón's original work was in functional-typological syntax. From a psycholinguistic perspective, Hatch (1983, 9), too, has noted that linguistic levels 'leak'. That is to say, each of the traditional levels – phonology, morphology, lexis, syntax and semantics is affected to varying degrees by one or more of the others. Few would argue with what may now seem such an obvious fact about language noted by these and other scholars. Yet it is a fact that IL studies have usually ignored. Most researchers specialize in such areas as IL phonology, IL syntax, and so on, and books and articles in the field continue to bear similar titles. Here, we briefly report some recent findings which illustrate the value of recognizing the interdependence of linguistic levels in IL development.

In her longitudinal study of two Vietnamese learners of English, Sato (1983, 1984) found syllable structure transfer from Vietnamese to have a delaying effect on the acquisition of the English past tense inflection. When neither learner produced any inflectional pasts during the ten-month period of the study, an explanation was sought and found in an analysis of the learners' syllable-initial and syllable-final consonant cluster production in English. As predicted from the fact that Vietnamese does not permit syllable-final consonant-clusters and that syllable-final position for clusters is more marked cross-linguistically, very low frequencies of such clusters were observed in the IL data. Since English past time marking on verbs often creates clusters in final position (walked: /kt/, missed: /st/, dragged: /gd/, etc.), it was concluded that the lack of such inflected forms in the learners' ILs stemmed to a large degree from syllable structure transfer. In short, this analysis demonstrated first-language transfer at the level of phonology to be a critical factor in accounting for a characteristic of the ILs at the morphological level.

To date, perhaps the most complex relationship between levels explored has been that between syntax and discourse. Hatch (1983, 9–10) describes, for example, the effect of discourse level 'plans' upon relative clause analysis at the level of syntax:

> Several researchers have found . . . that learners use few relative clauses. When they do, they put more of them in post-verb position than following sentence subjects. There is no obvious explanation for this at the sentence syntax level. However, it is not so surprising when we consult information at the discourse level. The subject position in narratives is usually held by the major character. Once she or he has been identified . . . we know who the subject is. There is no need for further identification (and that is the function a relative clause could have in post-subject position). The major character engages in a series of actions throughout the narrative. These actions affect various people or objects which may need to be identified. And they may be related to places or times which also may need to be identified. Therefore, given a discourse view, we would expect to find more relative clauses in post-verb position. And if the story were relatively unrehearsed, we would expect to find a rather small number of relative clauses overall, since much of the work of relative clauses can be presented more easily in other less complex ways.

Huebner's (1983) study, discussed earlier in the context of form-to-function analysis, provides another illustration of the discourse-syntax interface. One of the features examined in his Hmong learner's English IL was the form *isa*, which Huebner (1983, 92) notes is taken from Standard English 'it's' and 'it's a'. In the early stages of the study, *isa* functions as a topic-comment boundary marker, i.e. a *discourse* marker rather than a copular verb. Later, the learner begins to use the form more often in Standard English copula environments, 'first in equative constructions, then in adjective constructions, and finally in other environments' (Huebner 1983, 127). In the interest of pinpointing the functions of this form, Huebner found it necessary to attend to discourse-pragmatic constraints on the initial use of this form, which then allowed him to document its transformation into a copula in various syntactic structures.

Still other examples of the interdependence of discourse and morphosyntax are provided by the recent studies of past time reference in IL speech. All studies of this phenomenon report the prevalence of contextual indications of past time; 'implicit reference' or 'shared knowledge between interlocutors', rather than inflectional morphology or verbal auxiliaries, carry the burden of past time marking in early IL.

While other interactions undoubtedly occur among the phonological, morphological, syntactic and semantic levels, it is not our purpose to detail them here. It should be clear that broadening the scope of IL analysis to include, simultaneously or sequentially, more than one level of analysis, helps to integrate heretofore discrete, apparently unrelated areas of development. Further, and crucially, multilevel analyses have greater potential explanatory power both for phenomena within single linguistic levels and for IL development in general.

273

5. IL and Context

Since the mid-1970's, a major issue in IL studies has been the linguistic and conversational *context* of IL performance. This includes both the context second-language speakers create for themselves and the context created for them by their interlocutors. It also concerns the way data are gathered (the effect of task on IL performance), and the relationship between development of particular subsystems in the context of the wider IL grammar.

A common characteristic of contrastive, error and performance analysis was that the acquisition of a particular grammatical subsystem was studied in isolation from other subsystems in the developing IL. Studies focused upon single phonemes, grammatical morphemes, or single morphosyntactic constructions, such as negation, interrogatives, and relative clauses. More recently, however, researchers have attempted to broaden the range of such analyses by examining interactions between the development in two or more related subsystems of the language.

One example of this is the ZISA project's study of word order and certain movement rules in untutored migrant workers acquiring German. In that work (see, e.g. Meisel, Clahsen and Pienemann 1981), the researchers found that passage through the developmental stages in German word order temporarily involved learners in deleting other elements, such as verb or object-NP (over which one has to move) and subject or verb (one of the categories to be inverted), which they had previously displayed in their ILs, apparently in an attempt to incorporate the new, more complex sets of movement rules required at each stage. It would have been misleading, Meisel et al. point out, to classify learners as more or less 'advanced' in German on the basis of the presence or absence of the deleted elements in their ILs. Apparent 'acquisition' of those elements depended upon the stage of development attained (by learners of different types) in additional but related areas of the grammar.

Another example of the importance of context is again to be found in the work on IL reference to past time discussed earlier. Traditional methods of investigating this phenomenon would have involved pulling from a transcript all utterances containing some overt past time marking or, at best, pulling all utterances in which the learner seemed to have been trying to refer to past time or events, and then to see how he or she did so, with or without target-language forms. The very act of pulling those utterances, however, can now be seen to have eliminated the possibility of a researcher perceiving that, especially (but not only) in the early stages of IL development, second-language learners, like native speakers, often use temporal 'anchor points' *previously established* either by themselves or by their conversational partner.

An illustration of this process is provided by Sato (1984). While telling the researcher about a friend whom he had met on a camping trip, one of the

Vietnamese children produced the following:

> Learner: dei keim (fo) læs yia hi lIb wId m- wI- wId mai kæbIn
> (They came last year. He lived with me – with my cabin.)

In this case, the learner's own immediately preceding utterance establishes the temporal reference. In the next example, the same learner uses his interlocutor's immediately preceding utterance in the same way:

> (the child and the researcher are watching the boy's older brother fixing a broken car headlight)
> NS: Where did he learn? (i.e. how to fix cars)
> Learner: (If) hi nat lcr eniti hi no^w
> (He (did)n't learn anything. He know(s) (how))

Similar findings from the ZISA group's German as second-language data led Meisel (1982, 13) to comment:

> in initial stages, the markings seem to be limited to one instance per conversational unit, the latter being defined as a sequence of utterances dealing with the same topic and not changing temporal reference.

Use of an interlocutor's utterances as a means of establishing time reference is just one example of what is known as 'collaborative discourse', described in some detail in both first- and second-language research over the last decade (for review, see, e.g. Hatch 1983; Long 1983; Snow 1979), and recently recognized by Slobin (1982), who calls the phenomenon 'scaffolding'. For many researchers and not a few theoreticians today, in fact, *conversation* is the crucible for language *acquisition*. Investigators of developmental pragmatics, for example, have observed that propositions in child speech are first encoded *across utterances* and *across speakers* (Ochs, Schieffelin and Platt 1979). One form this process takes is the movement from what Scollon (1976) termed 'vertical' to 'horizontal' constructions, as illustrated in the following excerpt from a conversation between Scollon and an 18-month-old child, Brenda. Brenda was 'reading' from a picture story book:

> Brenda: Cook
>   Say
> Scollon: What'd the cook say?
> Brenda: Something

Each of Brenda's utterances: *cook, say,* and *something,* had a separate intonation contour and was bounded by a pause and/or her interlocutor's utterance. Taken together, they constitute a proposition – called a 'vertical construction' because of their arrangement in the transcript. Scollon argues that vertical constructions are the precursors of 'horizontal', syntacticized constructions in adult speech (The cook said something). Horizontal constructions appear as one unit, in one utterance, under a single intonation contour, and are produced without the collaboration of a conversational partner.

A similar claim has been made for the emergence of second-language syntax by Hatch (1978, 404), who argues that:

> language learning evolves out of learning how to carry on conversations. . . . One learns how to interact verbally, and out of this interaction syntactic structures are developed.

Hatch offers many examples of discourse collaboration similar to those found by first-language acquisition researchers. The following illustration comes from Itoh's (1973) study of the acquisition of English by a two-and-a-half-year-old boy, Takahiro:

Takahiro:	This
	Broken
NS:	Broken
Takahiro:	Broken
	This /z/ broken
	Broken
NS:	Upside down
Takahiro:	Upside down
	This broken
	Upside down
	Broken

The excerpt shows repetition and incorporation of the interlocutor's utterances, and recombination of these with the child's own output.

Commenting on this type of language-acquisition research, Ervin-Tripp (1977, 18) concludes:

> The analysis of discourse is not a distraction from the [traditional] study of the development of syntax. By clarifying structural organization at other levels, one can leave in clear relief the syntactic apparatus used to accomplish cohesion, procedural repair work, interpersonal goals, and the referential semantic communication that traditionally was thought to be the primary function of syntax.

That the collaborative/scaffolding phenomenon exists is undeniable. What is still highly controversial is its role, if any, in language acquisition. Showing that acquisition takes place when cooperative language experiences are available to learners does not, of course, constitute evidence of a causal role for conversation, merely of what could be two co-occurring but otherwise unrelated phenomena. Conversational assistance could, for example, serve only to facilitate communication, not acquisition.

Regretably, discussion of this issue would take us into questions of research design and theory construction beyond the scope of this paper. In the present context, suffice to say that several claimed effects of the linguistic and conversational environment have amassed sufficient empirical support to make consideration of that environment essential for anyone wishing to explain IL development. Thus, to cite just one example, while research by Gass (1982) and Zobl (1983c) strongly suggests a preemptive role for markedness over input frequency as a determining influence on acquisition sequences for various morphological and syntactic constructions, there is also evidence of an effect for frequency from several studies (see Larsen-

Freeman and Long, forthcoming, for review). Hatch (1978a, 431–3) has suggested how the process may work with respect to the acquisition of English morphology:

> It is *possible* that topic nomination for the beginning adult learner requires establishment of semantic relationships using precisely the morphemes that are acquired early. The vertical constructions may consist of a set of such relationships as object identification, time reference, action, . . . attribute description, etc. These would require such morphemes as the plural, the possessive, copula, etc. Secondly, it is *possible* that when the NS does not understand the learner, he asks for clarifications with questions like 'how many?', 'one?' . . . 'whose car?' Mistakes in the marking of verbs, however, would not be caught by 'when?' questions. Such question-corrections would more likely elicit a time adverb rather than a verb correction for morphology. This might explain late acquisition of certain verb functions in morphology. It is also likely that one would not question the third-person singular present tense if the subject were clear. So it is possible that conversations could also determine the order of acquisition of morphology for the adult.

Whatever one's view of the likely role of the linguistic environment in SLA, it is surely indisputable that the potential explanatory role of input is preempted by studies which simply ignore speech to the learner – the 'other side of the page' in IL studies. Yet the majority of IL studies to date do just that. (In like fashion, most input/conversation studies have ignored IL development, too.)

Also ignored in many studies is the last aspect of the context of IL which we wish to mention here, namely, the effect of task on IL performance. This is, however, an issue that has recently received increasing attention, with promising results.

While only a few researchers have focused on the theoretical aspects of task variation in IL (e.g. Hyltenstam 1983b; Tarone 1979, 1982, 1983), a number of studies have documented the phenomenon. The importance of the relationship between the means by which IL data are obtained and their shape and substance is that our explanations of the process of IL development are crucially constrained by the data we think most accurately reflect a learner's underlying competence.

In addition to free speech or spontaneous conversation, a number of tasks (see Beebe 1980; Tarone 1979, 1982, 1984, for a sociolinguistic perspective) have been used to obtain IL data. These include at least the following (adapted from a list in Hyltenstam 1983b, 58):

1) elicited production, often with pictorial stimuli
2) manipulation of given linguistic material, e.g. sentence-combining, sentence completion, oral reading
3) intuition and grammaticality judgment tests (see Chaudron 1983, for review)
4) introspection
5) cloze tests
6) imitation
7) dictation or partial dictation
8) translation.

Researchers have selected from among these, with studies interested in task variation usually contrasting free or elicited conversation with a more formal/controlled task such as word-list reading.

Using various combinations of tasks, investigators have observed task variation in both IL phonology and morphosyntax. At the level of phonology, studies have tended to focus on particular phonological segments, e.g. English /r/ in native speakers of Japanese (Dickerson 1974; Dickerson and Dickerson 1977) and Thai (Beebe 1980), and English /θ/ for native Egyptian Arabic speakers (R. Schmidt 1977). A longitudinal study by Sato (1983b) of the English IL of a Vietnamese adolescent extended this focus to word-final single consonants and word-final consonant clusters. In all of these studies, task variation was reported, the general finding being that more controlled tasks (e.g. word-list reading, minimal pair production) elicited a higher proportion of target-language variants of the phonological features in question than did less controlled tasks (free speech, elicited oral description).

An added dimension to both Schmidt's (1977) and Beebe's (1980) studies was apparent native-language sociolinguistic transfer to the IL. In Schmidt's study of English /θ/ production by Egyptian Arabic speakers, the segment /θ) also happens to be a prestige variant in the native language and manifested the same task variation in the native language as in the English IL data. In Beebe's study of the English IL of Thai speakers, another kind of L1 sociolinguistic pattern was transferred. Although final R (Beebe uses this symbol to represent the phonological variable which is phonetically realized as a flap, a trill, or a lateral continuant) in the IL data occurred more frequently in the careful style (word-list reading) than in the less careful style (interview conversation), the results for initial R showed 'rampant' phonetic interference in the word-list reading task (op. cit., 437). This interference was manifested as the most prestigious R variant – the trilled R – in the native language occurring most often in the formal (word-list) task and not at all in the less formal (conversation) task in the IL.

Other studies have demonstrated the influence of task on IL morphosyntax. In the first morpheme study to include task as a variable, Larsen-Freeman (1975b) reported that the rank orders of morpheme production varied in speaking, listening, reading, writing, and elicited imitation. Fairbanks (1982, reported in Tarone 1983) found that a Japanese learner of English produced the third person singular present -s inflection very rarely in casual speech but almost always produced it in careful style. Other features for which task variation has been described include the deletion of redundant elements in coordinate structures in English using and (e.g. 'Jack sang a song and (φ) read some poetry') (M. Schmidt 1980), and the production of pronominal copies in relative clauses and the formation of negatives in Swedish IL (Hyltenstam 1983b). More recently, Tarone (1984) has presented evidence of task variation in the production of English articles, third person singular -s, and third person direct object pronouns for Japanese and

Arabic speakers. Finally, it is salutary to note that Butler-Wall (1983) has shown that the very constructions *native speakers* produce vary with task. While a replication study with non-natives is urgently needed, there is, meanwhile, no reason to expect that IL performance will not pattern in the same way.

More research is needed on task variation in a broader array of morpho-syntactic features, e.g. complex syntactic structures, and for lexical choice. However, it is clear from this selective review that there already exists strong evidence for the effect of task on IL performance. This has at least three methodological implications:

1) Researchers need to *control for* task *within* studies in order to isolate that portion of variability in IL data which is related to acquisition processes (see the discussion of synchronic variation and diachronic change in section 3 of this paper).

2) Researchers need to gather data on a *range* of tasks before assuming that they have a representative or adequate sample of IL performance.

3) Researchers need to ensure that data are *comparable across* studies (in terms of the tasks set for learners) before concluding that any differences are due to acquisitional types as opposed to task types.

6. Summary and Conclusion

We have argued that four crucial methodological issues in IL studies have been, and continue to be: (1) the need to focus on the *process,* not just the product of IL development, (2) the need to treat *function* as well as form, (3) the need for *multiple levels* of linguistic analysis, and (4) the need to consider various aspects of the *context* of learners' performance. Further, we have claimed that the four issues are intrinsically *inter-related.* In our view, it is impossible to consider the process by which learners attain whatever product they finally exhibit without considering the (often non-target-like) functions of (both target-like and non-target-like) forms in their interim grammars. The functions of those forms, in turn, are often only apparent when the researcher looks across linguistic levels in an analysis. And the data analysed in this manner are known to vary with aspects of the context of second-language performance. In other words, the members of each set – process and product, form and function, levels of analysis, and contexts of performance – *interact* with one another *and* with members of each of the other sets.

We have provided evidence that the *findings* of IL studies are at least partly determined by the methodological decisions researchers make with respect to these four issues. As stated at the outset, we also assume that research methods reflect theoretical orientation. Hence, whatever form a theory of IL development may finally take, the kinds of data it purports to account for and – in the four areas defined – the methods it uses to do so, will have to be made explicit before the theory itself can be evaluated as an *explanation* of SLA.

25. Discussant

Both Lightbown's and Long and Sato's papers are concerned with the nature of 'scientific' enquiry in interlanguage (IL) research. Such enquiry deals with the methodological procedures by which means a research 'product' is achieved. I shall begin my discussion with a reminder that this 'product' is the result of a research 'process' that is far less polished than researchers often let on.

Dingwall (1982), in a critical assessment of applied linguistic research, makes a clear distinction between the research product and the research process. She notes that published research typically leaves out any mention of the countless decisions that go into the shaping, carrying out and writing up of research and provides instead an apparently faceless account that conforms to the accepted 'scientific' ideals of objectivity. The whole process of subjective decision making – the 'ad hocing' procedures in which ethno-methodologists such as Garfinkel (1967) set such store – is ignored in the public presentation of a piece of research. Kellerman (this collection) provides an interesting example of 'ad hocing' procedures. He notes that we habitually authenticate our pronouncements through reference to the pronouncements of others as if these constituted the proof itself. The way in which we authenticate is often far from 'scientific', yet because it is part of the conventional baggage of 'scientific' research it usually goes unchallenged. Another example of the messiness of objective research is to be found in differing interpretations of the same research data. Both Lightbown and Long and Sato rightly insist that the evidence supplied by the morpheme studies needs to be weighted against counterfactual evidence, yet, having practised what they preach the two papers arrive at noticeably different conclusions about the validity of the results reported by the morpheme studies. In a complex field such as IL research, where there are numerous and often indeterminate variables, it is inevitable that the research is unhygienic at times. This is not to excuse lack of rigour, but to warn that research in our field will always be, to a greater or lesser extent, fuzzy. It is doubtful whether a totally 'scientific' methodology is possible.

Lightbown contrasts the search for 'scientific' theory in IL studies with 'pedagogical' or 'educational' theory. Neither Lightbown nor Long and Sato concern themselves with educational issues. They are interested in describing the means by which 'pure' IL research can be carried out. This neglect of the educational issues of IL studies is a reflection of a major change in orientation since the early IL papers (e.g. Corder 1967). Whereas early IL research had a clear educational bias, recent research (as reflected in the papers of this collection – with some notable exceptions) is self-contained. If it does look outwards, then, it is to the contribution it can make to linguistic theory rather than classroom practice. I shall return to this point in my final comments, but first I wish to consider a number of other issues to do with 'scientific' theory and methodology, which are raised by the two papers.

There are two aspects of methodology which both papers address:

1) Theories of IL
2) The relationship between theory and IL methodology

Long and Sato's paper is given over to (1) almost entirely on the grounds that it is not possible to critique methodology without considering the underlying theory. Lightbown's paper looks at both (1) and (2).

The theoretical orientation of IL research determines how IL is conceptualized and, therefore, how it is investigated. Lightbown runs through a number of orientations; linguistics, social psychology, sociolinguistics, psychological learning theory and neurolinguistics. She makes no attempt to argue in favour of any one of these, however, her primary concern being to identify the foci and procedures associated with each contributing discipline. In contrast, Long and Sato argue strongly in favour of one particular theoretical approach. In their eyes an explanation of second language acquisition is best provided by an approach that is process rather than product oriented (i.e. avoids what Bley-Vroman (1983) has called the 'comparative fallacy'), considers function as well as form, examines the multiple levels of IL (phonology, lexis, grammar, discourse) and gives due recognition to the role of context in IL performance. Thus Long and Sato argue for what might be called a 'macro' theory of IL as the basis of research.

It is clear that not all subscribe to such a macro theory. This collection includes papers which are based on a 'micro' position. That is, they argue that IL can best be accounted for in terms of the linguistic properties of the target language and/or the learner's mother tongue. Felix, for instance, treats IL as a 'logical' and 'developmental' problem which can be solved with reference to hypotheses the learner generates on the basis of the universal principles of grammar that comprise his innate linguistic knowledge. In Felix's theory of IL, therefore, there is no place for language functions or for multiple level analysis, while input is of importance only as a means of confirming or disconfirming innately generated hypotheses. This micro position is in complete contrast to the macro position advocated by Long and Sato. This contrast is a testimony to the fact that the linguistic/ communicative competence debate begun in the sixties is still very much alive in IL studies today.

I lean strongly towards the Long and Sato position. The Hallidayan concept that language is as it is because of the functions it has to perform in communication is an attractive one and one that has received considerable support in IL studies in both first and second language acquisition. However, I am also impressed by the growing evidence that markedness factors in the target language and/or mother tongue determine at least some IL features. What is important surely is to recognize that input and context and linguistic universals may either co-determine IL features or work independently in influencing the course of development. As Lightbown notes apparent deviations from target language behaviour may be modelled in the input data, so that there is no need to attribute such features to 'complex unobservable mechanisms'. For example, external negation in IL can be accounted for by the 'scaffolding' that has been noted to occur in 'collaborative discourse' (Long and Sato's terms). It is still possible, of course, that external negation is the result of the 'maturational schedule of universal grammar', as described by Felix. The point is the importance of remaining open to both possibilities and the need to search for a way of choosing between them. The methodological danger of pursuing a purely linguistic account or a purely sociolinguistic one is to be avoided as unnecessarily blinkered.

If there is no general agreement about what theoretical orientation ought to inform IL research, there is also no clear and simple relationship holding between the theoretical orientation and the choice of methodology.

Long and Sato see a uni-directional relationship, from theory to methodology:

> . . . methodological issues have always reflected changes in theoretical orientation in the field.

Lightbown, however, recognizes that the availability of an attractive methodology can direct and shape the researcher's theoretical position. She quotes Bialystok and Swain (1978):

> . . . the formulation of research questions is often a function of available methodologies rather than . . . a function of theoretical motivations.

Thus researchers tend to use available methodologies. An example of this is the plethora of morpheme studies generated by Dulay and Burt's work.

In fact, theory and methodology constitute a symbiosis, each feeding off and contributing to the other. This is one reason why it is not desirable to restrict IL methodology to a single 'scientific' formula but to encourage diversity in order to foster theoretical development.

There is no necessary relationship between a particular theoretical position and a particular methodology, although there is often an historically preferred one (a point Lightbown makes strongly). Methodologies can be described as a series of choices with regard to three major dimensions (1) the temporality of the research, (2) the method of data collection and (3) the method of data processing, as shown:

1) Temporality: a. cross-sectional, b. longitudinal.

2) Data collection: a. natural language, b. experimental task, c. introspection.

3) Data processing: a. qualitative, b. quantitative.

Thus the morpheme studies have usually consisted of 1a,2b,3b. In contrast discourse studies (e.g. Hatch 1978a) have followed a methodology that can be described as 1b,2a,3a. But the link between the theories and the methodologies is not an essential one. Rosansky (1976) conducted a morpheme study using natural language data collected longitudinally. Allwright (1980) conducted a classroom discourse study that was cross-sectional and involved quantitative as well as qualitative data processing techniques. IL research affords an abundance of methodologies, each with their strengths and weaknesses, and each suited to one or more particular aspects of IL. This abundance needs to be encouraged and the temptation to popularize (and thus proliferate) one methodology over the others in the name of 'scientific' enterprise needs to be resisted.

Lightbown considers in some detail what is required to be 'scientific' in IL studies. The issues she sees as important are (1) whether the research is hypothesis testing or hypothesis generating and (2) the question of generalizability. These issues are problematic and so total agreement is not to be expected. I shall present my own views in the light of what Lightbown has to say.

Although Lightbown clearly states that there is a need for research that is both hypothesis testing and hypothesis generating, it would seem that she is wary of too much of the latter. She castigates the 'bits and pieces' approach where aspects of learner language are examined because they catch the researcher's eye. She writes:

> ... we have now passed through a period of nearly two decades during which a large proportion of SLA studies were simply descriptive and most analyses were of a pretheoretical or a-theoretical nature.

But I am not convinced that the 'bits and pieces' approach cannot provide explanations of a kind and therefore I am not convinced that the only route to explanatory adequacy is through a 'scientific' methodology that stresses hypothesis-testing. For a start the distinction between hypothesis-testing and hypothesis-formation is not a neat one. The researcher whose vision is restricted to the specific research question he is tackling does not exist. *All* research generates new questions and does not merely answer old ones. Also if we are honest the research question that is finally presented in the written-up account of the research is often not exactly that which the researcher started with. Perhaps what is required is not so much to distinguish hypothesis-testing and hypothesis-formation, which I do not believe is possible, but to be more open in reporting the research process rather than just its product, as Dingwall suggests.

Popper (1976) distinguishes 'dogmatic' and 'critical' thinking. He sees the former as a necessary precondition of the latter:

... there can be no critical phase without a preceding dogmatic phase in which
something – an expectation, a regularity of behaviour – is formed, so that error
elimination can begin work on it.

Lightbown is right if by her insistence on a 'scientific' approach to IL
research she means that it is time to focus on error-elimination by means of
critical thinking (although I think there is still plenty of room for dogmatic
thinking in our field). But if by 'scientific' approach she intends to eschew
qualitative analysis, then I must beg to differ. This would be to confuse
means and ends.

Lightbown is critical of what she calls 'anecdotes'. She comes down
firmly on the side of quantitative analysis. The careful detailed analysis of
corpora of learner language, selected with a view to examining the claims of
one or more theoretical positions, may be, as Allwright (this volume)
suggests, a laborious way of going about things, but it is capable of both
theory generation and theory testing, as, I believe the discourse work of
Hatch has shown. Quantitative research often screens important variability
or misses significant interactional processes. But there is no need to oppose
qualitative and quantitative research. Each is capable of 'critical thinking'
and each has its place in IL studies. The danger is in imagining that enquiry
that does not involve quantification is not scientific or in failing to acknowledge the contribution that can be made by 'hybrid' research (i.e. research
that employs both qualitative and quantitative procedures).

Lightbown is also in favour of circumscribing the generalization of
research findings. She comments:

The generalizability of any single study's results and conclusions may ... be
limited to subjects with the same characteristics performing the same type of
task.

The danger of over-generalization in a field which has, perhaps, been
overready to insist on the universal properties of language acquisition is
apparent. Yet, if we take Lightbown's suggestion at its face value the
possibility of the existence of such universal properties must be discounted
until every task and every learner characteristic has been identified, which,
surely, will never take place. Effectively such conditions would preclude the
current enquiry into the role of universal grammatical properties in IL. In
contrast to Lightbown, I would like to see both regulated enquiry where
specific hypotheses are examined empirically and the ensuing generalizations are carefully circumscribed *and* speculative theory building, of which I
take Corder's work (1981) to be such an excellent example. Also I would not
wish to attribute the task of critical thinking to the former and dogmatic
thinking to the latter; speculative theory building is a way in which we can
move forward critically. Again the danger is in trying to delimit the nature of
enquiry by projecting one methodology as inherently 'scientific' and therefore superior to others.

Ochsner (1979) distinguishes explaining and understanding SLA. Explaining involves the systematic description of SLA in order to predict how it takes place. It assumes that SLA can be accounted for by a single all-embracing model. Understanding involves the rejection of a single explanation and the acceptance of multiple-perspectives, as, for instance, in the reading of a poem. This is a useful distinction, although by no means a watertight one. It is tempting to link the kind of hypothesis-testing enquiry which Lightbown favours with explaining SLA and qualitative, 'bits and pieces' research and speculative theory-building with understanding. This, however, is a mistaken view. It is possible for explanation to occur using a variety of methodologies. Indeed, to borrow another of Popper's terms, this is more likely to ensure the 'critical imagination' which is required to attack the presuppositions which less critical thought accepts as delimiting the hypotheses that can be investigated. Like Larsen-Freeman, I see room for both research that seeks to explain and that seeks to increase understanding, but I also see explanation advancing not as the result of any single IL methodology, but as the result of many.

Neither Lightbown nor Long and Sato consider IL methodology from the point of view of educational issues. I should like to conclude with a few observations on this topic.

It is a feature of IL studies that they have grown progressively less concerned with educational matters. Whereas many of the early studies were conducted by researchers recently drawn from the ranks of teachers and motivated by a desire to understand the learning process in order to improve pedagogic practice, more recently IL research has gone 'pure'. There are, of course, notable exceptions to this – in particular the works of Corder and Krashen come to mind.

There is, of course, no unanimity that IL research should be applied at all. Tarone et al. (1976) and Tucker (1977) have both argued that the scope of research is too limited to warrant any firm applications. In contrast, Corder (1980) has argued that we have an obligation to answer practical questions using the best knowledge available. At the root of these disagreements is the question of generalization. If we follow Lightbown's advice the applications of research findings to the classroom will be prohibited as 'unscientific'. If the views I have projected in my discussion of Lightbown's paper are accepted then classroom applications will be in order.

There is, however, an alternative to applying IL findings. Lightbown distinguishes 'scientific' and 'pedagogical' theories of IL. Instead, then, of applying 'scientific' theory to classroom issues, we can develop 'pedagogical' theories. Elsewhere (Ellis 1984) I have proposed one way in which such theories might be developed. This consists of action research. This rests on the idea of 'research from the inside' rather than research conducted by those outside the classroom for the benefit of those inside (Nixon 1981). Its aims are to increase teachers' understanding by helping them to investigate and reflect on their own practice by identifying critical elements in the learning process. In action research importance is attached to the process of the teacher discovering for himself about how language learning takes place in the classroom, rather than extrapolating from non-classroom studies conducted by others.

In conclusion, let me return to my opening comments about the need to give due recognition to the research *process*. Where 'scientific' theory-building is concerned we need to be explicit not just in order to ensure that the research can be replicated (a point made in both papers) but to make more public the procedures that led to the published *product*. Where 'pedagogical' theory building is concerned we can give recognition to the role of the research process by involving teachers in it through action research.

26. Summary of Discussion

Lightbown responded to the discussant's criticism that her paper was not 'education-based' by pointing out that it was not intended to be. Her aim had been to consider the relevance of SLA research to classroom practice, and, in particular, to underline the importance of a 'research spiral' which would move the subject forward instead of repeatedly treading the same ground. On the quantification issue raised by the discussant, she stressed that she did not demand that quantifying measures should always be employed but only that they should be used when they were appropriate to the design of the research. Long and Sato were not present to reply to the discussant's comments.

The open discussion concentrated on the role of research in SLA and explored the relationship between researchers and teachers. There was a general consensus that the topic had increased in importance in recent years.

The early part of the debate concerned the definition of 'action research' (a new term to some participants) and its role in language education. In response to the criticism that it was often of poor quality and tended to distract attention away from professional work, the point was made that, despite its misleading label, action research, if properly managed, had a valuable part to play in helping teachers to explore the wider implications of their work and in sensitizing them to the issues involved. Learners, it was claimed, and researchers themselves could often benefit from participating in small-scale action research projects, but it was important to recognize that their objectives were localized, modest and did not aim at replicability or the testing of hypotheses through rigorously controlled research designs.

The debate then moved to more general topics, including the problem of communicating research findings to professional teachers. The point was made quite forcibly that well-designed experimental research in the classroom typically necessitated the simplification of complex teaching situations and that this could not in principle be replicated under ordinary classroom conditions. The value of research results, therefore, lay more in the questions they asked than in the solutions they appeared to advocate. Insofar as research findings offered guidance for educational change, it was the responsibility of the teaching profession to explore ways of assimilating this advice into the overall design of effective and efficient pedagogy.

The later stages of the discussion took up the more general topic of 'pure' versus 'applied' research and an analogy with industrial research suggested that the findings of both were significant for implementing change. It was pointed out, however, that the analogy missed the main point which was that educational research lacked the power and resources to initiate projects but had to rely on attracting funds from outside. One practical suggestion for deepening professional relationships between re-searchers and teachers might be the encouragement of joint project-teams.

PART FOUR

IMPLICATIONS FOR LANGUAGE TEACHING

27. The Interlanguage of Immersion Students and its Implications for Second Language Teaching

1. Introduction

In early French immersion as practised in Canadian schools, English-speaking students receive a substantial portion of their education via the medium of their second language, French. In light of current language teaching theory emphasizing the need for 'authentic' use of the target language in the classroom context, the development of second language proficiency by these students holds particular interest for language educators.

From previous research we have carried out (see e.g. Swain and Lapkin 1982), we know that immersion students develop a remarkable ability to comprehend oral and written discourse in the second language. For example, on a listening test involving authentic target language texts, such as extracts from radio broadcasts, grade 6 immersion students have been found to perform at a native-like level (Swain and Barik 1977). In subjects such as mathematics and science when immersion students have studied them in French and have then been tested in English, their test scores have almost always been equivalent to those of students from the regular English program (Swain and Lapkin 1982). On a multiple choice discourse test in French in which grade 6 immersion students were required to select one of three sentences to fill the gap in a short paragraph and make it coherent, the immersion students performed at a level comparable to a group of native speakers of the same grade level (Allen et al. 1983). The same immersion students also scored at a level close or equivalent to native speakers on two discourse production tasks, one oral and the other written. These tasks, which elicited narrative and argumentation, were scored for coherence and cohesiveness, but not for grammaticality.

Despite these indications of well developed discourse skills, there is evidence to show that after six to seven years of an immersion program, productive use of the second language still differs considerably in grammatical and lexical ways from that of native speakers (e.g. Harley and Swain 1978; Harley in press; Swain 1983). In what follows we first present a diagnostic view of some non-native characteristics of early immersion students' interlanguage, focusing on features of the verb system at beginning, intermediate and upper grade levels. This diagnostic information concerns (a) how target-like performance may outdistance L2 competence in early interlanguage; (b) the continuing role of the mother tongue in immersion interlanguage; (c) the extent to which fossilization occurs; and (d) the effect of task and function on interlanguage performance. Following the presentation of this diagnostic information, we go on to consider some general implications of these findings for language testing and for language teaching methodology and curriculum development.

In this paper, then, we see the results of our immersion interlanguage research as educationally relevant in three main respects:

1) as diagnostic information to teachers that can help them to interpret their students' second language development and monitor progress in particular domains;

2) as having implications for language testing;

3) as a basis for hypotheses about second language teaching methodology and curriculum content that require verification and experimental research in the classroom context.

	Grammar	Discourse	Sociolinguistic
Oral production	Structured interview	film retelling + argumentation	requests suggestions complaints
Multiple choice	45 items	29 items	28 items
Written Production	2 narratives 2 letters		1 letter 2 notes

FIGURE 1. Matrix of tasks used at Grade 6.

2. Subjects and Data Base

The data to be discussed were collected from students enrolled in early total French immersion programs in Toronto and Ottawa. These are programs in which English-speaking children receive their entire curriculum in French for the first few years of schooling. Between grades 2 and 4 (the exact grade level depending on particular programs), the children are gradually introduced to some classes in the mother tongue, English, so that by grade 6, they are receiving about half their curriculum in French and the other half in English. French continues to be used into the high school years, during which a smaller proportion of the day is devoted to French language arts and one or two other subjects (e.g. histoire, géographie). Some cross-sectional interlanguage data from samples of students in grades 1, 4, 6 and 10 of these programs will be discussed and compared where relevant to data from native French speakers in grades 1, 6 and 10. These data represent only a portion of all the data that have been collected over the years in the Modern Language Centre's projects concerned with French immersion programs.

Table 1 and Figure 1 summarize some key characteristics of the data sets at each grade level. At grades 1, 4 and 10 (see Table 1), speech data were collected in individual interviews (Harley 1982) with twelve immersion students at each grade level, and with twelve native speakers in each of grades 1 and 10. At grade 6 (see Figure 1), data are available from sixty-nine immersion students and ten native speakers on a variety of oral and written tasks designed to test aspects of grammatical, discourse and sociolinguistic competence (Allen et al. 1983; Swain 1983). The students in the grade 6 sample were randomly selected from six immersion classes in Ottawa schools and from a Francophone school in Montreal.

TABLE 1. Some sample characteristics at Grades 1, 4 and 10

Program	Location	Grade	Total N	N of boys	Task/ Method	Home language	$\bar{X}$ IQ†
Early imm.	Toronto	1	12	6	Oral interview + translation	Eng.	114.1
Early imm.	Toronto	4	12	6	Oral interview + translation	Eng.	113.4
Early imm.	Ottawa (75% of sample) + Toronto	10	12	5	Oral interview + translation	Eng.*	114.9
French L1	Quebec City	1	12	6	Oral interview	Fr.	111.2
French L1	Quebec City	10	12	6	Oral interview	Fr.	110.0

* One student regularly uses English and German at home.
  Three students report using French sometimes at home.
† The following IQ measures were used:
  Grade 1 immersion: Canadian Cognitive Abilities Test (CCAT), Primary 2, Form 1.
  Grade 4 immersion: CCAT, Verbal battery, Level A, Form 1.
  Grade 10 immersion: Otis-Lennon Mental Ability Test, Intermediate Level, Form J (admin. in grade 9).
  Grade 1 native speakers: Epreuve d'Habileté Mentale Otis-Lennon, Echelle primaire II, Forme J.
  Grade 10 native speakers: Epreuve d'Habileté Mentale Otis-Lennon, Echelle supérieure, Forme J.

3. Diagnostic Information

a) Performance Outdistancing Competence

It is frequently observed in interlanguage studies that native-like use of a target-language structure in a particular linguistic context is no guarantee that the underlying knowledge of the learner with respect to that structure is the same as that of a mature native speaker. In the early oral interlanguage of immersion students in grade 1, there are numerous examples of this 'performance outdistancing competence' phenomenon.

One example has to do with the internal structure of the passé composé. The appearance of forms such as j'ai vu or j'ai mang-E[1] in a past narrative context does not necessarily indicate that the structure has yet been analysed into a three- or four-place frame of the following kind: pronoun + auxiliary + verb stem (+ suffix). Instead there is evidence from about two-thirds of the children interviewed towards the end of their grade 1 year to indicate that only partial segmentation has taken place. In non-past time contexts, for example, we find the students using similar forms on occasion. When asked if she lives a long way from school, one child responds as follows:

EIO7: Euh non. J'ai march-E à la maison toujours.

Alternatively, j'ai may appear in a present-time context in association with a present-stem form, as in the following exchange about a picture cartoon:

Interviewer: Est-ce que tu crois qu'il dit quelque chose aux enfants?
EIO9:   Non, j'ai crois qu'il juste f-fait comme ça.

From this and other evidence (e.g. the limited appearance of je in the interviews with some students, the non-use of any other forms of avoir by two of the students, and the apparent lack of alternate forms such as marche beside march-E for at least some students and some verbs), we conclude that a form such as j'ai mang-E in a past context may for some learners have the status of only two constituents. These we can label: pronoun (j'ai) + verb (mang-E). As the learner comes to perceive that in second and third person past (singular) contexts, a three- or four-place construction is used which incorporates the auxiliary form a(s), this auxiliary element may be generalized to the first person context as in the following example:

Interviewer: Qu'est-ce que tu as aimé le mieux de ce que tu as vu?
EIO4:   Mm j'ai a(s) oublié.

The appearance of this 'extra' auxiliary may be the clearest evidence to an immersion teacher that j'ai has the status of a pronoun. Only two of the grade 1 students in our sample, however, produced such 'extra' auxiliaries in the first person, and we may well wonder how often and how long this apparently widespread segmentation problem goes undetected by teachers. There may, for example, be a tendency on the part of native speakers to interpret forms such as j'ai prends and j'ai fait (very common in the grade 1 data) automatically as instances of the passé composé, and provide misleading feedback accordingly. In the following exchange in one interview, for example, it is not clear that the child who is explaining how she 'plays karate' is referring to the past, although the native French-speaking interviewer interprets it that way:

EIO5:   Et umm . . . umm j'ai fait à William, j'ai 'duck' comme ça (gesture) et j'ai 'flip right ov-' umm (laughs)
Interviewer: Tu es bonne au karaté alors (laughs), n'est-ce pas?
EIO5:   Et euh umm Jason, j'ai fait (gesture) umm comment est-ce que tu dis 'back'?
Interviewer: Tu lui as donné un coup de poing
EIO5:   J'ai donn-E un coup de poing umm.

If indeed, as we suspect from the form of the English substitutions in this exchange, the child is referring to generalized, present-relevant time rather than to a specific past event, then she may have received the erroneous impression from the native speaker's positive feedback that j'ai is the appropriate form for referring to the first person in the present.

Clearly it is important for teachers not to be misled by the early use of superficially correct structures and to be aware that a segmentation problem exists in order to provide the kind of input that will facilitate the students' entry into the French verb system. That the problem is potentially a persistent one is suggested by the fact that there is at least one child in the grade 4 sample of twelve students who appears to be using j'ai as a pronoun form on occasion. In describing a recipe, for example, this student says:

EI412: ... puis j'ai mets les um 'rice krispies' dedans

While we do not yet know exactly which teaching methods are likely to be most effective in facilitating target-like segmentation, we can at least point to some key factors which will need to be taken into consideration.

Based on oral input, which is what students at the grade 1 stage of an early immersion program have mainly been exposed to, phonological salience can be expected to be an important factor in influencing early segmentation by language learners (Slobin 1973; Peters 1983). As an initial stressed syllable of an apparently universally preferred consonant-vowel phonological form (Tarone 1981), j'ai is a prime candidate for segmentation as an acquisition 'unit' (Peters 1983). It is relevant to note that there are other examples in the students' speech of mis-segmentations that adhere to a consonant-vowel-(consonant) principle: for example, le l'eau instead of l'eau, il j'aime ça instead of il aime ça, cet l'homme instead of cet homme. We may hypothesize that written input of some kind would be helpful in drawing attention to phonologically non-salient segments relevant in the target language. Indeed it appears significant that a group of twelve adolescent late immersion students, who had had a similar overall amount of in-class exposure to French as the grade 1 students but more emphasis on written texts, showed considerably less evidence of non-target-like segmentations in their oral production (j'ai appears to function at times as a first person pronoun for only three of these late immersion students) ((Harley 1982).

In addition to phonological salience in oral language input, we can point to L1 transfer as a contributing factor in the non-segmentation of j'ai by early immersion students in grade 1. Whereas the passé composé in French is a three- or four-place construction, the neutral past tense in English – the simple past – is a two- or three-place construction without auxiliary (pronoun + verb stem (+ suffix) as in 'I saw', 'I walked'). This characteristic of English may be seen as working in tandem with the natural segmentation process noted above to promote interpretation of j'ai as a pronoun form. The cooperation of L1 influence with natural acquisition processes in this manner is consistent with predictions made by Zobl (1980b) and Andersen

(1983b). In order for teachers to determine whether j'ai vu, for example, is functioning in obligatory contexts as a two- or a three-place construction, we suggest that it is important at least to observe whether the students are also saying il a vu in the third person instead of il vu, and, of course, whether j'ai is appearing in non-past contexts too.

In short, we believe that recognition by teachers of the existence of this potentially long-drawn-out segmentation problem is an important first step towards the realistic assessment of students' progress in learning the French verb system and the provision of maximally helpful input. As Corder (1973, 293) has pointed out, it is necessary for a teacher to

> understand the source of the errors so that he can provide the appropriate data and other information, sometimes comparative, which will resolve the learner's problems and allow him to discover the relevant rules.

b) The Continuing Role of L1

i) Present progressive. The learner's interpretation of a French verb construction in terms of an English verb frame is not limited to the passé composé in association with j'ai. There is evidence that some of the grade 1 early immersion students have interpreted the marked passé composé with auxiliary être in terms of the English progressive construction, be + verb stem + suffix (note that être is a translation equivalent for be in many other contexts). Some examples follow of this 'progressive' use of the marked passé composé:

> EIO7 (telling a story about Winnie-the-Pooh's encounter with a mirror): Winnie-the-Pooh est regard-E dans la mur et il dit – (continues in present tense) (interpreted by us as 'is looking')
> Interviewer (referring to a cartoon in which a boy is shovelling snow off a car): Et pourquoi le monsieur n'est-il pas content?
> EIO3: Parce que le garçon um est um 'scratch'-E le voiture (interpreted by us as 'is scratching')

At times the English progressive also appears as être + (non-first-conjugation) infinitive:

> EIO8 (describing a cartoon in which a wave is coming up behind a man): Maintenant elle(s) est content(s) parce que le 'wave' est venir (interpreted by us as 'is coming')

It should be pointed out that this type of transfer from English, also observed among late immersion students (Harley 1982) and anecdotally reported by teachers of Anglophone students in regular 'core' French programs too, does not appear to be constrained by markedness conditions. Contrary to the proposition that:

> unmarked categories will be preferred to marked ones in early stages of second language acquisition irrespective of the learner's L1 and L2. (Hyltenstam 1982, 14)

we interpret the last three examples as indicating that partial structural similarities between two specific languages – English and French – have led the immersion students to attempt to use a marked formal construction in the L2 to express a marked L1 function (the progressive aspect) even in those contexts where a simple unmarked verb stem form is all that is needed in French. These findings are more consistent with the hypothesis expressed by White (1983) that once a marked form in the L1 has been acquired, the form in question may be transferred to the L2.[2] In this instance, as in the j'ai + verb construction discussed above, similarity of syntactic frame in English and French appears to be an important factor.

The last three examples should lead teachers to be suspicious of target-like marked forms such as il est tombé when they occur in the early inter-language of immersion students. In the next example, for instance, it is likely that a present progressive, rather than a past completive meaning is intended:

Interviewer (pointing to a picture of a man just about to plunge into the water):
Qu'est-ce que qu'il fait ici?
EIO8: Elle est tomb-E dans le l'eau (interpreted by us as 'she is falling')

Significantly, in support of our interpretation of est tomb-E as progressive rather than completive in such early interlanguage contexts, we find grade 4 students later on almost invariably using il a tombé (with auxiliary avoir) to indicate completive aspect when referring to another picture where a man on skis has already fallen. The more widespread target rule involving the use of auxiliary avoir in the passé composé is also reflected in numerous errors at grades 4 and beyond of the following kind:

EI401: On a allé à Québec (ce) le um l'été passé

In the grade 4 sample, we find no further evidence of être + verb stem + suffix being used as an English-style progressive. Instead when the marked L2 construction, être + verb stem + suffix, does occur (relatively infrequently), it appears by this stage to have the target completive meaning. We may hypothesize that the contradiction in meaning between progressive and completive is one reason why transfer of the English present progressive does not appear to be a lasting phenomenon. However, the continued infrequent use of être + past participle in a completive sense partly reflects the functional non-congruence of the constructions with be and être in the two languages.

In short, the findings indicate that in its initial use, the marked target construction être + verb stem and suffix is often assigned the wrong function. The next stage, it would appear, is one in which the target construction is dropped from the students' interlanguage. The third stage, we hypothesize, will show the re-entry of the form with its target completive function.

ii) Word order. More persistent than present progressive constructions are word order errors which can be traced to English syntax. Every student in the grade 4 sample makes at least one word order error of the following type in which an adverb is inserted between subject and verb:

> EI404: je toujours prends l'auto
> EI406: je juste mets du lait et un oeuf

Other English-based syntactic errors of a type noted some years ago by Selinker, Swain and Dumas (1975) among grade 1 students still occur in the speech of grade 4 students. For example:

> EI411: Son voiture a beaucoup de neige sur le. 'His car has lots of snow on it'.

By grade 10, we find few word order errors of this kind among the immersion students. It may be relevant to note in this regard that Lepicq (1980), who had native speakers evaluate typical errors made by immersion students in grade 6, found that after lexical errors in verbs, word order errors were the most severely judged of several types of errors – i.e. considered the most serious impediment to comprehension. The general lack of word order errors among the grade 10 immersion students suggests that teachers have been supplying negative input (Schachter in press), and that this has had a positive effect in rubbing off the rough edges of L1 influence on the students' L2 performance.

iii) Impersonal verbs. While English-influenced errors such as those illustrated in the last three examples are relatively rare in the interviews with the group of grade 10 early immersion students, more subtle influences from English still remain in the constructions that are used. Typically, where there is more than one structural option in French for expressing a particular notion, the students will select that option which is most similar to English. One example has to do with the general lack of use of impersonal verbs, characteristic of French, and which would have been appropriate in the last example above (il y a beaucoup de neige sur sa voiture). None of the grade 10 students interviewed uses the impersonal il faut . . ., for example, which is used on average 3.8 times each by a subsample of six of the native French-speaking Quebec students who were also interviewed in grade 10, and on average 3.2 times each by a subsample of six of the Quebec students interviewed in grade 1. In expressing the notion of necessity, grade 10 early immersion students tended to personalize it in characteristically English fashion as follows:

> EIXO1: il a décidé qu'il devait se réveiller

In this example, no error results from this use of a construction that is more congruent with English, but on other occasions, the non-use of an impersonal construction does lead to error, as in the example below, where an English-style passive is produced instead of an impersonal on (on m'a donné . . .):

> EIX10: . . . il y avait xxx du um liquide dans mes poumons et j'ai j'étais donné du mé . . . beaucoup de médication

Such characteristic differences between the interlanguage of immersion students and the French produced by native speakers of the target language are probably less obtrusive than the kinds of word order errors illustrated from grade 4, and hence less likely to provoke negative reactions from native speakers.

iv) Direction. Overt errors that are L1-based are, we suggest, in general only the tip of the iceberg. That the English L1 affects more than surface tactics in immersion interlanguage at intermediate grade levels is indicated by a study of how direction is expressed in the French compositions of grade 6 immersion students (Harley in press). In contrast to a group of native French speakers in Quebec who generally expressed direction together with motion in the verb (e.g. partir, descendre), the immersion students tended to express motion with manner in the verb (e.g. courir), using prepositional phrases more frequently to carry the directional information. These differences between the groups were seen to reflect deep-seated differences between French and English. The way in which immersion students characteristically expressed direction, it should be noted, did not necessarily lead to the production of overt errors, although it sometimes did. Thus it is quite likely that teachers are unaware of the systematic nature of the transfer taking place.

This brief survey of some negative aspects of L1 influence at various grade levels of an immersion program suggests that at least in a classroom context where the learners share a mutually reinforcing L1 and are relatively cut off from speakers of the L2 other than their teacher, there is a distinct continuing effect of the L1 at all grade levels. This effect appears, however, to become less superficially obvious at the higher grades, perhaps in response to teachers' negative feedback when the errors (e.g. of word order) are plain. For language teachers and curriculum developers these findings suggest that one cannot ignore the students' L1 in such circumstances and expect it to melt away. The learners will continue to draw on their English L1 as an often fruitful source of hypotheses about the target language.

c) Fossilization: Does it Occur?

According to Selinker (1972, 215c):

> Fossilizable linguistic phenomena are linguistic items, rules, and subsystems which speakers of a particular NL will tend to keep in their IL relative to a particular TL, no matter what the age of the learner or amount of explanation and instruction he receives in the TL.

In the previous section, it was observed that even after six to ten years in the program, early immersion students appear to still favour those means of expressing themselves in the target language that are congruent with their L1, English. Does this mean that their interlanguage has fossilized? Does it indicate that they would not respond to further explanation or instruction aimed at clarifying some of the more subtle differences between English and French?

We should point out that there is currently no evidence that immersion students' interlanguage stops developing in any specific area. While growth towards target language norms in productive language use may seem remarkably gradual, we find at any grade level we look at closely that there is new development relative to earlier grades. Such development is not always evident from a simple count of errors made. With respect to gender distinctions, for example, Harley (1979) found that in grade 5, a small sample of early immersion students actually had a slightly higher rate of gender errors in their speech than did some grade 2 students. The figures, however, concealed the fact that the grade 5 students were further ahead than the grade 2 students in more regularly using feminine gender to refer to female referents, which represented a significant development in their interlanguage system.

TABLE 2. Median scores on 7 variables at Grades 1, 4 and 10

Item	Immersion			Native speakers	
	Gd. 1	Gd. 4	Gd. 10	Gd. 1	Gd. 10
a) % use of reflexive	0	0.25	1.00 *	1.00	1.00
b) % use of polite 2 pers.	0	0	0.50	1.00	1.00
c) % use of 2 pers. pl.	0	0	0.67 *	1.00	1.00
d) % use of 3 pers. pl.	0	0.13	0.76 *	1.00	1.00
e) use of imparfait (progressive context)	0	0	0.68 *	0.60	0.63
f) use of imparfait (habitual context)	0	0	0	0.78	0.74
g) use of conditional (hypothetical context)	0	0	0.58 *	1.00	1.00

* Based on Mann-Whitney U-Test, $p < 0.02$.

The appearance of errors following a period of correct use may at the same time be less an indication of fossilization than evidence of non-linear U-shaped development (Kellerman 1983a), which has been noted in various spheres of learning as well as in language development (e.g. Strauss 1982). When, for example, we find an immersion student in grade 1 making an error in the first person of the passé composé such as j'ai a(s) oublié, we may hypothesize that this is a new stage subsequent to the 'correct', but only partially analysed use of j'ai oublié. To complete the U-shaped curve of development, we would expect the final (correct) solution to re-occur only when j'ai itself is analysed as two morphemes rather than one. A similar pattern of correct use, followed by incorrect, then correct use again has been hypothesized to apply to the use of j'ai and je suis in expressions such as j'ai peur (je suis peur) by immersion students (Harley 1982).

Even though accuracy rates are thus not an entirely satisfactory way of measuring progress from one grade level to another, we present some cross-sectional findings in Table 2 which suggest that, with respect to a number of features of the target French verb system, significant developments take place between grades 4 and 10 in those areas where there is little or no apparent development between grades 1 and 4. From these data it is clear that we would not want to conclude that certain features of the verb system of immersion students in grade 4 have fossilized because we cannot measure any change from grade 1 to that point.

The variables presented in Table 2 are as follows: (a) percentage use in obligatory context of reflexive pronouns with pronominal verbs; (b) percentage use of polite second-person forms (vous + verb stem + -ez) in addressing a stranger; (c) percentage use in obligatory context of second person plural forms (same as polite form); (d) percentage use in obligatory context of phonologically distinct third person plural verb inflections; (e) use of the imparfait in a past progressive context (percentage of all verb forms used in response to a specific interview question); (f) use of the imparfait in a past habitual context (percentage of all verb forms used in response to a specific interview question); and (g) percentage use of the conditional in an obligatory hypothetical context.

Table 2 shows that, based on a Mann-Whitney U-test involving rank-order comparisons, grade 4 students appear to be no further ahead than the grade 1 students but the grade 10 students are significantly more target-like than the grade 4 students on almost all variables. In only one instance, the habitual past context, do grades 4 and 10 appear alike in making minimal use of the imparfait in contrast to the native speakers who used it about 75 per cent of the time. Two factors may help to explain why, in this context, grade 10 students do not show any improvement over the grade 4 students: (a) the context, in the shape of the question: L'hiver/l'été passé, qu'est-ce que tu faisais d'habitude les fins de semaine?, provides for optional, rather than obligatory, use of the imparfait; and (b) in English the simple past, usually translatable in French by the passé composé with respect to actions, would be the appropriate form to use. As suggested in section 3b(iii) above, it is in contexts for optional use of target forms that immersion students appear most likely to continue selecting those forms that are most congruent with their L1 system.

From the results presented in Table 2, we conclude that there does appear to be substantial L2 development taking place beyond the early years of an immersion program, but that we need to examine further data, preferably of a longitudinal nature, in order to document the students' progress in more detail. From an educational perspective, the main conclusion to be made is that there is to date no evidence of fossilization in any particular L2 domain at any particular grade level. Hence we would argue that it is by no means too late at the intermediate grade levels to consider ways of improving on the immersion students' L2 proficiency (see section 4 below).

d) The Effect of Task and Function on Interlanguage Performance

Our discussion of features of early immersion students' interlanguage has concentrated up to this point almost entirely on non-native aspects of their oral production with respect to the verb system. We now wish to consider the performance of the students on a particular target language structure, the conditional verb form, across a variety of language tasks. Our purpose in this section is to throw further light on the relationship between the students' use of a marked verb form in an oral interview setting and their ability to recognize and produce this form under other task conditions (see also Tarone 1984) and in the realization of different language functions. An explanation of the various tasks (oral production, multiple choice and written production) and functions (hypothetical and attenuation) follows.

i) Hypothetical contexts

1) Oral production. In the interviews with the students at grades 1, 4 and 10, production of the conditional form in a hypothetical context was elicited by two questions:

> Qu'est-ce que tu ferais si tu avais beaucoup d'argent? Si tu gagnais la loterie, par exemple?
> Et tes parents, qu'est-ce qu'ils feraient, eux?

At grade 6, only the first question was asked. These questions were considered to provide an obligatory hypothetical context for the use of conditional verb forms, which were in fact produced by virtually all the native speakers in grades 1 and 10 (except for one child in grade 1). As indicated in section 3(c) above, the score for the conditional in this context was obtained by taking the accurate uses of the conditional as a percentage of the obligatory contexts produced by each student.

A number of other tasks also involved the hypothetical use of the conditional:

2) Oral translation task. Following the interviews with grades 1, 4 and 10, the immmersion students were asked to translate a number of orally presented French sentences into English. One of these sentences was: Si j'avais une pomme, je la mangerais. Use of the conditional in English was simply scored as 1, and its non-use as 0.

3) Multiple-choice grammar items. In the matrix of tests administered to the grade 6 students (see Figure 1), two items on a multiple-choice grammar test required students to select a conditional form in preference to two other verb forms in order to fill the blank in a given sentence. The items were:

A ta place, je le ferais tout de suite au cas où quelqu'un . . . .
a) arriverait
b) arrivait
c) arrivera

Si j'avais le temps, je . . . . avec toi.
a) jouerais
b) jouerai
c) jouais

It should be noted that in the first of these items French requires the use of the conditional in both segments of the hypothetical sentence. In contrast, in standard English the use of a present-tense form in the second part of the sentence (. . . in case someone comes) is normal. A score of 1 was awarded for the choice of (a), and zero for (b) or (c). For the second item, 2 points were awarded for the choice of (a) where the correct conditional inflection -ais was indicated, 1 point was awarded for the choice of (b), in which the potentially homophonous futur simple inflection -ai could be regarded as simply a spelling error, and zero was awarded for the choice of (c).

4) Written compositions. Two letters written by the grade 6 immersion students in the context of the grammatical and discourse written production tasks (see Figure 1) provided contexts in which conditionals might optionally be used in a hypothetical sense. These letters were written to request a favour of an imaginary adult, and required students to think of arguments as to why that favour should be granted. In such circumstances, native speakers sometimes used conditionals or, more often, the futur simple to express their arguments, which frequently involved indicating what would happen if the request were granted (e.g. je serais très prudent pour ne pas la briser si vous vouliez bien me la prêter).

The choice of a conditional as opposed to a futur simple in such a context has sociolinguistic connotations. By envisaging the granting of the request as a hypothetical condition rather than an open condition (i.e. more likely to be actualized), the writer who uses a conditional can be regarded as putting slightly less pressure on the addressee to do what is asked. However, use of the 'distant' futur simple (Chevalier et al. 1964; Deshaies and Laforge 1981) still implies less expectation that the request will be granted than does the use of the immediate futur proche.

For the analysis, uses of the conditional in the two letters were summed for each student as were uses of the futur simple. Mis-spellings in the first person, ferais instead of ferai and vice versa, were ignored.

ii) Attenuation contexts

1) Written compositions. The letters also provided optional contexts for the sociolinguistically determined use of conditionals in the attenuation of the writer's expressed desires (e.g. j'aimerais . . ., je voudrais . . .) and of more direct requests (est-ce que je pourrais . . ., pourriez-vous . . .). In summing instances of such uses for each student, a third formal request letter (asking for information to be used in a class assignment), written by the students as a sociolinguistic written production task (see Figure 1), was also included.

2) Oral production. In the interviews with grades 1, 4 and 10, students were asked to role-play a polite request in which they had to approach an unknown adult to ask the time. In this context, the majority of the grade 10 native speakers (eight out of twelve students) used a conditional: e.g. Auriez-vous l'heure, s'il vous plaît? Use of the conditional was scored as 1, and non-use as 0.

The grade 6 students carried out a greater number of role-plays in a sociolinguistic oral production task (see Swain 1983 for details) involving both formal and informal variants of situations. Only the formal variants of the six situations (two requests, two complaints and two suggestions involving a higher status, adult addressee) were included in the analysis, since it was in these circumstances that grade 6 native speakers were most likely to use conditionals. However, even in these formal contexts, only a minority of the native speakers used attenuating conditionals such as: Est-ce que vous voudriez vous asseoir . . .? A score for each grade 6 student was obtained by summing uses of the conditional across the six formal situations.

TABLE 3. Use of conditionals in Grades 1, 4 and 10 (n = 12 in each group)

		Immersion			Native speakers	
		Gd. 1	Gd. 4	Gd. 10	Gd. 1	Gd. 10
Translation task	$\bar{X}$ correct	82%	100%	100%	—	—
Oral interview: hypothetical context	$\bar{X}$ correct	0	15%	56%	95%	98%
Oral interview: polite request context	$\bar{X}$ use	0	0	0	0.17%	0.66%

3) Multiple choice. In the multiple choice sociolinguistic test administered to the grade 6 students, one item involved an understanding of the socio-linguistic relevance of the attenuating conditional. From the three sentences presented in this item, the student needed to know that the conditional forms of options (a) and (b) were less appropriate in the informal request situation than the use of the present tense in option (c). All the native speakers in grade 6 in fact selected option (c).

A l'école, dans la cour de récréation dite par une élève à son ami
a) Pourrais-je te voir un instant?
b) Est-ce que je pourrais te parler quelques minutes?
c) Je peux te parler une minute?

Students who selected option (c) were awarded 1 point, whereas selection of (a) or (b) resulted in a zero score.

iii) Results. Looking first at the results from grades 1, 4 and 10 (see Table 3), we find that even in grade 1, the great majority of immersion students are able to translate the orally presented sentence, Si j'avais une pomme, je la mangerais, into English. From the tapes it is clear that they generally do this promptly and without hesitation. This we suggest they can do, not because they necessarily understand the meaning of the conditional form per se, but primarily because the bipartite sentence beginning with the conditional si serves as an excellent cue to meaning. A secondary cue is provided by the past tense form avais, but in this case it appears that at least some students do not recognize the tense of this form. Another sentence, Il en avait une, was incorrectly translated into the present tense in English by five of the twelve grade 1 students, four of the twelve grade 4 students and one of the twelve grade 10 students.

The immersion students thus have a remarkable ability to capture the meaning of a hypothetical sentence without necessarily paying attention to verb form. This ability is not matched by the production of conditionals by most students until after grade 4. Only two grade 4 students are using conditionals in the obligatory oral production context of a hypothetical condition (see also Harley and Swain (1977) with respect to grade 5 students). By grade 10, nine out of twelve students are using the conditional in this context at least some of the time, but their average accuracy rate is still only 56 per cent.

Turning to the grade 6 findings on the use of the conditional (see Table 4), we find that, as might be expected, recognition of a conditional form and of its use in a particular task and function is not necessarily associated with the ability to use similar forms in other tasks and functions. If, for example, we ignore spelling on the grammatical multiple choice test and count both jouerais and jouerai as correct choices, we find that 94 per cent of the grade 6 immersion students are able to select a conditional-sounding form to insert in the obligatory hypothetical context. In a similar obligatory context in the oral interview, however, the conditional is used accurately on average 41 per cent of the time, and on the first item of the grammatical multiple choice test where there is a different context for use of the conditional which does not coincide with English, only 20 per cent of the immersion students obtain correct scores. In an optional context such as that provided by the letters of suasion, the use of hypothetical conditionals is very infrequent, being used on average 0.2 times by each immersion student, in contrast to the native speakers who used on average 1.5 conditionals each. The same pattern may be observed for the futur simple, which is used more frequently than the conditional in this context by both the immersion students and the native speakers (immersion $\bar{x} = 0.9$ and native speaker $\bar{x} = 3.0$). Overall, the immersion students were twice as likely as the native speakers to use the futur proche in this context (immersion $\bar{x} = 2.0$ and native speaker $\bar{x} = 1.0$). While the use of this analytic, and thus presumably simpler verb form (Traugott

TABLE 4. Use of conditionals by Grade 6 students

	Immersion (n = 69)		Native speakers (n = 10)	
	X̄ use	Accuracy rate in obligatory context	X̄ use	Accuracy rate in obligatory context
Grammar oral production hypothetical contexts	1.13	41%	4.10	94%
Grammar multiple choice (1st item)		20%		100%
Grammar multiple choice (2nd item)		94% (chose a or b) 41% (chose a)		100% (chose a or b) 80% (chose a)
Written production: hypothetical contexts	0.20		1.50	
Sociolinguistic oral production: attentuating contexts	0.36		1.80	
Sociolinguistic multiple choice item		58% (chose c)		100% (chose c)
Written production: attentuating contexts	0.40		2.70	

1977), is grammatically correct and semantically acceptable, it may well be that it is sociolinguistically less appropriate than the use of the conditional or the futur simple.

It has previously been observed that immersion students are generally non-native-like in their performance on sociolinguistic tasks, which can be interpreted as a reflection of their lack of social contact with native speakers in or out of the classroom context (e.g. Swain 1983). Examination of the immersion students' performance on the attenuating function of the conditional supports the earlier findings. On the sociolinguistic multiple choice item, only 58 per cent of the immersion students chose response (c) without a conditional verb form, this being the response that was unanimously selected by native speakers. Since we know from the grammatical multiple choice second item that the immersion students can almost all recognize a conditional-sounding form, we can only conclude that they do not yet have adequate knowledge of its appropriate use in a sociolinguistically relevant context. Instead their performance on this task shows a tendency towards over-formal use in an informal context. Conversely, in the formal contexts of the sociolinguistic oral production task and the letters, we find them under-producing attenuating conditionals relative to native speakers (see

TABLE 5. Grade 6 immersion students' use of conditionals: principal-components analysis with varimax rotation

	Factor 1	Factor 2	Factor 3
Grammar oral production: hypothetical contexts	0.28922	0.49443	0.28646
Grammar multiple choice (1st item)	−0.16761	0.33456	0.67997
Grammar multiple choice (2nd item)	−0.00887	0.70842	0.14507
Written production: hypothetical contexts	0.18979	−0.19251	0.76770
Sociolinguistic oral production: attenuating contexts	0.87694	0.17944	0.10550
Sociolinguistic multiple choice item	0.03166	0.70525	−0.24604
Written production: attenuating contexts	0.87226	−0.04728	−0.04630

Table 4). In short they are too formal in an informal context and not formal enough in a formal context, indicating a general inability to shift register appropriately.

The findings provide evidence that the comprehension by early immersion students of the use of a conditional form in a specific hypothetical or attentuation context may far exceed their productive use of that form in a similar context. At the same time it is clear that the students are much more likely to produce conditionals in an obligatory context than they are to produce them in an optional context.

In order to determine the extent to which grade 6 performance on the various tasks involving the conditional represent separate dimensions of proficiency for the immersion students, a principal components analysis was carried out on their conditional scores on each variable. Three factors emerged with eigenvalues greater than 1 (see Table 5). These three factors were subjected to a varimax rotation.

The first factor reflects the ability to produce attenuating conditionals in both oral and written formal contexts. It is interesting to note that although the ability to produce attenuating conditionals in both oral and written contexts load together on the same factor, the ability to produce hypothetical conditionals in both oral and written tasks do not load on the same factor. This suggests that form, function and task interact in complex ways in determining actual performance.

The sociolinguistic multiple choice task loaded together with the second item of the grammatical multiple choice test on a second factor. Use of the conditional in the obligatory hypothetical context of the oral interview also loaded mainly on this factor. This second factor represents the ability to recognize or produce conditionals in those contexts where native speakers unanimously used, or unanimously avoided using, conditionals – those contexts, that is, where use or non-use can be considered as obligatory or conventional.

The interpretation of the third factor is less clear, but the two tasks represent the most difficult ones for the immersion students as indicated by their performance (see Table 4). The first task, the first grammar multiple choice item, would, in English, not call for the use of the conditional, while the second task, written production (hypothetical contexts), provides an optional context in which the conditional was also used least frequently by native speakers (see Table 4).

The results of this factor analysis indicate that it cannot be assumed that use of a form in one function or context automatically leads to its use in other functions or contexts.

4. General Implications

a) Language Testing

In our view there are two important implications for language testing that follow from the data which have been presented in this paper. The first point follows from the recognition that performance can outstrip target competence. The second point reflects the need to consider both form and function in assessing language development.

Our data, as well as those of many other researchers (see, for example, Kellerman 1983a; Lightbown 1983a), indicate quite clearly that the correct use of surface forms does not necessarily mean that learners are using them in native-like ways. Furthermore, the incorrect use of surface forms may indicate an advance in language development from a prior, superficially 'correct' stage. What this implies for language testing is that 'right' and 'wrong' responses on a test each need to be interpreted as positive or negative in relation to earlier performances of the learner. The interpretation of responses as such will be possible only when the test includes key diagnostic contexts (see section 3a).

The need to consider both form and function in assessing language development is clearly indicated by the conditional data presented in section 3(d) above. The data demonstrate that learners may have knowledge of a particular form but that they may not be able to use it appropriately to reflect its various functions. Furthermore, the use of a form to indicate a particular function may be dependent upon the nature of the task. From the standpoint of testing, this implies that in order to claim that learners have mastered, for example, the conditional, it will be necessary to measure instances of its use according to function as it interacts with task in obligatory and optional contexts.

b) Language Teaching Methodology and Curriculum Development

The L2 proficiency data from early immersion students that we have presented lead us to several observations relevant for L2 teaching methodology and curriculum development.

We noted first that incomplete segmentation of a second language structure may delay initial progress in sorting out the forms of the target French verb system, and that this was more of a problem for the grade 1 early immersion students than for a group of adolescents entering late immersion in grade 8. One advantage that the grade 8 students have had is greater access to written French. While this is clearly partly dependent on their maturity, we believe that it would be worth experimenting with activities – supplementary to communicative interaction – at the grade 1 level which would draw attention, for example, to the bi-morphemic status of j'ai and its opposition to je. One possibility would be a card-sorting game, in which the goal would be to construct simple sentences out of the given 'pieces' of language to match pictures or real-life events. In this sort of game, j' and ai would be on separate cards. A problem-solving game of this nature might be particularly appropriate for adaptation to a computer, a motivating 'toy' in a growing number of Ontario classrooms.

An added advantage of a computer game is that it could be used on an individual basis with those students who the teacher has identified as having a particular problem. Certainly we would suggest that there is great potential here for a variety of units focusing on specific features of French that have been seen to cause continuing problems for the early immersion students and that often appear to involve influence from the L1 (see section 3b). Such units would need to undergo carefully controlled experimental testing in order to determine their efficacy. The fact that there is as yet no evidence of long-term fossilization of grammatical subsystems in the interlanguage of immersion students (see section 3c) encourages us to think of ways and means of further developing the students' proficiency at various stages of their schooling.

What we are suggesting, in effect, is that the input that the students have been receiving is not adequate to promote target-like proficiency. With respect to the conditional (section 3d) for example, the results indicate that there may be many years intervening between the general comprehension of a form which is embedded in a discourse context and the ability to produce this form consistently in a similar obligatory context. In light of this finding we would argue that the simple provision of meaningful input which is comprehensible to the learner (Krashen 1982), while clearly necessary, is not in itself sufficient to promote productive use of a marked formal aspect of the L2 in a classroom setting, even in the context of an immersion program where students are exposed to the L2 for several hours per day (see also Swain 1983). Indeed, we suspect that such improvement as is observable

309

between the production of grade 4 and grade 10 students on several variables (section 3c) at least partly reflects the use of formal grammatical training by teachers rather than exclusive reliance on unanalysed meaningful input.

In case of misunderstanding, we hasten to add that we are in no way advocating a swing towards extensive use of explicit grammar teaching in an immersion program, although we do believe that there is room for some selective grammatical explanation, which is attuned to the maturity level and metalinguistic ability of the students. More important, we suggest, is the recognition that some forms (such as the conditional) are semantically relatively redundant and/or infrequent in the natural unplanned discourse that the students are mostly exposed to. They can extract the essential meaning of the discourse – and we know they do this very well (see page 291) – without paying attention to some forms. In order to promote greater accuracy in the production of French by immersion students, we hypothesize that there is a twofold need:

1) for the provision of more focused L2 input which provides the learners with ample opportunity to observe the formal and semantic contrasts involved in the relevant target subsystem (this does not necessarily involve explicit grammar teaching); and

2) for the increased opportunity for students to be involved in activities requiring the productive use of such forms in meaningful situations.

These needs, which have been expressed previously in relation to other immersion findings (see e.g. Harley 1982; Ireland 1981; Swain 1983) and which are clearly recognized in current L2 curriculum theory (e.g. Allen 1983; Yalden 1983), have a psycholinguistic analogue in the notions of knowledge and control proposed by Bialystok (e.g. Bialystok and Ryan in press). We suspect that in an immersion program students do more and more listening and reading as they progress through school, but that there is relatively little opportunity to develop productive processing control of the L2 even in those areas where they have developed analysed knowledge. From an L2 curriculum perspective, we see the immersion results as providing support for a 'variable focus' curriculum model in which provision is made for analytic structural and functional approaches to language teaching even in the context of a program with a predominantly non-analytic experiential focus (Allen 1983).

Based on our observations of linguistic outcomes at different grade levels of early immersion programs, we are currently in the process of conducting a classroom observation study at grades 3 and 6, in order to document some features of the L2 input that students are receiving (both from the teacher and their peers), and to test our hypothesis that immersion students generally have little opportunity to use the L2 productively. Later this year we shall be involved in the experimental testing of some classroom materials based on some of our specific findings concerning problems that the students are having (Harley and Ullmann 1983). Three groups of classes

310

are proposed for the study: one group will receive enriched focused input and plenty of opportunity for productive communicative use of the relevant features, together with some explicit grammatical or sociolinguistic explanation; a second group will have the same focused input and opportunities for use but without the explanation; and a third control group will receive no treatment. Through this kind of study, we hope to gain further insight into the L2 curriculum needs of second-language learners.

Acknowledgements. Some of the data on which this paper is based were collected in context of the Development of Bilingual Proficiency Project, funded by the Social Sciences and Humanities Research Council of Canada (No. 431-79-0003). We are grateful to project staff for assistance in transcription and data analysis, and would like to thank Patrick Allen for helpful comments on an earlier draft of this paper.

Notes

1) The forms [že] and [e] are indicated by j'ai and -E respectively. It should be emphasized that this choice of presentation is not a statement about the morphemic status of the forms in the students' interlanguage. That is, j'ai is not necessarily two forms, and -E is not necessarily an inflection separable from the verb stem. By using -E rather than -er, -é, or -ez, we are, however, obviating the need to choose between these target morphemes, homophonous in French.

2) White considers some evidence relating to the stranding of prepositions, a marked phenomenon in English which is also observable as L1 transfer in the French of immersion students at various grade levels. For example: Qu'est-ce que ça c'est pour?

28. Theoretical Implications of Interlanguage Studies for Language Teaching

This paper aims to assess the present state of language teaching, and particularly its more exciting trends, in relation to interlanguage studies. However, before attempting this task, it may be helpful for me to contextualize the discussion by considering the ways in which education does usually relate to descriptive studies. I shall do this fairly simply and starkly, for the issues raised are both important for my argument and inevitably (since they are primarily about the sociology of educational systems) not seen as significant in the basic research of linguists or psycholinguists.

Education and Description

Education involves the positive intervention of institutions or individuals in the lives of other individuals. Consequently the characteristics of institutions and of individuals who have identified themselves as educationalists or teachers need to be taken into account in assessing the relationship between theoretical and descriptive studies and practical activity. Since it is individual teachers who are most likely to respond to the concepts included in 'interlanguage studies', I shall concentrate on individual reactions rather than institutional ones. But teachers, of course, operate as members of institutions, and they have strong, if not always clear, perceptions of themselves as an institution, which influence their views of acceptable and unacceptable behaviour, the limits of their professional role, and so on. These perceptions and behaviours will often have become strongly conventionalized, but they have not necessarily arisen randomly, nor are they necessarily self-protective, though they will often represent coping-strategies in the context which teachers are placed in by decisions (about number of hours to be taught, size of classes, etc.) taken by administrators or politicians.

In the present (and foreseeable) state of education, teachers are likely to be the major influence over what happens in classrooms. Even when teaching materials are prescribed, it is they who will determine how or whether particular materials are used at any given moment in a class, and it is their slavish imitation of patterns of teaching advocated by textbooks – or their free improvization – which will determine the nature of productive language activity in the classroom. (This is not to deny the inevitable process of negotiation with students, whether explicit or implicit, but such negotiation takes place within limits conventionally accepted and imposed by the teacher, at least in the state school systems in which most language teaching in the world takes place.).

The teacher's relationship with the class, therefore, may be crucial in language teaching. And this relationship will inevitably reflect particular views of the nature of language, for the student can be expected to respond linguistically to the teacher in a number of possible ways.

One teaching model will see the student's role as imitation: the teacher performs and the student copies. This may have value at one level of skill performance, but is clearly an inadequate model either where a combination of complex operations interact with each other, or where learners have to establish criteria for when to perform a particular operation appropriately. On both these grounds the imitation model has only limited value for language teaching. This is Model i.

A slightly higher level of operation occurs when the teacher expects students to perform complex tasks on the basis of the limited data provided by the teachers's observable behaviour. This model presupposes some form of recreation by the student of an underlying system not explicitly demonstrated by the teacher. (Model ii.)

A third model specifies exactly what is to be done even less precisely. Essentially the teacher seems to be saying, 'Approach the task of language learning in this way; here is plenty of language data to work on: make use of it in any of these activities, but there will be no explicit language instruction, just imitate the kind of things I do'. (Model iii.)

In practice teachers will operate with all three of these levels of specificity in language teaching, just as they will call upon procedures not referred to here (overt explanation of what they are doing, for example) which could be associated with any of these models. But the attitude taken by teachers to descriptive and explanatory linguistic research will be different for each model. Work on articulatory phonetics has been incorporated closely into the teaching of pronunciation, following Model i. Much, perhaps all, inductive teaching of syntax has followed Model ii, and arguably all formal teaching of syntax has to follow such a model. The third model, however, appears to be less dependent on language description, though it does of course take a definite position on the nature of language acquisition. Yet this model may certainly entail accepting particular views of the nature of language, and such views will inform the nature of the linguistic data provided to students as well as the ways in which it is provided.

Although the examples given here are based on language, the three models can refer equally to other fields of education, and the extent to which teachers perceive their task as predominantly orientated towards one particular model is determined by a combination of tradition and intellectual and ideological pressures, to which the past experience of other teachers in similar situations is a major contributor. The research significance of this accumulated professional wisdom is a broader issue than this paper can address, but we do need to recognize that a research area like interlanguage studies which is making claims to be significant for the practice of teaching may be significant in different ways for each of those three models.

Irrespective, then, of views of the nature of language acquisition, teachers may incorporate linguistic descriptions into their work with varying intentions and in varying ways. Indeed, the influence of a particular approach may be more in the provision of a fruitful metaphor than in explicit direction of material and methods. This is particularly likely to be true with Model III, and since this model accords most closely with contemporary language teaching practice (among the most informed and committed teachers), its relation to interlanguage studies is worth exploring in some detail.

Language Theories and Language Teaching

Recent years have seen a substantial shift in the parts of linguistic theory called upon to validate language teachers' intuitions. Indeed, there has been something of a shift away from a narrow conception of linguistics which reflects arguments in the discipline itself. This shift is compatible with the underlying assumptions of interlanguage work, and Corder has undoubtedly been one of the major influences on commentators advocating the principles of the communicative approach, but there are other influences as well. The central issue is the insistence that language is fluid, dynamic and negotiable and that this fact needs to be recognized in the process of teaching. The research and theoretical discussions which support this view come from a variety of sources, and cannot be described in detail here, but they can be briefly summarized.

1) From linguistic discussion: the concept of communicative competence, with its demand that it is necessary to specify as clearly as possible not only the formal features of linguistic systems, but the ways in which these formal features may be legitimately operated (Canale and Swain, 1980).

2) From anthropology: views of the nature of linguistic performance in relation to specific social contexts, in which particular 'speech events' have their structures influenced by such factors as participants, setting, topic, etc. (Hymes 1967).

3) From sociolinguistics: analyses of language in which it is clear that there are systematic adjustments of (e.g.) syntactic rules according to social context, even if these rules have to be expressed as probabilities rather than absolutes (Labov 1972).

4) From social **psychology**: some suggestions which would motivate certain of the adjustments noted above. Learners develop strong in- and out-group perceptions on the basis of language, by the age of three (Day 1982), and these may be manipulated to distance speakers from interlocutors when there is bad feeling (Bourhis and Giles 1977), or to converge when relations are good (Giles 1977).

5) From philosophy: the concept of the speech act (Searle 1969) which, by its emphasis on performance, forces us to consider the relationships between speaker intention and listener interpretation; and also the co-operative principle (Grice 1975) with its emphasis on the process of making sense (see Schmidt and Richards (1980) for discussion of these in relation to language teaching).

6) From ethnomethodology: a particular strand in discourse analysis which emphasizes the negotiated conventions of much interaction and the systematic nature of much apparently spontaneous activity (Coulthard 1977).

All these examples of recent work related to language point to a modification of the implicit view of many language teachers that they should be concerned primarily with the formal properties of an idealized linguistic system. Much discussed work in syllabus design (Wilkins 1976), needs analysis (Munby 1978), methodology and materials design (Widdowson 1978a; Brumfit and Johnson 1979; Candlin 1981), has cited most of these areas of work in building up a justification of recommended changes. Work emerging directly from the Council of Europe projects (Richterich 1972; van Ek 1975, for example), and general discussions of the state of language teaching pedagogy (Rivers 1972; Alatis, Altman and Alatis 1981) have also been conscious of the varied theoretical influences.

This range of sources enables us to build up a general picture of language which may be sufficient to validate, in the minds of informed teachers, changes which they feel to be necessary on the basis of past experience. But it is not a picture which would be formalizable, or opera-tionalizable for research purposes. It operates at a high level of generality, and will presumably inform rather than direct specific language teaching activities. It could be argued that no research should have a closer relation-ship to the individual acts of language teachers than this. Then, inter-language studies would simply have to contribute towards such a general picture. But most researchers would probably wish to argue a stronger case. Let us, therefore, examine the field for its direct relevance to pedagogy.

Interlanguage Studies from a Pedagogical Perspective

Several commentators (Corder 1981; Faerch and Kasper 1983d) have noted the shift in interlanguage interest from a concern with a description of linguistic *systems* to a concern with *processes*, though there is some uncer-tainty over what exactly constitutes a process (Faerch and Kasper 1983d, 29–30). This shift relates to the general increase in social sensitivity of language studies described above, for the emphasis on process arises out of the need to specify criteria for the choices made by learners revealed in the descriptive studies, and these choices are – at least partially – made in response to social context. Indeed, the concept of interlanguage could fruitfully be applied to language behaviour in all of the areas isolated in the previous section of this paper, for all of them to refer to conventional systems requiring adjustment whenever new communities, with new conventions, are encountered.

In the early days of interlanguage studies, a reformulation of our attitude to pedagogy arose partly out of the psycholinguistic orientation to idealization in Chomsky's definition of competence, and partly out of the related recognition of the systematic and predictable nature of mother-tongue language acquisition. Errors could now be reclassified as systematic or non-systematic, or competence or performance, for L1 or L2 learners, and this had clear implications both for theory (the status of 'competence') and for the practice of teaching (appropriate identification and correction procedures). The idea that some errors at least were inevitable as part of the language acquisition process, suggesting that learners' production should be accorded, at least partially, the status accorded to the production of young children in L1, made it difficult to sustain previous implicit views of errors as either the result of laziness or of inadequate teaching methods (Corder 1975). Probably the most widely observable change in the attitudes of teachers in the last decade has been the increased volume of error, and the rejection of the view that every mistake (formally evaluated) will reinforce deviant forms in subsequent performance. Conversely, however, this change has produced something of a crisis of confidence, for a generalized guilt about the notion of correction does not provide an adequate base for principled intervention in students' learning activities.

Descriptive analyses of errors may, of course, be used more specifically for particular groups of learners; indeed, for advanced students the syllabus may be avowedly based around observed errors – but this will be for those who have already developed a fairly comprehensive generation system in the target language. Otherwise, the value of the description of interlanguage must be primarily for the light it sheds on the learning process, as data from which to make hypothesis about the nature of language acquisition. The problem is that this immediately leads us into areas which are both complex and more speculative, so that the implications for teaching may be harder to tease out. The study of 'underlying mechanisms which lead to a certain IL behaviour' (Faerch and Kasper 1983d, xvi) is certainly important in psycholinguistics, but major problems of generalizability need to be addressed before connection can be renewed by incorporating the results of such studies into syllabuses or teaching methods. Even the argument about communication and learning strategies (Tarone 1981b), which has clear implications for language teachers, needs care in assessment for classroom use, for the definition of 'learning' implied in much discussion of the distinction is narrower than the process with which teachers are concerned. Interpretation of underlying stategies on the basis of overt language production is a notoriously difficult task, and the controversy over Krashen's work (Krashen 1981; McLaughlin 1978; James 1980; Bibeau 1983) should make us wary of too rapid an application of hypothetical analyses to classroom practice – to name only one prominent example. I shall return to this point later.

The problem lies partly in the difficulty of establishing a framework for pedagogy. When two separate and stable systems were assumed, however fictitiously, it was not difficult for teachers to view their activities as super-imposing one system on another and helping students to make appropriate adjustments. Once linguistics accept that the notion of L1 or mother tongue is problematic (Bamgbose 1976; Cummins 1979), or that 'there is no clear or qualitative difference between so-called "language-boundaries" and "dialect-boundaries"' (Hudson 1981, 336), then the differences between mother-tongue 'acquisition' and second-language learning, and language learning and language use, are eroded. The major difference for the older learner of a foreign language will then lie in the extent to which the tokens of the system will have to be acquired independently of the cultural and semantic values of the foreign language system. In early language develop-ment it is hard to distinguish linguistic and social adaptation, but the older learner can (and often does) separate linguistic tokens from meaning. The general point that second-language use may be similar to that of first-language speakers has been demonstrated from a number of points of view. Schwartz (1980) has looked at the negotiation of meaning by second-language learners, and the use of language in context by children (e.g. Huang and Hatch 1978) and adults (e.g. Allwright 1980) has been demon-strably similar to that of native speakers. Learning failure may be attributed to inability to interact, or to unwillingness (Schumann 1976, 403). Hatch's contention that there are 'overall similarities in acquisition strategies whether the learner is child or adult' (Hatch 1978, 17) nonetheless poses problems for teachers as soon as she modifies it by saying that 'the studies show considerable variation among learners at one age group and also across the age range'. Variation in strategy, found both in classrooms (Naiman, Fröhlich, Stern and Todesco 1978, 100) and with children outside the classroom (Fillmore 1979) prevents clear implementation unless criteria for variation can be isolated.

One solution to this dilemma is to insist on the value of improvization, both by teachers and students. Sajavaara, indeed, has made this a theoreti-cal principle: 'production and reception are *creative* processes, and the establishment of communication between the two interactants is based only partially on rules which exist in the speech community and are available to its members through socialization and language acquisition. As important as such rules are various negotiation processes which are created ad hoc in each individual communication situation. The linguist's description of the lin-guistic system functioning in such an interactive process cannot catch the creative aspect, the rules that are made by participants' (Sajavaara 1980, 2).

Now, it may be felt that this position is too strong, for it denies the value of generalizations at all in at least some areas of language interaction. But it is important to distinguish the research issue from the pedagogical one. Even if it is possible to show that the negotiation processes are not ad hoc, as Sajavaara suggests, this need not result in teaching incorporating descriptions of underlying principle. There are a number of spheres of physical activity which are both complex and interactive – cross-country running, swimming and gymnastics, for example – where the physical and anatomical principles are clearly describable but where coaching will often be more effective through hints, corrections and tips than through conscious application of broad analytical systems.

An alternative solution, though, is to try to specify precisely the nature of learning and acquisition processes, and to build a methodology on these specifications. The problem here is the difficulty of producing convincing specifications. Clearly learners do acquire communication strategies as they develop linguistically, and clearly many of these strategies are operable, even in the most distant languages and cultures – otherwise we would rarely succeed in communicating at all in foreign languages. But what is it that goes on in classrooms? I shall refer briefly to two discussions of this issue, one by Widdowson and one by Krashen.

Widdowson (1978b) distinguishes between 'expression rules' (which govern what the learner does with language) and 'reference rules' (which characterize the learner's knowledge). He proposes an intuitively convincing motivation for the widely observed differences between learners' formal classroom responses and their natural use: 'What happens, I suggest, is that the learner is provided with a set of reference rules which he will act upon with a fair degree of success in those teaching situations which require simple conformity to them. The more he is required to use these rules for a communicative purpose, however, the more likely he is to adopt the normal communicative strategy of simplification; the more likely he is, in other words, to behave like a normal human being and develop expression rules to facilitate communication' (Widdowson 1978b, 15). This is a suggestive distinction, with the great virtue that it allows some motivation for learners operating both systems without trivializing one of them – as Krashen appears to by downgrading learning at the expense of acquisition. Expression rules are the rules of normal communication applied by the language learners to the language items they have so far been exposed to; and just as the rule systems of young mother tongue learners appear different from those of adult speakers, so the second-language-learner systems will differ from target rule systems. Widdowson's suggestions for language teaching which facilitate expression rules, notional-functional syllabus design and immersion teaching, lack explicit detail, and the role of reference rules needs careful consideration before a full methodology can be developed. The beginnings of this development can be seen in the extension of this distinction to different levels of language knowledge, 'systemic' and 'schematic'

(Widdowson 1983, 57–8). Since the schematic level will enable expression rules to operate, and since it depends on integration of general interpretative strategies with language activity, the methodology of the teacher in promoting genuine problem-solving becomes more important than syllabus specifications or descriptions of language product. Furthermore, the language-learning and -using capacity to be developed will not be isolable from general learning capacities, and the way forward will lie more in the close relationship between language acquisition and general cognitive development than in an isolation of language learning from other modes of learning.

But, suggestive as this is, it remains speculative, and requires carefully reported working out in normal classrooms before its value can be ascertained.

I shall discuss Krashen's response briefly with reference to the acquisition/learning distinction, for I have developed this argument more fully elsewhere (Brumfit, 1983). He has produced a distinction similar to Widdowson's, but insists (most of the time) on the separation of the two systems. The problem arises with the claim that conscious knowledge is available *only* as a monitor. Apart from the fact that this claim is unfalsifiable (McLaughlin 1978; James 1980), this has worried otherwise enthusiastic experienced teachers such as Stevick (1980, 267–82) into constructing interactionist versions of the same model to allow learning to influence acquisition. Certainly Krashen's strong position forces us to commit such illogicalities as rejecting from the data by which we 'acquire' language perfectly successful but consciously constructed sentences of our own while accepting similar ones from fellow-learners because we shall be unaware of their constructed status. Further, Krashen's view of 'learning' is excessively simple. The only benefits of conscious learning he allows are an increase in accuracy for optimal monitor users, irrelevant linguistic knowledge for those who like linguistics, and confidence in the creative construction process for those who need given rules to confirm their intuitions (Krashen 1978a, 25–6). But conscious learning need not involve consciousness of rules at all, and anyway, what criteria for accuracy are available independent of specified communicative acts? Further, automatic monitoring is acquired by native speakers and will be crucial to the necessary self-regulation for cooperative principles to be applied. Krashen seems to have a vision of undifferentiated language system being fluently churned out, to be self-consciously monitored by a completely independent system which turns it into socially acceptable units, rather like a machine carving bars of chocolate out of a stream of brown sludge.

It would not be worth mentioning this work at all, except that it is the most publicized basis for teaching emerging from second language acquisition research, and consequently raises problems of exact specifications in an acute form. Krashner's ideas have received their most practical presentation through 'The Natural Approach' (Krashen and Terrell 1983). This is not the

319

place for a detailed review of a particular book, but several areas of misinterpretation are worth referring to. First, there is a constant tendency throughout the book to equate 'knowledge' with 'learning' and to conflate 'knowledge of' with 'knowledge about'. 'Language learning is "knowing about", or "formal knowledge" of a language. While acquisition is subconscious, learning is conscious' (p.26). 'Knowing' a language, in Chomsky's sense defining competence (Chomsky 1965, 4), cannot be equated with knowledge about a language in the sense of being able to define rules. Conscious learning, whether learning by heart or audiolingual overlearning, or even self-forcing to communicate with rapid semi-conscious application of rules, may facilitate the former, but Krashen constantly attacks one and dismisses both.

A second problem is the relationship between 'teaching' and 'acquiring'. Acquisition in any class has to be effected by learners, and cannot result in any simple way from specific procedures adopted by the teacher. A key issue in pedagogic theory must be the discontinuity between specific teaching acts and the demonstration of satisfactory, automatic acquisition in language acts by particular students. Teaching cannot be seen simply as the obverse of learning.

A consequence of the view that learning does not assist acquisition is the dismissal of several traditional learning activities as peripheral. Examples are exercises and drills (pp.146–7) and grammatical explanation (p.144). Many language learners have testified to the usefulness of such procedures (Pickett 1978; Rivers 1979), and an authoritative rejection of such procedures needs to be based on firmer evidence than has been forthcoming. Much more useful would be to explore the role that such traditional practices have had for learners who have found them helpful.

This is not to say there is no value in the recommendations of 'The Natural Approach'. Many of the exercises contextualize language well, and demand from students participation in genuine communication tasks which might contribute to Widdowson's schematic level. The difficulty lies in the claim for uniqueness, for materials similar to these have been found in English-as-a-foreign-language work (Abbs, Ayton and Freebairn 1975; Abbs, Candlin, Edelhoff, Moston and Sexton 1978) and ESL work (Grant, Olagoke and Southern 1976) without requiring the support of Monitor Theory.

What Krashen and Terrell have raised as a key issue for current discussion is the role of overt knowledge. What are the pedagogic implications of a concern for communicative processes rather than linguistic products? Faerch and Kasper, for example, suggest (1983d, 31) that 'strategic competence' (Canale and Swain 1980) should be 'incorporated into foreign language teaching objectives'. Now if such competence emerges from the performance of specific types of communicative task, the responsibility of the teacher is limited to incorporating such tasks at appropriate points in the syllabus. If, however, the competence requires more overt teaching, explicit analytical description may be necessary. Teachers may claim with some justice, that they are in a better position to encourage such competence than to describe it, except in the negative sense of helping those who are manifestly failing. Further, we can accept that any aspect of language use which can be described should appear in the classroom as part of language behaviour (assuming it is needed by students), but this is not to say that it will need either to be 'taught' overtly or to be precisely defined. If the first task is to enable learners to be themselves as far as possible through the medium of another language, we shall have to await specifications of native-speaker variations in communicative competence before we have a way of defining the objectives for particular learners. The borderline between personality, in terms of ability to perform and willingness to perform is by no means easily drawn. On the one hand, we may wish everyone to have the opportunity to be an ideal communicator, but on the other we have to accept that communicative capacity is also a substantive part of what you are, and people need lack of communication as well as communication. Either way, we are still a long way from empirically

1) identifying specific strategic competences so that they can be incorporated in syllabuses;

2) establishing whether exposure to the conditions for particular strategies is enough to enable them to be integrated with other language work;

3) clarifying such conditions enough to be able to specify them for overt teaching at a conscious level.

If the second area for investigation reveals that exposure is enough, Faerch and Kasper's optimism (1983d, 56) on communicative syllabuses may be justified, but there remain a number of questions to be answered, including those above, but also the relationship between types of language course or teaching technique and learner strategy (Haastrup and Phillipson 1983, 156–7). The more precise the specification we demand, the more certain our research findings need to be on all significant aspects. We are not, therefore, in a position to be precise at this stage.

This position would appear to rule out an adoption of interlanguage studies as a basis for model one in our initial educational discussion. There appear to be two other possible positions to take up. One is to concentrate almost exclusively on the grading of tasks, as implied by Corder (1981, 78): 'The progressive elaboration of the interlanguage system of the learner is a response to his developing need to handle even more complex communicative tasks. If we can control the level of these correctly, the grammar will look after itself. Instead, then, of grading the linguistic material that we expose the learner to, we should consider grading the communicative demands we make on him, thereby gently leading him to elaborate his approximative system.' This is close to our Model III, and also close to what is implied by Widdowson's schematic requirement. One interesting project along these lines is Prabhu's Madras/Bangalore communicational project (Johnson 1982; Brumfit, forthcoming). This involves a sequence of problem-solving tasks, graded by trial and error, but with the intention of allowing no overt teaching of language whatsoever. Initial results, in comparison with classes exposed to conventional structuralist South Indian English teaching, are promising – but there are major issues of design and practice to be explored before the significance of this project can be assessed firmly.

The other position to take is one of cautious dualism. This may be defended on pragmatic grounds, because we are more likely to be successful with innovation if it does not deny the major premises of existing practice, but extends the strong points and diminishes the weak. It may also be defended on the grounds that learners' instincts are not necessarily wrong and a case can be made for most traditional practices. On this basis, the usefulness of accuracy work to establish security for learners, and enable them to have tokens of the language (whether vocabulary, syntactic and phonological patterns or cohesive devices in discourse) more readily available for integration into their developing interlingual system, can be accepted. But it is essential that accuracy work is not confused with the process of language acquisition; it is a useful preliminary, and a means of developing access, for some learners, to the beginnings of communicative fluency work. This is the position I have taken myself (Brumfit 1979). As with any of these positions, all decisions have to be seen in the context of broader educational criteria, based on general philosophical and ideological beliefs about the nature of knowledge and human aspirations as well as language (Brumfit 1984).

What does seem to be clear is that in practice interlanguage studies have had more metaphorical than specific influence on language teaching theory. Even before descriptive studies were available on a large scale, commentators were following the implications of the general contextualization of language studies (e.g. Long 1975) to demand native-speaker-like processes in the foreign-language classroom. If researchers are dissatisfied with this rather general level of acceptance, they should bear in mind that there are key areas where we shall need a much profounder understanding of interlanguage processes in order to address educational questions. Three of them are perhaps worth mentioning in conclusion.

1) The relationship between language use and ideology needs more careful consideration. To what extent are we entitled to assume that our views of the ideal language user, or of appropriate strategies for language use are universal, either socially or in relation to individual personalities?

2) The relationship between language deficit in L1 and interlanguage work needs fuller exploration. Tarone (1981b) points out that there is normally a gap between any speaker's linguistic and semantic systems, and all our semantic systems differ. There is a risk, in the absence of more understanding of native speaker behaviour, that IL characteristics are attri-

buted to the learning/acquisition condition simply because the issues are starker, and more susceptible to observation.

3) The nature of innovation in education needs to be considered with more sophistication if researchers claim to be contributing to language teaching as well as language description. The relationship between description and teaching is always complex, and it is often easier for academics with what look like clear answers to impress teachers who are only too aware of the weak points in their teaching. Establishing clear and usable categories from interlanguage work may, at this stage, be premature – but it is a task which still needs to be attempted.

29. Discussant

We are concerned in this session with what IL studies can tell us about the language-learning process which will enable language teachers to contrive the most effective conditions possible in classrooms for this process to take place. If the findings from IL research cannot be exploited in this way, as providing particular kinds of warrant for teacher intervention, then they are of little pedagogic value. We can acknowledge, as Brumfit does, that this research has helped to promote a more favourable attitude to the efforts of learners and a recognition of the inhibiting effect of uninformed control and correction on the part of the teacher. But we should surely expect more from it than that. If the study of IL tells us what learners do to develop second-language mastery, then this should provide teachers with a principled way of deciding what conditions they have to contrive so that learners do similar things in classrooms.

There is one theory of IL development which does claim to provide a principled basis for a particular approach to pedagogy. I refer, of course, to Krashen's direct derivation of 'The Natural Approach' from his theory of two distinct systems of interlingual development (Krashen and Terrell 1983). I do not think we need to devote too much attention to these proposals in the present company. As a number of people have made clear (most notably McLaughlin 1978; Gregg 1983), the theory is conceptually inept and empirically unfounded, and the pedagogy which is promoted as a practical corollary is in many ways naive and dangerously delusive. But it is instructive to consider the Krashen case as a cautionary tale to illustrate what sort of insight IL study *does* need to provide if it is to have implications of any pedagogic worth.

The essential argument in Krashen, as we all know, is that there is a natural order in which language rules are acquired (language *rules,* we should note, which is not the same, as we shall see, as all knowledge of a language), and that it is the purpose of pedagogy to encourage natural acquisition by providing comprehensible input, which will automatically activate the process. Teaching cannot have any effect on acquisition itself, since it is already pre-programmed and pre-destined, psychically sealed, and not subject to any outside influence. Nor is it, apparently, associated with any development in conceptual or communicative ability. It is a system of linguistic forms which spreads in the human mind like a growth, inaccessible to conscious awareness or control.

Such an impermeable system provides no opportunity whatever for pedagogic intervention. How much more satisfactory it would be if IL study of a more open minded and enlightened sort could find some principles, other than the working of the universal mind, which regulated the appearance of a certain order, if it could find some conditions which controlled their formation in some way, rather than simply presided over their inevitable emergence. Let me mention one or two such regulating conditions which it would be of considerable pedagogic advantage if IL studies *could* discover. First, conditions which have to do with conceptual implications of the acquisition of linguistic forms. Discussion here touches on the point made by Harley and Swain that both form and function need to be taken into account in the assessment of language development.

Consider first our familiar friend the acquisition order for grammatical morphemes, and let us suppose that it is empirically well-founded, and that it is indeed the case that the progressive *ing* and the copula (to be) (often in that order) occur before the past tense morpheme, irregular and regular. Why? This would seem to be an inadmissible question for Krashen: They occur in this order and that's that. Now it happens that these three morphemes can be closely associated with certain basic conceptual or ideational processes which have to do with states, changes of state and causes for such changes, as Keith Brown has recently demonstrated with admirable lucidity (Brown 1984, 213–18). Thus there are three kinds of related predication:

State:	The door *is* open.
Event (change of state):	The door is open*ing*.
Event (cause – change of state):	The man open*ed* the door.

Brown adds:

> This relationship between state and event predications is one of the fundamental relationships in any language, and its influence is . . . pervasive at many levels of linguistic structure. (p.215)

Given the significance of this conceptual relationship as a universal feature of language, it is a matter of considerable interest how it is acquired, and the question naturally arises: Are these three morphemes *-ing, be* and *-ed* associated with these semantic functions of state, change and cause? If they are not, what functions are they associated with?

If we could confidently assign some semantic function to them, and to other emerging morphemes, we would be in a position, Piaget-like, to talk about a natural process of conceptualization which the language forms are called in to service. And this in turn would provide some basis for setting up classroom conditions, devising tasks and so on, which focused attention on these functions in the preferred implicational order. As it is, the bare list of functionally undifferentiated forms gives us nothing to go on, and all we can do is feed the learners with comprehensible input and hope for the best.

Any IL research which simply gives a chronological account of the emergence of linguistic forms without any functional explanation for their occurrence is going to be of no use for teaching, since such an account provides no guidance as to the conditions which need to be contrived to induce acquisition, either those relating to conceptual development of the kind just mentioned, or those relating to the contexts of communicative interaction as mentioned in discourse studies (e.g. Hatch 1978b). But such guidance needs to go beyond explanation as to what conditions the occurrence of particular forms. We also require it to offer some indication of how rules in general get to be inferred in the learners' mind and what role they play in language learning; how the whole epistemological process of rule formation actually operates. This brings me to conditions for IL development of a rather different kind: conditions which have to do with the communicative contexts in which it occurs. Discussion here touches on the observation made by Harley and Swain that performance outstrips competence in the language ability of learners in the immersion programmes they have studied.

The aim of interlanguage studies is to specify the rules which define the language learners' interim system and how they get to be internalized, and in more recent work to indicate the variable status of these rules and the way they are constrained and used in communicative contexts. The assumption is that language learning is uniquely a matter of reduction to rule, that the language learner devotes all his attention to the deriving of a generative system from the language data at his disposal. But is this really the case? One can readily acknowledge that the identification of rules as they develop is of central concern for IL studies, but is it the *only* concern? What about items in the interlingual repertoire which do not conform to rule? Some of these may be regularized at a later stage. If so, why, under what pressure, and why did they not appear as conforming items in the first place? Some of these items may resist conformity to rule and remain as 'fossilized' forms. Why these and not others, and what is the reason for such resistance? These questions have to do with the very nature of the rule-making process itself and role in language learning in general. And if IL studies are to provide pedagogically relevant insights about learning and not just information about the language which results from it, these questions ought to be central to their enquiry. It is not enough to note the phenomena of variability, deferred regularization, or its fossilized arrest: they need to be considered as evidence for some integrated theory of language learning and language use. I sometimes get the impression that IL researchers are so busy with the accumulation of data, observed and elicited, that they (both literarily and figuratively) have no time for the kind of imaginative speculation which might yield such a theory. Pit Corder's work was of course always characterized by this kind of speculation. This is why it is so valuable.

But let me briefly indulge in speculation myself and elaborate a little on this issue of regular and irregular elements in interlanguage. Consider again the acquisition order of morphemes. There is one item in the sequence which is essentially different from the others and calls for some explanation. I refer to the irregular past. This occurs before the regular past. In other words, there is a set of language items which are exceptional, and which are, therefore, by definition, acquired without reference to rule, memorized as unique entities. Of course we do not know *which* irregular past forms are acquired at this stage, perhaps only one or two, but even so if language acquisition is a matter of internalizing rules as the Krashen theory requires their appearance here is anomalous: indeed one could say it undermines the whole theory. Could it be that the language learner is not so fixated on rule discovery as we imagined? Could it be that his first inclination, his primary strategy, is to process the language schematically, that is to say to remember words and phrases as indivisible units, tagged with contextual value, with the systematic process of analysis into formal rule being applied only as a secondary resource subsequently if and when required.

For of course it is not always required. Language is full of unanalysed 'schematic' units, pre-packaged, as it were, for use. A glance at any dictionary of idioms in English (e.g. Cowie and Mackin 1975) will indicate how many expressions have remained beyond the pale of rule jurisdiction. Indeed, so prevalent is this phenomenon that one is tempted to suggest that it is more satisfactory to describe language as a set of adaptable idioms supplemented by generative rules for composing expressions which are not already schematically preformulated, rather than in the orthodox way as a system of generative rules with a few unaccountable exceptions. The *learning* of language, one might then be led to suppose, is perhaps a matter of gradual modification of lexemes by syntactic elaboration as learners perceive that the *juxtaposition* of lexemes alone will not serve their conceptual and communicative purposes.

Now there is a fair amount of evidence that learners do go in for schematic rather than systemic processing. The findings in the Harley and Swain study point to such a conclusion: schematic performance precedes systemic competence. And such findings have been anticipated in first-language-acquisition research. Ruth Clark, for example, talks about the way her son Adam learned to produce expressions as unanalysed units and so, in this sense, to perform without competence. She comments:

> In Adam's speech at this time a number of routine unproductive sequences seemed to co-exist with a few simple productive rules. Many, though not necessarily all, the productive rules originated as invariable rules, which were in use for some time with the original lexical items before new lexical items were inserted. (Clark 1974, 4)

Other researchers, like Lily Wong-Fillmore and Evelyn Hatch, have pointed to the prominence of formulaic expressions or 'refabricated routines' in second-language acquisition (for a review see Vihman 1982). As

Jean Berko Gleason points out, this work indicates:

> ... that second language learners begin not so much with generative systems as with chunks, prefabricated routines, or unopened packages, as they have been called. . . . The importance of routines in language acquisition, in second language learning, and in the everyday use of non-exceptional speakers has yet to be recognized. It is probably safe to say that we are not as endlessly creative as we are wont to think, and that we rely heavily on memory and routinized phrases in our ordinary production of speech. Linguistic models need to make room for memory, and take into account that in retrieving language the size of the units we deal with is variable: there are times when language is produced generatively, one word or one morpheme at a time, and there are times when much larger units, too large for the individual to analyse, are produced. It is thus possible to learn to use language appropriately months or even years before understanding all the underlying units. (Gleason 1982, 355–6)

Krashen has also had things to say about such 'prefabricated routines' and his review of the evidence (Krashen 1981, ch.7) leads him, perhaps predictably, to a rather different conclusion, namely:

> ... that routines and patterns are fundamentally different from both acquired and learned language, and they do not 'turn into' acquired or learned language directly. (Krashen 1981, 9)

There are a number of points that might be made here. First, since such routines, or schematic units as I have called them, cannot be either learned or acquired since they do not by definition conform to rule, then how are they internalized? Presumably by some third kind of process. It is not unreasonable to expect that IL studies might reveal what such a process might be that internalizes without recourse to rule. Secondly, recent work on discourse interpretation would seem to indicate that it relies heavily on schematic processing rather than systemic decomposition. So the communicative use of language, the comprehensible input that Krashen insists on as a 'fundamental principle' and 'crucial ingredient', is not naturally a condition for the acquisition of linguistic rules. It is not therefore surprising to be told, as Harley and Swain tell us, that 'the simple provision of meaningful input which is comprehensible to the learner . . . is not in itself sufficient to promote productive use of a marked formal aspect of the L2 in a classroom setting'. How then *does* a schematic intake, necessary for interpretation, result in a systemic internalization? Thirdly, and more generally, if such routines loom as large in language as has been suggested, then any model of interlanguage development which cannot account for them must be regarded as seriously deficient.

And this brings me back to the main theme of the pedagogic relevance of IL studies in general. Such studies have tended to concentrate on the internalization of rules, categorical and variable, and to assume that irregularities are only interim and transitory phenomena traces of declining or incipient rules, or performance lapses. But as the appearance of the irregular past and other unanalysed units would seem to indicate (and as Rod Ellis in his paper points out), maverick forms occur which cannot so easily be explained away. I would suggest that their schematic value ensures their survival, outside the productive rules of grammar, as a crucial component of language mastery which is beyond competence, understood in its usual sense of a command of productive rules.

What bearing does all this have on pedagogy? The model of language teaching currently in fashion is Brumfit's Model III: one which emphasizes communicative activity on the assumption that this will lead to the natural internalization of rules. What evidence does IL study provide to sustain this assumption? What support does it give to my speculation that learners do not subject language data to analysis, driven by an urge to formulate rules, but learn what is schematically useful, only deriving rules by taking these patterns apart when they no longer serve their purposes? For if there is substance in this speculation, it would lead us to reconsider the current belief that rules are naturally derived from communicative experience and the exposure to comprehensible input and to make provision for a deliberate focusing on form. So what can IL study tell us about how these ready-made patterns are learned, which ones become analysed, and how; which ones remain, unanalysed but operative, as an essential part of the learner's repertoire? In general, how regular and irregular elements of language mastery are related in the learning process? Although, as Brumfit implies, the relationship between language description and language teaching is not one of direct relevance, some indication as to how these questions might be answered would give us some guidance as to what hypotheses were worth taking up as a basis for pedagogic experiment.

Teachers have to find out what kind of thinking and doing they should encourage by contrivance in classrooms to promote the process of language learning. It would give them some guidance if it were known what the conceptual and communicative coordinates were of natural language acquisition. Unless IL research can provide some indication of what these are then, interesting though its findings might be for the study of exceptional language, it can have little relevance to issues in education.

30. Summary of Discussion

Brumfit's comments in response to the discussant expanded on his view that developments in language teaching should be compatible with research in applied linguistics (including IL), but this did not mean they were derived from it. The general implications of the IL hypothesis, for instance, were illuminating for the language teacher, but detailed applications of research findings (e.g. on sequences of morpheme acquisition) were more problematical since the priorities of IL research did not necessarily match those of language teaching. Harley and Swain both echoed Brumfit's call for caution in interpreting and applying IL research in the classroom, but they stressed the value of research findings as an element in a 'cycle' of research which began with the identification of specific pedagogical problems. Swain also drew attention to the potential usefulness of IL analysis in language testing, possibly through the development of a 'longitudinal' approach.

The central issue in the general discussion concerned the notion of 'sequencing' in the design of language teaching programmes. One view, which was quite strongly expressed, held that a linguistically defined 'linear' sequence of 'teaching points' was a misguided approach to syllabus design since it distorted the overall pattern of L2 growth. It made better sense in second language teaching to try and identify broadly defined 'stages' of development rather than adopt a step-by-step approach. The problem was illustrated by a fairly detailed account of the complex pattern of learning observed in the acquisition of the progressive -ing form which, according to the morpheme studies, was acquired early. The learning history appeared to follow a 'U-shaped' pattern involving a pre-analytic stage during which performance accuracy appeared misleadingly high, followed by an analytic stage during which performance levels fell as the item was integrated into a more complex system of semantic and syntactic contrasts, and a final stage of increasing, though by no means 'perfect', control.

The argument was taken further by speakers who acknowledged the pedagogical value of IL research in tracing the developmental history of specific linguistic elements, but who doubted the wisdom of applying it on a large scale. Other participants were uneasy at what appeared to be a rather 'piecemeal' approach. Nevertheless, there was a broad measure of agreement that, outside the rather controversial sequencing issue, there was a considerable body of IL research data which would prove helpful to language teachers in designing courses and interpreting outcomes.

The discussion returned to the syllabus issue towards the end of the session when the suggestion was made that a clear distinction should be made between patterns of learning, to which IL research could contribute usefully, and patterns of teaching specified in the syllabus which reflected the social realities of the particular educational context for which it was designed.

The problems of immersion students were taken up in the closing minutes of the debate when it was pointed out that the serious issues did not include sequencing but were concerned with problems of input and of providing appropriate opportunities for language use. Considerable emphasis was also placed on the need to investigate the reasons for the high prevalence of language transfer among immersion learners and to seek for practical ways of alleviating the problem.

31. The Current State of IL Studies:
An Attempted Critical Summary

In this attempted critical summary[1] I agree with the Editors that no names be used, because we would like readers to try to concentrate as directly as possible on some of the more important critical issues in current IL studies. I will concentrate in this section on nine issues that I feel are central. Many other participants, it is clear,[2] would have chosen other issues, but most of my issues were, at least, on someone's list. My nine are:

1) Methodology in IL studies
2) Language transfer
3) Fossilization
4) The universal hypothesis
5) Universal grammar
6) (IL) grammar in one's head?
7) IL strategies
8) IL discourse
9) Context in IL studies

Much was discussed at the seminar and all the issues here came out of the papers that appear in this volume.

A few preliminary notes: first, I will attempt to be *obvious,* which, like others before me, I have found to be enormously difficult. But it is important to attempt to state where we are, as clearly as I know how.

Second, I am struck by the number of different perspectives represented in this volume. There are overlapping perspectives and, perhaps, mutually exclusive perspectives. We have classroom perspectives; immigrant perspectives; theoretical linguistic perspectives; grammatical perspectives; discourse perspectives; conversational analysis perspectives; sociolinguistic perspectives; ethnographic perspectives; ethnomethodological perspectives; cognitive psychological perspectives; social psychological perspectives; and perhaps others. We need to ask: Exactly how are we *constrained* by these outside perspectives brought from other fields into IL studies. This is not entirely clear and has not been seriously dealt with. Also, I cannot help wondering if there are IL perspectives which inform other fields and what they might be. We should look for this mirror-upon-ourselves and see what we learn from it.

Third, in these remarks, there is no separate section on pedagogical concerns since I feel unqualified to write one, but such concerns are brought up at various points where I feel competent to comment.

Fourth, I feel that we have come a long way since Corder's 1967 paper 'The Significance of Learner's Errors'. Whenever I feel that we are not making fast enough progress, I think of sibling fields, e.g. the study of grammar is 2,500 years old at least, as is the thinking and talking about language pedagogy. Our topic here – IL Studies – is no more than 17 years old.[3] What can we expect while we are struggling for a way to do things? In terms of quantity alone, in the late 1960s, we would cheer if we saw an empirical error-analysis study such as Ken Coulter's (1967) error-analysis study (MA thesis, University of Washington). Like most colleagues, today, I can hardly keep up with the literature. I feel that this is a success and not a trivial one. There are whole groups of things we do not have to 'call for' anymore:

– careful descriptive and analytical studies are being done;
– longitudinal studies are being done;
– methodology, in most cases, is clearly being stated;
– pidgin and creole studies are not being ignored;

and so on. I think we have come a long way in solidifying a subject matter and much of that is with Pit Corder's help.

Issue 1: Methodology in IL Studies

A long time ago I argued against using learner intuition in IL studies. I was wrong! Lots of interesting results and hypotheses have come out of elicitation procedures designed to tap learner intuitions. However, the Labov caution is still worth considering: That when two forms of a language are in a subordinate and superordinate relationship, the intuitions one gets from those in the subordinate relationship will (or, at least, may) reflect the superordinate system. I believe this does happen at times in IL studies and that the caution holds. That is, theoretically the following is still a possibility: That in some learners at least, co-existent systems are not to be discounted.

One has to ask how far intuition can get us? And I suppose that is an empirical question and we should judge each claim of intuitional data on its merits as it appears in the literature. But if, as has been strongly argued, intuition about linguistic forms underlies a different sort of competence than that competence which controls language use in conversation, writing and so forth, then those who use intuition as a tool (myself included) have a burden to temper claims made about what ILs are like and what they are not like, since it is clear that different tasks with the same learner at the same time regularly produce different IL facts.

It is good to know what is fact and what is not about all ILs and about IL learning.[4] For example, the existence of a universal IL placement-constraint concerning negative items is a good candidate for factual status. Though in some sense we may be drowning in certain types of data, I would personally like to know more facts about IL universals, i.e. what is universal to all ILs. Here the distinction between what is *universal* to all ILs versus what is *global* to an IL or to a set of ILs may prove helpful. In order to constraint theory building, I would argue that we need to gather certain types of facts as to what is universal to all ILs and what is global to a particular set of ILs, because descriptive work of this kind can in fact (and has) lead to useful theoretical advances.

Issue 2: Language Transfer

This issue has been around for a long time, perhaps the longest of any issue we can discuss. The phenomena of native language influence on the learning of a second language has been recognized for centuries. I agree, of course, that the term 'transfer' has to be carefully defined each time one uses it in a study. I also agree that transfer is most probably best thought of as a cover term for a whole class of behaviours, processes and constraints that have to do with the use of prior linguistic knowledge, especially native-language knowledge, in interacting with input from the target language.

How does the analyst unambiguously show transfer? The jury is still out on that. I think that the many discussions of the past few years on efforts to constrain a theory of language transfer have proved helpful though not conclusive. But we surely must broaden our concerns here to all the linguistic behaviours, including the real possibility of the existence of rhetorical transfer in terms of the organizational choices that learners make in producing IL discourse.

As pointed out long ago, structural congruence is not enough. Also error counts and simple percentages are clearly misleading. One improvement in our way of doing things is a comparison of behaviours in a common L2 by learners with different L1s. Contrastive analysis is a good place to begin, but we have to be sure to carefully define for each study concepts such as 'similarity of structures', 'congruence', and the like. Structural congruence (or at least partial structural similarity) is most probably necessary, though of course not sufficient, for many claims implying cross-linguistic influence in phonology and surface syntax and lexis, but may not be necessary in rhetoric and discourse where abstract argumentational patterns are often involved. Even in phonology learning, abstract principles may prove important as in the apparent case of Thai learners of English transferring principles of tonality but not the tone of Thai, to their Thai-English IL.

Studies that claim cross-linguistic influence should particularly be evaluated in terms of care in definitions, consistency in definitions, and explicit statements about argumentation used to establish facts. These are three important criteria that we need to pay more attention to.

Some colleagues still wish to deny a central role to cross-linguistic influence in the formation and structure of ILs and putative counterevidence is presented. I say putative because I think such evidence only shows that the

334

original position concerning language transfer is still probably the correct one – that language transfer interacts with other processes and constraints throughout the IL experience. Our research job is to find out the 'when and what and how and why' of cross-linguistic influence.

Issue 3: Fossilization

I especially liked the remark made during the seminar that 'Among fossilized Francophones in Canada, there is no English plural for generations'.[5] The concept of fossilization still seems to be both a viable and widely-used concept. It would be nice however to have some positive evidence as to when a particular structure fossilizes for what types of learners. Also, analogous to language transfer concerns, we need to know about fossilized forms: Why these and not others? The very real possibility of the cessation of IL learning, often far from IL norms, leads to thoughts about its inevitability and about innateness, which makes some colleagues nervous. It is impossible to show innateness so I guess that is where matters will stand. We can skirt this issue empirically by agreeing that 'non-development' in IL is an important research area and try to describe and understand that.

There is also a controversy as to how this non-development connects up with first-language acquisition. My position remains the same here. I read the evidence as saying children learning a first language do *not* cease learning far from target norms and I still maintain that this, and the concept of 'backsliding' are among the distinguishing features of IL learning.

Those of us also interested in classroom instruction have to take careful note of the claims regarding fossilization. Nowhere is it claimed that fossilization means that learners cannot be taught to communicate in the L2. Various teaching strategies have been proposed to deal with apparently fossilized learners, but the most important point I wish to make here concerns 'discourse domains'. Teachers might wish to become aware of those domains in which particular learners may wish to or need to communicate in. Teachers might thus wish to adjust teaching to that, since in my experience, system-wide changes appear to be more difficult to induce than domain-specific IL change. We might want to test this claim. Descriptive learning/teaching evidence would be nice here. Some rhetorical/grammatical 'safe rule' data, for example, exists as perhaps a new type of learning/teaching data uniting pedagogical and IL research. This I think could help, at least with writing instruction of apparently fossilized learners in particular domains (Selinker, forthcoming).

Issue 4: The Universal Hypothesis

First, we must distinguish between this hypothesis as a cover term and the particular concept of 'universal grammar'. One can hold to an important role for universals of language in IL learning while at the same time not necessarily believe in the innateness claims of universal grammar.

One important version of the universals claim relates to similarities in surface structures across languages, often in a statistical sense and IL development seems to relate to these constraints, but other factors such as language transfer are involved here as well.

Typological universals, i.e. universals within a certain typology, have been studied in IL and represent a growth industry and rightly so. It would be neat, e.g. if 'clustering' works out, i.e. if it works out that IL acquisition of more minor elements turns out to be predictable from the acquisition of major elements. Ideally we want a theory of IL to be able to predict what would happen (borrowing loosely from Givón's work) if a Chinese were to parachute into Colorado and had to learn to communicate in Ute. We have no such theory at present. What we do know is that it is impossible to have a theory of IL without incorporating linguistic universals of some type but as with transfer, it seems that we have the 'what, when, why and how' questions to consider. Just as there are first-language structures which appear to have no effect on L2 acquisition, it seems likewise to be the case that there are language universals which do not seem to have an effect on L2 acquisition. This result leads to a detailed question that keeps coming up in IL studies: Why is it that so many of the processes and constraints that concern us apply differentially? I suppose all we can say at present is that language contact makes a difference. I am not surprised therefore that L1- and L2-specific facts are needed to account for such differential effects regarding the role of language universals and IL development. This view does, however, fit in nicely I think with the original raison-d'etre of the IL concept as a (partially at least) separate linguistic system, separate from L1 and L2. Universals of IL whether or not they are connected to universals of language are most interesting here.

A nice research trend is that some of the more recent work relating universals of language to IL interconnects syntactic constraints in IL with discourse constraints and I will get to discourse below.

Issue 5: Universal Grammar

The major assumption here – and we must remember that it has the status of a postulate and that postulates can be wrong – is that adult L2 learners can *re*activate the language acquisition capacity, what Slobin interestingly calls the language-making capacity. I have several problems with this view. One is that of fossilization mentioned above, if one takes the strong inevitable view of fossilization. The second reservation involves the considerable individual differences one finds in SLA. There is such clear evidence of differential success in L2 (compared to L1) – which I feel might override surface similarities – that I feel one must come to the conclusion (if one holds a universal-grammar point of view) that adult learners reactivate latent capacities differentially and one wonders why this should be so. The third problem is methodological. Those of us who work in English for Academic Purposes and specific-purpose acquisition regularly see IL use involving large stretches of complicated discourse where language and subject matter concerns are intimately and structurally intertwined. In light of this experience, I personally pale at any approach to language that studies isolated sentences if it does not in principle try to show how this could be linked up with naturally occurring discourse. Well, I believe in live and let live and agree with the modular approach to research, but it would be nice if some of those interested in inserting universal grammar into IL studies were to try to show how this concept might, for example, link up, in principle, with IL conversation and IL technical writing.

Also some of the terms used by universal-grammar people are, I would maintain, as unclear as our use of 'strategy': What does it really mean, for example, to say that a second-language learner has 'triggered' or 'set off' parameters of universal grammar or that a 'trigger' activates a parameter of universal grammar? I personally find these metaphoric ideas quite vague. Furthermore, and importantly, implicit in universal grammar claims is in fact *discourse,* i.e. the claim that experience with the language is necessary to activate (or, in our case, reactivate) universal grammar and that experience must come through discourse. Why then is discourse ignored in this formal model building? It cannot be that it is too hard to do formal modelling of discourse. There are in fact a number of formal models of discourse analysis (see, e.g. the special issue of *Text,* 3.3, 1983 on 'Formal models of discourse'), but none that I know of thinks that it is reasonable to try to 'derive' itself from universal grammar and its interaction with other capacities.

Nevertheless, I am enthralled with the recent outburst of papers on this subject from some of the colleagues I most admire in this field. The renewed cross-fertilization with theoretical linguistics is to be welcomed. If nothing else, the rigour evident in their work can inform us constantly. But there is what I want to call the 'carry over' problem. Some colleagues insist that generalizations concerning universal grammar carry over to IL learning. I have no sympathy with this point of view. I hope we can agree that one should demonstrate carry over of models from other fields. In each case the researcher will show, I would hope, that the particular universal-grammar constraint and its parameters, whether subjacency, movements of any kind, pro-drop, whatever, do in fact carry over. One result seems clear from recent research, that universal grammar interacts with language-transfer concerns and that they constrain each other. It seems too early to be exactly sure how. Additionally, in spite of the fact that markedness is not always clear and that markedness evidence does not always fall out the way universal grammar claims would indicate, the precision of the model is seductive. But here too is another complication; the details and even the basic conception of this model keep changing and some colleagues, especially in child language acquisition, are clearly worried about this. We have been this route before. A cautionary tale: A few years back I argued strongly[6] for the reality in IL of the linguistic rule of subject-raising in object position on the basis of French immersion sentences such as:

il veut moi de dire français à il

There were quite a few unhappinesses with this proposal, least not the ever-changing role and even the existence of such rules in generative grammar. If we go this route we have the serious carry-over problem of deciding for IL grammar such questions as what to do with structures where markedness plays no role, do we want IL grammars with deletion or without deletion, and so on.

Issue 6: (IL) Grammar in One's Head?

I think the following will be hard for anyone trained in linguistics to accept: The assumption that one has a grammar in one's head (or even that one *builds* a grammar in one's head) is *only* an assumption. Too many of our studies treat this assumption as fact and claim that regularities in the data *necessarily* prove something about the grammar in one's head. For example, researchers may say that such and such accords with or violates a markedness condition, then they may also say that it follows that it confirms or disconfirms claims of *the* grammar, that is psychologically real. Not necessarily. We are too often a bit sloppy here.

There certainly is enough argument in the literature that universal grammar itself, set away from experience as it is, is just untestable. On the other hand, grammars, it has been argued, are nothing more nor less than cultural artefacts. In the final analysis, what is the evidence for the claim that the learner has or builds a grammar in his or her head? It must be remembered that the only evidence we have is regularity in the data and that there are other explanations for such regularity. The one that I find appealing is that of Becker (1983, for example) concerning 'prior text' and the 're-shaping' of such texts to new contexts (see also Geertz (1983) for a description of this approach in contrast with other approaches).

What is nice and clear, and most colleagues now accept this as fact, is that there exist patterns of regularity in IL data. We are exploring alternative approaches of IL and IL learning and since there is a good argument in the literature that units of native-speaker linguistic analysis are not necessarily those of IL, we should be cautious about IL grammatical claims. Jumping on the linguistic grammar bandwagon is dangerous for another reason. It has been argued strongly that one of the most important aspects of natural human languages is language transfer and also that no presently available linguistic theory comes anywhere near meeting the requirement of adequately handling language transfer. I buy this argument and add: Any theory of language that purports to be general *must* have as one of its ultimate goals the explanation of language transfer or it necessarily fails. I like this position if only because its adoption would, for once, make the theoretical concerns of theoretical linguists subordinate to the theoretical concerns of applied linguists.

Issue 7: IL Strategies

I feel as if I raised a hornet's nest when I suggested long ago (Selinker 1972) the distinction: communication strategies versus learning strategies. The distinction in principle is seductive, but seems to have proved impossible to distinguish in practice. Empirically, it appears that the only way out is to clearly operationalize what one means for each study. The approach of using a priori 'structured lists' is, as we now know, fraught with well-detailed difficulty.

Looking at Slobin's current forty-two operating principles (lecture, Univ. of Michigan, April 1984), I see an interesting mixture of perceptual, production and learning procedures and strategies of 'attention', 'storage', 'mapping' and 'problem solving'. What I do not think we have handled well, that he has thought a lot about, is storage, which is after all long-term memory. IL studies could make a general contribution here since so little is known about memory and language where content and context are concerned. But we will need hard and replicable evidence here. As I read the behaviour and brain literature, I am not too surprised that we have trouble with distinctions as to various types of strategies and procedures. After all (as has long been recognized) people in memory studies have trouble distinguishing and disentangling from their data whether they are in fact talking about storage or retrieval.

I may be wrong here but I suggest it is a mistake (which we seem to have made) to link up IL strategies with *problematicity*. This pulls us away from more general concerns with ways of organizing data. More important, a good deal of IL development must occur through the use of strategies where problems (however defined) are not involved and we do not want to lose touch with that.

What we seem to have is a lot of useful descriptive detail about something cognitive that involves the handling of IL information. There are two approaches to consider here: One common approach in experimental (especially mathematical) psychology is to search for some physical correlate to a hypothesized mental construct – as for example assuming the correlation of attention to eye movements. One gets precise measures and, if (sometimes a big if) one likes, what has been operationalized, then lots of insight is present. This has been tried in IL procedural discourse (see, e.g. the work of Russ Tomlin) and I recommend that those in IL strategy research look at such attempts.

Another approach is to relate inferred IL strategies to those strategies seemingly operating in other domains. This has of course been done successfully in first language acquisition where it has been claimed (Slobin, above-mentioned lecture) for example, that a child who knows at some point that he has finished building a tower versus not completing it has information that is the same (or at least highly similar) to that operating in language, e.g. in the Russian accusative constructions.

This approach would make particular sense to those involved in class-room research, I suggest, where instruction and explanation is meant to appeal to the learner's intellectualizing procedures.

One important set of strategies, discussed in the first-language litera-ture relates to the using of context, i.e. the child using contextual clues or cues, and in IL studies we have not even begun to scratch the surface of the rich array of phenomena we call context. I will discuss context below.

One strategy that has always interested me is 'simplification'. Even though I buy the following two arguments (from Corder 1981) I still believe there is a place for simplification in IL theory. One argument says that central to a theory of IL *must* be complexification and the second, is that 'simple codes' do not necesarily mean simplification has occurred. This is insightful. But the argument 'how can one simplify what one does not know, i.e. the target language?' is too general. Of course we get simplification of the native language; that is not in dispute. I would like to claim that learners, sometimes, and maybe quite consciously, also simplify target-language in-formation. There are many examples in the literature as, for example, the French immersion learners who use one form of the verb for the whole paradigm. Interestingly this also happens in West African French adult IL so that it may be a more general strategy.

I agree that a definition of strategy must be cognitive and not L2-specific, but I must confess that none of the ones proposed so far are convincing to me. They all seem to push the problem to another unclear term or to another unclear set of terms. Additionally, it is reasonable to suppose that IL communication strategies must at times further learning, but apparently no one has any idea how this happens.

Issue 8: IL Discourse

The study of text-acquisition or the acquisition of genres is in its infancy and IL studies can make a general contribution here. It has often been pointed out in the literature that many non-native speakers wish only to learn to read and write in the L2. Interestingly, for such learners fossilization may be as persuasive a characteristic in learner writing as it appears to be for spoken IL. We may want to study this.

One important research trend deals with this question. What does it mean to say that IL data from beginning learners had by and large a lack of morphological markers? One trend is not to rush into grand conclusions about this but to focus on IL interactive discourse since it has strongly been argued that acquisition of structure (or at least some parts of structure) comes through interactions. One research goal here is to try and map linguistic *and* discourse/pragmatic means of expressing various functional categories. Such studies show how dangerous it is to focus on one linguistic level at a time. Without some principled means of integrating various linguistic levels in an IL study, the researcher may be seriously distorting the data by hiding how the various linguistic levels are affected by each other.[7] This is something we should ponder, especially as we apply simple, but in fact complicating statistics to single-level IL data. Multi-level IL analysis with discourse and text as central is surely called for.

I would like to be a bit stronger here and assert (but I won't) that the burden of showing that an IL study is *not* misleading rests on the shoulders of the researcher who claims to 'show' anything at all in IL from a single-level, non-context-based analysis. We can be helped here perhaps by some of the exciting work done recently on discourse strategies and their linguistic correlates in inter-ethnic conversations (e.g. the work of Gumperz) and the work that attempts to apply formal models to discourse in organizational settings (e.g. the work of Goguen and Linde).

Also in this regard I applaud the effort to try to integrate pedagogy and IL by seeing what effect classroom discourse has on IL development. I would like to see classroom research expanded to include the development of genre learning in IL using a multi-level approach. A good place to begin a study of the learning of genres in IL is to integrate that with the learning of lexis since IL lexical acquisition as a problem for learners manifests itself quite often (functionally speaking) in negotiation of meaning and interpretation of texts.

Issue 9: Context in IL Studies

We have not done well here. In order to help us tackle the integration of context in IL studies, we need to be clear on what has been keeping us back. One main reason, as hinted above, is that many of us – myself included – have at times been very preoccupied with studying isolated sentences, preoccupied because of our training from linguistics. And even in discourse studies, we often get trapped by the machinery of countable things and stay away from sociofunctional reality. I always ask with such studies: How can one quantify, e.g. 'effective communication' or 'rhetorical strategy'? To make progress here in integrating context into IL studies I wish to minimally propose two criteria:

a) that the context studied be well defined and

b) that it be sociofunctionally real and important to the learners under study.

I urge the reader to look into the Language for Specific Purposes research literature for its very real relevance to IL learning.[8]

Much descriptive work has been done on scientific and technical contexts, on a macro-level by people in ethnomethodology, technical writing, sociology, etc. This background work already done should help us get away

341

from what some think is a current overemphasis on product research into a more theoretical hypothesis forming phrases.

On a micro-level, there is an applied linguistics literature of rhetorical/ grammatical correspondences in written Language-for-Specific-Purposes texts. One wonders how these rhetorical/grammatical principles are mirrored in the IL technical talk of second-language learners, for example, who are trying to master subject matter in a second language. These two sub-fields of applied linguistics – IL studies and Language-for-Specific-Purposes studies – hardly know each other and this is a shame. For example, recently I was talking to a British colleague in English-for-Specific-Purposes who is studying strategies used in coping with technical manuals and he is collecting (in delayed protocol form) IL data as well as native-speaker data. His work on these strategies could inform ours and our work could inform his. Yet today these appear to be separate worlds.

In arguing for IL studies to look to well-defined and sociofunctionally real areas of context, the area of what we are calling specific-purpose acquisition comes to mind. Do specific-purpose contexts shape IL behaviour? Is complexification of IL different in specific-purpose contexts? Are language transfer effects, fossilization effects and so on related in such contexts? I have a strong feeling that the answer is 'yes', in each case, and that IL specialists have been blind to this.

In pedagogical terms, on the other hand, it has been pointed out forcefully (Widdowson 1983) that there is no coherent theory of Language for Specific Purposes and that important decisions affecting learners are regularly being made on unprincipled grounds. I believe that Language for Specific Purposes will continue to lack that theory until it integrates into its concerns the IL talk and IL writing that Language-for-Specific-Purposes students produce in abundance. We intend to work on that. There is the possibility of a strong potential two-way series of benefits here.

Notes

1) Because of trying to finish this attempted critical summary before leaving Edinburgh after the seminar, the references presented here are not as many as might be wished. I hope this has caused no inconvenience.

2) At the end of the seminar, before hearing the oral version of this summary, we polled the participants for their views of critical issues in IL studies. They were not told in advance of this survey as we did not wish to bias their listening to the discussion. The raw survey data were coded by those participants who were able to attend the 'Workshop on data analysis' held for two days after the seminar. We refer now to those items (arranged alphabetically) that kept coming up again and again:

– Agreement on what IL is
– Context: use and acquisition (including input)
– General theory of language acquisition
– Language transfer
– Pedagogical implications
– Research methodology
– Variation

For historical reasons, it might be interesting to note some other issues that were mentioned: age, cognitive constraints, communicative success, comparison between language learning and other kinds of learning, competence/performance, fossilization, grammatical framework for IL, IL and other disciplines, initial IL hypothesis, interrelationships of IL subsystems, metalinguistic knowledge and use, relationships between non-native and native linguistic systems, relationship of perception and production, role of fixed expressions, schemata as a basis for IL, sequencing and stages, simplified languages, strategies, universal grammar, and universals and implicational clusterings. It would be most interesting, we felt, to compare these lists with ones gathered five or ten years from now.

3) I have searched the literature for several centuries back and there exists no previous systematic field of study of learner languages, under any name.

4) I use the term 'IL learning' since I propose that within a theory of IL, this is precisely what happens. This is not merely terminological since psycholinguistically speaking, it removes (or should remove) the inherent difficulty of conceiving of a third or a fourth language as 'second'.

5) Of course, the facts for French-English plural are more complicated than portrayed in this statement.

6) An argument, as is made evident in one of the footnotes (Selinker, Swain and Dumas 1975), my co-authors were not too eager to buy.

7) I believe it was acknowledged in the seminar that we have a conundrum here that has important theoretical and methodological implications: Given level X and Y in IL,

a) One cannot relate X and Y unless one knows X and Y independently, and

b) One cannot understand X (or Y) unless one knows how Y (or X, respectively) affects it.
The important point is that there is now strong evidence in IL research, for the reasonableness of (b).

8) For those readers interested in IL who wish to become acquainted with the Language-for-Specific-Purposes field, I recommend beginning by reading the last two to three years of the *English for Specific Purposes Newsletter,* available from the English Language Institute, Corvallis, Oregon, USA.

32. Epilogue

The following is a transcript (with minor editorial amendments) of the remarks made by Pit Corder at the close of the Seminar.

I have never been at a seminar that had an Epilogue before, but then I have never been at such a pleasant seminar, surrounded entirely by friendly and familiar faces. I am going to commit one of the worst sins, and that is make a reference without saying where I got it from, because I frankly cannot remember. Somebody pointed out that this was in effect the 'Fest' part of a 'Festschrift', and that most so-called Festschrifts lack Fests. This for me has been a Fest.

I had thought of several things I wanted to say, but most of them have in fact cropped up in the course of our discussion. You might perhaps expect me to offer you wisdom as a result of years of experience before I finally disappear, and suggest to you the way that you should go in future. But these suggestions have all been made already, not only by me but by others in the course of our discussions, so this has left me bereft of anything to say of a relevant nature in connection with interlanguage. All the things I would like to stress have in fact been stressed, such as, for example, the respectability of speculation. I had thought the Epilogue might carry a title like 'In Praise of Speculation', but speculation has already been praised amongst us, so there is nothing for me to add. I had thought that it would be interesting to say something about what I believe to be the relation between theory and practice, in other words, the role of applied linguistics. But that has been aired fairly extensively to the point of suggesting, to me at least, that we really ought to drop the term 'applied linguistics' and replace it, as I was saying to someone earlier on, by 'implied linguistics'.

One point, however, which has not I think come up, and which I would be happy to see developed, is that, if we are really going to get into the business of universalist hypotheses, it might not be a bad idea to look at rather more languages than we have traditionally done. We are, I think, seriously liable to the criticism that we are altogether too English-oriented in our work. This is a criticism which has been levelled at others, of course. I think we have to be careful that it is not levelled at ourselves. We want to look at the acquisition of many more languages than we have done so far before we start making any serious general claims of one sort or another.

Those are, I think, all things I would have included if I had been making a longer contribution. However, this is not really the occasion for an addition to our academic activities, but an opportunity for me to express some personal feelings. Obviously, I am deeply moved by the honour that you have done me by coming here. There is no other way in which I could wish to leave the profession, which is what I am in fact doing, than in a circumstance of this kind. To see myself surrounded by people whose work I have followed and whom I have in many cases personally known over the years, to see them all gathering together on an occasion of this sort, makes it for me a fitting rounding to whatever I may have been able to do in this field myself. I am, therefore, very grateful to my colleagues at Edinburgh for the imaginative, very imaginative, way in which they decided to mark my retirement. And I should thank you not only for going to the trouble of finding the time and means to come to Edinburgh, but also for producing papers which I have found consistently interesting and stimulating. Even though I am saying good-bye to the field, I was still able to participate in your own interest and excitement in the work you are doing. Thank you.

References

Abbs, B., Ayton, A. and Freebairn, I. (1975) *Strategies,* London: Longman.
Abbs, B., Candlin, C., Edelhoff, C., Moston, T. and Sexton, M. (1976) *Challenges,* London: Longman.
Adjémian, C. (1976) On the nature of interlanguage systems, *Language Learning* 26, 297-320.
— (1983a) The transferability of lexical properties. In Gass, S. and Selinker, L. (eds) (1983), 250-68.
— (1983b) L'idéalisation des langues secondes. In Gueron, J. and Sowley, T. (eds) (1983), *Grammaire Générative,* Presses Universitaires de Vincennes, Paris.
Adjémian, C. and Liceras, J. (1982) Accounting for adult acquisition of relative clauses: universal grammar, L1, and structuring the intake. Paper presented at the 11th UWM Linguistics Symposium: Universals of Second Language Acquisition, University of Wisconsin-Milwaukee, March 1982.
Adorno, T. (ed.) (1969) *Der Positivismusstreit in der deutschen Soziologie,* Darmstadt: Luchterhand.
Aissen, J. (1974) The syntax of causative constructions. Unpublished Ph.D. dissertation, Harvard University.
Alatis, J., Altman, H. and Alatis, P. (eds) (1981) *The Second Language Classroom: Directions for the 1980s,* New York: Oxford University Press.
Albert, M. and Obler, L. (1978) *The Bilingual Brain,* New York: Academic Press.
Allen, J. P. B. (1983) A three-level curriculum model for second-language education, *The Canadian Modern Language Review* 40, 23-43.
Allen, J. P. B. and Corder, S. P. (eds) (1973, 1974, 1975) *Edinburgh Course in Applied Linguistics,* vols 1, 2, 3, London: Oxford University Press.
Allen, J. P. B., Cummins, J., Mougeon, R. and Swain, M. (1983) *Development of Bilingual Proficiency: Second Year Report,* Toronto: Ontario Institute for Studies in Education (mimeo).
Allendorf, S. (1980) Wiedererwerb einer Zweitsprache, dargestellt am Beispiel der englischen Negation. Doctoral dissertation, Kiel University.
Allwright, R. L. (1975) Problems in the study of the language teacher's treatment of learner error. In Burt and Dulay (eds) (1975), pp.96-109.
— (1980) Turn, topics and tasks: patterns of participation in language learning and teaching. In Larsen-Freeman, D. (ed.) (1980).
— (1984) The importance of interaction in classroom language learning, *Applied Linguistics* vol.5, no.2, Summer, pp.156-71.
Andersen, R. W. (1977) The impoverished state of cross-sectional morpheme acquisition/accuracy methodology (or: The leftovers are more nourishing than the main course). In Henning, C. (ed.), *Proceedings of the Los Angeles Second Language Research Forum,* Los Angeles: University of California.
— (1978) An implicational model for second language research, *Language Learning* 28, 21-82.

References

— (1979a) Expanding Schumann's pidginization hypothesis, *Language Language* 29, 105-19.
— (1979b) The relationship between first language transfer and second language overgeneralization: data from the English of Spanish speakers. In Andersen, R. W. (ed.) (1979c), 43-58.
— (ed.) (1979c) *The Acquisition and Use of Spanish and English as First and Second Languages,* Washington, DC: TESOL.
— (1980) Creolization as the acquisition of a second language as a first language. In Valdman, A. and Highfield, A. (eds) (1980), *Theoretical Orientations in Creole Studies,* New York: Academic Press, 273-95.
— (1981a) Two perspectives on pidginization as second language acquisition. In Andersen, R. W. (ed.) (1981b), 165-95.
— (ed.) (1981b) *New Dimensions in Second Language Acquisition Research,* Rowley, Mass.: Newbury House Publishers.
— (1982a) The expression of temporality in interlanguage. MS, UCLA.
— (1982b) What's gender good for, anyway? Paper presented at the Fourth Los Angeles Second Language Research Forum, Los Angeles, California.
— (1982c) Determining the linguistic attributes of language attrition. In Lambert, R. D. and Freed, B. F. (eds), *The Loss of Language Skills,* Rowley, Mass.: Newbury House Publishers, 83-118.
— (1983a) A language acquisition interpretation of pidginization and creolization. In Andersen, R. W. (ed.) (1983d), 1-56.
— (1983b) Transfer to somewhere. In Gass, S. and Selinker, L. (eds) (1983).
— (1983c) The one-to-one principle of interlanguage construction. Paper presented at the 17th Annual TESOL Conference, Toronto, Ontario, Canada, 15th-20th March.
— (ed.) (1983d) *Pidginization and Creolization as Language Acquisition,* Rowley, Mass.: Newbury House Publishers.
— (in press) A cross-linguistic perspective for second language research. In Andersen, R. W. (ed.), *Second Languages: A Cross-linguistics Perspective,* Rowley, Mass.: Newbury House Publishers, 13-26 (MS pages).
Anglin, J. M. (1977) *Word, Object and Conceptual Development,* New York: Norton.
Arabski, J. (1979) *Errors as Indications of the Development of Interlanguage,* Katowice: Uniwersytet Slaski.
Ard, J. (1975) Raising and word order in diachronic syntax. Ph.D. dissertation, UCLA.
— (1983) Towards an applied phonology. Paper presented at the Conference on the Uses of Phonology, Southern Illinois University, Carbondale.
Arditty, J. and Perdue, C. (1979) Variabilité et connaissances en langue étrangère, *Encrages,* Presses Universitaires de Vincennes, Paris.
Bach, E. (1974) *Syntactic Theory,* New York: Holt, Rinehart and Winston.
Bahns, J. (1976) Der L2-Erwerb der englischen Pluralflexion unter naturlichen Bedingungen bei Kindern mit Deutsch als L1, mimeo, Kiel University.
Bailey, B. L. (1966) *Jamaican Creole Syntax. A Transformational Approach,* Cambridge: Cambridge University Press.
Bailey, C.-J. (1971) Trying to talk in the new paradigm, *Working Papers in Linguistics* (University of Hawaii), 4.2, 312-39.
— (1973) *Variation and Linguistic Theory,* Washington, DC: Center for Applied Linguistics.
Bailey, N., Madden, C. and Krashen, S. D. (1974) Is there a 'natural sequence' in adult second language learning? *Language Learning* 24, 235-43.
Baker, C. (1978) *Introduction to Generative Transformational Syntax,* New York.

References

— (1979) Syntactic theory and the projection problem, *Linguistic Inquiry* 10, 533-81.

Baker, C. and McCarthy, J. (eds) (1981) *The Logical Problem of Language Acquisition*, Cambridge, Mass.: MIT Press.

Bamgbose, A. (ed.) (1976) *Mother Tongue Education: The West African Experience*, London: Hodder and Stoughton and Paris: UNESCO.

Bar-Adon, A. and Leopold, W. (eds) (1971) *Child Language: A Book of Readings*, Englewood Cliffs, NJ: Prentice Hall.

Baron, N. S. (1977) *Language Acquisition and Historical Change*, Amsterdam/New York/Oxford: North Holland.

Bartelt, H. G. (1983) Transfer and variability of rhetorical redundancy in Apache English interlanguage. In Gass, S. and Selinker, L. (eds) (1983).

Bartsch, R. and Vennemann, T. (1972) *Semantic Structures: A Study in the Relation between Syntax and Semantics*, Frankfurt: Athenaeum Verlag.

Bartsch, R., Lenerz, J. and Ullmer-Ehrich, V. (1977) *Einfuhrung in die Syntax*, Kronberg: Scriptor.

Bates, E. and MacWhinney, B. (1979) A functionalist approach to the acquisition of grammar. In Ochs, E. and Schieffelin, B. (eds), *Developmental Pragmatics*, New York: Academic Press.

— (1981) Functionalist approaches to grammar. In Gleitman, L. and Wanner, E. (eds), *Language Acquisition, The State of the Art*, New York: Cambridge University Press.

Bates, E., MacWhinney, B. and Smith, S. (1982) Pragmatics and syntax in psycholinguistic research. In Felix, S. W. and Wode, H. (eds), *Language Development at the Crossroads*, Tübingen, West Germany: Tübingen, 11-28.

Bates, E., McNew, S., MacWhinney, B., Deviscovi, A. and Smith, S. (1982) Functional constraints on sentence processing: a cross-linguistic study, *Cognition* 11, 245-99.

Baudouin de Courtenay, J. (1972) *A Baudouin de Courtenay Anthology*, translated and edited by Stankiewicz, E., Bloomington, Indiana: Indiana University Press.

Bauer, A. (1974) Das melanesische und chinesische Pidginenglisch, *Linguistische Kriterien und Probleme*, Regensburg: Carl.

Beebe, J. (1977) The influence of the listener on code-switching, *Language learning* 27, 331-40.

— (1983) Input: choosing the right stuff. Paper presented at the 10th University of Michigan Conference of Applied Linguistics.

Beebe, L. (1979) Implications of research on cohesion for ESL teaching. Paper presented at TESOL, Boston, Mass.

— (1980) Sociolinguistic variation and style shifting in second language acquisition, *Language Learning* 30.2, 433-77.

— (in press) Risk-taking and the language learner. In Seliger, H. and Long, M. (eds) (1983).

Behagel, O. (1924) *Deutsche Syntax: Eine geschichtliche Darstellung*, Heidelberg: Winter.

Bell, R. (1973) The English of an Indian immigrant. *ITL: A Review of Applied Linguistics* 22, 11-61.

Bellugi, U. (1967) The acquisition of negation. Doctoral dissertation, Harvard University.

Bellugi, U. and Brown, R. (eds) (1964) The acquisition of language. *Monographs of the Society of Research on Child Development* 29, Part I, Chicago: University of Chicago Press.

Berent, G. (1983) Control judgments by deaf adults and by second language learners, *Language Learning* 33, 37-54.

References

Berko, J. B. (1958) The child's learning of English morphology, *Word* 14, 150-77.
— (1982) Converging evidence for linguistic theory in the study of aphasia and child language. In Obler, L. K. and Menn, L. (eds) (1982).
Berman, R. (1980) The case of an (s)vo language. Subject-less constructions in Modern Hebrew, *Language* 56, 759-76.
Bever, T. G. (1970) The cognitive basis for linguistic structures. In Hayes, J. (ed.), *Cognition and the Development of Language*, New York: John Wiley & Sons.
Bialystok, E. (1978) A theoretical model of second language learning, *Language Learning* 28, 69-83.
— (1979) The role of conscious strategies in second language proficiency, *Canadian Modern Language Review* 35, 372-94.
— (1981) The role of linguistic knowledge in second language use. *Studies in Second Language Acquisition* 4, 31-45.
— (1983a) Inferencing: testing the 'Hypothesis-testing' hypothesis. In Seliger, H. W. and Long, M. (eds) (1983).
— (1983b) Some factors in the selection and implementation of communication strategies. In Faerch, C. and Kasper, G. (eds) (1983d), 100-18.
— (1983c) Learning language form and language function, *Interlanguage Studies Bulletin*.
Bialystok, E. and Frolich, M. (1980) Oral communication strategies for lexical difficulties, *The Interlanguage Studies Bulletin* 5, 1, 3-30.
Bialystok, E. and Ryan, E. B. (in press) A metacognitive framework for the development of first and second language skills. In Forrest-Pressley, D. L., MacKinnon, G. E. and Waller, T. G. (eds), *Meta-cognition, Cognition, and Human Performance*, New York: Academic Press.
Bialystok, E. and Sharwood Smith, M. (1984) Interlanguage is not a state of mind. Unpublished ms, York University, Toronto.
Bialystok, E. and Swain, M (1978) Methodological approaches to research in second language learning, *McGill Journal of Education* 13, 137-44.
Bibeau, G. (1983) La Theorie du Moniteur de Krashen: aspects critiques, *Bulletin of the CAAL*, 99-123.
Bickerton, D. (1971) Inherent variability and variable rules, *Foundations of Language* 7, 457-92.
— (1973) On the nature of a creole continuum, *Language* 49, 640-69.
— (1974) Creolization, linguistic universals, natural semantax and the brain, *Working Papers in Linguistics* (University of Hawaii), 6.3, 124-41.
— (1975) *Dynamics of a Creole System,* Cambridge: Cambridge University Press.
— (1976) Pidgin and creole studies, *Annual Review of Anthropology* 5, 169-93.
— (1981a) *Roots of Language,* Ann Arbor, Mich.: Karoma Publishers.
— (1981b) Discussion. In Andersen, R. W. (ed.).
Bickerton, D. and Givón, T. (1976) Pidginization and language change: from svx and vsx to svx. In *Papers from the Parasession on Diachronic Syntax*, Chicago: Chicago Linguistic Society.
Bierwisch, M. and Heidolph, K. (eds) (1970) *Progress in Linguistics*, Den Haag: Mouton.
Blaas, L. (1982) *Fossilisation in the Advanced Learner's Lexicon*, Department of English, University of Utrecht.
Blatchford, C and Schachter, J. (1978) *On TESOL '78*, Washington, DC: TESOL.
Bley-Vroman, R. (1983) The comparative fallacy in interlanguage studies: the case of systematicity, *Language Learning* 33, 1, 1-17.
Bloom, L. (1970) *Language Development: Form and Function in Emerging Grammars*, Cambridge, Mass.: MIT Press.
— (1973) *One Word at a Time*, Den Haag: Mouton.

References

Blum, S. and Levenston, E. (1977) Strategies of communication through lexical avoidance in the speech and writing of second language teachers and learners and in translation. Ontario Institute for Bilingual Education. ED139280.

— (1978a) Lexical simplification in second language acquisition, *Studies in Second Language Acquisition* 2.2, 43-64.

— (1978b) Universals of lexical simplification, *Language Learning* 28, 399-415.

Boete, H. and Herrlitz, W. (eds) (1983) *Kommunikation im (Sprach)-Unterrichts,* Utrecht.

Bongaerts, T. (1983) The comprehension of three complex structures by Dutch learners, *Language Learning* 33, 159-82.

Bourhis, R. Y. and Giles, H. (1977) The language of intergroup distinctiveness. In Giles, H. (ed.) (1977).

Bowerman, M. (1973) *Early Syntactic Development. A Cross-linguistic Study with Special Reference to Finnish,* Cambridge, England: Cambridge University Press.

— (1979) The acquisition of complex sentences. In Fletcher, P. and Garman, M. (eds), *Language Acquisition; Studies in First Language Development,* Cambridge: Cambridge University Press.

— (1982) Starting to talk worse: clues to language acquisition from children's late speech errors. In Strauss, S. (ed.) (1982).

— (1983) How do children avoid constructing an overly general grammar in the absence of feedback about what is not a sentence? *Papers and Reports on Child Language Development* 22.

Braine, M. (1963) The ontogeny of English phrase structure: the first phase, *Language* 39, 1-13.

Brainerd, C. J. (1983) Varieties of strategy training in Piagetian concept learning. In Pressley, M. and Levin, J. R. (eds) (1983).

Bransford, J. D. and Johnson, M. K. (1973) Conceptual prerequisites for understanding: some investigations of comprehension and recall, *Journal of Verbal Learning and Verbal Behavior* 11, 717-26.

Bresnan, J. (1970) On complementizers: towards a syntactic theory of complement types, *Foundations of Language* 6, 297-321.

— (1982) Polyadicity. In Bresnan, J. (ed.), *The Mental Representation of Grammatical Relations,* Cambridge, Mass.: The MIT Press, 149-72.

Broselow, E. (1983) Nonobvious transfer: on predicting epenthesis errors. In Gass, S. and Selinker, L. (eds) (1983).

Brown, A. (1975) The development of memory: knowing, knowing about knowing, and knowing how to know. In Reese, H. W. (ed.), *Advances in Child Development and Behavior,* vol.10, New York: Academic Press.

Brown, G. (1977) *Listening to Spoken English,* London: Longman.

Brown, H. D., Yorio, C. and Crymes, R. (eds) (1977) *On TESOL '77,* Washington DC: TESOL.

Brown, J. D. (1983) An exploration of morpheme-group interactions. In Bailey, K. M., Long, M. H. and Peck, S. (eds), *Second Language Acquisition Studies,* Rowley, Mass.: Newbury House Publishers.

Brown, K. (1984) *Linguistics Today,* Fontana.

Brown, R. (1973) *A First Language,* Cambridge, Mass.: Harvard University Press and London: George Allen and Unwin.

Brown, R. and Fraser, C. (1963) The acquisition of syntax. In Cofer, C. and Musgrave, B. (eds) (1963).

Brown, R. and McNeill, D. (1966) The tip of the tongue phenomenon, *Journal of Verbal Learning and Verbal Behavior* 5, 325-37.

Brumfit, C. J. (1979) Accuracy and fluency as polarities in foreign language teaching materials and methodology, *Bulletin CILA* 29, 89-99.

— (1983) Some problems with Krashen's concepts 'Acquisition' and 'Learning', *Nottingham Linguistics Circular*.

— (1984) *Communicative Methodology in Language Teaching*, Cambridge: Cambridge University Press.

— (forthcoming) The Bangalore procedural syllabus, *ELTJ*.

Brumfit, C. J. and Johnson, K. (eds) (1979) *The Communicative Approach to Language Teaching*, Oxford: Oxford University Press.

Burmeister, H. (1977) Experimentelle vs. spontane Spracherwerbsdaten am Beispiel der L2-Englischen Negation, mimeo, Kiel University.

Burt, M. K. and Dulay, H. C. (eds) (1975) *On TESOL '75: New Directions in Second Language Learning, Teaching and Bilingual Education*, Washington, DC: TESOL.

— (1980) On acquisition orders. In Felix, S. W. (ed.) (1980), 265-328.

Burtoff, M. (1983) Organisational patterns of expository prose: a comparative study of native Arabic, Japanese and English speakers. Paper presented at TESOL, Honolulu, Hawaii.

Butler-Wall, B. (1983) Optional syntax in oral discourse: evidence from native speakers English. In Campbell, C. et al. (eds), *Proceedings of the Los Angeles Second Language Research Forum*, vol.II, Los Angeles: University of California.

Canale, M. and Swain, M. (1980) Theoretical bases of communicative approaches to second language teaching and testing, *Applied Linguistics* 1, 1, 1-47.

Cancino, H., Rosansky, E. and Schumann, J. H. (1978) The acquisition of English of English negatives and interrogatives. In Hatch, E. M. (ed.) (1978b).

Candlin, C. N. (1981a) Discoursal patterning and the equalizing of interpretive opportunity. In Smith, L. (ed.), *English for Cross-cultural Communication*, London: Macmillan, 166-98.

— (ed.) (1981b) *The Communicative Teaching of English*, London: Longman.

Carr, E. B. (1972) De kine talk. From pidgin to standard English in Hawaii. Honolulu, Hawaii: University of Hawaii Press.

Carrell, P. L. (1981) Background knowledge in second language comprehension. Paper presented at AILA, Lund, Sweden.

— (1983) Three components of background knowledge in reading comprehension, *Language Learning* 33, 183-207.

Carroll, M. and Dietrich, R. (1983) Bestimmtheit, Unbestimmtheit, Wortstellung, European Science Foundation Progress Report II, Heidelberg.

Carton, A. S. (1971) Inferencing: a process in using and learning language. In Pimsleur, P. and Quinn, T. (eds) (1971), 45-58.

Cavalcanti, M. D. C. (1983) The pragmatics of FL reader-text interaction: key lexical items as source of potential reading problems. Unpublished Ph.D. thesis, University of Lancaster.

Cazden, C., Cancino, H., Rosansky, E. and Schumann, J. H. (1975) Second language acquisition sequences in children, adolescents and adults. Final Report submitted to the National Institute of Education, Washington, DC.

Chaudron, C. (1983a) Foreigner talk in the classroom – an aid to learning? In Seliger, H. W. and Long, M. H. (eds) (1983), 127-45.

— (1983b) Research on metalinguistic judgements: a review of theory, methods, and results, *Language Learning* 33.3, 343-77.

Chevalier, J.-C., Blanche-Beneviste, C., Arrive, M. and Peytard, J. (1964) *Grammaire Larousse du Français Contemporain*, Paris: Larousse.

Chomsky, C. (1969) *The Acquisition of Syntax in Children from 5-10*, Cambridge: MIT Press.

References

— (1972) Stages in language development and reading exposure, *Harvard Educational Review* 42, 1-33.

Chomsky, N. (1964) *Current Issues in Linguistic Theory*, The Hague: Mouton.

— (1965) *Aspects of the Theory of Syntax*, Cambridge, Mass.: MIT Press.

— (1973) *Language and Mind*, enlarged edition, New York: Harcourt Brace Jovanovitch, Inc.

— (1976) *Reflections on Language*, New York, NY: Pantheon Books.

— (1981a) Principles and parameter in syntactic theory. In Hornstein, N. and Lightfoot, D. (eds) (1981).

— (1981b) *Rules and Representations*, Oxford: Basil Blackwell.

— (1981c) *Lectures on Government and Binding*, Dordrecht: Foris.

— (1982) *Some Concepts and Consequences of the Theory of Government and Binding*, Cambridge, Mass.: MIT Press.

Chomsky, N. and Halle, M. (1968) *The Sound Pattern of English*, New York: Harper and Row.

Chomsky, N. and Lasnik, H. (1977) Filters and control, *Linguistic Inquiry* 8. 425-504.

Chomsky, N. and Miller, G. A. (1963) Introduction to the formal analysis of natural languages. In Luce, R. D., Bush, R. R. and Galanter, E. (eds), *Handbook of Mathematical Psychology*, vol.2, New York, 323-418.

Clahsen, H. (1980) Psycholinguistic aspect of L2 acquisition. In Felix, S. W. (ed.) (1980), 57-79.

— (1982) Spracherwerb in der Kindheit. Eine Untersuchung zur Entwicklung der Syntax ei Kleinkindern, Tübingen.

— (in press) The acquisition of German word order: a test case for cognitive approaches to L2 development. In Andersen, R. W. (ed.), *Second Languages: A Cross-linguistic Perspective*, Rowley, Mass.: Newbury House Publishers.

Clahsen, H. and Muysken, P. (1983) The accessibility of 'move alpha' and the acquisition of German word order by children and adults. Unpublished MS, University of Dusseldorf and the University of Amsterdam.

Clahsen, H., Meisel, J. and Pienemann, M. (1983) *Deutsch als Fremdsprache. Der Spracherwerb auslandischer Arbeiter*, Tübingen: Gunther Narr.

Clark, E. V. (1973a) Non-linguistic strategies and the acquisition of word meanings, *Cognition* 2, 161-82.

— (1973b) What's in a word? On the child's acquisition of semantics in his first language. In Moore, T. E. (ed.), *Cognitive Development and the Acquisition of Language*, New York: Academic Press.

Clark, H. and Haviland, S. (1974) Psychological processes as linguistic explanation. In Cohen, A. D. (ed.) (1974), 91-124.

Clark, H. H. (1970) The primitive nature of children's relational concepts. In Hayes, J. R. (ed.), *Cognition and the Development of Language*, New York/London: John Wiley & Sons, 260-78.

— (1975) Bridging. In Schank, R. C. and Nash-Webber, B. L. (Chairpersons), *Theoretical Issues in Natural Language Processing*, Cambridge, Mass.

Clark, H. H. and Clark, E. (1977) *Psychology and Language: An Introduction to Psycholinguistics*, New York: Harcourt Brace Jovanovich.

Clark, R. (1974) Performing without competence, *Journal of Child Language* 1, 1-10.

Clarke, M. A. (1979) Reading in Spanish and English: evidence from adult ESL students, *Language Learning* 29, 121-50.

Clements, G. and Keyser, S. J. (1983) *CV Phonology: a Generative Theory of the Syllable*, Cambridge, Mass.: MIT Press.

Closs-Traugott, E. (1977) Natural semantax: its role in the study of second language acquisition. In Corder, S. P. and Roulet, E. (eds), *The Notions of Simplification, Interlanguage and Pidgins and Their Relation to Second Language Pedagogy*,

References

132-62, Geneva: Librairie Droz.

Cofer, C. and Musgrave, B. (1963) *Verbal Behavior and Learning: Problems and Processes,* New York: Holt, Rinehart and Winston.

Cohen, A. D. (ed.) (1974) *Explaining Linguistic Phenomena,* Washington, DC: Hemisphere.

— (1983) Introspecting about second language learning, *Studia Anglica Posnaniensia,* vol.15, 139-46.

Cohen, A. D. and Hosenfeld, C. (1981) Some uses of think-aloud and self-observational data in second language research, *Language Learning* 31.

Comrie, B. (1976) *Aspect,* Cambridge: Cambridge University Press.

— (1981) *Language Universals and Linguistic Typology,* Chicago: Chicago University Press.

— (1984) Why linguists need language acquirers? In Rutherford, W. (ed.), *Second Language Acquisition and Language Universals,* Amsterdam: John Benjamins Press.

Cook, V. J. (in press) Universal grammar and second language learning, *Applied Linguistics.*

Cooper, R., Olshtain, E., Tucker, G. and Waterbury, M. (1979) The acquisition of complex English structures by adult native speakers of Arabic and Hebrew, *Language Learning* 29, 255-75.

Corder, S. P. (1960a) *An Intermediate English Practice Book,* London: Longmans.

— (1960b) *English Language Teaching and Television,* London: Longmans.

— (1966) *The Visual Element in Language Teaching,* London: Longmans.

— (1967) The significance of learners' errors, *International Review of Applied Linguistics,* vol.5, no.4, pp.161-70, reprinted in Richards, J. C.. (ed.) (1974).

— (1971) Idiosyncratic dialects and error analysis. *IRAL* 9, 147-59.

— (1973a) The elicitation of Interlanguage. In Svartvik, J. (ed.) (1973), *Errata. Papers in Error Analysis,* Gleerup, Lund.

— (1973b) *Introducing Applied Linguistics,* Harmondsworth: Penguin Books.

— (1975) Error analysis, interlanguage and second language acquisition, *Language Teaching and Linguistics Abstracts* 8, 4, 201-18. (1981) *Error Analysis and Interlanguage,* Oxford: Oxford University Press.

— (1977a) Simple codes and the source of the second language learner's initial heuristic hypothesis, *Studies in Second Language Acquisition* 1, 1-10.

— (1977b) Language continua and the interlanguage hypothesis. In Corder, S. P. and Roulet, E. (eds), *The Notions of Simplification, Interlanguage and Pidgins and Their Relation to Second Language Pedagogy,* 11-17.

— (1978) Language distance and the magnitude of the language learning task *Studies in Second Language Acquisition* 2, 27-36.

— (1980) Second language acquisition research and the teaching of grammar, *BAAL Newsletter* 10.

— (1981) *Error Analysis and Interlanguage,* Oxford: Oxford University Press.

— (1983a) A role for the mother tongue. In Gass, S. and Selinker, L. (eds) (1983).

— (1983b) Strategies of communication. In Faerch, C. and Kasper, G. (1983d), 15-19 (originally published 1978).

Courthard, R. M. (1977) *An Introduction to Discourse Analysis,* London: Longmans.

Cowie, A. P. and Mackin, R. (1975) *Oxford Dictionary of Current Idiomatic English,* Oxford: Oxford University Press.

Cummins, J. (1979) Linguistic interdependence and the educational development of bilingual children, *Review of Educational Research* 49, 2, 222-51.

Cutler, A. (1978) Lexical complexity and sentence processing. In Flores d'Arcais, F. B. and Jarvella, R. (eds).

References

D'Anglejan, A. and Renaud, C. (1981) Learner characteristics and second language acquisition. Paper presented at the First European North American Workshop on Cross Linguistic Research in Second Language Acquisition, Lake Arrowhead, CA.

D'Anglejan, A. and Tucker, G. (1975) The acquisition of complex English structures by adult learners, *Language Learning* 25, 281-96.

Dahl, O. (1979) Typology of sentence negation, *Linguistics* 17, 79-106.

Davidson, D. and Harman, G. (1972) *Semantics of Natural Language*, Dordrecht: Reidel.

Day, R. R. (1982) Children's attitudes towards language. In Ryan, E. B. and Giles H. (eds) (1982), *Attitudes towards Language Variation*, London: Edward Arnold.

— (1983) Rocky Horror Picture Show: a speech event in three acts. In Wolfson, N. and Judd, E. (eds) (1983).

Dechert, H. W. (1982) How a story is done in a second language. In Faerch, C. and Kasper, G. (eds) (1983d), 175-95.

Dechert, H. W. and Raupach, M. (eds) (forthcoming) *Transfer in Production*, Norwood, NJ: Ablex.

Deshaies, D. and Laforge, E. (1980) Le futur simple et le futur proche dans le français parlé dans la ville de Quebec. Paper presented at ACFAS.

Dickerson, L. (1974) Internal and external patterning of phonological variability in the speech of Japanese learners of English. Unpublished Ph.D. dissertation, University of Illinois.

Dickerson, L. and Dickerson, W. (1977) Interlanguage phonology: current research and future direction. In Corder, S. P. and Roulet, E. (eds), *The Notions of Simplification, Interlanguages and Pidgins: Acts du 5ème Colloque de Linguistique Appliqué de Neuchâtel*, Paris: AIMAV/Didier.

Dietrich, R. (1982) Bestimmtheit und Unbestimmtheit im Deutschen eines türkischen Arbeiters – eine Hypothese, Universität Kassel.

Dik, S. (1978) *Functional Grammar*, Amsterdam: North-Holland.

Dingwall, S. (1982) Critical self-reflection and decisions in doing research: the case of questionnaire survey of EFL teachers. In Dingwall, S. and Mann, S. (eds), *Methods and Problems in Doing Applied Linguistic Research*, Department of Linguistics and Modern English Language, University of Lancaster.

Dittmar, N. (1981a) 'Regen bisschen Pause geht' – More on the puzzle of interference. Paper presented at the 1st Eunam Workshop on Second Language Acquisition, Lake Arrowhead, August.

— (1981b) On the verbal organization of L2 tense marking in an elicited translation task by Spanish immigrants in Germany, *Studies in Second Language Acquisition* 3.2, 136-64.

Donaldson, M. (1978) *Children's Minds*, Glasgow: Fontana.

Dressler, W. (1977) *Grundfragen der Morphonologie*, Vienna, Verlag der Osterreichischen Akademie der Wissenschaften.

Drubig, B. (1972) Zur Analyse syntaktischer Fehlleistungen. In Nickel, G. (ed.), *Fehlerkunde*, 78-91, Bielefeld: Cornelsen, Velhagen and Klasing.

Dryer, M. (1980) The positional tendencies of sentential noun phrases in universal grammar, *Canadian Journal of Linguistics* 25, 123-95.

Dulay, H. C. and Burt, M. K. (1972) Goofing, an indicator of children's second language strategies, *Language Learning* 22.2, 234-52.

— (1973) Should we teach children syntax? *Language Learning*, vol.24, 253-78.

— (1974a) Errors and strategies in child second language acquisition, *TESOL Quarterly* 8, 129-36.

— (1974b) Natural sequences in child second language acquisition, *Language Learning* 24, 37-53. Reprinted in Hatch, E.M. (ed.) (1978b).

References

— (1974c) A new perspective on the creative construction process in child second language acquisition, *Language Learning* 24, 235-78.

— (1978) Some remarks on creativity in language acquisition. In Ritchie, W. C. (ed.) (1978).

Dulay, H. C., Burt, M. K. and Krashen, S. D. (1982) *Language Two*, Oxford and New York: Oxford University Press.

Duranti, A. (1979) Object clitic pronouns in Bantu and the topicality hierarchy, *Studies in African Linguistics* 10, 31-45.

Eckman, F. (1977) Markedness and the contrastive analysis hypothesis, *Language Learning* 27, 315-30.

— (1981) On the naturalness of interlanguage phonological rules, *Language Learning* 31, 195-216.

— (1984) Universals, typologies and interlanguages. In Rutherford, W. (ed.) (forthcoming).

Eckman, F., Moravcsik, E. and Wirth, J. (eds) (forthcoming) *Proceedings of the 12th Annual University of Wisconsin-Milwaukee Symposium on Markedness*, New York: Plenum.

Ellis, R. (1983) Research styles in second language acquisition. Paper given at the 1983 BAAL Annual Conference, Leicester Polytechnic.

— (1984) Can syntax be taught? *Applied Linguistics*, vol.5, no.2, Summer, pp.138-55.

Emonds, J. (1976a) *A Transformational Approach to English Syntax: Root, Structure-preserving, and Logical Transformations*, New York: Academic Press.

— (1976b) A principled limit on differences in the grammar of French and English, *U.C.L.A. Papers in Syntax* 7, 76-94.

Engdahl, E. (1983) Parasitic gaps, *Linguistics and Philosophy* 6, 5-34.

Ervin-Tripp, S. (1977) From conversation to syntax, *Papers and Reports on Child Language Development* no.13, K1-21.

Faerch, C. (1979) Describing interlanguage through interaction. Problems of systematicity and permeability, *Working Papers on Bilingualism* 19, 59-78.

— (1982) Inferencing procedures and communication strategies in lexical comprehension. Paper read at the BAAL Seminar on Interpretive Strategies, University of Lancaster.

— (1984) Giving transfer a boost – describing transfer variation in learners' interlanguage performance, *Scandinavian Working Papers on Bilingualism* 2, 1984, 1-22.

Faerch, C. and Kasper, G. (1980a) Process and strategies in foreign language learning and communication, *Interlanguage Studies Bulletin Utrecht* 5, 47-118.

— (1980b) Stratégies de communication et marqueurs de stratégies. In Arditty, J. and Mittner, M. (eds), *Encrages*, numéro spécial, Université Paris VIII – Vincennes à Saint-Denis, 17-24.

— (1982) Phatic, metalingual and metacommunicative functions in discourse: gambits and repairs. In Enkvist, N. E. (ed.), *Impromptu Speech: A Symposium*, Åbo: Åbo Akademi, 71-103.

— (1983a) Introduction. In Faerch, C. and Kasper, G. (1983d), xv-xxiv.

— (1983b) On identifying communication strategies in interlanguage production. In Faerch, C. and Kasper, G. (1983d), 210-38.

— (1983c) Two ways of defining communication strategies. Mimeo paper, University of Copenhagen.

— (eds) (1983d) *Strategies in Interlanguage Communication*, London: Longmans.

— (1983e) Plans and strategies in foreign language communication. In Faerch, C. and Kasper, G. (1983d), 20-60.

References

— (1984) Communication strategies in the foreign language classroom. In Kasper, G. (ed.) (in press a).

— (forthcoming a) Cognitive dimensions of language transfer. To appear in Kellerman, E. and Sharwood Smith, M. (eds) (forthcoming a).

— (forthcoming b) Introspektive Verfahren in der Interimsprachenanalyse. To appear in Borsche, S. (ed.), *Psychologie und Sprachlehrforschung,* Tübingen: Gunther Narr.

— (forthcoming c) Procedural knowledge as a component of foreign language learners' communicative competence. In Bolte, H. and Herrlitz, W. (eds), *Kommunikation im (Sprach-)unterrickt,* Utrecht: University of Utrecht.

— (in press) Strategic competence in foreign language teaching. In Kasper, G. (in press a).

Faerch, C., Haastrup, K. and Phillipson, R. (1984) *Learner Language and Language Learning,* Copenhagen: Gyldendal/Clevedon: Multilingual Matters.

Fairbanks, K. (1982) Variability in interlanguage. Unpublished MS, University of Minnesota, Minneapolis.

Farkas, D., Jacobsen, W. and Todrys, K. (eds) *Papers from the Parasession on the Lexicon,* Chicago Linguistic Society.

Fathman, A. K. (1975) Language background, age and the order of acquisition of English structures. In Burt, M. K. and Dulay, H. C. (eds) (1978).

— (1978) ESL and EFL learning: similar or dissimilar? In Blatchford, C. and Schachter, J. (eds) (1978).

Favreau, M. and Segalowitz, N. S. (1982) Second language reading in fluent bilinguals, *Applied Psycholinguistics* 3, 329-41.

Felix, S. W. (1976) Wh-pronouns in first and second language acquisition, *Linguistische Berichte* 44, 52-64.

— (1977a) Naturlicher Zweitsprachenerwerb und Fremdsprachenunterricht, *Linguistik und Didaktik* 31, 231-47.

— (1977b) Entwicklungspronzesse im naturlichen und gesteuerten Zweitsprachen-erwerb, *Anglist und Englischunerricht* 1: *Sprachdidaktik,* 39-60.

— (1978) *Linguistische Untersuchungen zum naturlichen Zweitsprachenerwerb,* Munchen: Wilhelm Fink.

— (ed.) (1980) *Second Language Development. Trends and Issues,* Tübingen: Gunther Narr.

— (1981) The effect of formal instruction on second language acquisition, *Language Learning,* vol.31, no.1, June, 87-112.

— (1982a) *Psycholinguistische Aspekte des Zweitsprachenerwerbs,* Tübingen: Gunther Narr.

— (1982b) What you always wanted to know about cognition and language development. Paper presented at the Second European-North American Workshop on Cross Linguistic Second Language Research, Gohrde, West Germany.

Ferguson, C. A. and Slobin, D. (eds) (1973) *Studies in Child Language Development,* New York: Holt, Rinehart and Winston.

Flanders, N. A. (1963) Teacher and classroom influences on individual learning. Paper presented at the Seventh Annual Curriculum Research Institute, Eastern Section, Association for Supervision and Curriculum Development.

Flashner, V. (1982) The interlanguage of three native speakers of Russian: two perspectives. MA thesis, UCLA.

— (1983) A functional approach to tense-aspect-modality in the interlanguage of a native Russian speaker. In Campbell, C. et al. (eds), *Proceedings of the Los Angeles Second Language Research Forum,* vol.II, Los Angeles: University of California.

References

Flavell, J. H. (1977) *Cognitive Development,* Englewood Cliffs, NJ: Prentice-Hall.

Flores D'Arcais, G. and Jarvella, R. (198) *The Process of Language Understanding,* New York: John Wiley & Sons.

Flynn, K. (1983) The acquisition of form and function in interlanguage: a preliminary study. Paper given at The Second Language Research Forum, USC, November.

Flynn, S. (1981) Effects of the reversal of principal branching direction in L2 acquisition, *Cornell Working Papers,* vol.2 (Spring 1981).

— (1984) Similarities and differences between first and second language acquisition: setting the parameters of Universal grammar. In Rogers, D. R. and Sloboda, J. (eds), *The Acquisition of Symbolic Skills,* London and New York: Plenum.

Fodor, J. (1978) *The Language of Thought,* Cambridge, Mass.: MIT Press.

— (1980) Fixation of belief and concept acquisition. In Piattelli-Palmarini, M. (ed.), *Language and Learning,* London, 143-9.

— (1981) *Representations: Philosophical Essays on the Foundation of Cognitive Science,* Cambridge, Mass.: MIT Press.

Fodor, J., Bever, T. and Garrett, M. (1974) *The Psychology of Language: An Introduction to Psycholinguistics and Generative Grammar,* New York: McGraw-Hill.

Frauenfelder, U. and Porquier, R. (1979) Les voies d'apprentissage en langue étrangére, *Working Papers on Bilingualism* 17, 37-64.

Frauenfelder, U., Noyau, C., Perdue, C and Porquier, R. (1980) Connaissance en langue étrangére, *Langages* 57, 43-60.

Frawley, W. (1981) The complement hierarchy, evidence for language universals from L2. Paper presented at Winter LSA.

Fries, C. C. (1945) *Teaching and Learning English – as a Foreign Language,* Ann Arbor, Mich.: University of Michigan Press.

Frith, M. (1977) Second language learning: a study of form and function at two stages of developing interlanguage. Indiana University Linguistics Club.

Gaies, S. J. (1983) The investigation of language classroom processes, *TESOL Quarterly,* vol.17, no.2, June, 205-17.

Gardner, R. C., Smythe, P. C., Clement, R. and Gliksman, L. (1976) Second language learning: a social psychological perspective, *The Canadian Modern Language Review,* vol.32, no.3, February, 198-213.

Garfinkel, H. (1967) Studies of the routine grounds of everyday activities. In Garfinkel, H., *Studies in Ethnomethodology,* Englewood Cliffs, NJ: Prentice Hall.

Gaskill, W. (1980) Correction in native speaker–non-native speaker conversation. In Larsen-Freeman, D. (ed.) (1980).

Gass, S. (1979) Language transfer and language universals, *Language Learning* 29, 327-44.

— (1980) An investigation of syntactic transfer in adult second language learners. In Scarcella, R. and Krashen, S. D. (eds) (1980).

— (1982) From theory to practice. In Hines, M. and Rutherford, W (eds), *On TESOL '81,* Washington, DC: TESOL.

— (1983) Interlanguage syntax state of the art: language transfer and language universals. Paper presented at the 17th Annual TESOL Conference, Toronto, Ontario, Canada, 15th-20th March.

— (1984) Language transfer and language universals, *Language Learning* 34(2), in press.

— (forthcoming) Interaction in second language acquisition.

Gass, S. and Ard, J. (1980) L2 data, their relevance for language universals, *TESOL Quarterly* 14, 443-52.

References

— (1984) Second language acquisition and the ontology of language universals. In Rutherford, W. (ed.) (forthcoming).

Gass, S. and Selinker, L. (eds) (1983) *Language Transfer in Language Learning,* Rowley, Mass.: Newbury House.

Geest, T. van der and Heckhausen, J. (1978) Sprachentwicklungsprozesse in semantischer und interaktionalistischer Sicht, Zeitschrift für Entwicklungspsychologie und pädagogische, *Psychologie* 10, 286-304.

Genesee, F. (1982) Experimental neuropsychological research on second language processing, *TESOL Quarterly* 16, 315-22.

Genesee, F. and Hamayan, E. (1980) Individual differences in second language learning, *Applied Psycholinguistics* 1, 95-110.

George, H. (1972) *Common Errors in Language Learning,* Rowley, Mass.: Newbury House.

Giles, H. (ed.) (1977) *Language, Ethnicity and Intergroup Relations,* London: Academic Press.

Givón, T. (1971) Historical syntax and synchronic morphology, an archaeologist's field trip, *Paper from the Seventh Regional Meeting.* Chicago Linguistics Society.

— (1975) Promotion, NP accessibility and case marking, toward understanding grammars, *Working Papers on Language Universals* 19, 55-125.

— (1976) Topic, pronoun and grammatical agreement. In Li, C. (ed.), *Subject and Topic,* New York: Academic Press.

— (1979a) From discourse to syntax: grammar as a processing strategy. In Givón, T. (ed.), *Discourse and Syntax, Syntax and Semantics,* vol.12, New York: Academic Press.

— (1979b) *On Understanding Grammar,* New York: Academic Press.

— (1981) Typology and functional domains, *Studies in Language* 5.2.

— (1982) Tense-aspect-modality: the creole prototype and beyond. In Hopper, P. (ed.), *Tense and Aspect: Between Semantics and Pragmatics, Typological Studies in Language,* vol.1, Amsterdam: John Benjamins.

— (1983) Topic continuity in discourse. An introduction. In Givón, T. (ed.), *Topic Continuity in Discourse: A Quantitative Cross-Language Study,* Amsterdam/ Philadelphia: John Benjamins Publishing Company, 1-41.

— (forthcoming) Function, structure and language acquisition. In Slobin, D. (ed.), *Cross Linguistic Studies of Language Acquisition,* Hillsdale, NJ: Lawrence Erlbaum Associates.

— (in press) Universals of discourse structure and second language acquisition. In Rutherford, W. (ed.) (forthcoming).

Glahn, E. (1980) Introspection as a method of elicitation in interlanguage studies, *Interlanguage Studies Bulletin Utrecht* 5, 119-28.

Goffman, E. (1976) Replies and responses, *Language in Society* 5, 254-313.

Gough, J. (1975) Comparative studies in second language learning, *CAL/ERIC Series on Language and Linguistics,* No.26.

Gransfors, T. and Palmberg, R. (1976) Errors made by Finns and Swedish-speaking Finns learning English at a commercial college level. In Ringbom, H. and Palmberg, R. (eds), *Errors Made by Finns and Swedish-speaking Finns in the Learning of English,* AFTIL, vol.5, Åbo, Finland.

Grant, N. J. H., Olagoke, D. O. and Southern, K. R. (1976) *Secondary English Project,* London: Longmans.

Greenberg, J. H. (1966) Some universals of grammar with particular reference to the order of meaningful elements. In Greenberg, J. H. (ed.), *Universals of Language,* Cambridge, Mass.: MIT Press.

— (1968) *Anthropological Linguistics: An Introduction,* New York: Random House.

References

Greenberg, J. H., Ferguson, C. and Moravcsik, E. (eds) (1978) *Universals of Human Language, 4, Syntax,* Stanford: Stanford University Press.

Gregg, K. (1984) Krashen's monitor and Occam's razor, *Applied Linguistics* 5.2, 79-100.

Grice, H. (1975) Logic and Conversation. In Cole, P. and Morgan, J. (eds) (1975), *Syntax and Semantics,* vol.3, *Speech Acts,* New York: Academic Press.

Grosu, A. and Thompson, S. (1977) Constraints on the distribution of NP clauses, *Language* 53, 104-51.

Gundel, J. (1978a) Stress, pronominalisation and the given-new distinction, *University of Hawaii Working Papers in Linguistics* 10, 1-13.

— (1979b) A universal constraint on deletion. In Dressler, W. and Meid, S. (eds), *Proceedings of the Twelfth Internation Congress of Linguists.* Innsbrucker Beitrage zur Sprachwissenschaft.

— (1980) Zero NP-anaphora in Russian, a case of topic prominence, *Papers from the Parasession on Pronouns and Anaphora,* Chicago: Chicago Linguistics Society.

Gundel, J. and Tarone, E. (1983) Language transfer and the acquisition of pro-nominal anaphora. In Gass, S. and Selinker, L. (eds) (1983).

Haastrup, K. and Phillipson, R. (1983) Achievement strategies in learner/native speaker interaction. In Faerch, C. and Kasper, G. (eds) (1983d).

Hahn, A. (1982) Spracherwerb und Fremdsprachenunterricht. Doctoral dissertation, Passau University.

Haiman, J. (1980) The iconicity of grammar, *Language* 56, 515-40.

Hakuta, K. (1974a) A preliminary report on the development of grammatical morphemes in a Japanese girl learning English as a second language, *Working Papers in Bilingualism* 3, Toronto, Ontario Institute for Studies in Education, pp.13-43.

— (1974b) Prefabricated patterns and the emergence of structure in second language learning, *Language Learning* 24, 287-97.

— (1976) A case study of a Japanese child learning English as a second language, *Language Learning* 26, 321-51.

— (1981) Some common goals for second and first language acquisition research. In Andersen, R. W. (ed.) (1981).

Hall, R. A. (1943) *Melanesian Pidgin English: Grammar, Texts, Vocabulary,* Baltimore: Linguistic Society of America.

Halliday, M. A. K. and Hassan, R. (1976) *Cohesion in English,* London: The Longman Group Ltd.

Hamayan, E. V. and Tucker, G. R. (1980) Language input in the bilingual classroom and its relationship to second language achievement, *TESOL Quarterly,* vol.14, no.4, December, 453-68.

Hammarberg, B. (1979) On intralingual, interlingual and developmental solutions in interlanguage. In Hyltensham, K. and Linnarud, M. (eds), *Interlanguage,* Stockholm: Almqvist and Wiksell.

Hammarberg, B. and Viberg, A. (1977) The place-holder constraint, language typology and the teaching of Swedish to immigrants, *Studia Linguistica* 31, 106-63.

Harbert, W. (1977) C.e union and German accusative plus infinitive constructions. In Cole, P. and Sadock, J. (eds), *Syntax and Semantics, Vol.8: Grammatical Relations,* 121-49, New York: Academic Press.

Harley, B. (1979) French gender 'rules' in the speech of English-dominant, French-dominant and monolingual French-speaking children, *Working Papers on Bilingualism* 19, 129-56.

— (1982) Age-related differences in the acquisition of the French verb system by anglophone students in French immersion programmes. Unpublished Ph.D. thesis, University of Toronto.

— (forthcoming) Transfer in the written compositions of French immersion students. In Dechert, H. W. and Raupach, M. (eds) (forthcoming).

Harley, B. and Swain, M. (1977) An analysis of verb form and function in the speech of French immersion pupils, *Working Papers on Bilingualism* 14, 31-46.

— (1978) An analysis of the verb system used by young learners of French, *Interlanguage Studies Bulletin* 3, 35-79.

Harley, B. and Ullmann, R. (1983) Focussing language input in the communicative L2 classroom. A research proposal submitted to the Ontario Institute for Studies in Education (mimeo).

Hatch, E. M. (1978a) Discourse analysis and second language acquisition. In Hatch, E. M. (ed.) (1978b).

— (ed.) (1978b) *Second Language Acqusition: A Book of Readings,* Rowley, Mass.: Newbury House Publishers.

— (1983) *Psycholinguistics: A Second Language Perspective,* Rowley, Mass.: Newbury House Publishers.

Hatch, E. M. and Farhady, H. (1982) *Research Design and Statistics for Applied Linguistics,* Rowley, Mass.: Newbury House.

Hatch, E. M. and Wagner-Gough, J. (1976) *Explaining Sequence and Variation in Second Language Acquisition,* Ann Arbor: University of Michigan.

Hatch, E. M., Shapira, R. and Gough, J. (1978) Foreigner talk discourse, *IRAL* 39/40, 39-60.

Hawkins, B. (1983) Is an 'appropriate response' always appropriate? Paper presented at 10th Conference on Applied Linguistics – Input in Second Language Acquisition, Ann Arbor, Michigan.

Hawkins, J. (1980) On implicational and distributional universals of word order, *Journal of Linguistics* 16, 193-235.

— (1981) The semantic diversity of basic grammatical relations in English and German, *Linguistische Berichte* 75, 1-25.

— (1982) Cross-category harmony, X-bar and the predictions of markedness, *Journal of Linguistics* 18, 1-35.

— (1983) *Word Order Universals,* New York: Academic Press.

Hawkinson, A. and Hyman, L. (1974) Hierarchies of natural topic in Shona, *Studies in African Linguistics* 5, 147-70.

Hebb, D. O., Lambert, W. E. and Tucker, G. R. (1971) Language thought and experience, *Modern Language Journal* 60, 212-22.

Heidelberger Forschungsprojekt 'Pidgin-Deutsch': Arbeitsberichte III, IV, V. Universitat Heidelberg (1976-9).

Hinds, J. (1982) Contrastive rhetoric: Japanese and English. Paper presented at TESOL, Honolulu, Hawaii.

Hodge, C. (1970) The diachronic cycle, *Language Sciences* 13, 1-7.

Hoekstra, T., van der Hulst, H. and Moortgat, M. (1980) *Lexical Grammar,* Dordrecht: Foris.

Hoffmann, A. and Rudeloff, B. (1982) Negation in Pidgin- und Kreolsprachen, mimeo, Kiel University.

Hopper, P. (1979) Aspect and foregrounding in discourse. In Givón, T. (ed.), *Discourse and Syntax, Syntax and Semantics,* vol.12, New York: Academic Press.

Hopper, P. and Thompson, S. (1980) Transitivity in grammar and discourse, *Language* 56, 251-99.

Hornstein, N. and Lightfoot, D. (eds) (1981) *Explanation in Linguistics,* London: Longmans.

References

Hottel-Burkhart, G. (1983) Native-language writing ability, cohesive features, and ESL proficiency. Unpublished MS, Texas A and M University. (See also Ph.D. dissertation, University of Texas, 1981.)

Huang, J. (1971) A Chinese child's acquisition of English syntax. Master's thesis, University of California at Los Angeles.

Huang, J. and Hatch, E. M. (1978) A Chinese child's acquisition of English. In Hatch, E. M. (ed.) (1978b).

Hudson, R. A. (1981) Some issues on which linguists can agree, *Journal of Linguistics* 17.2, 333-43.

Huebner, T. (1979) Order of acquisition vs. dynamic paradigm: a comparison of methods in interlanguage research, *TESOL Quarterly* 13, 21-8.

— (1983) *A Longitudinal Analysis of the Acquisition of English*, Ann Arbor: Karoma Press.

— (forthcoming) Linguistic system and linguistic change in an interlanguage, *Studies in Second Language Acquisition*.

Hughes, A. (1979) Aspects of a Spanish adult's acquisition of English, *Interlanguage Studies Bulletin* 4, 49-65.

Huttenlocher, J. (1974) The origins of language comprehension. In Solso, R. L. (ed.), *Theories of Cognitive Psychology: The Loyola Symposium*, Potomac, MD: Erlbaum Associates.

Hyams, N. M. (1983) The acquisition of parametrited grammar. Dissertation, City University of New York.

Hyltenstam, K. (1977) Implicational patterns in interlanguage syntax variation, *Language Learning* 27.2, 383-411.

— (1978a) A framework for the study of interlanguage continua. Working Papers No. 18, Department of Linguistics, University of Lund.

— (1978b) Variation in interlanguage syntax. Working Papers, Phonetics Laboratory, Department of General Linguistics, Lund University.

— (1982) Language typology, language universals, markedness, and second language acquisition. Paper presented at 2nd European-North American Workshop on Cross-linguistic Second Language Acquisition Research, Görhde, W. Germany, 22nd-29th August.

— (1983a) Teacher talk in Swedish as a second language classrooms. Quantitative aspects and markedness conditions. In Felix, S. W. and Wode, H. (eds), *Language Development at the Crossroads*. Papers from the Interdisciplinary Conference on Language Acquisition at Passau, Tübingen: Gunther Narr.

— (1983b) Data types and second language variability. In Ringbom, H. (ed.) (1983).

— (in press) The use of typological markedness conditions as predictors in second language acquisition, the case of pronominal copies in relative clauses. In Andersen, R. W. (ed.), *Second Language: A Cross-linguistic Perspective*, Rowley, Mass.: Newbury House.

Hymes, D. (1967) Models of the interaction of language and social setting, *Journal of Social Issues* 23.2, 8-28.

Ioup, G. and Kruse, A. (1977a) Interference versus structural complexity as a predictor of second language relative clause acquisition. In Henning, C. (ed.), *Proceedings of the Second Language Research Forum*, Los Angeles.

— (1977b) Interference vs. structural complexity in second language acquisition: language universals as a basis for natural sequencing. In Brown, H. D., Yorio, C. and Crymes, R. (eds), *Teaching and Learning English as a Second Language: Trends in Research and Practice*, Washington: TESOL.

Ireland, D. (1981) The implications of teaching behavior for language practice. Paper presented at the OMLTA Conference, Kingston, Ontario, 1981.

References

Issatchenko, A. (1974) On Be-languages and Have-languages. In Heilmann, L. (ed.), *Proceedings of the 11th International Congress of Linguistics*, 71-2, Bologna: Il Mulino.

Itoh, H. (1973) A Japanese child's acquisition of two languages. MA-TESL thesis, University of California at Los Angeles.

Jackson, H. (1981) Contrastive analysis as a predictor of errors with reference to Punjabi learners of English. In Fisiak, J. (ed.), *Contrastive Linguistics and the Language Teacher*, Oxford: Pergamon Press.

Jakobson, R. (1971) Zur Struktur des russischen Verbums, Selected Writings, The Hague: Mouton, 3-15.

James, C. (1980) *Contrastive Analysis*, Harlow: Longman.

James, J. (1980) Learner variation: the monitor model and language learning strategies, *Interlanguage Studies Bulletin* 5.2, 99-111.

Jansen, B., Lalleman, J. and Muysken, P. (1981) The alternation hypothesis: acquisition of Dutch word order by Turkish and Moroccan foreign workers, *Language Learning* 31, 315-36.

Jeffers, R. and Lehiste, I. (1979) *Principles and Methods for Historical Linguistics*, Cambridge: MIT Press.

Jespersen, O. (1917) *Negation in English and Other Languages*, Copenhagen: Andr. Fred. Host & Son.

Jisa, H. and Scarcella, R. (1981) Discourse markers in adult second language performance. Paper presented at CATESOL conference.

Johansson, S. (1978) Studies in error gravity. Native reactions to errors produced by Swedish learners of English, *Gothenburg Studies in English* 44.

Johns, A. M. (1979) Cohesive error in the written discourse of non-native speakers. Paper presented at TESOL, Boston.

Johnson, K. (1982) *Communicative Syllabus Design and Methodology*, Oxford: Pergamon Press.

Jordens, P. (1977) Rules, grammatical intuitions and strategies in foreign language learning, *Interlanguage Studies Bulletin Utrecht* 2/2, 5-76.

— (1983a) Discourse functions in interlanguage morphology. In Gass and Selinker (eds) (1983).

— (1983b) *Das Deutsche Kasussystem im Fremdspracherwerb*, Tübingen: Gunter Narr Verlag.

— (forthcoming) The cognitive function of case marking in German as a native and a foreign language. In Kellerman, E. and Sharwood Smith, M. (eds) (forthcoming).

Kadar-Haffmann, G. (1977) Der Erwerb der Negation bei einem dreisprachigen Kind. In Hartig, M. and Wode, H. (eds) (1978), *Kongressberichte der 8. Jahrestagung der Gesellschaft für angewandte Linguistik*, GAL e.V. Mainz, 1977, vol.4, Stuttgart: Hoehschul Verlag, 47-53.

Karmiloff-Smith, A. (1984) Children's problem solving. In Lamb, M., Brown, A. and Rogoff, B. (eds), *Advances in Developmental Psychology*, Vol.III, Hillsdale, NJ: Erlbaum.

Kasper, G. (1981) *Pragmatische Aspekte in der Interimsprache*, Tübingen: Gunter Narr.

— (forthcoming) Pragmatic comprehension in learner-native speaker discourse. To appear in *Language Learning* 35.

— (ed.) (in press a) *Learning, Teaching and Communication in the Foreign Language Classroom*, Aarhus: Arkona.

— (in press b) Repair in foreign language teaching. In Kasper, G. (in press a).

Katz, J. and Postal, P. (1974) *An Integrated Theory of Linguistic Descriptions*, Cambridge, Mass.: MIT Press.

References

Kayne, R. (1983) Connectedness, *Linguistic Inquiry* 14, 223-50.

Keenan, E. (1975) Variation in universal grammar. In Fasold, R. and Shuy, R. (eds), *Analysing Variation in Language*, Washington, DC: Georgetown University Press.

— (1976) Towards a universal definition of 'subject'. In Li, C. (ed.), *Subject and Topic*, New York: Academic Press.

— (1978a) The syntax of subject-final languages. In Lehmann, W. (ed.), *Syntactic Typology*, Austin: University of Texas Press, 267-327.

— (1978b) Language variation and the logical structure of universal grammar. In Seiler, H. J. (ed.), *Language Universals*, 89-123, Tübingen: Gunter Narr.

— (1979) On surface form and logical form, *Studies in the Linguistic Sciences*, Special Issue, vol.8, no.2, 163-204.

Keenan, E. and Bimson, K. (1975) Perceptual complexity and the cross-language distribution of relative clauses and NP-question types, *Papers from the Parasession on Functionalism*, Chicago: Chicago Linguistics Society.

Keenan, E. and Comrie, B. (1977) Noun phrase accessibility and universal grammar, *Linguistic Inquiry* 8, 63-99.

Keller-Cohen, D. (1979) Systematicity and variation in the non-native child's acquisition of conversational skills, *Language Learning* 29, 27-44.

Kellerman, E. (1974) Elicitation, lateralisation and error analysis, *York Papers in Linguistics* 4, 165-89. Reprinted in *Interlanguage Studies Bulletin* 1.176, 79-116.

— (1975) Review of J. Richards (ed.) 'Error Analysis', *Dutch Quarterly Review* 5, 319-24.

— (1977) Towards a characterisation of the strategy of transfer in second language learning, *Interlanguage Studies Bulletin* 2, 58-145.

— (1978a) Giving learners a break: native language intuitions as a source of predictions about transferability, *Working Papers on Bilingualism* 15, 59-92.

— (1978b) Transfer and non-transfer, where are we now, *Studies in Second Language Acquisition* 2, 37-57.

— (1979) The problem with difficulty, *Interlanguage Studies Bulletin* 4, 27-48.

— (1980) Oeil pour oeil, *Encrages*, Presses Universitaires de Vincennes, Paris.

— (1983a) If at first you do succeed . . . Paper presented at the Xth University of Michigan Conference on Applied Linguistics, Ann Arbor. In Gass, S. and Selinker, L. (eds) (1983).

— (1983b) Now you see it, now you don't. In Gass, S. and Selinker, L. (eds) (1983).

Kellerman, E. and Sharwood Smith, M. (eds) (forthcoming a) *Cross-linguistic Influence in Second Language Acquisition*, Oxford: Pergamon Press.

— (forthcoming b) The interpretation of second language output. In Dechert, H. C. and Raupach, M. (eds) (forthcoming).

Kellerman, E. and Wekker, H. (1982) On the acquisition of conditional syntax by Dutch learners of English. Paper given at the International Conference of Contrastive Projects, Jyväskylä, June.

Kelz, H. (1971) *Phonologische Analyse des Pennsylvaniadeutschen*, Hamburg: Helmut Buste.

Kerkman, H. (1981) The organisation of the lexicon in bilingual subjects. Paper presented at the AILA congress in Lund, 1981.

Kerlinger, F. N. (1977) The influence of research on education practice, *Educational Research* 6, 5-12.

Kielhoefer, B. (1975) *Fehlerlinguistik des Fremdsprachenerwerbs*, Kronberg, Germany: Scriptor.

Kirkwood, H. (1969) Aspects of word order and its communicative function in English and German, *Journal of Linguistics* 5, 85-107.

Klein, W. (1981a) Knowing a language and knowing how to communicate. In Vermeer, A. R. (ed.), *Language Problems of Minority Groups*, Tilburg.

References

— (1981b) Réponse à Felix et Simmet, *Encrages*, Presses Universitaires de Vincennes, Paris.

Klein, W. and Dittmar, N. (1979) *Developing Grammars*, Berlin: Springer.

Kleinmann, H. (1977) Avoidance behavior in adult second language acquisition, *Language Learning* 27.1, 93-108.

— (1978) The strategy of avoidance in adult second language acquisition. In Ritchie, W. (ed.) (1978).

Klima, E. and Bellugi, U. (1971) Syntactic regularities in the speech of children. In Bar-Adon, A. and Leopold, W. (eds) (1971).

Knapp-Potthoff, A. and Knapp, K. (1982) *Fremdsprachenlernen und -lehren*, Stuttgart: Kohlhammer.

Kohrt, M. (1976) *Koordinationsreduktion und Verbstellung in einer generativen Grammatik des Deutschen*, Tübingen: Niemeyer.

Koster, J. 1975) Dutch as an s o v language. *Linguistic Analysis* 1, 111ff.

— (1978a) *Locality Principles in Syntax*, Dordrecht: Foris.

— (1978b) Conditions, empty nodes and markedness, *Linguistic Inquiry* 9, 551-93.

Krashen, S. D. (1976) Formal and informal linguistic environments in language acquisition and language learning, *TESOL Quarterly* 10, 157-68.

— (1977) Some issues relating to the Monitor Model. In Brown, H. D. et al. (eds) (1977).

— (1978a) The monitor model for second language acquisition. In Gingras, R. C. (ed.) (1978), *Second Language Acquisition and Foreign Language Teaching*, Arlington, Va.: Center for Applied Linguistics.

— (1978b) Individual variation in the use of the monitor. In Ritchie, W. C. (ed.) (1978).

— (1980) The input hypothesis. In Alatis, J. (ed.), *Current Issues in Bilingual Education*, Washington, D C: Georgetown University Press.

— (1981) *Second Language Acquisition and Second Language Learning*, Oxford: Pergamon Press.

— (1982) *Principles and Practice in Second Language Acquisition*, Oxford: Pergamon Press.

Krashen, S. D. and Seliger, H. W. (1975) The essential contribution of formal instruction in adult second language learning, *TESOL Quarterly* 9/2 June, 173-81.

Krashen, S. D. and Terrell, T. D. (1983) *The Natural Approach*, Oxford: Pergamon Press.

Krashen, S. D., Ferlazza, V. S., Feldman, L. and Fathman, A. (1976) Adult performance on the S L O P E test: more evidence for a natural sequence in adult second language acquisition, *Language Learning*, vol.26, no.1, 145-51.

Krashen, S. D., Houck, N., Giunchi, P., Bode, S., Birnbaum, R. and Strei, G. (1977) Difficulty order for grammatical morphemes for adult second language performers using free speech, *TESOL Quarterly* 11.3, 338-41.

Kumpf, L. (1981) An approach to tense/aspect/modality in the analysis of inter-language. M S, University of California at Los Angeles.

— (1982) An analysis of tense, aspect and modality in interlanguage. Paper presented at T E S O L, Honolulu.

— (1983) A case study of temporal reference in interlanguage. In Campbell, C. et al. (eds), *Proceedings of the Los Angeles Second Language Research Forum*, Los Angeles: University of California.

Kuno, S. (1974) The position of relative clauses and conjunctions. *Linguistic Inquiry* 5, 117-36.

Labov, W. (1963) The social motivation of a sound change, *Word* 19, 273-309.

References

— (1966) The social stratification of English in New York City, *Urban Language Series 1,* Washington, DC: Center for Applied Linguistics.

— (1969) Contraction, deletion, and inherent variability of the English copula, *Language* 45, 715-492.

— (1972) *Sociolinguistic Patterns,* Philadelphia: University of Pennsylvania Press.

Labov, W., Cohen, P., Robins, C. and Lewis, J. (1968) *A Study of the Non-standard English of Negro and Puerto Rican Speakers in New York City,* vol.I: Phonological and grammatical analysis (Cooperative Research Project 3288), New York: Columbia University.

Lado, R. (1957) *Linguistics Across Cultures. Applied linguistics for language teachers,* Ann Arbor: University of Michigan Press.

Lakoff, G. (1970) *Irregularity in Syntax,* New York, NY: Holt, Rinehart and Winston.

Lamendella, J. (1977) General principles of neurofunctional organisation and their manifestations in primary and non-primary language acquisition, *Language Learning* 27, 155-96.

Lamotte, J., Pearson-Joseph, D. and Zupko, K. (1982) A cross-linguistic study of the relationships between negation stages and the acquisition of noun phrase morphology. Term paper, Ed. 676, Philadelphia, University of Pennsylvania.

Lange, S. and Larsson, K. (1973) Syntactical development of a Swedish girl Embla, between 20 and 42 months of age, part I: Age 20-25 months, Stockholm: Stockholms Univ. Inst. för nordiska språk.

Larsen-Freeman, D. (1975a) The acquisition of grammatical morphemes by adult ESL students, *TESOL Quarterly,* vol.9, no.4, 409-19.

— (1975b) The acquisition of grammatical morphemes by adult learners of English. Unpublished doctoral dissertation, University of Michigan, Ann Arbor.

— (1976) ESL Teacher speech as input to the ESL learner, *UCLA Workpapers in TESOL,* vol.10, 45-9.

— (1978) An explanation for the morpheme accuracy order of learners of English as a second language.

— (ed.) (1980) *Discourse Analysis in Second Language Research,* Rowley, Mass.: Newbury House.

Larsen-Freeman, D. and Long, M. H. (forthcoming) *An Introduction to Second Language Acquisition,* Rowley, Mass.: Newbury House.

Lauerbach, G. (1982) Face-work in Reparaturen – ein Charakteristikum von Lerner/ Native Speaker-Diskursen, *LAUT Paper,* no.81, Series B, Trier: University of Trier.

Lavandera, B. (1975) Linguistic structure and sociolinguistic conditioning in the use of verbal tenses in S1-clauses (Buenos Aires Spanish). Unpublished Ph.D. dissertation, Pennsylvania.

Lehmann, C. (1982) On some current views of the language universal. In Dirven, R. and Radden, G. (eds), *Issues in the Theory of Universal Grammar,* 75-94, Tübingen: Gunter Narr.

Lehmann, W. (1973) A structural principle of language and its implications, *Language* 49, 47-66.

Lenerz, J. (1977) *Zur Abfolge nominaler Satzglieder im Deutschen,* Tübingen: Gunther Narr.

Lenneberg, E. H. (1967) *Biological Foundations of Language,* New York: John Wiley & Sons.

— (1969) On explaining language, *Science* 164, 634-43.

Lepicq, D. (1980) Aspects théoriques et empiriques de l'acceptabilité linguistique: Le cas du français des éléves des classes d'immersion. Unpublished Ph.D. thesis, University of Toronto.

Lesgold, A. M. and Perfetti, C. A. (eds) (1981) *Interactive Processes in Reading,*

References

Hillsdale, NJ: Lawrence Erlbaum Associates

Levenston, E. (1971) Overindulgence and underrepresentation aspects of mother tongue interference. In Nickel, G. (ed.), *Papers in Contrastive Linguistics,* Cambridge: Cambridge University Press.

— (1979) Second language vocabulary acquisition: issues and problems, *The Interlanguage Studies Bulletin* 4.2, 147-60.

Levenston, E. and Blum, S. (1977) Aspects of lexical simplification in the speech and writing of advanced adult learners. In Corder, S. P. and Roulet, E. (eds), *Actes du 5éme Colloque de Linguistique Appliquée de Neuchâtel,* Geneva: Droz.

— (1978) Discourse completion as a technique for studying lexical features of interlanguage, *Working Papers in Bilingualism* 15, 2-13.

Li, C. and Thompson, S. (1976) Subject and topic: a new typology of language. In Li, C. (ed.), *Subject and Topic,* New York: Academic Press.

Liceras, J. (1983) Markedness, contrastive analysis and the acquisition of Spanish syntax by English speakers. Unpublished Ph.D. thesis, Toronto.

Lightbown, P. M. (1978) Question form and question function in the speech of young French L2 learners. In Paradis, M. (ed.), *Aspects of Bilingualism,* Columbia, SC: Hornbeam Press, Inc.

— (1980) The acquisition and use of questions by French L2 learners. In Felix, S. W. (ed.) (1980).

— (1983a) Acquiring English L2 in Quebec classrooms. In Felix, S. W. and Wode, H. (eds), *Language Development at the Crossroads. Papers from the Interdisciplinary Conference on Language Acquisition at Passau,* Tübingen: Gunter Narr Verlag.

— (1983b) Exploring relationships between developmental and instructional sequences in L2 acquisition. In Seliger, H. W. and Long, M. H. (eds) (1983), 217-45.

Lightbown, P. M., Spada, N. and Wallace, R. (1980) Some effects of instruction on child and adolescent ESL learners. In Scarcella, R. C. and Krashen, S. D. (eds) (1980).

Lightfoot, D. (1979) *Principles of Diachronic Syntax,* Cambridge: Cambridge University Press.

— (1982) *The Language Lottery: Towards a Biology of Grammars,* Cambridge, Mass.: MIT Press.

LoCoco, V. (1975) An analysis of Spanish and German learners' errors, *Working Papers on Bilingualism* 7, 96-124.

Long, M. H. (1975) Group work and communicative competence in the ESOL classroom. In Burt, M. K. and Dulay, H. C. (eds) (1975).

— (1981) Input interaction and second language acquisition. In Winitz, H. (ed.), *Native Language and Foreign Language Acquisition,* Annals of the New York Academy of Sciences, vol.379, 259-78.

— (1983a) Does second language instruction make a difference? *TESOL Quarterly* 17/3 September, 359-82.

— (1983b) Linguistic and conversational adjustments to non-native speakers, *Studies in Second Language Acquisition* 6.2, 177-93.

— (in press) Input and second language acquisition theory. In Gass, S. and Madden, C. (eds) (in press), *Input and Second Language Acquisition,* Rowley, Mass.: Newbury House.

Long, M. H. and Sato, C. J. (1983) Classroom foreigner talk discourse: forms and functions of teachers' questions. In Seliger, H. W. and Long, M. H. (eds) (1983), 268-86.

Ludwig, J. (1977) Vocabulary acquisition and use by learners of French. Ph.D. thesis, University of Michigan.

References

Lynch, B. K. (1983a) Fossilisation? Who knows? Paper for Psycholinguistics seminar, UCLA.

— (1983b) A discourse-functional analysis of interlanguage. In Campbell, C. et al. (eds), *Proceedings of the Los Angeles Second Language Research Forum*, Los Angeles: University of California.

Maccoun, W. (1980) On the acquisition of argumentative discourse from a comprehension point of view. M.A. thesis, UCLA.

Mace-Matluck, B. J. (1979) The order of acquisition of English structures by Spanish-speaking children: some possible determinants. In Andersen, R. W. (ed.). (1979c).

Macnamara, J. (1972) The cognitive basis of language learning in infants, *Psychological Review* 79, 1-13.

Mafeni, B. (1971) Nigerian Pidgin. In Spencer, J. (ed.), *The English Language in West Africa*, London: Longman.

Makino, T. (1979) English morphemes acquisition order of Japanese secondary school students, *TESOL Quarterly*, vol.13, no.3, September, 428.

Maling, J. (1972) On 'gapping and the order of constituents', *Linguistic Inquiry* 3, 101-8.

Mallinson, G. and Blake, B. (1981) *Language Typology*, Amsterdam: North Holland.

Marantz, A. (1982) On the acquisition of grammatical relations, *Linguistische Berichte* 80, 32-69.

Martin, A. V. (1980) First language differences in processing spatial, chronological and hierarchical information. Unpublished Ph.D. dissertation, University of Southern California.

Masny, D. (1983) Cognitive and linguistic correlates of second language grammaticality judgements. Doctoral thesis, Université de Montreal.

Mazurkewich, I. (1980) Second language acquisition of the dative alternation and markedness: the best theory. Dissertation, University of Montreal.

— (1984) The acquisition of dative alternation by second language learners and linguistic theory, *Language Learning*, in press.

— (forthcoming) Dative questions and markedness. In Eckman, F., Bell, L. and Nelson, D. (eds), *Universals of Second Language Acquisition*, Rowley, Mass.: Newbury House.

McDonough, S. H. (1981) *Psychology in Foreign Language Teaching*, London: George Allen and Unwin.

McLaughlin, B. (1978a) *Second Language Acquisition in Childhood*, Hillsdale, NJ: Erlbaum.

— (1978b) The monitor model: some methodological considerations, *Language Learning* 28.2, 309-32.

— (1980) Theory and research in second language learning: an emerging paradigm, *Language Learning* 30, 331-50.

McNeill, D. (1970) *The Acquisition of Language: The Study of Developmental Psycholinguistics*, New York: Harper & Row.

— (1979) *The Conceptual Basis of Language*, Hillsdale, NJ: Erlbaum.

Meara, P. (1980) Vocabulary acquisition: a neglected aspect of language learning, *Language Teaching and Linguistics: Abstracts* 13.4, 221-46.

— (1983a) *Vocabulary in a Second Language*, London Centre for Information on Language Teaching and Research.

— (1983b) Psycholinguistics and language learning: some reservations. In Ringbom, H. (ed.) (1983), 126-32.

Meisel, J. (1980) Strategies of second language acquisition: more than one kind of simplification. In Andersen, R. W. (ed.)(1983d).

References

— (1982) The role of transfer as a strategy in natural second language acquisition / processing, mimeo. Hamburg University.

— (1982) Reference to past events and actions in the development of natural second language acquisition. Paper presented at the 2nd European-North American Cross-linguistic Second Language Acquisition Workshop, Görhde, West Germany, 22nd-29th August.

— (1983a) Transfer as a second-language strategy, *Language and Communication* 3, 11-46.

— (1983b) Strategies of second language acquisition. More than one kind of simplification. In Andersen, R. W. (ed.) (1983d), 120-57.

Meisel, J., Clahsen, H. and Pienemann, M. (1981) On determining developmental stages in natural second language acquisition, *Studies in Second Language Acquisition* 3.2, 109-35.

Meyer-Ingwersen, J. et al. (1977) *Zur Sprachentwicklung tuerkischer Schueler in der Bundesrepublik*, 2 vols, Kronberg, Germany: Scriptor.

Miller, W. and Ervin, S. (1964) The development of grammar in child language. In Bellugi, U. and Brown, R. (eds) (1964).

Milne, A. A. (1926) *Winnie-the-Pooh*, London: Methuen.

Milon, J. (1974) The development of negation in English by a second language learner, *TESOL Quarterly* 8, 137-43.

Möhle, D. and Raupach, M. (1983) *Planen in der Fremdsprache*, Frankfurt: Peter Lang.

Moravcsik, J. (1978) On the distribution of ergative and accusative patterns, *Lingua* 45, 233-79.

Morolong, M. and Hyman, L. (1977) Animacy, objects, and clitics in Sesotho, *Studies in African Linguistics* 8, 199-217.

Munby, J. (1978) *Communicative Syllabus Design*, Cambridge: Cambridge University Press.

Myint Su (1971) The analysis of lexical errors. M.Litt. thesis, Edinburgh University.

Naiman, N., Frohlich, M., Stern, H. H. and Todesco, A. (1978) *The Good Language Learner*, Toronto: Ontario Institute for Studies in Education.

Nemser, W. (1971) Approximate systems of foreign language learners, *IRAL* 9.2, 115-23.

Neufeld, G. (1979) Vers une théorie de la capacité d'apprentissage linguistique, *Encrages*, Presses universitaires de Vincennes.

Nicholas, H. and Meisel, J. (1983) Second language acquisition: the state of the art. In Felix, S. and Wode, H. (eds), *Language Development at the Crossroads*, Tübingen: Gunter Narr Verlag.

Nixon, J. (1981) *A Teacher's Guide to Action Research*, Grant McIntyre.

Obanya, P. (1974) Lexical and structural error in the written French of Nigerian pupils, *Audio-Visual Language Journal* 12, 29-32.

Obler, L. K. (1977) Right hemisphere participation in second language acquisition. In Diller, K. (ed.), *Individual Differences and Universals in Language Learning Aptitude*, Rowley, Mass.: Newbury House.

Obler, L. K. and Menn, L. (eds) (1982) *Exceptional Language and Linguistics*, New York: Academic Press.

Ochs, E., Schieffelin, B. and Platt, M. (1979) Propositions across utterances and speakers. In Ochs, E. and Schieffelin, B. (eds), *Developmental Pragmatics*, New York: Academic Press.

Ochsner, R. (1979) A poetics of second language acquisition, *Language Learning* 29, 53-80.

Oller, J. and Redding, E. (1971) Article usage and other language skills, *Language Learning* 22, 85-95.

References

Olshtain, E. (1979) The acquisition of English progressive: a case study of a seven-year-old Hebrew speaker, *Working Papers on Bilingualism* 18, 81-102.

Omar, M. (1973) *The Acquisition of Egyptian Arabic as a Native Language,* Den Haag: Mouton.

Orestrom, B. (1983) *Turn-taking in English Conversation,* Lund: Gleerup.

Ostler, S. and Kaplan, R. (1982) Contrastive rhetoric revisited. Paper presented at TESOL, Honolulu, Hawaii.

Painchaud, G., D'Anglejan, A. and Vincent, D. (1982) Acquisition du français par un groupe d'immigrants asiatiques. Université de Montreal, Rapport de Recherche, Faculté des Sciences de l'Education.

Palmberg, R. (1979) Investigating communication strategies. In Palmberg, R. (ed.), *Perception and Production of English: Papers on Interlanguage,* Åbo: Åbo Akademi.

— (1982) On the use of lexical avoidance strategies in foreign-language communication. Paper read at the 18th International Conference on Polish-English Contrastive Linguistics, Blazejewko, 2-4 December 1982.

Paribakht, T. (1983) The relationship between the use of communication strategies and aspects of target language proficiency: a study of Persian ESL students. Unpublished Ph.D. thesis, University of Toronto.

Park, T. (1974) A study of German language development. MS, Universität Bern.

Peck, S. (1978) Child-child discourse in second language acquisition. In Hatch, E. (ed.) (1978b).

Peters, A. (1980) The units of acquisition, *University of Hawaii Working Papers in Linguistics* 21.1, 1-72.

— (1983) *The Units of Language Acquisition,* Cambridge: Cambridge University Press.

Pfaff, C. (1982) Functional approaches to interlanguage. Paper presented at the Second European-North American Workshop on Cross-Linguistic Second Language Acquisition Research, Jagdschloss Görhde, West Germany, 22nd-28th August.

Piaget, J. (1954) *The Construction of Reality in the Child,* New York: Ballantine Books.

Piatelli-Palmarini, M. (ed.) (1980) *Language and Learning: The Debate between Jean Piaget and Noam Chomsky,* London: Routledge and Kegan-Paul.

Pica, T. (1983) Adult acquisition of English as a second language under different conditions of exposure, *Language Learning,* vol.33/4, 465-97.

— (1984) Methods of measuring overall morpheme production accuracy: suppliance in obligatory contexts vs. target-like use analyses. Paper presented at the 18th Annual TESOL Conference, Houston, Texas, 6th-11th March.

Pickett, G. D. (1978) *The Foreign Language Learning Process,* London: The British Council.

Pienemann, M. (1980) The second language acquisition of immigrant children. In Felix, S. W. (ed.) (1980).

— (1982) Psychological constraints on the teachability of languages. Paper presented at the Second European-North American Workshop on Cross-linguistic Second Language Acquisition Research, Göhrde, West Germany.

Pimsleur, P. and Quinn, T. (eds) (1971) *The Psychology of Second Language Learning,* Cambridge: Cambridge University Press.

Plann, S. (1979) Morphological problems in the acquisition of Spanish in an immersion classroom. In Andersen, R. W. (ed.), *The Acquisition and Use of Spanish and English as First and Second Languages,* Washington, DC: TESOL.

Popper, K. (1969) Die Logik der Sozialwissenschaften. In Adorno, T. (ed.) (1969), 103-23.

— (1976) *Unended Quest,* Fontana.

Porter, J. H. (1977) A cross-sectional study of morpheme acquisition in first language learners, *Language Learning* 27.1, 47-62.

Posner, R. (197) The relevance of comparative and historical data for the description and definition of a language.

Prabhu, N. S. (1980) Theoretical background to the Bangalore project, *New Approaches to Teaching English,* Regional Institute of English Bulletin, Bangalore, no.4(1), 19-26.

Pressley, M. and Levin, J. R. (eds) (1983) *Cognitive Strategy Research: Education Applications,* New York: Springer-Verlag.

Py, B. (forthcoming) Competence attrition in the native language of migrant workers: towards an extension of the concept of interlanguage. In Kellerman, E. and Sharwood Smith, M. (eds) (forthcoming).

Quine, W. V. O. (1972) Methodological reflections on current linguistic theory. In Davidson, D. and Harman, G. (eds) (1972), 442-54.

Quirk, R. and Greenbaum, S. (1973) *A University Grammar of English,* London: Longman.

Raabe, H. (1982) Ist 'ne . . . pas' denn keine doppelte Verneinung? Die Analyse von Fragereaktionen in ihrer Bedeutung für die Vermittlung von Fremdsprachen. In Gnutzmann, C. and Stark, D. (eds), *Grammatikunterricht,* Tübingen: Gunter Narr, 61-99.

— (in press) The influence of L1 and L3 in the foreign language classroom: An analysis of learners' questions in foreign language teaching. In Kasper, G. (in press a).

Radford, A. (1981) *Transformational Syntax,* Cambridge: Cambridge University Press.

Raupach, M. (1983) Analysis and evaluation of communication strategies. In Faerch, C. and Kasper, G. (eds) (1983d).

Ravem, R. (1968) Language acquisition in a second language environment. In Richards, J. C. (ed.) (1968).

— (1974a) Second language acquisition. A study of Norwegian children's acquisition of English syntax in a naturalistic setting. Doctoral dissertation, University of Essex.

— (1974b) The development of Wh questions in first and second languages learners. In Richards, J. C. (ed.) (1968). First published in *Occasional Papers,* University of Essex, Language Centre, Colchester, December 1970.

Rehbein, J. (1977) *Komplexes Handeln,* Stuttgart: Metzler.

Reynolds, P. D. (1971) *A Primer in Theory Construction,* Indianapolis: Bobbs-Merrill.

Richards, J. C. (1971) A non-contrastive approach to error analysis, *English Language Teaching* 25, 204-19. Reprinted in Richards, J. C. (ed.) (1974), 172-88.

— (ed.) (1974) *Error Analysis Perspectives on Second Language Acquisition,* London: Longman.

Richterich, R. (1972) *A Model for the Definition of Language Needs of Adults Learning a Modern Language,* Strasbourg: Council of Europe.

Ringbom, H. (1978) The influence of the mother tongue on the translation of lexical items, *Interlanguage Studies Bulletin* 3, 80-101.

— (ed.) (1983) *Psycholinguistics and Foreign Language Learning,* Åbo: Åbo Akademi.

Ritchie, W. C. (ed.) (1978) *Second Language Acquisition Research,* New York: Academic Press.

Rivers, W. M. (1972) *Speaking with Many Tongues,* Rowley, Mass.: Newbury House.

References

— (1979) Learning a sixth language: an adult learner's daily diary, *CMLR* 36.1, 67-82.

Rizzi, L. (1978) Violations of the wh-island constraint in Italian and the subjacency condition, *Montreal Working Papers in Linguistics* 11, 155-90.

Roeper, T. (1972) Approaches to a theory of language acquisition with examples from German children. Dissertation, Harvard.

— (1981) On the deductive model and the acquisition of productive morphology. In Baker, C. and McCarthy, J. (eds) (1981), 129-50.

— (1982) On the importance of syntax and the logical use of evidence in language acquisition. In Kuczai, S. (ed.), *Language Development, Vol.1: Syntax and Semantics*, 137-58, Hillsdale, NJ: Lawrence Erlbaum.

Rosansky, E. (1976) Methods and morphemes in second language acquisition research, *Language Learning* 26.2, 409-25.

Rosenbaum, P. (1967) *The Grammar of English Predicate Complement Constructions*, Cambridge, Mass.: The MIT Press.

Ross, J. (1970) Gapping and the order of constituents. In Bierwisch, M. and Heidolph, K. (eds) (1970), 249-59.

— (1974) Three batons for cognitive psychology. In Weimer, W. and Palermo, D. (eds), *Cognition and the Symbolic Process*, 63-124, Hillsdale, NJ: Lawrence Erlbaum.

Rubin, J. (1975) What the 'good language learner' can teach us, *TESOL Quarterly* 9, 41-51.

— (1981) Study of cognitive processes in second language learning, *Applied Linguistics*, 2.2, 117-31.

Rudska, B., Channell, J., Putsyes, Y. and Ostyn, P. (1982) *The Words You Need*, London: Macmillan.

Ruke-Dravina, V. (1963) Zur Sprachentwicklung bei Kleinkindern: 1. Syntax: Beitrag auf der Grundlage lettischen Sprachmaterials, *Slaviska och Baltiska Studier* 6, Lund: Slaviska Institutionen vid Lunds Universitat.

Rumelhart, D. E. (1975) Note on a schema for stories. In Bobrow, D. G. and Collins, A. (eds), *Representation and Understanding: Studies in Cognitive Science*, New York: Academic Press.

Rutherford, W. (1982) Markedness in second language acquisition, *Language Learning* 32, 85-108.

— (1983a) Description and explanation in interlanguage syntax. Paper presented at TESOL, Toronto, March.

— (1983b) Language typology and language transfer. In Gass, S. and Selinker, L. (eds) (1983).

— (ed.) (forthcoming) *Language Universals and Second Language Acquisition*, Amsterdam: Benjamins.

Safir, K. (1982) Inflection-government and inversion, *The Linguistic Review* 1, 417-66.

Sajavaara, K. (1980) Psycholinguistic models, second language acquisition, and contrastive analysis, mimeo. University of Jyväskylä.

— (1981) The nature of first language transfer: English as an L2 in a foreign language setting. Paper presented at the First European-North American Workshop on Second Language Acquisition Research, Lake Arrowhead, California.

Sampson, G. P. (1984) Exporting language teaching methods from Canada to China, *TESOL Canada Journal* 1, 19-31.

Sampson, J. (1979) A non-nativist account of language universals, *Linguistics and Philosophy* 3, 99-104.

Sato, C. J. (1982) Form and function in the English interlanguage of two Vietnamese children. Paper presented at the Georgetown University Round Table on Lan-

References

guages and Linguistics Pre-Conference Session on Analysis of Spoken Discourse: Second Language Research and Teaching Practice.

— (1983a) Phonological processes in second language acquisition: another look at interlanguage syllable structure. Paper presented at the 17th Annual TESOL Conference, Toronto, Ontario, Canada, 15th-20th March. To appear in *Language Learning* 34.4.

— (1983b) Task variation in interlanguage phonology. Paper presented at the Tenth University of Michigan Conference on Applied Linguistics, Ann Arbor, Michigan, October. To appear in Gass, S. and Madden, C. (eds), *Proceedings of the Tenth University of Michigan Conference on Applied Linguistics,* Rowley, Mass.: Newbury House Publishers.

— (1984) The syntax of conversation in interlanguage development. Unpublished Ph.D. dissertation, University of California at Los Angeles.

Scarcella, R. C. (1983a) In Gass, S. and Selinker, L. (eds) (1983).

— (1983b) Developmental trends in the acquisition of conversational competence by adult second language learners. In Wolfson, N. and Judd, E. (eds) (1983).

— (1984) Ph.D. dissertation, University of Southern California.

Scarcella, R. C. and Krashen, S. D. (1980) *Research in Second Language Acquisition,* Rowley, Mass.: Newbury House.

Schachter, J. (1974) An error in error analysis, *Language Learning* 24, 205-14.

— (in press) A universal input condition. In Rutherford, W. and Scarcella, R. (eds), *Universals and Second Language Acquisition,* Amsterdam: John Benjamin.

Schachter, J. and Celce-Murcia, M. (1977) Some reservations concerning error analysis, *TESOL Quarterly* 11.4, 441-51.

Schachter, J. and Rutherford, W. (1978) Discourse function and language transfer. Paper presented at Los Angeles Second Language Research Forum.

— (1979) Discourse function and language transfer, *Working Papers on Bilingualism* 19, 1-12.

Schachter, J., Tyson, A. and Diffley, F. (1976) Learner intuitions of grammaticality, *Language Learning* 26, 67-76.

Schiefelbusch, E. and Lloyd, L. (eds) (1974) *Language Perspectives: Acquisition, Retardation and Intervention,* Baltimore: University Park Press.

Schlesinger, J. (1974) Relational concepts underlying language. In Schiefelbusch, E. and Lloyd, L. (eds) (1974), 129-51.

Schmidt, M. (1980) Coordinate structures and language universals in interlanguage, *Language Learning* 30.2, 397-416.

Schmidt, R. (1977) Sociolinguistic variation and language transfer in phonology, *Working Papers in Bilingualism* 12, 79-95.

— (1983) Interaction, acculturation, and acquisition of communicative competence: a case study of an adult. In Wolfson, N. and Judd, E. (eds) (1983).

Schmidt, R. W. and Richards, J. C. (1980) Speech acts and second language learning, *Applied Linguistics* 1.2, 129-57.

Schröder, A. (1979) Aussprachenfehler bei Sextanern im English-Anfangs Unterricht im Lichte des natürlichen L2-Erwerbs, mimeo. Kiel University.

Schumann, J. H. (1975) Second language acquisition: the pidginization hypothesis. Unpublished Ph.D. dissertation, Harvard University.

— (1976) Second language acquisition: the pidginization hypothesis, *Language Learning* 26.2, 391-408.

— (1978a) *The Pidginization Process: A Model for Second Language Acquisition,* Rowley, Mass.: Newbury House Publishers.

— (1978b) The relationship of pidginization, creolization and decreolization to second language acquisition, *Language Learning* 28.2, 367-88.

References

— (1979) The acquisition of English negation by speakers of Spanish: a review of the literature. In Andersen, R. W. (ed.) (1979c).

— (1980) The acquisition of English relative clauses by second language learners. In Scarcella, R. C. and Krashen, S. D. (eds) (1980).

— (1981) Discussion of 'Two perspectives on pidginisation as second language acquisition'. In Andersen, R. W. (ed.) (1981b).

— (1982) Simplification, transfer, and relexification as aspects of pidginisation and early second language acquisition, *Language Learning* 32, 337-65.

Schumann, J. H. and Stauble, A.-M. (1983) A discussion of second language acquisition and decreolization. In Andersen, R. W. (ed.) (1983d).

Schwartz, J. (1980) The negotiation of meaning: repair in conversations between second language learners of English. In Larsen-Freeman (1980), 138-53.

Schwarze, G. (1982) Die historische Entwicklung der englischen Negation im Spiegel ausgewahlter Textsorten. Master's thesis, Kiel University.

Scollon, R. (1976) *Conversations with a One Year Old,* Honolulu: University of Hawaii Press.

Searle, J. (1969) *Speech Acts,* Cambridge: Cambridge University Press.

Seliger, H. W. (1977) Does practice make perfect? *Language Learning,* vol.27, no.2, 263-75.

— (1980) Data sources and the study of L2 speech performance: some theoretical issues, *Interlanguage Studies Bulletin Utrecht* 5, 31-46.

Seliger, H. W. and Long, M. H. (eds) (1983) *Classroom-oriented Research in Second Language Acquisition,* Rowley, Mass.: Newbury House.

Selinker, L. (1969) Language transfer, *General Linguistics* 9, 67-92.

— (1971) The psychologically relevant data of second language learning. In Pimsleur and Quinn (eds) (1971), 35-43.

— (1972) Interlanguage, *IRAL* 10.3, 209-31.

Selinker, L. and Douglas, D. (forthcoming) Wrestling with 'context' in interlanguage theory.

Selinker, L., Swain, M. and Dumas, G. (1975) The interlanguage hypothesis extended to children, *Language Learning* 25, 139-52.

Shapira, R. (1978) The non-learning of English: a case study of an adult. In Hatch, E. (ed.) (1978b).

Sharwood Smith, M. (1979) Strategies, language transfer and the simulation of the second language learner's mental operations, *Interlanguage Studies Bulletin Utrecht* 4, 66-83.

— (1980) Contrastive studies and acquisition theory. Paper presented at the Conference on Contrastive Projects, Charkowy, Poland.

— (1981) The competence/performance distinction in the theory of second language acquisition and the pedagogical grammar hypothesis. Unpublished MS, University of Utrecht.

— (1983a) Adverbial placement and intake: theoretical implications. Paper given at Xth Conference on Applied Linguistics: 'Input in Second Language Acquisition', University of Michigan, October.

— (1983b) From input to intake: on argumentation in second language acquisition. Paper presented at the 10th University of Michigan Conference on Applied Linguistics: 'Input in Second Language Acquisition', Ann Arbor, 28-30 October 1983.

Shibatani, M. (1982) Japanese grammar and universal grammar, *Lingua* 57, 103-23.

Shiffrin, R. M. and Schneider, W. (1977) Controlled and automatic human information processing: II. Perceptual learning, automatic attending, and a general theory, *Psychological Review* 84, 127-90.

Silva-Corvalán, C. Subject expression and placement in Mexican-American Spanish.

References

In Amstae, J. and Elías-Olivares, L. (eds), *Spanish in the United States: Sociolinguistic Aspects,* Cambridge: Cambridge University Press, 93-120.

Silverstein, M. (1972) Chinook jargon: language contact and the problem of multi-level generative systems, *Language* 48, 378-406, 596-624.

Simon, H. A. (1979) *Models of Thought,* New Haven: Yale University Press.

Sinclair, J. McH. and Coulthard, R. M. (1975) *Towards an Analysis of Discourses: The English Used by Teachers and Pupils,* London: Oxford University Press.

Sjoholm, K. (1983) Problems in 'measuring' L2 learning strategies. In Ringbom, H. (ed.) (1983).

Slama-Cazacu, T. (1974) Theoretical interpretation and methodological consequences of 'regularisation'. In *Further Developments in Contrastive Studies,* Bucharest: Bucharest University Press.

Slobin, D. (1973) Cognitive prerequisites for the development of grammar. In Ferguson, C. A. and Slobin, D. (eds) (1973).

— (1982a) Reference to the not-here and not-now. Pre-Workshop Paper, Nijmegen: Max-Planck-Institut.

— (1982b) Universal and particular in the acquisition of language. In Wanner, E. and Gleitman, L. R. (eds) (1982), *Language Acquisition: The State of the Art,* Cambridge: Cambridge University Press, 128-70.

— (1984) Crosslinguistic evidence for the language-making capacity. In Slobin, D. (ed.), *The Crosslinguistic Study of Language Acquisition,* Hillsdale, NJ: Lawrence Erlbaum.

Smith, D. (1978) Mirror images in Japanese and English, *Language* 54, 78-122.

Smith, N. (1973) *The Acquisition of Phonology. A Case Study,* Cambridge: Cambridge University Press.

Snow, C. (1979) Conversations with children. In Fletcher, P. and Garman, M. (eds) (1979), *Language Acquisition,* Cambridge: Cambridge University Press.

Snow, C. and Ferguson, C. A. (1977) *Talking to Children: Language Input and Acquisition,* Cambridge: Cambridge University Press.

Snow, C. and Meijer, G. (1977) On the secondary nature of syntactic intuitions. In Greenbaum, S. (ed.) (1977), *Acceptability in Language,* The Hague: Mouton.

Snow, C., van Eeden, R. and Muysken, P. (1981) The interactional origins of foreigner talk: municipal employees and foreign workers, *International Journal of the Sociology of Language* 28, 81-92.

Sportiche, S. (1982) Bounding nodes in French, *Linguistic Review* 1, 219-46.

Stauble, A.-M. (1978) The process of decreolization: a model for second language development, *Language Learning* 28.1, 29-54.

— (1981) A comparison of a Spanish-English and Japanese-English second language continuum: verb phrase morphology. Paper presented at the European-North American Workshop on Cross-linguistic Second Language Acquisition Research, Lake Arrowhead, California, September. To appear in Andersen, R. W. (ed.) (in press).

Stauble, A.-M. and Schumann, J. H. (1983) Toward a description of the Spanish-English basilang. In Bailey, K. M., Long, M. H. and Peck, S. (eds), *Second Language Acquisition Studies,* Rowley, Mass.: Newbury House Publishers.

Stedje, A. (1982) Sprechabsicht und Luckenindikatoren, *Zeitschrift für germanistische Linguistik* 10.2, 156-72.

— (1983) Deception and dissociation markers as indicators of communication strategies. In Ringbom, H. (ed.) (1983), 201-11.

Stegmuller, W. (1974) *Probleme und Resultate der Wissenschaftstheorie und analytischen Philosophie. Bd. 1. Wissenschaftliche Erklarung und Begrundung,* Berlin: Springer.

References

Stern, H. H. (1975) What can we learn from the good language learner? *Canadian Modern Language Review* 31, 304-18.

Sternefeld, W. (1982) Konfigurationelle und nicht-konfigurationelle Aspekte einer modularen Syntax des Deutschen. Arbeitspapiere des SFB 99, Universitat Konstanz.

Stevick, E. W. (1980) *Teaching Languages: A Way and Ways,* Rowley, Mass.: Newbury House.

Stockwell, R. P., Bowen, J. D. and Martin, J. W. (1965) *The Grammatical Structures of English and Spanish,* Chicago: University of Chicago Press.

Stowell, T. (1981) Origins of phrase structure. Dissertation, Massachusetts Institute of Technology, Cambridge, Mass.

Strauss, S. (ed.) (1982) *U-Shaped Behavioral Growth,* New York: Academic Press.

Stutterheim, C. V. (1982) *Temporality in Learner Varieties _ A First Report,* Nijmegen: Max-Planck-Institut für Psycholinguistik.

Swain, M. (1983) Communicative competence: some roles of comprehensible input and comprehensible output in its development. Paper presented at Xth University of Michigan Conference on Applied Linguistics, Ann Arbor.

Swain, M. and Barik, H. (1977) Report to Ottawa Board of Education and Carleton Board of Education re: evaluation of the 1976-77 French immersion program in grades 4-6 (mimeo). Ontario Institute for Studies in Education, Toronto.

Swain, M. and Lapkin, S. (1982) *Evaluating Bilingual Education: A Canadian Case Study,* Clevedon, Avon: Multilingual Matters.

Swain, M. and Wong-Fillmore, L. (1984) Child second language development. Views from the field on theory and research. Paper presented at the Academic Session of the Research Interest Section, TESOL Convention, Houston, Texas.

Taeschner, T. (1983) *The Sun is Feminine,* Berlin: Springer.

Talmy, L. (1975) Semantics and syntax of motion. In Kimball, J. (ed.), *Syntax and Semantics,* vol.4, New York: Academic Press.

Tarallo, F. and Myhill, J. (1983) Interference and natural language processing in second language acquisition, *Language Learning* 33, 55-76.

Tarone, E. (1977) Conscious communication strategies in interlanguage. In Brown, H. D., Yorio, C. A. and Crymes, R. C. (eds) (1977), 194-203.

— (1979) Interlanguage as Chameleon, *Language Learning* 29.2, 181-91.

— (1980a) Some influences on the syllable structure of interlanguage phonology, *IRAL* 18, 139-52.

— (1980b) Communication strategies, foreigner talk and repair, *Language Learning* 30, 417-31.

— (1981a) Decoding a Nonprimary Language: the Crucial Role of Strategic Competence. Paper read at the BAAL Seminar on Interpretive Strategies, University of Lancaster.

— (1981b) Some thoughts on the notion of 'community strategy', *TESOL Quarterly* 15/3. Reprinted in Faerch and Kasper (eds) (1983d).

— (1982) Systematicity and attention in interlanguage, *Language Learning* 32.1, 69-84.

— (1983) On the variability of interlanguage systems, *Applied Linguistics* 4.2, 142-63.

— (1984) Variability in interlanguage use: a study of style-shifting in morphology and syntax. Paper presented at the 18th Annual TESOL Conference, Houston, Texas, 6th-11th March.

— (in press) The role of the syllable in interlanguage phonology. In Eliasson, S. (ed.), *Theoretical Issues in Contrastive Phonology,* Heidelberg: Julius Groos Verlag.

Tarone, E., Cohen, A. D. and Dumas, G. (1976) A closer look at some interlanguage

References

terminology: a framework for communication strategies, *Working Papers in Bilingualism* 9, 76-90. Reprinted in Faerch and Kasper (1983d), 4-14.

Tarone, E., Frauenfelder, U. and Selinker, L. (1976) Systematicity/variability and stability/instability in interlanguage systems. In Brown, H. D. (ed.), *Papers in Second Language Acquisition, Ann Arbor, Michigan: Language Learning,* 93-134.

Tarone, E., Swain, M. and Fathman, A. (1976) Some limitations to the classroom applications of current second language acquisition research, *TESOL Quarterly* 10.1, 19-33.

Tarone, E. and Yule, G. (1983) Communication Strategies in East-West Interactions. Paper prepared for the Conference on English as an International Language: Discourse Patterns across Cultures. East-West Center, Honolulu, Hawaii, 1-6 June 1983.

Tavakolian, S. (ed.) (1981) *Language Acquisition and Linguistic Theory,* Cambridge, Mass.: MIT Press.

Taylor, B. (1975) The use of overgeneralisation and transfer learning strategies by elementary and intermediate students in ESL, *Language Learning* 25, 73-108.

Terrell, T., Gomez, E. and Mariscal, J. (1980) In Scarcella, R. and Krashen, S. D. (eds) (1980).

Thiersch, C. (1978) Topics in German syntax. Dissertation, Massachusetts Institute of Technology, Cambridge, Mass.

Thompson, S. (1978) Modern English from a typological point of view: some implications of the function of word order, *Linguistische Berichte* 54, 19-35.

Tiphine, U. (1983) The acquisition of English statements and interrogatives by French-speaking children. Doctoral dissertation, Kiel University.

Todd, L. (1974) *Pidgins and Creoles,* London: Routledge and Kegan Paul.

Traugott, E. C. (1972) *The History of English Syntax,* New York: Holt, Rinehart and Winston.

— (1977) Natural semantax: its role in the study of second language acquisition. In Corder, S. P. and Roulet, E. (eds), *The Notions Simplifications, Interlanguage and Pidgins and Their Relation to Second Language Pedagogy,* Geneva: Droz.

Trévise, A. (1979) Spécificité de l'énonciation didactique dans l'apprentissage de l'anglais par les étudiants francophones, *Encrages* 44-52.

— (forthcoming) Is it transferable, topicalisation? In Kellerman, E. and Sharwood Smith, M. (eds) (forthcoming).

Trosborg, A. (1982) Communication strategies: relating theory and practice, *Finlance* 2, 111-36.

Trubetzkoy, N. S. (1936a) Essai d'une theorie des oppositions phonologique, *Journal de Psychologie* 33, 5-18.

— (1936b) Die Aufhebung der phonologischen Gegensatze, *Travaux des Cercles Linguistiques de Prague* 6, 29-45.

Trudgill, P. (1974) *The Social Differentiation of English in Norwich,* Cambridge: Cambridge University Press.

Tucker, G. (1977) Can a second language be taught? In Brown, H., Yorio, C. and Crymes, R. (eds) (1977).

Ufert, D. (1980) Der natürliche Zweitsprachenerwerb des Englischen: die Entwicklung des Interrogationssystems. Doctoral dissertation, Kiel University.

Ultan, R. (1978) Some general characteristics of interrogative systems. In Greenberg, J. H. (ed.), *Universals of Human Language,* vol.4, Stanford, Calif.: Stanford University Press, 221-48.

Upshur, J. A. (1968) Four experiments on the relation between foreign language teaching and learning, *Language Learning* XVIII, nos 1 and 2, 111-24.

Van D'Yk, T. A. (1972) *Some Aspects of Text Grammars,* The Hague: Mouton.

References

— (1977) *Text and Context,* London: The Longman Group Ltd.

Van Ek, J. A. (1975) *The Threshold Level,* Strasbourg: The Council of Europe.

Váradi, T. (1980) Strategies of target language learner communication: message adjustment, *IRAL* 18, 59-72. Reprinted in Faerch, C. and Kasper, G. (eds) (1983d), 79-99.

Vennemann, T. (1972) Analogy in generative grammar. In Heilmann, L. (ed.), *Proceedings of the 11th International Congress of Linguists,* Bologna: Il Mulino.

Vihman, M. M. (1982) Formulas in first and second language acquisition. In Obler, L. K. and Menn, L. (eds) (1982).

Vincent, N. (1976) Perceptual factors and word order change in Latin. In Harris, M. (ed.), *Romance Syntax: Synchronic and Diachronic Perspectives,* 54-68, University of Salford.

Visser, F. (1963) *An Historical Syntax of the English Language,* Leiden: E. J. Brill.

Von Stutterheim, C. (forthcoming) Temporalitat im Zweitspracherwerb turkischer Arbeiter. Ph.D. thesis, University of Berlin.

Wagner, J. (1983) Dann du tagen eineeeee – weisse Platte – an analysis of interlanguage communication in instruction. In Faerch, C. and Kasper, G. (eds) (1983d), 159-74.

Wagner-Gough, J. (1975) Comparative studies in second language learning, *CAL-ERIC/CLL Series on Languages and Linguistics* 26.

— (1978) Excerpts from comparative studies in second language learning. In Hatch, E. M. (ed.) (1978b).

Wardaugh, R. (1970) The contrastive analysis hypothesis, *TESOL Quarterly* 4, 123-30. Reprinted in Schumann, J. H. and Stenson, N. (eds), *New Frontiers in Second Language Learning,* Rowley, Mass.: Newbury House, 11-19.

Watabe, M. and Brown, C. (1983) An analysis of form and function in the compositions of ESL and JSL learners. Paper presented at Second Language Research Forum, Los Angeles.

Weeks, L.-A. (1983) Spanish patterns of lexicalisation for motion events: a validation study? Unpublished paper, Max-Planck-Institut for Psycholinguistics, Nijmegen.

Weinreich, U. (1953) *Languages in Contact. Findings and Problems.* New York: Publication of the Linguistic Circle of New York, No.1.

Weinreich, U., Labov, W. and Herzog, M. (1968) Empirical foundations for a theory of language change. In Lehmann, W. and Malkiel, Y. (eds), *Directions for Historical Linguistics,* Austin, Texas: University of Texas Press.

Wekker, H., Kellerman, E. and Hermans, D. (1981) Trying to see the would for the trees. Paper presented at the 17th International Conference on Polish-English Contrastive Linguistics, Blazejewko, Poland, December 1981.

Wenk, B. (forthcoming) Cross-linguistic influence and second language phonology: speech rhythms. In Kellerman, E. and Sharwood Smith, M. (eds) (forthcoming a).

Wesche, M. and Ready, D. (in press) Foreigner talk discourse in the university classroom. In Gass, S. and Madden, C. (eds) (in press), *Input and Second Language,* Rowley, Mass.: Newbury House.

Wexler, K. and Culicover, P. (1980) *Formal Principles of Language Acquisition,* Cambridge, Mass.: The MIT Press.

Whinnom, K. (1971) Linguistic hybridization and the 'special case' of pidgins and creoles. In Hymes, D. (ed.), *Pidginization and Creolization of Languages,* Cambridge: Cambridge University Press.

Whitaker, H. (1978) Bilingualism: a neurolinguistic perspective. In Ritchie, W. C. (ed.) (1978).

References

White, L. (1980) Error analysis and error correction in adult learners of English as a second language, *Working Papers on Bilingualism* 13, 42-58.

— (1981) The responsibility of grammatical theory to acquisitional data. In Hornstein, N. and Lightfoot, D. (eds) (1981), 241-71.

— (1982) *Grammatical Theory and Language Acquisition*. Dordrecht: Floris.

— (1983a) Markedness and parameter setting: some implications for a theory of adult second language acquisition. Paper presented at 12th Annual University of Wisconsin-Milwaukee Linguistics Symposium on Markedness, Milwaukee, Wisconsin.

— (1983b) The 'pro-drop' parameter in adult second language acquisition. Paper presented at the 8th Annual Boston University Conference on Language Development, Boston, October.

— (forthcoming) Markedness and parameter setting: some implications for a theory of adult second language acquisition. In Eckman, F., Moravcsik, E. and Wirth, J. (eds) (forthcoming).

Whitman, R. and Jackson, K. (1972) The unpredictability of contrastive analysis, *Language Learning* 22.1, 29-41.

Widdowson, H. G. (1978a) *Teaching Language as Communication,* Oxford: Oxford University Press.

— (1978b) The significance of simplification, *Studies in Second Language Acquisition* 1, 11-20.

— (1983) *Language Purpose and Language Use,* Oxford: Oxford University Press.

Wikberg, K. (1979) Lexical errors made by Finnish and Swedish senior secondary school students: a comparison. Paper presented at the Nordic Interlanguage Symposium, Hanasaari, Finland.

Wilkins, D. A. (1976) *Notional Syllabuses,* Oxford: Oxford University Press.

Williams, E. (1981) Language acquisition, markedness and phrase structure. In Tavekolian, S. (ed.) (1981).

Winterowd, R. (1975) *The Contemporary Writer: A Practical Rhetoric,* New York: Harcourt Brace.

Wode, H. (1974) Natürliche Zweitsprachigkeit: Probleme, Aufgaben, Perspektiven, *Linguistische Berichte* 32, 15-36. Engl. translation in Wode, H. (ed.) (1983a).

— (1976a) Some stages in the acquisition of questions by monolingual children. In Raffler-Engel, W. von (ed.), *Child Language 1975.* Word 27 (Special issue), 261-310. Reprinted in Wode, H. (ed.) (1983a).

— (1976b) Development sequences in naturalistic L2 acquisition, *Working Papers on Bilingualism* 11, 1-31.

— (1977a) On the systematicity of L1 transfer in L2 acquisition. In Henning, C. (ed.), *Proceedings of the Los Angeles Second Language Research Forum, Los Angeles, Calif.,* 160-9. Reprinted in Wode, H. (ed.) (1983a).

— (1977b) The L2 acquisition of /r/, *Phonetica* 34, 200-17.

— (1977c) Four early stages in the development of L1-negation, *Journal of Child Language* 4, 87-102.

— (1978a) L1-Erwerb, L2-Erwerb und Fremdsprachenunterricht, *Die Neueren Sprachen* 77, 452-65.

— (1978b) The L1 vs. L2 acquisition of English interrogation, *Working Papers on Bilingualism* 15, 37-57. Revised version in *Indian Journal of Applied Linguistics (IJOAL)* 4, 31-46.

— (1978c) The beginnings of non-school room L2 phonological acquisition, *IRAL* 16, 109-25. Reprinted in Wode, H. (ed.) (1983a).

— (1978d) Developmental sequences in naturalistic L2 acquisition. In Hatch, E. (ed.) (1978b).

References

— (1979) Operating principles and 'universals' in L1, L2, and FLT, *IRAL* 17, 217-31. Reprinted in Wode, H. (ed.) (1983a).

— (1980) Phonology in L2 acquisition. In Felix, S. W. (ed.) (1980), 123-36. Reprinted in Wode, H. (ed.) (1983a).

— (1981) *Learning a Second Language. I. An Integrated View of Language Acquisition,* Tübingen: Gunter Narr.

— (1982) Language transfer, language learning, and the functioning of natural languages. Arbeitspapiere zum Spracherwerb (APSE) 28, English Department, Kiel University.

— (ed.) (1983a) *Papers on Language Acquisition, Language Learning, and Language Teaching,* Heidelberg: Julius Groos.

— (1983b) Contrastive analysis and language learning. In Wode, H. (ed.) (1983a).

— (1983c) Language acquisition, pidgins and creoles, *Studies in Second Language Acquisition* 3, 193-200. Revised version in Wode, H. (ed.) (1983a).

— (forthcoming) Language transfer: a cognitive, functional, and developmental view. To appear in Kellerman, E. and Sharwood-Smith, M. (eds) (forthcoming a).

Wode, H. and Ruke-Dravina, V. (1977) Why 'Kathryn no like celery?', *Folia Linguistica* 10, 361-75.

Wode, H., Bahns, J., Bedey, H. and Frank, W. (1978) Developmental sequence: an alternative approach to morpheme order, *Language Learning* 28, 175-85.

Wolfson, N. (1983) An empirically based analysis of complimenting in American English. In Wolfson, N. and Judd, E. (eds) (1983).

Wolfson, N. and Judd, E. (eds) (1983) *Sociolinguistics and Second Language Acquisition,* Rowley, Mass.: Newbury House.

Wong, S. (1983) Overproduction, under-lexicalisation and unidiomatic usage in the 'make' causatives of Chinese speakers: a case for flexibility in interlanguage analysis, *Language Learning and Communication* 2, 151-63.

Wong-Fillmore, L. (1976) The second time around: cognitive and social strategies in second language acquisition. Ph.D. dissertation, Stanford University, Palo Alto, CA.

— (1979) Individual differences in second language acquisition. In Fillmore, C. J., Kemples, D. and Wang, W. S.-Y. (eds), *Individual Differences in Language Ability and Language Behaviour,* New York: Academic Press.

Yalden, J. (1983) *The Communicative Syllabus: Evolution, Design and Implementation,* Oxford: Pergamon Press.

Zobl, H. (1980a) The formal and developmental selectivity of L1 influence on L2 acquisition, *Language Learning* 30, 43-57.

— (1980b) Developmental and transfer errors: their common bases and (possibly) differential effects on subsequent learning, *TESOL Quarterly* 14, 469-79.

— (1982) A direction for contrastive analysis: the comparative study of developmental sequences, *TESOL Quarterly* 16, 169-83.

— (1983a) Markedness and the projection problem, *Language Learning* 33, 293-314.

— (1983b) Contact-induced language change, learner language, and the potentials of a modified contrastive analysis. Paper read at the Third Los Angeles Second Language Research Forum, February 1980. Also in Bailey, C., Long, M. H. and Peck, S. (eds), *Second Language Acquisition Studies,* 104-12, Rowley, Mass.: Newbury House.

— (1983c) Grammars in search of input and intake. Paper presented at the Tenth University of Michigan Conference on Applied Linguistics, Ann Arbor, 28th-30th October.

— (1983d) L1 acquisition, age of L2 acquisition, and the learning of word order. In Gass, S. and Selinker, L. (eds) (1983).

References

— (forthcoming) The Wave Model of linguistic change and the naturalness of interlanguage systems, *Studies in Second Language Acquisition.*

— (in press a) Aspects of reference and the pronominal syntax preference in the speech of young child L2 learners. In Andersen, R. W. (ed.), *A Cross-linguistic Perspective for Second Language Research,* Rowley, Mass. : Newbury House.

— (in press b) Source language variation across developmental continua. In Rutherford, W. and Scarcella, R. (eds), *Language Universals and Second Language Acquisition,* Philadelphia: John Benjamins.

Zydatiss, W. (1973) Fehler in der englischen Satzgliedfolge, *IRAL* 11, 319-55.

— (1974) Some instances of over-indulgence and under-representation, *Linguistische Berichte* 33, 47-53.

Index